CW00417918

MARRIED SAINTS AND BLESSEDS
THROUGH THE CENTURIES

FERDINAND HOLBÖCK

MARRIED SAINTS AND AND BLESSEDS

THROUGH THE CENTURIES

Translated by
Michael J. Miller

IGNATIUS PRESS   SAN FRANCISCO

From the second edition of the original German:
*Heilige Eheleute: Verheiratete Selige
und Heilige aus allen Jahrhunderten*
© 2001 Christiana-Verlag, Stein am Rhein, Salzburg
Published with ecclesiastical approval

Illustration credit: Photographic archive Christiana-Edition,
CH–8260 Stein am Rhein, Switzerland.

Cover photographs:
Top: Gianna Beretta-Molla
Middle: Thomas More; Marie-Azélie Martin and Louis-Joseph Martin
Bottom: Emperor Karl von Österreich and Empress Zita

Cover design by Riz Boncan Marsella

© 2002 Ignatius Press, San Francisco
All rights reserved
ISBN 0–89870–843–5
Library of Congress Control Number 2001095550
Printed in the United States of America ∞

Husbands, love your wives, as Christ loved the church and gave himself up for her. . . . This is a great mystery, and I mean in reference to Christ and the church; however, let each one of you love his wife as himself, and let the wife see that she respects her husband.

Letter of Paul to the Ephesians, 5:25, 32–33

CONTENTS

ABBREVIATIONS

CD   *Canons and Decrees of the Council of Trent*, trans. H. J. Schroeder, O.P. (St. Louis: B. Herder Book Co., 1941)

CSEL *Corpus Scriptorum Ecclesiasticorum Latinorum* (Vienna, 1866ff.)

DS   *Enchiridion Symbolorum*, ed. Heinrich Denzinger and Adolf Schönmetz, S.J., 22nd ed. (Barcelona and Freiburg: Herder, 1963)

LThK *Lexikon für Theologie und Kirche*

PG   *Patrologia Graeca*

PL   *Patrologia Latina*

AUTHOR'S PREFACE

Marriage and the family "in the modern world, as much as and perhaps more than any other institution, [have] been beset by the many profound and rapid changes that have affected society and culture". So says the introduction to the apostolic letter *Familiaris consortio* of November 22, 1981.

In the years that have passed since then, the position of marriage has become still more critical. Frequently it is in a serious crisis, not merely in concrete particular instances, but in general as an institution. In many countries, one out of every two or three marriages fails, and many young couples today live together "without benefit of marriage certificate", to say nothing of the Sacrament of Matrimony, as long as it suits them and then go their separate ways again when it no longer does. Why is this? Is it just a lack of the serious resolve required to bind oneself to another person in an indissoluble marriage? Or is the overall situation such that it seems to many people today impossible to live in a genuinely Christian, indissoluble marriage according to the demands of God, of Jesus Christ, and of the Church?

Many concerned pastors ask: How can a couple succeed, even today, in leading a happy married life that is loving and faithful until death and therefore good both in this world and for the next, while taking into consideration all the problems related to correct conduct in a Christian marriage, for example, the legitimate and responsible transmission of life, which is much debated today, the formation and education of the children who are begotten, or the perfect marital fidelity that is radically demanded by Christ in the Sermon on the Mount (see Mt 5:27)?

Can those saints who were married themselves give us any insight into this question? Or are the saints, in this regard also, merely our "companions in the human condition", as the Second

Vatican Council said about the saints in general [*Lumen Gentium*, no. 50]?

In any case it would certainly be very illuminating in many respects to investigate the lives of married blesseds and saints and to see whether and how they managed to deal with the problems that came up in their marriages.

Did the marriages of the canonized saints and blesseds always correspond to what is set forth about Christian marriage and its demands in Sacred Scripture and in the Church's magisterial documents, those issued by councils as well as papal encyclicals? Or do the lives of married blesseds and saints also exhibit marital break-ups and the improper use of marriage? Can Christian married couples of our time learn from the way in which married saints lived as spouses and dealt with the difficulties that came up? One question after another arises when you broach the subject of "married saints", yet these are often brushed aside with the remark that married saints, after all, constitute an extremely rare exception. Is that really the case?

The topic of "the married life of wedded saints and blesseds" has scarcely ever been treated until now. So far, only one slim Italian book, *I Santi sposati*,[1] with portraits of ten married saints, has come to the attention of the author of this book, together with one chapter, "Das Leben in der Ehe" [Married life], in Walter Nigg's book *Heilige im Alltag* [Everyday saints],[2] which lists eight saintly couples and considers in a few sentences the married life of each. But have there not been many more than eight to ten married saints? The search for such witnesses in ancient, modern, and most recent times produced almost a hundred married couples of this sort, in which one or both spouses was declared by the Church to be a saint or a blessed.

Now the question arises once more: Can it be demonstrated for the married people of our time, from the example of the lives of these married blesseds and saints, how a person can become holy—not in spite of, but precisely through marriage? In this regard the

---

[1] Milan, 1989.

[2] Walter Nigg, *Heilige im Alltag* (Olten 1974), pp. 47–72.

deceased Protestant theologian Walter Nigg, in his book *Heilige im Alltag*, accurately wrote the following lines:

> It is wrong to claim that marriage does not enable a person to attain the full perfection of the Christian life. If this view were correct, then the sacrament of marriage would be the most miserable of all sacraments. We maintain, on the contrary and quite emphatically, that marriage too is a path to holiness. Why should it not be? We defend this stance against the contemporary cynical ridicule of marital intimacies, but also and just as much against the theological depreciation of marriage that resulted from an ascetical ideal. Instead we unswervingly advocate the belief that marriage and sanctity can be united, because we are convinced that only this understanding will put a stop to the present-day disintegration of marriage.[3]

The question here is merely in which state—in marriage or in virginal celibacy consecrated to God—it is *easier* to become holy. The words of Saint Paul in 1 Corinthians 7:25–35 are probably pertinent. And the teaching of the Council of Trent is probably still pertinent also, even today: "If anyone says that the married state excels the state of virginity or celibacy, and that it is better and happier to be united in matrimony than to remain in virginity or celibacy, let him be anathema."[4]

In any case, looking to married blesseds and saints can and should help put a stop to the "present-day disintegration of marriage".

I dedicate this book to my deceased parents, Josef Holböck and Leopoldine, née Windischbauer, who for forty-six years strove together honestly and conscientiously, in love and fidelity—indeed, in difficult and trying times, especially during the two World

---

[3] Ibid., p. 70.

[4] The original Latin text of Canon 10 can be found in *Enchiridion Symbolorum*, ed. Heinrich Denzinger and Adolf Schönmetz, S.J., 22nd ed. (Barcelona and Freiburg: Herder, 1963) (hereafter cited as DS), no. 1810, p. 1417. English version from *Canons and Decrees of the Council of Trent*, trans. H. J. Schroeder, O.P. (St. Louis: B. Herder Book Co., 1941)(hereafter cited as CD), p. 182.

Wars—to lead a truly Christian married life. They gave the gift of life to twelve children: three of them died in early childhood in their baptismal innocence; nine were raised in such a way that four of them dedicated themselves to Christ and to his Church in the priesthood or the religious life, while five of them handed on the blessings of life and the Catholic faith through the vocation of Christian marriage.

As to the contents of this book, the author wishes to make another remark. One or another reader may perhaps notice that between the saintly married couples from the Bible and the first Christian married couples there is a gap of almost three hundred years. One might then ask: Were there no saintly married couples during the first Christian centuries? No doubt there were some, even in the midst of the severe persecutions of Christians—for instance, the Roman Titus Flavius Clemens and his wife, Domitilla, who both stood fast by their Christian faith and their indissoluble marriage and, condemned by their relative, the pagan emperor Domitian, shed their blood in A.D. 95 and died as martyrs. We should also mention Perpetua and Felicity, whom the Church commemorates in the Roman Canon of the Mass. Perpetua, the daughter of a patrician, was twenty-two years old and married. With her little boy on her arm, she was arrested because she had received Baptism, and together with Felicity, a slave, and other Christians she was thrown to the wild animals during a circus in the great arena of Carthage on March 7, 202. Her heroic witness to Christ caused many pagans likewise to accept the Christian faith. Tradition is silent as to the name of Perpetua's husband and whether he too became a Christian.

The first saintly married couple named by their names and portrayed in detail, in fact, we encounter only in the middle of the fourth century: Saint Basil the Elder and his saintly wife, Emmelia.

Feast of the Betrothal of Mary and Joseph
January 23, 1994
Ferdinand Holböck

NOTE BY THE PUBLISHER OF
THE GERMAN EDITION

Attitudes toward marriage and the family have swung back and forth like a powerful pendulum in the course of human history. At present the pendulum is completing its swing in one direction. We are experiencing an all-engulfing sexual revolution and destruction of the family. Sex has become, with mammon and drug consumption of every sort, an idol of our time. The consequence of this is that people have quickly lost all appreciation for purity and virginity, because they pursue only their own self-fulfillment, which causes many to drift about in the crassest forms of egotism. This is why celibacy—the renunciation of marriage for the sake of the kingdom of heaven, as Christ recommended—also meets with vehement opposition.

In the Middle Ages the pendulum had swung to the other extreme. This is also reflected in the lives of the saints of that era. A certain exaggerated esteem for the virginal state was part of a trend at that time. Naturally this was not always a flight from marriage. It was the custom among the nobility, for political reasons, for families to arrange marriages for their sons and daughters while they were still children. Among those who were thus compelled to marry there were also some who felt called to a life of complete dedication to God and who experienced marriage as a straitjacket. Such people, by mutual consent, renounced the consummation of their marriage, preferring to enter the cloister; this was legitimate and must not be interpreted as contempt for marriage. We are grateful to the learned author Monsignor Ferdinand Holböck that he has not withheld such examples from us. Given today's one-sided perspective, it might benefit the people of our time, especially, to reconsider the genuine values expressed in virginity and the necessity of occasional continence within marriage, which also confronts modern couples, whether because of illness or the long absence of one spouse.

The apostles already posed the question to Christ whether it is better to marry or not. Throughout all the centuries since, people have wrestled with this question. Both ideals are legitimate paths to God. Every man must prayerfully strive to be sure he is setting out on the way God has destined for him. In this book individuals are presented who were able to realize both ideals—for instance, Saint Nicholas von Flüe, Saint Bridget [Birgitta] of Sweden, and Saint Rita of Cascia. This book, however, primarily shows that many Christians, in and through marriage, have followed Christ's command: "Be perfect, as your heavenly Father is perfect" (Mt 5:48).

On the occasion of the International Year of the Family, the Catholic–Jewish Liaison Committee emphasized the "sacred value of stable marriage and the family". The Common Declaration mentions the crises to which the family, as "humanity's most precious resource", is exposed today throughout the world. Society is called to stand up for the rights of the family. For Jews and Christians, the family is much more than a legal, social, or economic unit; in fact, it is a divinely ordained "stable community of love and solidarity".[1]

With all this concern about the family, we Christians can still be confident. The real guarantor of the family is Christ himself, who by his Incarnation sanctified the family. This magnificent thought is found in the "Letter to Families" that Pope John Paul II wrote for the Year of the Family on the Feast of the Presentation, February 2, 1994; there it says:

> The family has its origin in that same love with which the Creator embraces the created world . . . . The *only begotten Son*, of one substance with the Father, "*God from God* and Light from Light", *entered into human history through the family*: "For by his

---

[1] The "Common Declaration on the Family" issued by the Catholic-Jewish Liaison Committee for the Year of the Family is quoted from *L'Osservatore romano*, weekly English ed., June 8, 1994, p. 6.

incarnation the Son of God united himself in a certain way with every man. He laboured with human hands . . . and loved with a human heart. Born of Mary the Virgin, he truly became one of us and, except for sin, was like us in every respect." If in fact Christ "fully discloses man to himself", he does so beginning with the family in which he chose to be born and to grow up. We know that the Redeemer spent most of his life in the obscurity of Nazareth, "obedient" (Lk 2:51) as the "Son of Man" to Mary his Mother, and to Joseph the carpenter. . . . *The divine mystery of the Incarnation of the Word thus has an intimate connection with the human family.* [2]

The majority of the faithful are married. How is it, though, that there are so few married people who have been raised to the honors of the altar? The explanation is very simple. Anyone who has ever attended a beatification or a canonization knows that the expenditure of time and resources for the process is considerable. The veneration of the saints is a momentous thing, and the Church does well to proceed in this matter with all possible care and thoroughness. Saints should be prayed for, since they have a decisive, leading role in the interior life of the Church. Religious orders and congregations are in a better position than individual dioceses to conduct processes of beatification and canonization. In addition, the chances of living a life of Christian perfection are greater in the cloister than in the hectic confusion of the world. I am convinced, though, that in all times there have been countless married people who have led lives of heroic virtue in silence and obscurity and who in God's sight have the status of sainthood. The great French scientist Pasteur once declared that he would be happy if he had the faith of a Breton peasant woman.

Today, so many marriages break up that soon in many countries one out of every three marriages will end in divorce. The spiritual need of divorced persons and, above all, of their children is indescribable. Where there is a need, again and again God sends someone to help. Would it not be appropriate if those in marital and

---

[2] *L'Osservatore romano*, February 23, 1994, p. 5.

familial difficulties would call on saintly married people to intercede with God? Here too, Christ's word is true: "Make friends for yourselves in heaven" (Lk 16:9).

I. MARRIAGE IN SACRED SCRIPTURE

1. Genesis 1:27–28.

God created man in his own image, in the image of God he created him; male and female he created them. And God blessed them, and God said to them, "Be fruitful and multiply, and fill the earth and subdue it."

2. Genesis 2:22–25.

And the rib which the LORD God had taken from the man [Adam] he made into a woman and brought her to the man [Adam]. Then the man [Adam] said, "This at last is bone of my bones and flesh of my flesh; she shall be called Woman, because she was taken out of Man." Therefore a man leaves his father and his mother and cleaves to his wife, and they become one flesh. And the man [Adam] and his wife were both naked, and were not ashamed.

3. Matthew 19:3–12.

And Pharisees came up to him and tested him by asking, "Is it lawful to divorce one's wife for any cause?" He answered, "Have you not read that he who made them from the beginning made them male and female, and said, 'For this reason a man shall leave his father and mother and be joined to his wife, and the two shall become one'? So they are no longer two but one. What therefore God has joined together, let no man put asunder." They said to him, "Why then did Moses command one to give a certificate of divorce, and to put her away?" He said to them, "For your hardness of heart Moses allowed you to divorce your wives, but from the beginning it was not so. And I say to you: whoever divorces his wife, except for unchastity, and marries another, commits adultery; and he who marries a divorced woman, commits adultery."

The disciples said to him, "If such is the case of a man with his wife, it is not expedient to marry." But he said to them, "Not all men can receive this precept, but only those to whom it is given. For there are eunuchs who have been so from birth, and there are eunuchs who have been made eunuchs by men, and there are eunuchs who have made themselves eunuchs for the sake of the kingdom of heaven. He who is able to receive this, let him receive it."

4. Ephesians 5:21–32.

Be subject to one another out of reverence for Christ. Wives, be subject to your husbands, as to the Lord. For the husband is the head of the wife as Christ is the head of the church, his body, and is himself its Savior. As the church is subject to Christ, so let wives also be subject in everything to their husbands. Husbands, love your wives, as Christ loved the church and gave himself up for her, that he might sanctify her, having cleansed her by the washing of water with the word, that he might present the church to himself in splendor, without spot or wrinkle or any such thing, that she might be holy and without blemish. Even so husbands should love their wives as their own bodies. He who loves his wife loves himself. For no man ever hates his own flesh, but nourishes and cherishes it, as Christ does the church, because we are members of his body. "For this reason a man shall leave his father and mother and be joined to his wife, and the two shall become one." This is a great mystery, and I mean in reference to Christ and the church.

5. Romans 7:1–3.

Do you not know, brethren—for I am speaking to those who know the law—that the law is binding on a person only during his life? Thus a married woman is bound by law to her husband as long as he lives; but if her husband dies she is discharged from the law concerning the husband. Accordingly, she will be called an adulteress if she lives with another man while her husband is alive. But if her husband dies she is free from that law, and if she marries another man she is not an adulteress.

6. 1 Corinthians 7:1–11.

Now concerning the matters about which you wrote. It is well for a man not to touch a woman. But because of the temptation to immorality, each man should have his own wife and each woman her own husband. The husband should give to his wife her conjugal rights, and likewise the wife to her husband. For the wife does not rule over her own body, but the husband does; likewise the husband does not rule over his own body, but the wife does. Do not refuse one another except perhaps by agreement for a season, that you may devote yourselves to prayer; but then come together again, lest Satan tempt you through lack of self-control. I say this by way of concession, not of command. I wish that all were (unmarried) as I myself am. But each has his own special gift from God, one of one kind and one of another.

To the unmarried and the widows I say that it is well for them to remain single as I do. But if they cannot exercise self-control, they should marry. For it is better to marry than to be aflame with passion.

To the married I give charge, not I but the Lord, that the wife should not separate from her husband (but if she does, let her remain single or else be reconciled to her husband)—and that the husband should not divorce his wife.

7. 1 Corinthians 7:39.

A wife is bound to her husband as long as he lives. If the husband dies, she is free to be married to whom she wishes, only in the Lord.

It follows from these Scripture passages that:
1. Marriage was instituted, not by men, but by God.
2. Marriage is a true, real sacrament, because Christ has raised it to this dignity. Thereby Christ unites husband

and wife in a sacred, indissoluble covenant and grants abundant graces to the marriage partners, so that they may fulfill conscientiously the duties of this covenant.

3. The essential characteristics of marriage are unity (one man with one woman) and indissolubility, which is to say that the marriage bond can be dissolved only through the death of one of the marriage partners.

II. MARRIAGE IN THE DOCUMENTS OF THE MAGISTERIUM

1. The Council of Florence (1438–1445), in its doctrinal decision for the Armenians, spoke clearly about the sacramentality of marriage, about its essential form, and about its threefold good (offspring, fidelity, and indissolubility).[1]

2. The Council of Trent at its twenty-fourth session (1563) set forth its teaching on the Sacrament of Matrimony in one chapter[2] and in twelve propositions.[3]

3. Leo XIII, encyclical *Arcanum divinae sapientiae*, February 10, 1880, on Christian marriage.[4]

4. Pius XI, encyclical *Casti connubii*, December 31, 1930.[5]

5. Second Vatican Council, pastoral constitution *Gaudium et spes*, The Church in the Modern World, December 7, 1965:[6]

No. 47: Marriage and the Family in the Modern World.
No. 48: Holiness of Marriage and the Family.
No. 49: Married Love.
No. 50: The Fruitfulness of Marriage.
No. 51: Married Love and Respect for Human Life.
No. 52: Fostering Marriage and the Family: A Duty for All.

6. Paul VI, encyclical *Humanae vitae*, July 25, 1968.

---

[1] *Bulla unionis Armeniorum "Exsultate Deo"*, November 22, 1439, DS 1327, pp. 336–37.

[2] DS 1797–1800, pp. 415–16; English translation in "Doctrine of the Sacrament of Matrimony", CD (sess. 24, November 11, 1563), pp. 180–81.

[3] DS 1801–12, pp. 416–17; English translation in CD (sess. 24, November 11, 1563), pp. 181–82.

[4] DS 3142–46, pp. 612–14; Encyclical of Pope Leo XIII on Christian Marriage, *Arcanum divinae sapientiae*, February 10, 1880, in *The Papal Encyclicals: 1878–1903*, ed. Claudia Carlen, I.H.M., A Consortium Book (McGrath Publishing Co., 1981), pp. 29–40.

[5] DS 3700–42, pp. 718–27; Encyclical of Pope Pius XI on Christian Marriage, *Casti connubii*, December 31, 1930, in *The Papal Encyclicals: 1903–1939*, ed. Claudia Carlen, I.H.M., A Consortium Book (McGrath Publishing Co., 1981), pp. 391–414.

[6] Pt. 2, chap. 1.

7. John Paul II, apostolic exhortation *Familiaris consortio*, November 22, 1981, in which it says,[7]

This conjugal communion sinks its roots in the natural complementarity that exists between man and woman, and is nurtured through the personal willingness of the spouses to share their entire life-project, what they have and what they are: for this reason such communion is the fruit and the sign of a profoundly human need. But in the Lord Christ God takes up this human need, confirms it, purifies it and elevates it, leading it to perfection through the sacrament of Matrimony: the Holy Spirit who is poured out in the sacramental celebration offers Christian couples the gift of a new communion of love that is the living and real image of that unique unity which makes of the Church the indivisible Mystical Body of the Lord Jesus.

8. The Code of Canon Law promulgated by John Paul II on January 25, 1983:

Canon 1055—§ 1. The matrimonial covenant, by which a man and a woman establish between themselves a partnership of the whole of life, is by its nature ordered toward the good of the spouses and the procreation and education of offspring; this covenant between baptized persons has been raised by Christ the Lord to the dignity of a sacrament.

§ 2. For this reason a matrimonial contract cannot validly exist between baptized persons unless it is also a sacrament by that fact.

Canon 1056—The essential properties of marriage are unity and indissolubility, which in Christian marriage obtain a special firmness in virtue of the sacrament.

Canon 1057—§ 1. Marriage is brought about through the consent of the parties, legitimately manifested between persons who are capable according to law of giving consent; no human power can replace this consent.

[7] No. 19.

§ 2. Matrimonial consent is an act of the will by which a man and a woman, through an irrevocable covenant, mutually give and accept each other in order to establish marriage.

Canon 1058—All persons who are not prohibited by law can contract marriage.

Canon 1059—Even if only one party is baptized, the marriage of Catholics is regulated not only by divine law but also by canon law, with due regard for the competence of civil authority concerning the merely civil effects of such a marriage.

Canon 1060—Marriage enjoys the favor of the law; consequently, when a doubt exists the validity of a marriage is to be upheld until the contrary is proven.

Canon 1061—§ 1. A valid marriage between baptized persons is called ratified only if it has not been consummated; it is called ratified and consummated if the parties have performed between themselves in a human manner the conjugal act which is per se suitable for the generation of children, to which marriage is ordered by its very nature and by which the spouses become one flesh.

§ 2. After marriage has been celebrated, if the spouses have cohabited consummation is presumed until the contrary is proven.

§ 3. An invalid marriage is called putative if it has been celebrated in good faith by at least one of the parties, until both parties become certain of its nullity.

III. MARRIED BLESSEDS AND SAINTS

The Blessed Virgin Mary

and

Saint Joseph

In a book portraying married blesseds and saints and their marriages, we cannot remain silent about the holiest married couple of all; rather, their marriage and its unique character, significance, and purpose in God's plan of salvation must be placed at the very beginning.

In current opinion about the marriage of Mary and Joseph, among some who consider themselves Catholics, we encounter two quite contrary attitudes. Some have very strong inhibitions about admitting that there was a true, real, validly contracted, indissoluble marriage between Mary and Joseph. Others today not infrequently maintain—at the expense of Mary's perpetual virginity, a dogma to which the oldest professions of faith already testify—that Saint Joseph made use of his marriage to Mary with regard to sex as well and that the "firstborn" Son of Mary, the incarnate Son of God, Jesus Christ, was conceived and born in a completely natural way and was the son of Mary and of Joseph in exactly the same way, and that subsequent to this "firstborn", as a result of continued sexual relations, additional sons and daughters sprang from this marriage, precisely those "brothers and sisters of Jesus" mentioned in Sacred Scripture.

First of all, let us hold fast to the truth that between Mary and Joseph a marriage existed, not just figuratively or metaphorically, but in the full, true, and real sense. The betrothal of the two was brought to a conclusion by their wedding, when Saint Joseph took Mary into his home according to the instruction of the angel: "Joseph, son of David, do not fear to take Mary [as] your wife" (Mt 1:20).

There is actually no doubt at all as to the existence of a true marriage between Mary and Joseph: Joseph was not merely betrothed to Mary in the colloquial sense of being her "fiancé", as we understand the word today, but rather he was really, in the full legal sense, the husband, the spouse of Mary, and, conversely, Mary was really the wife, the spouse of Joseph. Indeed, Sacred Scripture explicitly uses the title corresponding to this, for instance in Matthew 1:16, where it says: "and Jacob [was] the father of Joseph the husband of Mary, of whom Jesus was born, who is called Christ." In Luke 2:4–5, in the report of the journey of the two saintly persons to Bethlehem to be enrolled in the census, it says: "And Joseph also went up from Galilee, from the city of Nazareth, to Judea, to the city of David, which is called Bethlehem, because he was of the house and lineage of David, to be enrolled with Mary his betrothed [or: his espoused wife (Douay-Rheims); *desponsata sibi* (Vulgate)], who was with child."

Furthermore, there is the fact, clearly attested in the Gospels, that Mary and Joseph really lived together, sharing a household, and that their life together was considered within the circle of their relatives and acquaintances to be marital cohabitation. Since the Israelites of that day had a strict concept of the requirements of morality and decency in married and family life, mature adults not of the same sex and not belonging to the same family could not possibly live under one roof and keep house together unless they were united in marriage as husband and wife.

Now Sacred Scripture explicitly says of Saint Joseph that he took Mary into his home, that he faithfully and conscientiously fulfilled the duties of a husband with respect to Mary, and, conversely, that Mary fulfilled the duties of a wife with respect to

The wedding of Joseph and Mary

Joseph. They made their way together to Jerusalem for the religious festivals; they fled together to Egypt from the persecution by Herod; after their return from Egypt they lived together in Nazareth.

Therefore, according to all we find reported in Sacred Scripture, there is no doubt that Mary and Joseph were united with one another in a completely legitimate marriage. It was a beautiful custom that previously the Church's liturgy celebrated the wedding of the Blessed Virgin Mary with a separate feast day on January 23. After 1914, it is true, this feast was no longer prescribed as a general obligation, because of the calendar reform of Pope Saint Pius X, but remained only a particular feast of various local churches, and this Marian feast was completely abolished in the 1969 reform of the calendar. This does not make us any less justified in recalling the mystery commemorated in this former Marian feast; even less does it alter the biblical fact that Mary, the most Blessed Virgin and the Mother of God, was not merely engaged to Saint Joseph but was married to him.

It is a question of the most noble, most beautiful, and holiest marital union, which—without impugning in the least the virginity of the Queen of Virgins—made Mary the real, lawfully wedded wife of Saint Joseph. Of course Mary had promised God or even vowed perpetual virginity—we can assume that this was by a special inspiration of the Holy Spirit. For a healthy girl who had reached sexual maturity to remain single and unmarried, however, was for the people of Israel at that time something almost unthinkable and impossible. So it was certainly part of God's plan that Mary should be espoused, despite her promise to God or her vow of virginity. Now the carpenter Joseph, from the house and lineage of David, was the husband whom Divine Providence had destined for Mary and surely prepared, too, with the requisite noble-mindedness and upright character so as to guarantee that in this marriage the husband would always respect the virginity of the wife.

As with any marriage, the marriage of Mary and Joseph had as its purpose the most intimate union of these two persons with one

"While they were there, the time came for her to be delivered. And she gave birth to her first-born son and wrapped him in swaddling cloths, and laid him in a manger"
(Lk 2:6–7).

33

another; in this case, though, both of them had agreed to renounce sexual relations.

In marriage, of course, the legitimate, natural use of the God-given sexual powers for the mutual delight of the spouses and for the transmission of life is also willed by God and therefore in order. Use does not necessarily have to be made of a right, however; it can certainly also be renounced so as to make the spiritual union of the two spouses even stronger. The right must be renounced, in fact, when there is a divine command to this effect or when it has to happen for the sake of the kingdom of God. Temporary or permanent abstinence from loving sexual relations within marriage, as was the case with Mary and Joseph, shows that the satisfaction of carnal desires and sexual appetites is by no means absolutely necessary for true marital happiness. The spiritual joys of a marriage lived in this way can become that much more beautiful and delightful in return.

We have arrived now at that unique quality which exalted the marriage of Mary and Joseph above every other marriage, however intimate and tender the mutual love of the spouses might be: It was a virginal marriage, that is, the parties to this marriage, with complete freedom and understanding, renounced forever the exercise of the right to sexual relations with one another. The evidence for this is quite clear in Sacred Scripture, after all: In the Gospel passage about the Annunciation (Lk 1:26–38) we read that Mary solemnly declared to the angel Gabriel in clear terms that she "did not know man". To the most momentous and honorific message that had ever come down from heaven to a human being—that she, Mary, was to become the mother of the Messiah, the Son of God—she gave the reply: "How can this be [that I will become a mother] since I do not know man [in sexual relations]?" [Lk 1:34, NAB]. Mary, this wise and humble virgin, by no means intended with these words to shirk the task that God presented to her; yet she did not understand how the angel's announcement, that she was to conceive and bear a child, could be fulfilled! She asked the heavenly messenger for an explanation: "How can this be since I do not know man?" Is not the saying, "Out of the abundance of

The Holy Family during their flight into Egypt

the heart the mouth speaks [Mt 12:34]", true of Mary's reply as well? Mary's heart was filled with the desire and the resolution to remain completely and utterly consecrated to God in perpetual virginity. Until now she had preserved her virginity spotlessly in both a physical and spiritual sense; she was determined to continue preserving this precious treasure. Moreover, she was surely convinced as well that this decision of hers to promise perpetual virginity had been approved and blessed by God; otherwise Mary's question would have made no sense. It must have been that the decision to remain perpetually a virgin was something that Mary had already settled, and no offer, no matter how honorable or from what quarter, could make her change her mind.

From such a stance on Mary's part we can then reasonably conclude that she consented to the betrothal with Joseph, which had been proposed earlier, only on the condition that her virginity would be preserved inviolate in the ensuing marriage.

If Joseph agreed to this condition, though, then we can also draw conclusions about his spiritual outlook and his moral views. If he agreed to the betrothal and the wedding with Mary on such an unusual condition, as mentioned above, then he—who at that time had no idea of the great salvific event that was to come, the Incarnation of the Son of God in the womb of his bride—must have considered Mary to be such an exceedingly precious individual, just as she was, with the crown of her virginity intact, that he wanted to unite himself forever with Mary in spite of that, or even for that very reason. But if this man thought so highly of Mary's virginity, then he himself was probably a thoroughly upright, noble, and chaste person, who with heartfelt gladness wanted to renounce the legitimate joys of sex within marriage and the blessings of children, so as to be able to protect a yet more precious good: the purity and virginity of his bride.

In this way, then, our attention is called here to the fact that Mary and Joseph entered upon their betrothal and their marriage covenant only after promising one another perpetual virginity, that is, after mutually agreeing to abstain forever from marital relations. For without Saint Joseph's agreement to Mary's perpetual virginity, which was so pleasing to God, such a decision on Mary's part alone would have made the marriage contract null and void in the first place.

We must keep in mind the fact that the marital bond between Mary and Joseph was entered into by both parties with clear understanding and complete freedom as a virginal covenant, in order to appreciate rightly the great reverence that Saint Joseph must have had for his immaculate bride—and this, remarkably, at a time when he had no idea that Mary had been specially chosen and called by God.

Let us reflect further on this fact, that Saint Joseph was betrothed to establish a virginal marriage covenant with Mary. Until then the world had never seen such a thing. The world probably would not have considered it possible, either. In any case, the entire Old Covenant knows of nothing like it. Even in the New Covenant, imitations of such a virginal marriage covenant are extremely rare, as we will see. Certainly, again and again in the course of the Church's history there have been generous individuals who, with a view to Christ and for the sake of the kingdom of heaven, enthusiastically consecrated their virginity to God in steadfast fidelity, especially in the clerical and the religious state. But such noble souls, who kept their promise to observe perpetual virginity with lifelong fidelity, renounced marriage entirely in the first place and lived in the unmarried, celibate state, instead of entering a marriage while renouncing all use of particular marital rights. Men and women who deliberately decided to live their married life as virgins after the example of Mary and Joseph, and in fact lived in that way, are—as will become apparent—very much the exception, even among the blesseds and the saints. Here the frequently asked question arises whether it would not have made more sense and been more conducive to perfection for Mary and Joseph to renounce marriage entirely instead of entering a virginal marriage. Did not Jesus Christ, and after him the Apostle Paul especially, prize very highly the unmarried state and a life of virginity? And is this not precisely the reason that the Church requires her priests to be unmarried and adheres to the discipline of obligatory celibacy for priests? And did not the Council of Trent issue a particular doctrinal statement concerning the preeminence of the virginal state over the marital state, in these words: "If anyone says that the marital state is to be preferred to the state of virginity or celibacy, and that it is not better and happier to remain in virginity or celibacy than to be united in matrimony, let him be anathema" (DS 1810)?[1]

In order to understand correctly the marriage of Mary and Joseph, we must of course take into account the circumstances of that time and the plans of Divine Providence.

A whole series of reasons, as listed early on by great Church Fathers such as Ambrose and Augustine, must have made entering a marriage contract seem to Mary and Joseph advisable, or even necessary, despite their decision to observe perpetual virginity:

1. First of all, among the Israelite people of that time the prevailing view was that an adult, sexually mature person could not possibly forgo marriage. Of course there was no commandment absolutely requiring marriage, but it would have been viewed as an offense against tradition and public decorum not to marry.

There was another important religious reason for this. At that time among the Israelite people, all eyes were directed toward the promised Messiah who was to come. In his children or his children's children, in his grandchildren and great-grandchildren, the Israelite believer hoped that he would at last have some share in the messianic blessing. The blessing of children was viewed as the fulfillment of God's promise to Abraham; childlessness, on the other hand, was considered a very serious affliction, often even a punishment from God. Therefore it is understandable that in the entire Old Testament not one single virgin can be named about whom it can be said with certainty that she voluntarily and deliberately renounced the married state.

2. We must also realize that, in the Israelite view at that time, the married state was held in much higher esteem than virginity.

---

[1] Council of Trent (sess. 24, November 11, 1563), can. 10. English trans. from *The Sources of Catholic Dogma*, trans. Roy J. Deferrari from the 13th ed. of Henry Denzinger's *Enchiridion Symbolorum* (St. Louis: B. Herder Book Co., 1957), p. 297.

We find a similar situation nowadays in a superficially Christian society; today there is scarcely a trace left of the former high opinion of virginity. In any case it was most fitting, for various reasons, for Mary to conceal her decision to remain forever a virgin under the cloak of marriage. The same can be said, of course, about Saint Joseph. He, too, was to a certain extent compelled by the circumstances of the day to contract marriage, despite his previous decision to practice celibacy. The one who arranged the circumstances of the time in that way, ultimately, was God in his all-wise Providence. Saint Thomas Aquinas explains in his *Summa Theologiae* [2] the wisdom behind God's provision that the two virginal individuals, Mary and Joseph, should enter a marriage—a virginal marriage, to be sure.

a. If the birth of the incarnate Son of God, in the eyes of the world—which at that time would have found a virginal conception and birth utterly incomprehensible—had not been protected by a legal father, then the Savior would have been exposed to the calumny that he was a bastard or an illegitimate child and that his blessed, virginal Mother was an unwed mother. It was necessary that Christ and his Mother be able to appear in public honorably and without reproach. That was possible only if Jesus, despite his virginal conception, was born into a legal marriage.

b. Furthermore, the promised Messiah had to come from King David's line. Without the marital bond of Joseph (a descendant of David) with Mary, Jesus Christ could never have legitimately assumed the role of the "Son of David", even though Mary herself was also from the house and lineage of David.

c. Besides this, it is easy to see why it was much more advantageous for Mary that the virginally conceived Divine Child be born into a marriage, since in this way Mary—especially during the childhood and boyhood years of the God-Man—had Saint Joseph at her side as a helper and protector in every predicament and danger.

There are quite a few other reasons why it was fitting for Mary

---

[2] Pt. 3, q. 29, art 1.

to espouse Joseph. If the saying "Marriages are made in heaven" was ever true, then it certainly was so for the sacred bond between Mary and Joseph: From all eternity the triune God had predestined Mary to be the Mother of the Redeemer and accordingly had also prepared most exquisitely everything that could serve this purpose. Since therefore the great mystery of the Incarnation of the Son of God was to be accomplished beneath the veil of a marriage, it was necessary to provide the future Mother of the Son of God with a worthy spouse. "Let us make her a helper fit for her." Thus the triune God may have spoken on this occasion, too—much as he did at the completion of the first man. To the extent that it was possible, the bridegroom and spouse chosen for the most chaste bride would have to be of equally high birth, especially with regard to the dispositions of his heart. When we consider all this as part of God's providential plan, we begin to understand that Saint Joseph, who gave his hand to Mary in a virginal marriage, greatly surpassed all his contemporaries, and indeed all men of all times, in the fullness of his virtues. We can see, then, also how these two virginal souls found each other and understood one another so well and how one spouse offered to the other the invaluable treasure of virginity. In offering Mary his hand and his heart so as to enter a virginal marriage, and in commending his own virginity to her as a precious engagement gift, Joseph gave Mary more than if he, the impoverished scion of the royal line of David, had brought with him into his marriage a kingdom instead of a modest dwelling with a carpenter's shop. Because Mary, furthermore, in the same way selected and chose Saint Joseph to be forever the protector, indeed, the legitimate master and proprietor of her own immaculate purity and virginity, a treasure fell to the lot of Saint Joseph with which nothing on earth can compare.

Saint Ann and Saint Joachim

That noble married couple, those parents who through their daughter find a place in the New Covenant, cannot be passed over in a book about married saints, even if there is scarcely anything historically certain that can be reported about them; we are speaking, of course, about the parents of the most Blessed Virgin Mary and the grandparents of the God-Man, Jesus Christ.

The names and the legendary lives of Saint Ann and her husband, Joachim, are written in the apocryphal *Protoevangelium of James*, which was composed around the middle of the second century. Further details come from the so-called *Gospel of Pseudo-Matthew* and also the *Book on the Origin of the Blessed Virgin Mary* (*liber de ortu beatae Mariae virginis*) from the fifth century, and from the likewise apocryphal *Gospel about the Birth of Mary* from the sixth century.[1]

The information contained in these sources, briefly summarized, gives us the following portrait of Joachim and Ann. Joachim came from Ephoris in Galilee. He married Ann and lived at the

[1] Cf. W. Michaelis, *Die Apokryphen zum Neuen Testament* (Bremen, 1956), pp. 72–98; B. Kleinschmidt, *Die hl. Anna: Ihre Verehrung in Geschichte, Kunst und Volkstum* (Düsseldorf, 1931).

Sheep Gate of Jerusalem. He led an exemplary life together with his wife and was very charitable. For decades this couple remained without the blessing of children. One day, when Joachim went to offer a sacrifice, the priests at the temple turned him away because he was childless. Because of this grievous insult he withdrew to the desert, where he lived a life of even greater piety and charity. After twenty years of childless marriage, Ann was the first to be consoled by an angel: "Ann, Ann, the Lord has heard your prayer: You shall conceive and bear a child, and your offspring shall be known throughout the world." Similarly an angel came to Joachim as well and said to him: "Joachim, Joachim, the Lord God has heard your prayer. Go down from here (to Jerusalem to your wife, Ann)!" Ann stood at the door and saw Joachim coming. Then she ran to him and threw her arms around his neck and said: "Now I know that the Lord God will bless me abundantly: For behold, I, who finally had to live as a widow, am a widow no longer; and I, though childless, shall be with child."

Then came about the conception and the birth of the long-desired child: It was to have the name Mary!

Instead of further elaborations from the apocryphal gospels, let us cite the last Father of the Church in the East, John Damascene (d. ca. 750), who contributed much toward the worldwide spread of devotion to Saint Ann and Saint Joachim. In a discourse on the birth of Mary he said the following:

Ann was to be the mother of the Virgin Mother of God, and hence nature did not dare to anticipate the flowering of grace. Thus nature remained sterile, until grace produced its fruit. For she who was to be born had to be a first-born daughter, since she would be the mother of the first-born of all creation, *in whom all things are held together* [cf. Col 1:17].

Joachim and Ann, how blessed a couple! All creation is indebted to you. For at your hands the Creator was offered a gift excelling all other gifts: a chaste mother, who alone was worthy of him.

And so rejoice, Ann, that *you were sterile and have not borne*

"The Holy Family". After a woodcut by Hans Baldung Grien. On the left Joseph and Mary; on the right Joachim and Anne; and in the middle the Christ Child can be seen.

children; break forth into shouts, you who have not given birth [Is 54:1]. Rejoice, Joachim, because from your daughter *a child is born for us, a son is given us, whose name is Messenger of great counsel and universal salvation, mighty God* [Is 9:6]. For this child is God.

Joachim and Ann, how blessed and spotless a couple! You will be known by the fruit you have borne, as the Lord says: *By their fruits you will know them* [Mt 7:16]. The conduct of your life pleased God and was worthy of your daughter. For by the chaste and holy life you led together, you have fashioned a jewel of virginity; she who remained a virgin before, during and after giving birth. She alone for all time would maintain her virginity in mind and soul as well as in body.

Joachim and Ann, how chaste a couple! While safeguarding the chastity prescribed by the law of nature, you achieved with God's help something which transcends nature in giving the world the Virgin Mother of God as your daughter. While leading a devout and holy life in your human nature, you gave birth to a daughter nobler than the angels, whose queen she now is. Girl of utter beauty and delight, daughter of Adam and mother of God, blessed the loins and blessed the womb from which you come! Blessed the arms that carried you, and blessed your parents' lips, which you were allowed to cover with chaste kisses, ever maintaining your virginity.[2]

[2] Saint John Damascene, *Orat.* 6, in *Nativitatem B. Mariae* 5:2, 4–6; *Patrologia Graeca* (PG) 96:663, 667, 670; English trans. from *The Liturgy of the Hours according to the Roman Rite*, trans. International Commission on English in the Liturgy (New York: Catholic Book Publishing Co., 1975), 3:1556–57.

Saint Elizabeth and Saint Zechariah

Elizabeth greets Mary. (Waanrode, Church of Saint Bartholomew, sixteenth century)

In the transition from the Old to the New Covenant, we encounter a couple upon whom Sacred Scripture bestows high praise:

> In the days of Herod, king of Judea, there was a priest named Zechariah, of the division of Abijah; and he had a wife of the daughters of Aaron, and her name was Elizabeth. And they were both righteous before God, walking in all the commandments and ordinances of the Lord blameless. But they had no child, because Elizabeth was barren, and both were advanced in years. (Lk. 1:5–7)

According to this passage, Zechariah (Zachary) was from the priestly class of Abijah, the eighth of twenty-four classes in all into which the entire Old Testament priesthood was divided and which were assigned in turn by lot to offer incense each day in the temple (cf. 1 Chron 24:7–19). This man Zechariah (in Hebrew: *zekaryāh, Zacharya* = "Yahweh thinks"), then, was a priest's son. It was not really an obligation for the son of a Jewish priest to take a priest's daughter as his wife, but this was considered a sign of particular fidelity to the Law of Yahweh. So it is still today in Orthodox rabbinical families. Zechariah, in any case, adhered to the custom and married a virgin from the tribe of the high priest Aaron whose name was Elizabeth (in Hebrew: *elisheba* = "God has sworn"; others interpret it: "God is seven", that is, perfection; still others claim that it is derived from the Hebrew name of God, *El*, and *beth* = "house", hence "house of God").

Having contracted marriage in reverent fidelity to their ancestral custom, this couple then lived their married life strictly according to God's commands and precepts. They were—as the Scripture verse Luke 1:6 was formerly translated—"just before God, walking in all the commandments and justifications of the Lord without blame" [Douay-Rheims]. Such a judgment upon the conduct of an Israelite couple was indeed very high praise. "A deeply rooted interior religious sense and exemplary external piety gave the life of this couple its character."[1]

Not all married people then lived like that, not even all the priestly families in Israel. There was also a less demanding approach. These believed they were more liberal, went along with the times, did not want to quarrel with God, but not with the world either. Being cultured was more important for them than living strictly according to the Torah. Especially in the higher priestly classes there were proponents of this Sadducee way of thinking.

In praising the virtuousness of the spouses Zechariah and Elizabeth, Luke the Evangelist intended especially to put the childlessness of this couple in the proper light. Among the people of Israel this condition was not only felt to be a heavy burden, but was also considered a divine judgment, as punishment for serious sins against God. Now if Zechariah and Elizabeth, despite their profound sorrow on account of their childlessness, did not cease to live righteously, then their piety had withstood the trial by fire.

[1] P. Ketter, *Christus und die Frauen* (Düsseldorf 1935), pp. 241–44; L. Ballarini, "Elisabetta", in *Bibliotheca Sanctorum* 4:1079–89; B. Mariani, "Zaccaria", in *Bibliotheca Sanctorum* 12:1443–45.

Elizabeth (center, with the child) and Zechariah (right foreground), who has asked for a writing tablet and written on it: "His name is John."

They humbly carried their cross. That is why they merited God's special favor: "Your prayer is heard", says the angel Gabriel to Zechariah in the temple. "Your wife Elizabeth will bear you a son, and you shall call his name John" (Lk 1:13. *Iōannēs* is the Greek form of the Hebrew *yehôhanān* = "the Lord is gracious"). That was in fact the proper name for this child of grace, who was to prepare the way of the Redeemer and announce a time of favor from the Lord.

It is humanly understandable that Zechariah was overwhelmed with astonishment at the announcement of the angel and asked incredulously: "How shall I know this? For I am an old man, and my wife is advanced in years" (Lk 1:18). Nevertheless, Zechariah's doubt merited an expiatory punishment, because it was, after all, an angel, a messenger of God, who had held out the prospect of this miracle and had done so in a holy place, in the temple. For an Old Testament priest, that should have been enough to elicit faith and a joyous, grateful affirmation of what had been revealed to him.

For Elizabeth's part, there is no report of doubting in Sacred Scripture. The opinion of P. Ketter is probably correct: "Her womanly soul dwelt more in that realm of mystery, where nature meets the supernatural, than did the priestly soul of her husband."

A new stage of life began now for this married couple, especially for Elizabeth. Only mothers can understand sympathetically what a transformation took place now in her entire being, as the Creator enlisted her in his service even though she was advanced in age.

"And when his time of service [in the temple] was ended, he went to his home. After these days his wife Elizabeth conceived, and for five months she hid herself, saying, 'Thus the Lord has done to me in the days when he looked on me, to take away my reproach among men'" (Lk 1:23–25). What can we deduce from Elizabeth's soliloquy, which Luke has handed down to us? For one thing, that she was really conscious that the child she had conceived was a blessing and a sign of God's favor. After all, she and her husband had yearned for so long to have a child and therefore had prayed together year after year for this intention. Second, she was grateful to God for freeing her from the shame she bore in the sight of men. But why did Elizabeth remain in complete seclusion for five months? Did she want to make an appearance again among her neighbors only when it had become apparent to all that God had taken away from her the shame of childlessness? A much higher motive kept her back in the silence and seclusion of her house: She fled the activities of the world in order to be alone with God and so to provide for her child, in those five months of silent retreat, a proper setting for his development and the abundant blessing of undisturbed converse with God. It has been noted astutely that in this silent advent time that Elizabeth observed, the love of the solitude that her son later sought in the desert must have become part of his flesh and blood. And the foundation laid during those first five months of silent growth in the womb of his mother was then brought to completion by the breath of the Holy Spirit when Mary visited Elizabeth in the sixth month. The first meeting of these two blessed mothers was accompanied by miracles of grace; how much more abundantly the stream of blessings must have flowed during the three months that those two expectant women spent together (cf. Lk 1:39–56).

When at the end of the nine months Elizabeth had given birth to her child and held him in her arms, it was a joyful day not only for her and for her husband, Zechariah. "And her neighbors and kinsfolk heard that the Lord had shown great mercy to her [Elizabeth], and they rejoiced with her" (Lk 1:58). To Zechariah the angel Gabriel had said, after announcing the birth of a child to Elizabeth: "And you will have joy and gladness, and many will rejoice at his [John's] birth" (Lk 1:14). Zechariah rejoiced, moreover, that the punishment of being struck dumb was taken away from him. His power of speech restored, he used it to praise and thank God prophetically with all his heart: "And his father Zechariah was filled with the Holy Spirit, and prophesied, saying, 'Blessed be the Lord God of Israel'" (Lk 1:67ff.).

What happened later in the life of the married couple Elizabeth and Zechariah, we do not know. Sacred Scripture is silent on this subject. In any case, the divine praises sung by Zechariah continue to resound as the canticle known as the *Benedictus* at Morning Prayer each day in the Divine Office prayed by priests and religious. According to the apocryphal *Apocalypse of Zechariah* from the turn of the fourth century, Zechariah was murdered by Herod in the temple. At any rate he was considered a saint even in early Christian times, and his feast day is November 5, the same as that of his holy spouse, Elizabeth. Whereas only after the reform of the liturgical calendar initiated by the Second Vatican Council were married saints commemorated together on the same day, not on separate days (for example, the parents of the Blessed Virgin, Joachim and Ann, or the imperial couple, Saints Henry and Cunegund), the parents of John the Baptist have always been commemorated on the same day and are mentioned together in the Roman Martyrology, where it says for November 5: "The holy priest and prophet Zechariah, father of John the Baptist, the Forerunner of the Lord, and Saint Elizabeth, mother of the eminently holy Forerunner."

Saint
Salome
and
Zebedee

We turn now to a biblical married couple who, at the beginning of the New Covenant, experienced the joy and honor of placing two sons at the disposal of the Lord Jesus for the college of apostles: Saint Salome and her husband, Zebedee.

James the Great and his younger brother, John, are the only two apostles whose father and mother are named in the New Testament. Zebedee (*Zebedaios* is the Greek form of the Hebrew name *zabdî* = "The Lord grants", "gift of God") is mentioned three times by name in the New Testament as the father of the apostles James and John (see Mt 20:20; 27:56; and Lk 5:10), who were born of his wife, Salome. Whether she bore him other children as well is not known. Other than that, Sacred Scripture mentions only that he was a fisherman by profession, plied his trade on the lake of Gennesaret, and probably lived in Bethzatha. Since he owned a boat with fishing nets and, besides his two sons, also employed day laborers, we can reasonably conclude that his family was among the more affluent in that locality.

Nowhere in the New Testament does it say that Zebedee, like his two sons, eventually decided to join the close followers of Jesus. Later legends, too, seem to have nothing more to say about him. Presumably he died during Jesus' public ministry, because his wife very soon joined the company of the other women who followed the Lord and served Him.

Zebedee's wife, Salome ("peaceable") by name, was a sister or a close relation of the Mother of Jesus (cf. Jn 19:25; Mk 15:40; Mt 27:56). Nothing is known of her childhood or youth.

Unlike so many other Jewish women at the time of Jesus,

Salome presumably did not have to contend with want and privation, because her husband, Zebedee—as was noted above—most likely conducted a prosperous fishing business. The greatest treasure of her house, though, and also her pride and joy, were her two sons, James and his younger brother, John. Like their father, they, too, devoted themselves to the fishing trade and went about their business together with their father and often with another pair of brothers, Simon Peter and Andrew (cf. Lk 5:9).

Sacred Scripture reports nothing further about the life of the married couple Zebedee and Salome. We can assume, though, of course, that their married and family life was very good and happy because, in the first place, it was blessed with children—to whom Israelite husbands attached great importance. Furthermore, the basic requirement for any happy and peaceful life together was fulfilled: the magnanimity of the spouses and the deeply religious spirit that pervaded the entire family. This can be inferred from the fact that the two sons of Zebedee and Salome joined early on the messianic movement that had started with the appearance of John the Baptist. Their younger son, John, together with his friend and compatriot Andrew, was the first to whom the Forerunner pointed out Jesus as the Lamb of God; he then experienced that blessed meeting with the Messiah, the exact hour and circumstances of which remained quite vivid in his memory even when he had reached an advanced age (cf. Jn 1:35ff.). John then brought his brother, James, to the Lord, as Andrew brought his brother, Simon Peter.

The definitive call of the two sons of Zebedee occurred later, while they were at their father's side, when Jesus was walking—and recruiting—one day on the shore of the lake of Gennesaret (cf. Mk 1:19–21). Jesus then saw in a boat the father Zebedee with his two sons and his hired men, as they were cleaning their fishing nets and preparing to make another catch. The eye of the best judge of men discovered in the two sons of Zebedee and Salome generous souls full of ardor, admirably suited for apostolic work. Jesus called them—and without hesitation they left the boat, their father, and their usual tasks and joined up with the poor, as yet little-known wandering preacher from Nazareth. Their mother, Salome, may have been terribly alarmed that evening when her husband, Zebedee, approached his house, slowly and pensively, and haltingly shared with her the news that her two sons had joined Jesus' company for good and would hardly ever return again to the family.

Salome—who, as we learn from Sacred Scripture, thought the world of her two sons and was devoted to them—would not have been a real mother had she let her sons go off without tears and laments. Yet she probably got hold of herself soon enough when she heard that both sons already belonged to the inner circle of Jesus' favored disciples and that John was even referred to as "the disciple whom Jesus loved"; Jesus himself gave him and his brother, James, the nickname "Boanerges—Sons of Thunder"; the scenes depicted in Luke 9:54 and Mark 9:38 show that this name suited their temperament.

What speaks most highly of Salome is the fact that, ultimately, not only did she gladly give up her two sons—whom she had raised with all the ingenuity that a pious, believing Jewish mother could muster—so that they could become close followers of Jesus; but she also—most likely after the death of her husband, Zebedee—placed herself at the Lord's disposal, serving him and helping financially along with other women (cf. Mk 15:40; Lk 8:2). In this way she would then observe, often at close range, how highly Christ thought of her sons and favored them over the others. They were permitted to be present when Jesus awoke the little daughter of Jairus from death back to life, and likewise when he was transfigured on the height of Mount Tabor; they were with him, too, however, when he was baptized on the Mount of Olives with a baptism of bitter suffering. On that occasion Salome may have recalled the answer that the Lord had given her when she, a mother, all too ambitiously had made a rather exorbitant request of the Lord on behalf of her sons.

Then the mother of the sons of Zebedee came up to him, with her sons, and kneeling before him she asked him for something.

And he said to her, "What do you want?" She said to him, "Command that these two sons of mine may sit, one at your right hand and one at your left, in your kingdom." But Jesus answered, "You do not know what you are asking. Are you able to drink the cup that I am to drink?" (Mt 20:20–22)

"Are you able . . . to be baptized with the baptism with which I am baptized?" And they said to him, "We are able." And Jesus said to them, "The cup that I drink you will drink; and with the baptism with which I am baptized, you will be baptized; but to sit at my right hand or at my left is not mine to grant, but it is for those for whom it has been prepared." (Mk 10:38–40)

What brought Salome to make this request, which not only neglects to take into consideration the other apostles, but also appears on its face to be very presumptuous? Not long before that, Peter on behalf of all the Twelve had asked the Lord the question about their reward, after Jesus had presented a magnificent prospect to the rich young man if he would leave everything and follow him. "Then Peter said in reply, 'Lo, we have left everything and followed you. What then shall we have?' Jesus said to them, 'Truly, I say to you, in the new world, when the Son of man shall sit on his glorious throne, you who have followed me will also sit on twelve thrones, judging the twelve tribes of Israel'" (Mt 19:27–28). Salome knew, then, that two thrones in the future messianic kingdom had been promised to her sons. That still did not satisfy her or them.

What must the mother, Salome, have thought when she heard Jesus' answer about drinking the cup with him and about being immersed in a baptismal bath like his, when both of these images, according to biblical usage, referred to great sufferings? Was this mother frightened, and did she have a dark premonition that something very difficult and painful was in store for her sons? The relevant Scripture passage tells us nothing about that, but we learn later from the same evangelists, Matthew and Mark, who gave us the report about Salome's maternal ambition, that she was not only an ambitious mother but also a fearless, courageous woman, who still stood by Jesus under the Cross when everything turned out to be very different from what she had hoped. Nor did she feel slighted when Jesus, dying on the Cross, finally entrusted the most precious thing he had left, namely, his Mother, to her son John (cf. Jn 19:27). After the death of Jesus, Salome nobly made a contribution so that spices could be bought for Jesus' burial. Salome was, then, one of those women, too, who on Easter morning hurried to the grave so as to render their dead Master one last service but, instead, were privileged to see the Risen One. Salome probably also lived to see her son James become the first apostle to offer his life for Christ as a martyr when he was beheaded around the year 42.

The wife of Zebedee, the mother of those two apostles, requested honors; she was assured of sacrifices. Because the mother Salome and her two sons nonetheless accepted and affirmed the sacrifice, God, who is not to be outdone in generosity, rewarded them accordingly. In many dioceses in Italy, the feast of the holy spouse and mother of apostles, Salome, is celebrated on October 22. Certainly we are justified in thinking on that date also of the husband and father of the family, Zebedee, who was an instructor and an example to his two sons not only in the fishing trade but also in faith-filled, confident hope for the Messiah, whom James and John then served with outstanding fidelity.[1]

---

[1] Cf. *Acta Sanctorum* 11:435–76; Fr. Spadafora, "Santa Salomè, madre degli Apostoli Giacomo e Giovanni", in *Bibliotheca Sanctorum* 11:583; P. Ketter, *Christus und die Frauen* (Düsseldorf, 1935), pp. 283–87; Fr. Zoepfl, "Salome, die Mutter der Zebedäussöhne", in *Biblische Mütter* (Donauwörth, 1922), pp. 171–84.

Saint
Basil the Elder
and
Saint
Emmelia

Basil:
> b. ca. 270 in Cappadocia
> d. before 349

Emmelia:
> d. ca. 372

Parents of ten children

Basil was the son of wealthy Christian parents from Caesarea in Cappadocia, who, during the persecution of Christians by the emperor Maximus, had to leave house and home and eke out a living for seven years (from 304 to 311) hidden in the wooded mountains of Pontus. In the funeral oration for his friend Basil the Great, Saint Gregory Nazianzen[1] mentions only the grandmother, Saint Macrina the Elder, but not the grandfather.

Basil the Elder, the father of Basil the Great, grew up in Caesarea in Cappadocia, studied law and rhetoric, and then made a career for himself in Caesarea as a lawyer and professor of rhetoric. Gregory Nazianzen the Younger portrays the father of his friend Basil the Great, in his aforementioned funeral oration for the latter, as an upright Christian and a master of every virtue.

Basil the Elder was married to Saint Emmelia, a woman of excellent and virtuous character and of outstanding beauty; she had lost her parents at an early age and married Basil the Elder so as to avoid the many dangers of the world. The reputation of this Christian married couple spread very quickly through all of

---

[1] *Oratio 53 in laudem Basilii Magni,* PG 36:500–504.

Pontus and Cappadocia, especially because they showed great zeal in establishing works of corporal mercy for the poor and pilgrims.

From the marriage of this noble, saintly couple, Basil the Elder and Emmelia, came ten children, the most famous among them being Saint Basil the Great, Saint Gregory of Nyssa, Saint Macrina the Younger, and Saint Peter of Sebaste.

With extraordinary love and care, Saint Emmelia saw to the Christian upbringing of her children; she taught them very early on to know and to treasure the Word of God in Sacred Scripture. By means of the Old Testament book of Wisdom she made them thoroughly acquainted with the fundamentals of Christian life.

Basil the Elder died soon after the birth of his last-born child (who later became Bishop Peter of Sebaste), around 349. His wife, Saint Emmelia, after providing for the care of all her children, withdrew to a cloister in Annesi. Emmelia died there at a ripe old age around 372, supported by the presence of her saintly daughter Macrina and her saintly son Peter of Sebaste.

C. Baronius inserted the names of Saint Basil the Elder and his wife Emmelia in the Roman Martyrology under the date of May 30. On this day the Italo-Greek monks of Calabria observe the "Feast of the Relatives of Saint Basil the Great".

Let us look briefly at the lives of the holy daughters and the holy sons of this holy married couple, Basil the Elder and Emmelia:

1. Saint Macrina the Younger—so named after her saintly grandmother Macrina the Elder—was born around 327 in Caesarea in Cappadocia. She must have been a great beauty and therefore much sought after; from among the many suitors, her father Basil the Elder chose as the bridegroom for his beautiful daughter one young man who, as he judged, would best correspond to his expectations. This bridegroom, though, died suddenly, even before the wedding, and then Macrina, who had been more and more inclined to the virginal state, acted as though she wanted to remain true to her deceased bridegroom even beyond the grave. At first she helped her mother, who was widowed soon after the birth of the youngest child, Peter of Sebaste, and assisted her in raising her younger brothers and sisters. Once all the children

were well educated and provided for and no longer needed a mother, Macrina convinced her mother that she should now live a life consecrated to God in the wilderness of Annesi near Hore in Pontus, on the bank of the river Iris. Her mother, Emmelia, agreed and followed her daughter's example. Together with several servant girls they began to live a cloistered life at the place mentioned. When Emmelia died there around the year 373, after having acted as a holy superior in the monastery thus founded, her daughter Macrina the Younger succeeded her in this office. Besides the monastery for women, one for men was founded as well, to which Peter, the youngest brother of Saint Macrina the Younger, had withdrawn. Both of the older brothers, Saint Basil and Great and Saint Gregory of Nyssa, were greatly influenced during their childhood and youth by their sister Macrina the Younger; even in their mature years as bishops they remained in contact with their saintly sister, who now was a nun. Macrina's oldest brother, Basil the Great, who in 370 had become bishop of Caesarea in Cappadocia, visited his saintly sister in the convent at Annesi and ordained his brother Peter, who lived as a monk in the nearby monastery, to the priesthood so that he could care for the souls of his sister Macrina and the other sisters in her community.

A younger brother of Saint Macrina the Younger, Saint Gregory of Nyssa, who in 371 had become Bishop of Nyssa, likewise called on his sister Macrina in the convent at Annesi; this took place around the beginning of the year 380. At this meeting very detailed religious conversations developed, which were then reflected in the work by Saint Gregory of Nyssa entitled *On the Soul and the Resurrection.*[2] Soon afterward Saint Macrina died. She was buried in the church nearby the convent that had been built in honor of the forty martyrs of Sebaste. There her saintly parents, Basil the Elder and Emmelia, were also laid to rest. C. Baronius spread liturgical devotion to Saint Macrina the Younger to the West as well by listing her name in the Roman Martyrology, where it says for

[2] PG 46:16–140.

July 19: "In Cappadocia memoria sanctae Macrinae Virginis, sororis sanctorum Basilii Magni et Gregorii Nysseni."

2. Basil the Great was born around 329 or 330 in Caesarea in Cappadocia, the oldest son of the saintly married couple Basil the Elder and Emmelia. A sickly child, he spent his earliest years on their country estate at Annesi, not far from Neocaesarea, where he was cared for lovingly by his grandmother Saint Macrina the Elder. Then, after an almost fatal illness from which, to the astonishment of his relatives, he completely recovered, he returned to live with his parents in Caesarea. He attended schools in Caesarea in Cappadocia, then the academies in Constantinople and, finally, in Athens, where he struck up a lifelong friendship with his compatriot Gregory Nazianzen. Having returned home around 356, Basil the Great taught rhetoric for a short time but soon decided to renounce the world. He received Baptism and visited the most famous ascetics in Syria, Palestine, Egypt, and Mesopotamia so as to become acquainted with the spirit of monasticism. Next he lived with a group of like-minded men in a wilderness not far from Neocaesarea in Pontus. When Gregory Nazianzen visited him there in 358, they worked together to compile the *Philokalia*, a collection of excerpts from the writings of Origen; it was here, too, that they wrote monastic rules that were to be of decisive importance for the further development and spread of the "cenobitic" or monastic life.

Bishop Eusebius induced Basil the Great to return from solitude to his home in Caesarea. He was ordained a priest and began pastoral work. Then, in the year 370, Basil became bishop of Caesarea and thus metropolitan of Cappadocia. His wide-ranging activities as a spiritual advisor, a founder of charitable works, and a leading archbishop earned for him even during his lifetime the surname "the Great". Especially important was his successful battle against Arianism, which had regained strength under the emperor Valens. His efforts as a mediator and an arbitrator contributed significantly to bringing about the collapse of Arianism in 381. He died in 379, and he is commemorated on January 2.

3. Gregory of Nyssa, a younger brother of Saint Basil the Great

and Saint Macrina the Younger, was born around 335 in Caesarea in Cappadocia. We do not know much about his childhood and youth or about his studies. At any rate his pious parents did not finance protracted studies for him as they did for his older brother Basil. Gregory never left Cappadocia; he had to pursue his education in the schools of Caesarea. Did his parents love him less? Presumably they had already decided that he was destined for the clergy and did not leave the choice of a career to him. Instead of devoting himself to the clerical state, however, Gregory became a rhetorician.

> Was it hesitation, or the desire to have his own way, or the inconstancy of an anxious nature? It is difficult to say. Apparently the pagan culture captivated him; indeed, at that time the emperor, Julian the Apostate, lent it new brilliance. Gregory married Theosebeia, an extraordinarily gifted woman with an excellent education, and was passionately devoted to her. One should not take him too literally when he reproaches himself in the *Treatise on Virginity* for having chosen "the common way of life", for that work contains all sorts of bombast that must be discounted. He renounced rhetoric, but not marriage. He remained married even when his brother Basil the Great made him bishop of the little town of Nyssa in the eastern part of Cappadocia in 371. Married life seems not to have hindered him in his spiritual development any more than it did Saint Hilary of Poitiers.

So writes A. Hamman in his little volume *Die Kirchenväter* (The Church Fathers).[3]

> Theosebeia died around A.D. 385. A letter of condolence sent by Bishop Gregory Nazianzen to the widowed Bishop Gregory of Nyssa is still extant, in which the departed is praised as "genuinely holy and a true wife of a priest". Gregory of Nyssa recognized the legitimacy of marital pleasures, and he left us a

---

[3] A. Hamman, *Die Kirchenväter* (Freiburg im Breisgau, 1967), pp. 114–15.

moving description of them. The doubt that he expressed with regard to the body and sexual relations may have come not from his own experience but from his philosophy, which was influenced by Platonism. Besides this we have little information about the further life of Gregory of Nyssa. Evidently he led a secluded life with Theosebeia and was so engrossed in study and spiritual exercises that he did not even call on his brother Basil at his monastic retreat, despite his invitations. He remained in constant contact with his sister Macrina and was profoundly attached to her; to him it was as though he found in her something of the heritage of their ancestors. She led a cloistered community of women in the same locality. Gregory of Nyssa called Macrina the "directress of his soul" and describes her life and her death, at which he was present, in a little book (*Vita sanctae Macrinae*) that is a masterpiece of sentiment. At that time—after 371, to be precise—Gregory occupied the episcopal see of Nyssa; it was, as he said, "forced upon him" by his brother Basil. Nevertheless, he was in fact a zealous bishop who devoted himself to his diocese and was highly esteemed in turn. He matured, moreover, into a great theologian and mystic and became the father of mystical theology.

4. Peter of Sebaste, the youngest son and the tenth child of the holy married couple Basil the Elder and Emmelia, was born before 349. He was greatly influenced by his saintly sister Macrina the Younger, who guided his spiritual education. He became a monk in the monastery in Pontus founded by Saint Basil the Great and later its abbot. In 370 he received priestly ordination from the hands of his brother Basil. Between 379 and 381 he became bishop of Sebaste in Armenia. He died in 392.

So much for the most important four out of the ten children of the holy married couple Basil the Elder and Emmelia.[4] They tower over the other six children, who died prematurely, not only on account of their preeminent ecclesiastical posts (three bishops, two

---

[4] *Acta Sanctorum Maii* 7:238–42; Gregory Nazianzen, *Oratio 43 in laudem Basilii Magni*, PG 36:503ff. Gregory of Nyssa, *Vita sanctae Macrinae virginis*, PG 46:962ff.

of them very important Doctors of the Church, and a daughter who founded a cloister and served as abbess), but also through the sanctity of their lives. They are a credit to their saintly grandparents and parents and bring honor to the entire Church of the East.

Saint Gregory Nazianzen the Elder

and

Saint Nonna

Gregory:
  b. ca. 274
  d. 374 at the age of almost 100

Nonna:
  d. 374

Parents of three saintly children

*Gregory Nazianzen the Elder
(eighteenth-century Russian icon)*

Saint Gregory Nazianzen the Elder is a saint of the Eastern Church who was married to a saint, namely, Saint Nonna, who gave him three saintly children.

He was born around 274. He was a rich landowner in Arianzus, near Nazianzus, and at the same time a high-ranking government official. As for his world view, he belonged at first to a peculiar sect that included in its beliefs a mixture of pagan and Jewish elements and worshipped "Zeus hypsistos".

Thanks to his Christian wife, Saint Nonna, the forty-five-year-old government official was converted to Christianity. He was baptized in 325 and then devoted himself wholeheartedly to living his faith in the Christian congregation of Nazianzus in Cappadocia, which four years later, in 329, elected him its bishop.

By approving the arianizing formula of the Synod of Rimini (359), Bishop Gregory the Elder turned the monks of Nazianzus against him. His son Gregory the Younger was able to intervene in this quarrel and make peace because of his prestige and his gift of eloquence.

In the year 374 Bishop Gregory Nazianzen the Elder died at the age of almost one hundred. His son Gregory Nazianzen the Younger, also a bishop, gave the funeral oration.[1]

The wife of Gregory Nazianzen the Elder, Saint Nonna, was the daughter of a certain Philantios. Judging from the portrait that her son Saint Gregory Nazianzen the Younger sketched in the funeral oration for his father,[2] as well as in his funeral orations for his brother, Caesarius,[3] and his sister, Gorgonia,[4] Saint Nonna must have been the model of a Christian wife and mother: she strove always to practice the Christian virtues and to lead a genuinely Christian life; she was extraordinarily pious and modest and demonstrated a heart-felt love of the poor; above all she raised her three children in such a manner as to lay within them the foundation for their future sanctity.

Saint Nonna concluded her holy life in 374; she died in the church that she customarily attended, during the celebration of the Eucharist. The great Church historian Caesar Baronius did much to promote liturgical devotion to this noble woman and mother in the West as well by including her in the Roman Martyrology for August 5.

If we look briefly now at the lives of the three saintly children of the holy married couple Saint Gregory Nazianzen the Elder and Saint Nonna, we can determine the following:

1. Gregory Nazianzen the Younger was born around 330. He studied in Caesarea in Cappadocia as well as in Caesarea in Palestine, thereafter in Alexandria in Egypt, and finally for almost ten years in Athens, where he struck up a lifelong friendship with Saint Basil. Around 358 he returned to Nazianzus and worked for a short time as a professor of rhetoric. Only then did he decide to

[1] *Oratio funebris in patrem*, PG 35:985–1044.
[2] Ibid., 993 and 997–98.
[3] Ibid., 257–60.
[4] Ibid., 793–94.

be baptized. For a while he wanted to become a monk. In 362, against his will and at the urging of the congregation, he was ordained a priest by the bishop, his father. Indignant at the "violence" done him, he fled to the wilderness and to justify his actions wrote *Apologia for His Flight* (on the dignity and burden of the priesthood). Soon, however, he returned to Nazianzus and helped his father in the administration and pastoral care of his diocese.

The division of the metropolia of Cappadocia reduced Saint Basil's influence as archbishop, and to consolidate his position he began to found new episcopal sees. When he also consecrated his reluctant friend Gregory bishop of the little town of Sasima, the latter never took office in the "accursed, miserable spot". After the death of his father in the year 374, he governed for a time the orphaned diocese of Nazianzus. Soon, however, he devoted himself again to the contemplative life in Seleucia (Isauria). In 379, though, he followed the call that had been issued to him and accepted the task of leading and reorganizing the diocese of Constantinople, which at that time had practically melted away, although it was orthodox in the spirit of the Council of Nicaea (325). Various intrigues embittered Gregory the Younger so much that he resigned his new position as bishop of Constantinople. For two years he cared for the still orphaned diocese of Nazianzus, his hometown. Gregory the Younger spent the last years of his life, until his death in 390, on the estate in Arianzus near Nazianzus that he had inherited from his father, composing important theological works in which he expounded and defended the mystery of the Holy Trinity and the consubstantiality of the Son of God with his Heavenly Father, as well as the consubstantiality of the Holy Spirit with the Father and the Son.[5]

2. The second son of the saintly married couple Gregory the Elder and Nonna was Caesarius. In Alexandria in Egypt he devoted himself to the study of geometry, astronomy, and medicine. After returning to his hometown of Nazianzus, he practiced medicine with such great success that he won the confidence of

[5] Cf. J. M. Sauget, "St. Gregorio di Nazianzo", *Bibliotheca Sanctorum* 7:194–204.

the emperor Constantius, who summoned him to Constantinople. The next emperor, too, Julian the Apostate, endorsed Caesarius as court physician, although the latter did not share in the least the emperor's pagan world view. Caesarius was then named quaestor of Bithynia by Emperor Jovinian. There he quasi-miraculously escaped death under the rubble of an earthquake in 368. He was so shocked by this painful incident that he then retired from all public offices, intent only on saving his own soul. He received Baptism and from then on led a life of penance and of Christian service to the poor, to whom he bequeathed everything he owned. Caesarius died quite suddenly in 369. His brother, the bishop, gave his funeral oration.[6]

3. Besides the two holy sons of the holy couple Gregory Nazianzen the Elder and Nonna, there was also a holy daughter, Saint Gorgonia. While still young she was married to a certain Alipius from Iconium, to whom she bore two sons and three daughters. She led an exemplary Christian life as a wife and mother. At her deathbed her spiritual father, Saint Basil, was present, but her brother Bishop Gregory gave her funeral oration.[7] Saint Gorgonia died in 370, a year after her brother Caesarius and four years before her aged parents. The only one of this family of five saints from Nazianzus to survive his parents and siblings for long was the saintly bishop and Doctor of the Church Gregory Nazianzen the Younger, who by his funeral orations and his poetry canonized, so to speak, his parents and siblings and made them famous. He did not die until 390, his heart full of longing to see his brother and sister, Caesarius (d. 369) and Gorgonia (d. 370), as well as his father, Gregory the Elder (d. 374), and his dearly beloved mother, Nonna (d. 374), and also his great and faithful friend Saint Basil (d. 379) once again in the communion of saints.

---

[6] Gregory Nazianzen, *Oratio* 7, PG 35:756–88.
[7] Gregory Nazianzen, *In laudem sororis suae Gorgoniae*, PG 35:789–818.

Saint
Hilary of Poitiers
and Spouse

b. ca. 315 in Poitiers, in Aquitaine,
 France
d. ca. 367

Father of a child

Hilary of Poitiers
Engraving by Béthume d'Ydewalle
(nineteenth century)

Is there such a thing as a married bishop, Father of the Church, and Doctor of the Church? One might question this, and yet it is true of Saint Hilary, the meritorious bishop of Poitiers and valiant opponent of the Arian heresy, which denied the divinity of Jesus Christ and reduced him to the status of God's first creature. In many biographies of Saint Hilary, the fact that he was married and had a daughter is not mentioned, as though that were an embarrassment. In other biographies of this important Father and Doctor of the Church it is noted that Saint Hilary was married, perhaps even in order to use this as an argument against priestly celibacy. This case, however, has to be examined carefully.

Hilary was born around 315 in Poitiers, in Aquitaine (France), the son of wealthy pagan parents. In his native city and, later, in Bordeaux, he received a scholarly education, mainly in grammar and rhetoric. Although Hilary was a pagan, he was repelled by the

67

pagan ways of his fellow citizens, who for the most part led lives of luxury and moral depravity. He was employed in a high-ranking administrative position. As was usual for a well-situated official, he married, and his marriage was blessed with a child, a daughter, who was given the name Abra.

Hilary had a great thirst for truth, which more and more bestirred his upright, noble heart, and pagan philosophy did not satisfy it. In his struggle to discover the truth, especially with regard to the meaning of human life, he was led as though by chance to read Sacred Scripture and then through this reading, with the help of God's grace, to the Christian faith. Around the year 345, Hilary was baptized with his wife and his daughter, Abra, at the Easter Vigil.

As he had already done as a pagan, so now as a Christian he led an even more exemplary life, together with his wife and his daughter. All three soon proved to be examples to their fellow Christians in Poitiers, and they enjoyed the best possible reputation. So it is understandable that when the episcopal see of Poitiers became vacant, around 350, Hilary was unanimously considered the worthiest candidate to succeed the departed bishop.

Hilary submitted to the will of the Christian people and accepted the dignity and burdens of the episcopacy. It is sometimes noted, explicitly and emphatically, that Bishop Hilary lived in perfect continence from the moment he was consecrated a bishop. If that was the case, it no doubt suited Bishop Hilary, for even as a pagan he was disgusted by the unrestrained and to a great extent immoral and corrupt way of life led by many of his fellow citizens who were pagans. One might also speculate that at the time Hilary was elevated to the episcopacy, his wife was no longer among the living. Only his daughter, Abra, remained, and Bishop Hilary was concerned about her, as his letter to her demonstrates. Even though this letter (*Ad Abram filiam*)[1] is considered spurious today,[2] the content of the letter would still apply very well to Hilary as a father and a bishop.

---

[1] Published in CSEL (the latest German edition of the Church Fathers), 65:237–44.
[2] Cf. B. Altaner, *Patrologie*, 5th ed. (Freiburg im Breisgau, 1958) p. 327.

On account of his orthodox, anti-Arian stance, Hilary was banished in 356 to Phrygia in Asia Minor. In 360 or 361, he was sent back again to Poitiers. There his chief activity was always to maintain or to reintroduce the true faith. He gathered his clergy together into a society, from which the first monastic communities in Gaul developed, through the efforts of his saintly disciple Martin of Tours. Hilary's character united the orderliness and sense of responsibility of a Roman administrative official with the zeal of an orthodox pastor of souls: he sought to combine clarity with piety, conciliatory mutual understanding with ecclesiastical unity. It was in this spirit, certainly, that he lived with his wife in matrimony as well, before he received episcopal orders. Because Hilary had become acquainted with Eastern theology during his exile in Phrygia, he understood—once he returned to his Gallic homeland—how to combine Eastern and Western theology harmoniously, how to "wed" one with the other, so to speak. Can we not draw inferences from this also as to the harmonious way in which he—before he became a bishop—lived harmoniously in marriage? Hilary was also—as this Doctor of the Church emphasizes in his theological works—profoundly convinced of the compatibility of faith and reason. He makes clear in his writings "how essential it is for a true theologian to have not only a clear-thinking mind, but above all a faith-filled heart."[3] "A clear-thinking mind and a faith-filled heart": Is that not needed especially by Christian married couples as well in order to conduct themselves correctly and harmoniously in a good marriage? In this Hilary could be an example for Christian spouses.

Hilary died around 367.

[3] Cf. H. Melzer, *Lexikon der Namen und Heiligen* (Innsbruck, 1982), p. 370.

Saint Monica

and

Patricius

b. 331 in Tagaste, North Africa
d. 387 in Ostia

Married 352
Mother of three children

Monica, the mother of Augustine, the great Father of the Church in the West, was born in 331 in Tagaste into an extremely pious Christian family, which probably belonged to that small circle of townspeople in North Africa who had assimilated the Roman culture and morality. Monica's parents entrusted the supervision and education of their daughter, for the most part, to a strict governess, who trained the little girl to control and mortify herself and also to hold Christian morality in great esteem.

In the bloom of youth Monica was given in marriage to a certain Patricius, who had a small estate in Tagaste and belonged to the town council. He was still a pagan, not yet a Christian like Monica, but a good and upright man who, nevertheless, was inclined to anger or even to violence. He did love Monica affectionately, but that did not keep him from being boorish and unfaithful to her. By her kindness and meekness, though, Monica succeeded in gaining the victory over the character flaws of her husband and also over the gossip of her maids and the touchiness of her mother-in-law. By her conduct through all this she won the admiration of her women friends.

Monica was twenty-three years old when she gave birth to her son Augustine, who to all appearances was her firstborn. Besides him, she had another son, named Navigius, and a daughter, whose name is not known. With great zeal and effort she provided the three children with a genuine Christian upbringing. We learn that Augustine was scarcely born when he was enrolled in the list of catechumens, but according to the custom of the time he did not yet receive Baptism. Still, as he himself reports, he imbibed the name of the Lord Jesus with his mother's milk, so that the Christian faith became rooted in the marrow of his bones. About the anonymous daughter of Monica we learn that she married but

Monica's wedding with Patricius

soon became a widow and then remained a widow, and that, until her death, she was the superior of the convent, the *monasterium feminarum*, in Hippo.

In the year 371 Monica lost her husband, Patricius, who died. Through Monica's efforts he had been baptized a year before his death and died as a believing Christian.

The sixteen years from the death of her husband until the conversion of her son Augustine make up the most sorrowful and painful period in Monica's life, which is at the same time the most beautiful, because during these years Monica brought her vocation and mission to its completion. In the year 385, after Augustine, deceiving his mother, had left Africa and arrived in Rome, his mother, Monica, set sail to follow her son. She was fifty-four years old at the time; after a stormy passage she landed in Italy and began to search in vain for Augustine in Rome. She followed his trail farther and finally found him in Milan. There he had already freed himself from the contagion of the Manichaean heresy, but he was still vacillating as far as his relationship to Christianity was concerned. With loving concern Monica now remained at her son's side. A year later she was able at last to rejoice over his conversion, for which she had shed so many tears and sent up so many prayers to heaven.

With her son, who had already undergone a conversion but was not yet baptized, Monica at first withdrew to Cassiciacum. There, during the Easter Vigil, on April 24, 387, Augustine received the Sacrament of Baptism from Bishop Ambrose. Monica was present at this Baptism.

Mother and son wanted to return to Africa together a few months later. While they waited in Ostia Tiberina for a ship to make the crossing to Africa, Monica came down with a serious illness that led to her death. She died in Ostia and was also buried there, according to her wishes.

Let us examine more closely now the portrait of this holy wife, mother, and widow, as sketched for us by her son in his *Confessions*.[1]

---

[1] Principally in chap. 9 of bk. 9. [The excerpt is from the translation by John K. Ryan (Garden City, N.Y.: Image Books, 1960), pp. 218–21.]

Brought up modestly and soberly in this manner, and made subject by you[, O God,] to her parents rather than by her parents to you, when she arrived at a marriageable age, she was given to a husband [Patricius] and served him as her lord. She strove to win him to you, speaking to him about you through her conduct, by which you made her beautiful, an object of reverent love, and a source of admiration to her husband. She endured offenses against her marriage bed in such wise that she never had a quarrel with her husband over this matter. She looked forward to seeing your mercy upon him, so that he would believe in you and be made chaste. But in addition to this, just as he was remarkable for kindness, so also was he given to violent anger. However, she had learned to avoid resisting her husband when he was angry, not only by deeds but even by words. When she saw that he had curbed his anger and become calm and that the time was opportune, then she explained what she had done, if he happened to have been inadvertently disturbed.

In fine, when many wives, who had better-tempered husbands but yet bore upon their faces signs of disgraceful beatings, in the course of friendly conversation criticized their husbands' conduct, she would blame it all on their tongues. Thus she would give them serious advice in the guise of a joke. From the time, she said, they heard what are termed marriage contracts read to them, they should regard those documents as legal instruments making them slaves. Hence, being mindful of their condition, they should not rise up in pride against their lords. Women who knew what a sharp-tempered husband she had to put up with marveled that it was never reported or revealed by any sign that Patricius had beaten his wife or that they had differed with one another in a family quarrel, even for a single day. When they asked her confidentially why this was so, she told them of her policy, which I have described above. Those who acted upon it, found it to be good advice and were thankful for it; those who did not act upon it, were kept down and abused.

By her good services and by perseverance in patience and meekness, she also won over her mother-in-law who at first was stirred up against her by the whispered stories of malicious servants. She told her son about the meddling tongues of the servants, by which peace within the house had been disturbed between herself and her daughter-in-law, and asked him to punish them. Afterward, both to obey his mother and to improve discipline within his household and promote peace among its members, he punished by whippings the servants who had been exposed, in accordance with the advice of her who had exposed them. Afterward she promised that the same reward might be expected by whoever tried to please her by telling any evil tale about her daughter-in-law. Since nobody thereafter dared to do this, they lived together with extraordinary harmony and good will.

Moreover, upon that good handmaiden of yours, in whose womb you created me, "my God, my mercy," [Ps 58:18] you bestowed this great gift: wherever she could, she showed herself to be a great peacemaker between persons who were at odds and in disagreement. When she heard from either side many very bitter things, like something a swollen, undigested discord often vomits up, when a rough mass of hatred is belched out in

Saint Monica with her son Augustine (Bavarian National Museum, fifteenth century)

74

biting talk to a present friend about an absent enemy, she would never betray a thing to either of them about the other except what would help towards their reconciliation. This might have seemed a small thing to me, if from sad experience I had not known unnumbered throngs who, through some kind of horrid wide-spreading sinful infection, not only report the words of angry enemies to angry enemies, but even add things they did not say. On the contrary, to a man who is a man it should be a little thing not to stir up or increase men's enmities by evil speaking, or else he even strives to extinguish them by speaking well of others. Such was she, and she had you as her inward teacher in the school of her heart.

Finally, towards the very end of his earthly life, she gained her husband for you. After he became one of the faithful, she did not have to complain of what she had endured from him when he was not yet a believer. She was also a servant of your servants. Whosoever among them knew her greatly praised you, and honored you, and loved you in her, because they recognized your presence in her heart, for the fruit of her holy life bore witness to this. She had been "the wife of one husband" (cf. 1 Tim 5:9); she "repaid the duty she owed to her parents"; she had "governed her house piously" (cf. 1 Tim 5:10); she "had testimony for her good works"; she had brought up children, being as often in labor in birth of them as she saw them straying from you. Lastly, Lord, of all of us, your servants—for out of your gift you permit us to speak—who, before she fell asleep in you already lived together, having received the graces of your baptism, she took care as though she had been mother to us all, and she served us as though she had been a daughter to all of us.

In his *Confessions*,[2] Saint Augustine goes on to describe the pious death of his saintly mother in Ostia and how he said farewell to her, who had been an exemplary wife, mother, and widow and who could truly serve as a model for all Christian married people.

---

[2] In chaps. 10, 11, and 12 of bk. 9.

Saint Paula of Rome

and

Toxotius

b. May 5, 347, in Rome
d. January 26, 404, in Bethlehem

Married 362
Mother of five children

Paula, the daughter of noble parents—her father, Rogatus, traced his lineage back to Agamemnon, while her mother, Blesilla, was a descendant of the Scipios and the Gracchi and was related to Paulus Aemilius—was born on May 5, 347, in Rome. She was

> raised in the magnificence and wealth that was customary in the aristocratic families of fourth-century Rome. People were Christians because it was a mark of good breeding and because the imperial house was Christian, but besides that they paid no attention to the teaching of Christ and lived a worldly life, read Greek and Roman classics, and devoted themselves to music and dancing.[1]

In 362, the fifteen-year-old Paula was married to Senator Toxotius, from the noble Julian race, who was still a pagan. That was the beginning of a marriage that was not only very fruitful but also very happy; it lasted for only sixteen years, however. Paula mourned

---

[1] E. and H. Melchers, *Das grosse Buch der Heiligen* (Munich, 1978), p. 62; *Acta Sanctorum Januarii* 3:326–37; G. Del Ton,: *S. Paola Romana* (Milan, 1950).

her loss intensely; as Saint Jerome later wrote about the death of Toxotius, which occurred in 378, "her grief was so great that she nearly died herself." After sixteen years of happy married life, the thirty-one-year-old widow was left alone with five children. Nevertheless, Paula raised her children to be good Christians, indeed, to be saints. They are as follows:

1. Saint Blesilla, who was born in 364 (d. 384). She married young, as her mother had done, and became a widow after only seven months of marriage. As a result of a serious illness, she began quite radically to renounce her former, rather superficial way of life and, following her mother, joined the company of Saint Jerome. After her all-too-premature death in October or November of 384, he dedicated to her an enthusiastic commemorative address.

2. The second child of Saint Paula, her daughter Paulina, became the wife of Saint Pammachius (d. 410), the boyhood friend and fellow student of Saint Jerome. After the premature death of his wife, Paulina, in the year 397, Pammachius led an ascetical life, used his great fortune to care for the poor, founded in Porto (near Rome) a hospice for pilgrims, and constructed a basilica on the Mons Caelius [Caelian Hill] in Rome.

3. The third child of Saint Paula was Saint Eustochium, who was born around 368. She remained a virgin and went with her mother in 385 to the East, settling in 386 with her in Bethlehem. After her mother's death in 404, she succeeded her as superior of the convent that Saint Paula had founded. Saint Jerome devoted several letters[2] and several shorter works to Eustochium; she died on September 28, 420, in Bethlehem.

About the fourth and the fifth child of Saint Paula, nothing further is known, except that the fourth child, her daughter Rufina, "by her early death heavily burdened her loving mother's heart"—as Saint Jerome has reported—and that the fifth child, Toxotius, was married and that the daughter from this marriage, Paula, not only bore the name of her saintly grandmother but also followed her to Bethlehem.

[2] Especially letters 22, 46, 54, 107, and 108.

At about the time that Paula's husband, Toxotius, died in 378 and she became a widow, there was a Christian renewal movement in Rome, centered in the palace on the Aventine Hill occupied by the widow Marcella (d. 410), together with her widowed mother and her adoptive daughter. Saint Marcella, born in Rome sometime between 325 and 335, a daughter of the noble Marcelli line, had become a widow after only seven months of marriage; she turned down a subsequent marriage proposal, consecrated herself to the Lord, and assembled in her palace a circle of pious widows and young maidens from the city's aristocracy in order to pursue a Christian, cultural life. Marcella studied Sacred Scripture zealously and had Saint Jerome instruct her in philological and exegetical questions during his stay in Rome in the years 382 to 385. During the sack of Rome, on August 24, 410, Marcella was barbarously struck down by the soldiers of Alaric I, but she was able to flee with her adoptive daughter, Principia, to safety in the Basilica of Saint Paul.

In this circle surrounding Saint Marcella, the widow Paula found refuge and consolation; she cared for the sick and the poor, liberally distributed alms, and unsparingly devoted herself to the education of her children. The needs of other people made her forget her own sorrow. She gradually began to give away more and more of her wealth.

In the year 385, Paula decided, on the advice of her spiritual director, Jerome, to leave Rome and everything that was dear to her and to make a pilgrimage to the East, that is, to the Holy Land. She settled in Bethlehem, where Jerome led a community of monks, and founded nearby a convent with three divisions (for noblewomen, for free women, and for slaves). From then on she lived there with her daughter Eustochium a strictly ascetical life and earnestly strove for perfection, while devoting herself to prayer, penance, and diligent study of the Word of God in Sacred Scripture, until her death on January 26, 404. Eustochium was the only one of her children still living then; the others had all been called to their eternal reward before their mother.

The exemplary life of this early Christian wife, mother, and widow has been described by her saintly spiritual director, Jerome, as follows:

> If all the members of my body were to be converted into tongues, . . . I could still do no justice to the virtues of the holy and venerable Paula. Noble in family, she was nobler still in holiness; rich formerly in this world's goods, she is now more distinguished by the poverty that she has embraced for Christ. [So inflamed was she with zeal for Christ, that she decided to leave her home in Rome.] . . . Not to prolong the story: she went down to Portus [Rome's seaport] accompanied by her brother, her kinsfolk and above all her own children eager by their demonstrations of affection to overcome their loving mother. At last the sails were set and the strokes of the rowers carried the vessel into the deep. On the shore the little Toxotius stretched forth his hands in entreaty, while Rufina, now grown up, with silent sobs besought her mother to wait till she should be married. But still Paula's eyes were dry as she turned them heavenwards; and she overcame her love for her children by her love for God. . . . Yet her heart was rent within her, and she wrestled with her grief, as though she were being forcibly separated from parts of herself. . . .
>
> [When Paula arrived in the Holy Land,] although the proconsul of Palestine, who was an intimate friend of her house, sent forward his [agents] and gave orders to have his official residence placed at her disposal, she chose a humble cell in preference to it. . . . She rested not on an ordinary bed but on the hard ground covered only with a mat of goat's hair. . . . She . . . said, "I must disfigure that face which contrary to God's commandment I have painted with rouge, white lead, and antimony. I must mortify that body which has been given up to many pleasures. I must make up for my long laughter by constant weeping. I must exchange my soft linen and costly silks for rough goat's hair. I who have pleased my husband and the world in the past, desire now to please Christ."

After recounting then many other admirable things about this Roman noblewoman, Saint Jerome finally tells of her death:

Who could tell the tale of Paula's dying with dry eyes? She fell into a most serious illness. . . . Paula's intelligence shewed her that her death was near. Her body and limbs grew cold and only in her holy breast did the warm beat of the living soul continue. Yet as though she were leaving strangers to go home to her own people, she whispered the verses of the psalmist: "Lord, I have loved the habitation of thy house and the place where thine honour dwelleth" (Ps 26:8) and "How amiable are thy tabernacles, O Lord of hosts! . . . I would rather be an outcast in the house of my God than to dwell in the tents of wickedness" (Ps 83:2, 10 Vulgate). When I asked her why she remained silent refusing to answer my call, and whether she was in pain, she replied in Greek that she had no suffering and that all things were to her eyes calm and tranquil. After this she said no more but closed her eyes as though she already despised all mortal things, and kept repeating the verses just quoted down to the moment in which she breathed out her soul, but in a tone so low that we could scarcely hear what she said. . . . And now, Paula, farewell, and aid with your prayers the old age of your votary [Jerome].[3]

---

[3] The obituary notice of St. Paula of Rome by St. Jerome (letter 108), in CSEL 55:306–51, and *Patrologia Latina* (PL), 22:878ff. The English translation is from *Nicene and Post-Nicene Fathers*, second series, eds. Philip Schaff and Henry Wace, vol. 6, *St. Jerome: Letters and Select Works* (New York, Christian Literature Publishing Co., 1893), pp. 195–212.

Saint
Paulinus of Nola
and
Therasia

b. ca. 353–355 near Bordeaux
d. June 22, 431, in Nola

Married 385
Father of one child

Paulinus of Nola[1] is an interesting figure from the patristic age, not only because of the fifty-one letters and thirty-one poems (*Carmina*) of his that have been preserved, but also on account of the fact that he was married—quite happily, too—and the father of a son.

Around 353 to 355, at about the same time that Augustine was born in North Africa, he was born in the vicinity of Bordeaux in western France as the son of a high-ranking Roman official. His family belonged to the Roman nobility and owned productive estates in the western part of the Roman Empire, that is, in southern Italy, Gaul, and Spain. He received a very good education, especially from the rhetor Ausonius, with whom he maintained long-lasting ties of genuine friendship. After Ausonius became the tutor of Gratian, the son of Emperor Valentinian I in Trier, he managed to obtain from the emperor for his former pupil Paulinus, who was destined for a career in civil service, the rank of consul and senator while still very young and an appointment as

---

[1] S. Prete: "Santo Ponzio Meropio Ancio Paolino, vescovo di Nola", in *Bibliotheca Sanctorum* 10:156–62; B. Kötting: "Paulinus von Nola", in P. Manns, *Die Heiligen in ihrer Zeit* (Mainz, 1966), 1:257–59; Communità di Caresto: "San Paolino di Nola, Monaco e vescovo", chap. 5 of *I Santi sposati* (Milan, 1989), pp. 78–97; letter no. 28, "Ambrose to Sabinus, bishop (c. 395)", in *St. Ambrose: Letters*, trans. Sr. Mary Melchior Beyenka, O.P. (New York: Fathers of the Church, 1954), pp. 144ff.

vice-regent of the imperial government in the province of Campania (southern Italy) at the age of about twenty-six.

Probably because of the victory of the Goths at Adrianople (378) and the impending collapse of the empire, Paulinus gave up his government post after a short time. In 385 he married a young woman of Spanish descent, Therasia, and returned with her to his properties near Bordeaux.

Although Paulinus was the son of Christian parents, he put off being baptized until he had reached mature adulthood. In this he was only following the custom of the time; great saints like Ambrose, Augustine, Gregory of Nazianzen, and so on, had not done any differently. Now, however, Paulinus was probably pressured to receive Baptism by his devoutly Christian wife, who had a very strong influence on him. Some time before 389, Paulinus was baptized by Bishop Delphinus of Bordeaux; for him this was to be no merely external ceremony, but rather the beginning of a profound interior conversion. He began to sell off his tremendously large properties and to place the proceeds at the disposal of the poor. His former tutor, Ausonius, and probably many others of his social stratum showed little understanding for his change of heart. His like-minded wife, Therasia, though, accompanied him every step of the way in his gradual detachment from the passing things of this world and its pleasures, until they reached the point of living a monastic, ascetical life, "in humility and poverty", as an expression of their Christian faith.

Together with his wife he moved first to Spain, where he also owned properties, and spent the next few years there. The only child granted to Paulinus and Therasia, their son, Celsus, died eight days after birth and was buried in Complutum (Alcalá). This bitter sorrow at losing so quickly the son they had longed for so ardently and received with immense joy—the lament of the grieving father in *Carmen V* is very moving—and very likely also the pain he experienced when his brother was murdered,[2] confirmed Paulinus and his wife even more in their decision to live the rest of

[2] Cf. *Carmen* 21.

their lives in poverty and renunciation, but especially in union with God and in pious practices. Paulinus yielded to the urging of the people of Barcelona and agreed to be ordained on Christmas Day, 394, by Bishop Lampius in Barcelona.

The married couple, who now practiced complete sexual abstinence, did not remain long in Barcelona, however. Both were irresistibly drawn to solitude.

During the time that Paulinus was vice-regent in Campania, he had come to know and prize the meditative silence and solitude surrounding the tomb of his favorite saint, the early Christian martyr Felix of Nola. Now he moved to that place with his wife, Therasia. In 395 Paulinus occupied a cell constructed nearby the tomb of Saint Felix and tried to live a plain and simple monastic life in complete seclusion, separated by only a short distance from Therasia, who began to live a very similar ascetical life in the same vicinity. Therasia was for Paulinus now, in the fullest sense, his "companion in faith" on the path to holiness, as Saint Augustine wrote in his fifty-eighth letter. And Saint Ambrose wrote in letter 28, addressed to Bishop Sabinus of Piacenza:

> I have learned that Paulinus, second to none of the Aquitanians in luster or birth, has sold his and his wife's possessions, and has taken up these practices of faith that he is giving his property to the poor by changing it into money. . . . Word has it that he has chosen a retreat in the city of Nola where he will pass his days out of reach of the tumult of the world. His wife, too, closely followed the example of his zeal and virtue. She has transferred her property to the jurisdiction of others and is following her husband, where, perfectly content with her little patch of ground, she will comfort herself with the riches of religion and charity. They have no children, but their desire is a posterity of good deeds.

From the two isolated cells, in which Paulinus and Therasia lived a life of poverty and humility near the burial place of the holy martyr Felix, gradually developed—as it is believed—a double monastery in a building with two wings. The consecrated men lived on the upper floor of one wing, and the upper floor of the other wing housed the nuns, while the rooms on the ground floor were available for travelers and the homeless. Adjoining the little chapel where Saint Felix was entombed, Paulinus constructed a large church beautifully decorated with frescos portraying scenes from the Bible; this church formed the center of the monastic structure. The enlargement of the monastery had become necessary because other couples had joined Paulinus and Therasia: Turcius and Avita, with their grown children Eunomia and Asterius, as well as Pinianus and Melania the Younger with her mother, Albina. This charismatic monastic household, consisting of five married couples who had consecrated themselves to God and practiced continence within marriage, was—as Paulinus portrays the community in his poem, *Carmen XXI*—a mystical harp with ten strings, which was to resonate in perfect harmony for the glory of God. In his letters Paulinus describes the simplicity of their way of life with regard to living quarters, food, and clothing, because the community sought to remain faithful to the two key concepts of *humilitas et paupertas* (humility and poverty). Their spiritual food was the Word of God in Sacred Scripture.

In the first decade of the fifth century the Western Goths roved through southern Italy and plundered it. During those days of unrest, Bishop Paulus of Nola died, and in 409 Paulinus was elected to be his successor and was consecrated a bishop. Little is known about the episcopacy of Saint Paulinus. On June 22, 431, the faithful husband who had become a bishop died; more than twenty years earlier, in 409, his equally noble wife had gone before him to her eternal reward.

Saint
Melania the Younger
and
Valerius Pinianus

b. 383 in Rome
d. December 31, 439, in Jerusalem

Married 396
Mother of two children

In describing those great noble female personages of Rome who, during the fourth century, in the midst of a superficially Christian culture, gave a living example of Christian marriage and widowhood, it is only fitting for us to mention, besides Saint Paula of Rome, Saint Melania the Younger.[1]

She was born in the year 383 in Rome, the daughter of Senator Valerius Publicola (d. 404), who was the son of Saint Melania the Elder, and of Albina, who came from a pagan family and whose father even held a high office as a pagan priest. The high-ranking noble family into which Melania was born possessed enormous estates and thus owned thousands of male and female slaves also. Because she took her Christian faith quite seriously, young Melania was afraid of becoming like those rich men who are excluded from the kingdom of heaven because of their wealth. From early

[1] Cf. Gerontius, *Vita sanctae Melaniae*, ed. D. Gorce, in Sources chrétiennes (Paris, 1962), no. 90; G. D. Gordini: "S. Melania, la Giovane", in *Bibliotheca Sanctorum* 9:282–85; B. Kötting: "Melania die Jüngere" in P. Manns, *Die Heiligen in ihrer Zeit* (Mainz, 1966), 1:245–48; E. Melchers, *Das grosse Buch der Heiligen* (Munich, 1978), 832–33.

youth, in the simplicity of her heart, she wanted to offer everything to God, including herself with her virginity intact.

Very soon she experienced the stark contrast between the life of the noble families in Rome and that of the oppressed caste of poor slaves who were reduced to servitude and regarded by Roman society as little more than beasts of burden. The Gospel, on the contrary, teaches that all men are brothers and sisters. Melania's longing for a plain and simple virginal life set her in opposition to her surroundings and also to her father. He wanted to dissuade her from her strange plans, and in 396 he abruptly married her to his wealthy nephew Valerius Severus Pinianus. Melania was only thirteen years old at the time, while her husband and cousin was seventeen.

Melania tried to convince her husband to renounce all sexual relations. He was willing to do so, provided that there were two children first to carry on the line. Melania had to resign herself to this plan. First she gave birth to a girl, who died a few years later. The second child, a son, survived a premature birth by only a few hours, whereas the mother remained in imminent danger of death. Pinianus prayed fervently, at the grave of the saintly deacon Lawrence in Rome, that God would keep his young wife alive; he promised that, if his prayer was granted, he would henceforth practice perfect continence in his marriage with Melania. She lived, but her parents would not permit them to carry out what he had pledged to God. Only after the death of her father in the year 404 could the twenty-one-year-old Melania and Pinianus (now twenty-five) make good their promise. From then on they kept it faithfully until death.

Besides the pledge of marital continence, Melania also convinced her husband to renounce all extravagance in their way of life and to use their enormously large combined wealth for charitable purposes and for the support of the Church. This began with the liberation of eight thousand slaves.

In order to overcome any attachment to their gigantic estate, the couple departed from Rome and traveled first in 406 to Nola to visit their distant relative Paulinus. Because of the advancing

Goths, they then retreated in 408 to their lands on the eastern coast of Sicily. Here the idea occurred to Melania and Pinianus of a simple common life in the sort of conventual arrangement that so many found inspiring in those days and for which Saint Augustine around that time had compiled a kind of religious rule. Melania, with sixty other women, began to form such a cloistered community. Not far away lived Pinianus, with thirty monks.

Fearing the onslaught of the Germanic tribes, the couple, who had now become consecrated religious, moved again from Sicily to Tagaste (North Africa), the home of Saint Augustine, where his friend Alypius was at that time bishop. Each of them founded here a monastery, one for women and one for men. After a two-year sojourn in Tagaste, Melania left North Africa with Pinianus in 413 and traveled—this time in the footsteps of her saintly grandmother, Melania the Elder—farther to Palestine. After short visits with the monks in the Egyptian desert and with Saint Cyril of Alexandria and then with Saint Jerome, they settled in Bethlehem and later in Jerusalem. Melania founded there a cloister with ninety sisters; she herself, though, occupied a very modest cell near the Mount of Olives and lived a strictly penitential life in the most austere poverty, after distributing all of her enormous wealth to churches and monasteries and to the poor. At her death, she who had once been the richest woman in the Roman Empire had only fifty gold pieces left, which she gave to the bishop. Her husband, Pinianus, had done the same with his possessions. He died in 437, while Melania survived him by two years. She died on December 31, 439. After a successful pastoral journey to Constantinople, she had spent Christmas of the year 439 in Bethlehem with her relative, the like-minded Paula "the Younger", the granddaughter of Saint Paula of Rome. She had also celebrated the feast of Saint Stephen in Jerusalem when she felt the approach of death; she had her attendants carry her into the church and received the Viaticum three times, according to the custom then; finally, she passed away, saying "As it has pleased the Lord, so let it be."

Saint
Alexius of Edessa
and
Spouse

b. ca. 400
d. ca. 450

The originally anonymous man of God, Alexius, who is said to have lived as an ascetic and beggar in Rome, or else in Edessa in Mesopotamia in the fifth century, is to a great extent a legendary figure with some historical basis; this figure should be mentioned, though, in a book about married saints, not merely because it played a considerable role in the poetic and theatrical arts from the early Middle Ages up until the recent past, but also because it broached a problem of morality in marriage.

The Alexius legend, which dates from the fifth century, originated in Syria, was expanded upon by the Greeks of Byzantium, and was finally accepted in the West. The essential elements of the legend are as follows: A young Roman patrician, for whom his wealthy parents had arranged a marriage, fled the Eternal City on the evening of his wedding day. He then lived abroad for a long time incognito. He spent seventeen years of his life in the service of the Blessed Virgin Mary in a church dedicated to the *Theotokos* in Edessa (Mesopotamia). After his origins were discovered, however, he returned to Rome. He lived another seventeen years in his parents' house, unrecognized, as a poor beggar, reluctantly tolerated and often mistreated, like poor Lazarus, by the household servants. Only on his deathbed was he recognized by his parents as their son.[1]

[1] Cf. *Acta Sanctorum Julii* 4:238–70; G. Rohlfs, *St. Alexius* (Tübingen, 1968); E. Josi, "St. Alessio, confessore", in *Bibliotheca Sanctorum* 1:814–23.

During the sixth through the ninth centuries, this legend became widespread and first received poetic treatment when the Byzantine hymnographer Joseph the Melodist (d. 833) made it the theme of one of his hymns.

The "Song of Alexius", which originated around 1040 in France, is written in verses of ten feet, some of which are rhymed; it consists of twenty-five strophes of five verses each. The song tells the very moving story of Alexius, the only son of the aristocratic, wealthy Roman couple Euphemianus and Aglae, who are said to have lived at the time of Pope Innocent I (402–417). Alexius, whose parents have destined him to marry against his will, forsakes his bride on the evening after his wedding, after telling her of his decision to remain a celibate forever and leaving her his ring and his costly belt as mementos. On the shore of the sea he finds a ship that brings him to the East, whereupon he makes his way to Edessa.

There he exchanged his clothes for a beggar's garment and gave all that he had to the poor. Whereupon he sat down in the square in front of a church and begged from passersby; he then took for himself, however, only what was absolutely necessary from the alms he received and gave the rest away to the sick and the needy.

Meanwhile there was great mourning in the house of his parents. His father sent out servants to all the countries in the world to look for his son, but they found no trace of him. The parents wept over their son and could not be consoled, while his bride put on mourning and spent her days as a widow. Alexius, though, spent seventeen years serving God by a hard life of penance.

Then it happened that the sacristan of the church in front of which Alexius used to sit begging one day clearly heard a voice coming from the picture of Mary that hung there, which said, "Bring Alexius, God's faithful servant, into the church, for he is worthy to live in the sanctuary itself." So the sacristan hastened to the square and brought Alexius into the church. It was not long until the story was known everywhere. People began to esteem highly the poor beggar Alexius.

Alexius, however, disdained all honors and slipped secretly away from the city of Edessa and set sail for Tarsus in Cilicia. Yet God arranged that the ship, buffeted by an unfavorable wind and tossed onto the shore of Italy, landed not far from the city of Rome. So Alexius decided to live in his father's house as a poor, unknown stranger. When he arrived at the marketplace of the city, he saw his father walking by with his attendants. He ran after him and asked, "Noble Sir, allow me, a poor stranger, to live in your house and to eat the crumbs that fall from your table. God will reward you for your kind-heartedness." Scarcely had Alexius said this, when Euphemianus remembered his son, and his heart was wondrously moved. He commanded his servants to take the traveler into his house, to give him something to eat and drink and to assign him a room to live in. But Alexius chose for himself a narrow, dingy compartment under the stairs of the house and made do with the most wretched food.

Soon the servants had forgotten their master's orders to treat the stranger well; they mocked the poor fool who chastised himself with fasting and keeping vigil—indeed, often they poured rinse water over his head and tossed crumbs to him as though to a dog and caused him all sorts of mischief. He bore everything patiently, however, and said not a word about it to Euphemianus; indeed, he rejoiced to suffer disgrace for Christ's sake. Every day he saw his dear father and often his mother and his bride, too, and heard their laments over him. That almost broke his heart, but he stood by his decision to remain unrecognized until his death. Alexius continued in this way for seventeen years, despised, living under the stairs as a humble beggar who had abandoned everything, even his identity, in order to gain Christ. When he felt the end of his life approaching, however, he had parchment and ink brought to him and wrote down who he was.

Now it happened one Sunday after Holy Mass that they

were astonished to find the beggar lying dead on a miserable bed of straw. His face was radiant as if with heavenly glory. In his hand he held a letter. When, with great sorrow, Euphemianus learned from the letter, which was read to him, that the poor beggar was no one else but his son, he fell unconscious to the floor. Streaming with tears, his mother and his bride came running and threw themselves, lamenting, upon the body. The servants, though, who had mistreated the saint and tormented him, trembled in fear and remorse. Meanwhile, the news of the wondrous occurrence spread rapidly. People hastened to the bier of the saint, where immediately many miracles took place.

Just as in the French version of the "Song of Alexius", the life of Saint Alexius is embellished with legendary elements in the poetry of the Middle High German bourgeois poet Konrad von Würzburg (d. 1287). The legend of Saint Alexius was dramatized in an opera composed by Stefano Landi (d. 1639), *Il Sant' Alessio*, the libretto of which was written by Giulio Rospigliosi, who later became Pope Clement IX (1667–1669); after almost four hundred years this opera was performed once again in August 1977 at the Salzburg Festival. We should also mention the play written by the French dramatist Henri Ghéon (d. 1944), *Le Pauvre sous l'escalier* (The poor man under the stairs).

Literary treatments in recent times have often raised the question of the moral justification for the way that Saint Alexius treated his bride, and most of them have answered in the negative. In fact, one could rightly ask: If Alexius had higher motives for separating from his bride, should he not have taken that step long before the wedding? Was he not man enough to tell his bride sooner about his reluctance to be married to her? Or did his bride fail to understand his decision to practice perpetual sexual continence, so that he then had to take that unusual step? Many saints have mutually agreed soon after their weddings—as is evident from examples in this book—to live in what is called a Josephite wedding. B. de Gaiffier has compiled a whole list of such saints' lives, in which the young newlyweds, having reached an agreement, decide to practice perfect continence within marriage.[2]

In conclusion, let us refer here to canons 1141 and 1142 in the new *Code of Canon Law*, which has been binding since the First Sunday of Advent in 1983:

A ratified and consummated marriage cannot be dissolved by any human power or for any reason other than death.

A non-consummated marriage between baptized persons or between a baptized party and non-baptized party can be dissolved by the Roman Pontiff for a just cause, at the request of both parties or of one of the parties, even if the other party is unwilling.

It should also be mentioned that the feast day of Saint Alexius is celebrated on March 17 by the Byzantine Church and on July 17 in the Western Church. In the year 978 a church on the Aventine Hill in Rome, which was formerly consecrated to Saint Boniface, was dedicated to Saint Alexius; even today in this church you will be shown the steps under which the saint is said to have lived as a beggar.

---

[2] Cf. B. de Gaiffier, "Intactam sponsam relinquens: À propos de la vie de Saint Alexis", *Analecta Bollandiana* 65 (1947): 157–95.

Saint Hilarius

and

Saint Quieta

Hilarius:
   b. ca. 410–420
   d. ca. 463–467

Parents of one child

Almost nothing is known about the couple Hilarius and Quieta, who lived in the fifth century, belonged to the Gallic nobility in Burgundy, and owned extensive lands in the region of Coutangy, near Montbald (Côte d'Or), and in the vicinity of Dijon, except the fact that they gave life to a son, John, who, thanks to the virtuous example of his pious parents, attained sanctity with maturity. Saint John of Réomé was born in the year 440 in Coutangy, the son of a senator, Hilarius, and his wife, Quieta. The monk Jonas of Bobbio (d. ca. 665), in the introduction to his biography of Saint John of Réomé,[1] describes the virtues of this saint's parents. Above all, their love for one another and their fidelity must have been exemplary. We learn this from a legendary miracle handed down by Saint Gregory of Tours (d. 594) in the eighth book of his hagiographic anthology *Miraculorum libri octo*, which bears the title *In gloria confessorum*.[2] The French poet Marie Noël also recalled it in her diary.[3]

---

[1] Jonas of Bobbio, *Vita sancti Johannis Reomaensis*, ed. B. Krusch, Monumenta Germaniae historica, Scriptores rer. merov. 3:505–17.

[2] Gregory of Tours, *Miraculorum libri octa, In gloria confessorum*, 41.

[3] Translated into English from the German edition, Marie Noël, *Erfahrungen mit Gott* (1961), pp. 254–55.

In the legend of Hilarius and Quieta, their life is not narrated in detail, but in a few golden words are contained some of the most beautiful things that could be recorded about their marriage. They led an exemplary married life and loved one another so much that their love was glorified after their death by a miracle. Hilarius died first. He was laid to rest in a richly appointed tomb in the church of Saint John in Dijon. Quieta died when her turn came. As they started to bury her in the tomb beside her husband, Hilarius lifted his right arm, put it around her neck, and drew her to his heart. Amid the rejoicing of the faithful, the spouses were later raised to the honors of the altar. In the ninth century the husband and wife were transferred to the crypt of the Cathedral of Dijon and placed in two separate tombs.

The poet then complains about the "impious priests" who did that, because they had not understood the meaning of the legendary miracle and had divided again those who wanted to be intimately united by marital love and fidelity, even in the grave. W. Nigg adds the comment: "The priests were able only to prevent them from being together in the grave, whereas we are firmly convinced that Hilarius and Quieta are united in heaven as well, to their indescribable happiness and ours!"

Saint Clotilda and Clovis

b. ca. 474
d. June 3, 545

Married 493
Mother of three children

Saint Clotilda was a saintly wife whose strong faith enabled her to bring her pagan husband to the Catholic faith, with the magnificent result that an entire populace found its way to the faith.[1]

She was of the royal line of Burgundy. King Gundobad, in the pursuit of absolute monarchy, had put his co-regent and brother Chilperic to death by the sword and had had the latter's wife drowned with a stone hanging around her neck. He allowed Chilperic's two daughters, Chroma and Clotilda, to live. Chroma, the elder of the two, took the veil as a consecrated virgin; Clotilda, though, Chilperic's younger daughter, who had been born around 474 in Lyons, was raised at the court of King Gundobad, her parents' murderer. Since Clotilda's parents had professed the Catholic faith and Gundobad, although an Arian, was tolerant enough now that he alone held power, Clotilda was allowed to remain true to the Catholic faith and also to practice it at the royal court.

---

[1] Cf. *Acta Sanctorum Junii* 1:292–98; A. Codaghengo, "Clotilde", in *Bibliotheca Sanctorum* 4:64–65.

Whereas most of the Germanic tribes at that time had already accepted Christianity, though in the heretical Arian form, the Franks living somewhat apart in the lower Rhine Valley at first remained pagan. The pagan King Clovis was typically Germanic in his thinking when he deliberated: Only if the Christians' God proves mightier than our gods will I believe in him and give up paganism.

Now Clovis' envoys often had business at the king's court in Burgundy. They were more and more impressed by Clotilda's beauty and by her prudent conduct. They reported it to King Clovis. Finally he asked Gundobad, the king of Burgundy, to give him Clotilda as his wife, and he did. That happened around 493.

Now married to King Clovis, Clotilda did not rest until she had won her husband to the Catholic faith, as we learn from the report of Saint Gregory of Tours (d. ca. 594).[2] There he writes:

The first child which Clotild bore for Clovis was a son. She wanted to have her baby baptized, and she kept on urging her husband to agree to this. "The gods whom you worship are no good," she would say. "They haven't even been able to help themselves, let alone others. They are carved out of stone or wood or some old piece of metal. The very names which you have given them were the names of men, not of gods. . . . You ought instead to worship Him who created at a word and out of nothing heaven, and earth, the sea and all that therein is, who made the sun to shine, who lit the sky with stars, who peopled the water with fish, the earth with beasts, the sky with flying creatures, at whose nod the fields became fair with fruits, the trees with apples, the vines with grapes, by whose hand the race of man was made, by whose gift all creation is constrained to serve in deference and devotion the man He made." However often the Queen said this, the King came no nearer to belief. "All these things have been created and produced at the

[2] In the second book of his history of the Franks, *Historiam libri decem*. The English translation from Gregory of Tours, *The History of the Franks*, trans. Lewis Thorpe (London: Penguin Books, 1974), 2:29–31, pp. 141–144.

The picture on the left, after a woodcut by Pierre le Rouge, depicts how King Clovis, at the request of his wife, consented to receive Baptism from Bishop Remigius.

The picture on the right: The Battle of Zülpich. On that occasion Clovis witnessed the power of prayer and was subsequently baptized with three thousand Franks.

command of *our* gods," he would answer. "It is obvious that *your* God can do nothing, and, what is more, there is no proof that he is a God at all."

The Queen, who was true to her faith, brought her son to be baptized. She ordered the church to be decorated with hangings and curtains, in the hope that the King, who remained stubborn in the face of argument, might be brought to the faith by ceremony. The child was baptized; he was given the name Ingomer; but no sooner had he received baptism than he died in his white robes. Clovis was extremely angry. He began immediately to reproach his Queen. "If he had been dedicated in the name of my gods," he said, "he would have lived without question; but now that he has been baptized in the name of your God he has not been able to live a single day!" "I give thanks to Almighty God," replied Clotild, "the Creator of all things, who has not found me completely unworthy, for He has deigned to welcome to His kingdom a child conceived in my womb. I am not at all cast down in my mind because of what has happened, for I know that my child, who was called away from this world in his white baptismal robes, will be nurtured in the sight of God."

Some time later Clotild bore a second son. He was baptized Chlodomer. He began to ail and Clovis said: "What else do you expect? It will happen to him as it happened to his brother: no sooner is he baptized in the name of your Christ than he will die!" Clotild prayed to the Lord and at His command the baby recovered.

Queen Clotild continued to pray that her husband might recognize the true God and give up his idol-worship. Nothing could persuade him to accept Christianity. Finally war broke out against the Alamanni and in this conflict he was forced by necessity to accept what he had refused of his own free will. It so turned out that when the two armies met on the battlefield there was great slaughter and the troops of Clovis were rapidly being annihilated. He raised his eyes to heaven when he saw this, felt compunction in his heart and was moved to tears.

"Jesus Christ," he said, "you who Clotild maintains to be the Son of the living God, you who deign to give help to those in travail and victory to those who trust in you, in faith I beg the glory of your help. If you will give me victory over my enemies, and if I may have evidence of that miraculous power which the people dedicated to your name say that they have experienced, then I will believe in you and I will be baptized in your name. I have called upon my own gods, but, as I see only too clearly, they have no intention of helping me. I therefore cannot believe that they possess any power, for they do not come to the assistance of those who trust in them. I now call upon you. I want to believe in you, but I must first be saved from my enemies." Even as he said this the Alamanni turned their backs and began to run away. As soon as they saw that their King was killed, they submitted to Clovis. "We beg you," they said, "to put an end to this slaughter. We are prepared to obey you." Clovis stopped the war. He made a speech in which he called for peace. Then he went home. He told the Queen how he had won a victory by calling on the name of Christ. This happened in the fifteenth year of his reign.

The Queen then ordered Saint Remigius, Bishop of the town of Rheims, to be summoned in secret. She begged him to impart the word of salvation to the King. The Bishop asked Clovis to meet him in private and began to urge him to believe in the true God, Maker of heaven and earth, and to forsake his idols, which were powerless to help him or anyone else. The King replied: "I have listened to you willingly, holy father. There remains one obstacle. The people under my command will not agree to forsake their gods. I will go and put to them what you have just said to me." He arranged a meeting with his people, but God in his power had preceded him, and before he could say a word all those present shouted in unison: "We will give up worshipping our mortal gods, pious King, and we are prepared to follow the immortal God about whom Remigius preaches." This news was reported to the Bishop. He was greatly pleased and he ordered the baptismal pool to be made ready. The public squares were draped with coloured cloths, the churches were adorned with white hangings, the baptistry was prepared, sticks of incense gave off clouds of perfume, sweet-smelling candles gleamed bright and the holy place of baptism was filled with divine fragrance. God filled the hearts of all present with such grace that they imagined themselves to have been transported to some perfumed paradise. King Clovis asked that he might be baptized first by the Bishop. Like some new Constantine he stepped forward to the baptismal pool, ready to wash away the sores of his old leprosy and to be cleansed in flowing water from the sordid stains which he had borne so long. As he advanced for his baptism, the holy man of God addressed him in these pregnant words: "Bow your head in meekness, Sicamber. [The Merovingians claimed to be descended from the Sicambri.] Worship what you have burnt, burn what you have been wont to worship."

King Clovis confessed his belief in God Almighty, three in one. He was baptized in the name of the Father, the Son and the Holy Ghost, and marked in holy chrism with the sign of the Cross of Christ.

After his Baptism on Christmas Day, 499—three years after the battle of Zülpich—King Clovis lived together with his wife Clotilda for twelve more years. He died in 511, scarcely forty-five years of age; Clotilda was at that time only thirty-eight years old.

Widowed after about twenty years of married life, Clotilda had many more sorrows to bear before her death on June 3, 545, especially on account of her son Chlodomer's death and on account of the crimes committed by her other two sons, Chlotar and Childebert, against Chlodomer's children.

She withdrew to Tours and lived there as a nun. Renouncing all her property, she opulently endowed the burial place of Saint Martin and other shrines and lived "not like a queen, but like a handmaid of God", as Gregory of Tours wrote. Though never officially canonized, she has always been revered as a saint.

Saint
Ethelbert
and
Bertha

b. ca. 552
d. February 24, 616

Married 588
Father of Saint Ethelburga

Bertha, the great-granddaughter of the Frankish King Clovis, is a very good example of how important the faith and courageous witness of a Christian wife can be, for her husband personally and for his entire country. Ethelbert was still a pagan when he married her, but she led him to the Christian faith. Thus she became, with her husband, Saint Ethelbert,[1] and with Saint Augustine of Canterbury, the foundress of Christianity in England.

Ethelbert, a descendant of the legendary King Hengist, the founder of the royal house of Kent, was born around 552. While still very young he succeeded his father Eormenric, who died in 560, on the royal throne of Kent. Soon he had gained preeminence among the various Anglo-Saxon kings.

Ethelbert was—as we have said—still a pagan in 588 when he went to Paris to marry a staunch Christian, Bertha, a great-granddaughter of the Frankish King Clovis. Bertha agreed to marry her royal bridegroom on one condition: that he would not prevent her from practicing her Christian faith or hinder her chaplain, Lindhard, in the discharge of his priestly duties.

Through his wife, Bertha, who was a pious believer, King Ethelbert not only came in contact with Christianity, but also became

---

[1] Cf. N. Del Re, "Santo Etelberto, re del Kent", in *Bibliotheca Sanctorum* 5:116–17 and 120; *Acta Sanctorum Februarii* 3:474–79; F. Caraffa: "Santa Etelburga di Lyminge", in *Bibliotheca Sanctorum* 5:120; *Acta Sanctorum Septembris* 3:205.

more and more sympathetic toward it. This was particularly evident in 596, when he received very amicably the missionaries, under the direction of Saint Augustine, who had been sent by Pope Gregory the Great; he even did all that he could to promote their missionary activity. Ethelbert is supposed to have been baptized by Saint Augustine during the Vigil of Pentecost (June 1), 597. It has been correctly ascertained, however, that this must have taken place later, because Pope Gregory the Great, in a letter written in June 601, reproached Queen Bertha for having neglected the conversion of her royal consort.[2] King Ethelbert assigned his royal palace in Canterbury to the monk Augustine, who had been consecrated a bishop in Arles on November 16, 597; he transferred his own residence to Reculver, and from there he promoted the evangelization work of Bishop Augustine in every respect. He also helped him with the reconstruction of an abandoned, ruined early Christian church. From this house of God, once rebuilt, arose "Christ Church", the first cathedral in England.

The royal couple Ethelbert and Bertha earned the greatest of all merit in the christianization of England. In the year 601 they received Mellitus—as they had received Augustine and his companions five years before—who brought the king a letter from Pope Gregory the Great, which contained instructions for him to continue his efforts to repress paganism and to propagate Christianity in England. Ethelbert succeeded also in converting his nephew Sabert, the son of his sister Ricula, and admonished him, the viceroy of Essex, that he should follow Mellitus' directions and build a cathedral in London dedicated to Saint Paul.

God also blessed the high-minded royal couple by bringing about the conversion of their daughter Ethelburga to Christianity through Saint Augustine. When she was given to King Edwin of Northumbria to be his wife, Saint Paulinus, one of Saint Augustine's companions, was given to her as her chaplain. King Edwin was at that time still a pagan; his father-in-law, Saint Ethelbert, demanded that he promise not to hinder the spread of the Chris-

[2] Cf. S. Brechter, *Die Quaestionen zur Angelsachsenmission Gregors des Grossen* (Münster, 1941).

tian faith in his kingdom and that he endeavor to become a Christian himself. In fact, King Edwin was baptized in 627, two years after his marriage with Ethelburga. In 633, when King Edwin fell in a battle against pagan foes near Hatfield Chase, Ethelburga withdrew to the convent of Lyminge, which she had founded, and served as superior of this cloistered community until her death on April 5, 647. She, just like her father, King Ethelbert, is revered in England as a saint.

Ethelbert lost his pious wife, Bertha, in 613. The widower married a second time, but tradition does not know the young woman's name. He soon died, though, three years after the death of his first wife, on February 24, 616, in the fifty-sixth year of his reign. Saint Gregory the Great in one document compared King Ethelbert with the emperor Constantine and called attention to the laudable services he had performed in propagating the Christian faith in England.

Saint Plectrude

and

Pepin of Herstal

b. ca. 650 near Trier
d. August 10, 725, in the Convent
of Saint Mary in the Capitol,
Cologne

Mother of two children

Tomb of Saint Plectrude, Church of
Saint Mary in the Capitol, Cologne,
twelfth century

Plectrude, who is revered in Alsace, Luxemburg, and in the Rhine Valley as a holy wife and mother and as the foundress of a cloister, was born around 650 near Trier, the daughter of the Frankish nobleman Hugobert and Blessed Irmina. Plectrude was married to the Frankish mayor of the palace, Pepin of Herstal. He conquered the Neustrian mayor Berchar in a battle at the French town of Tertry (near Saint-Quentin). He thereby initiated the rise of the Carolingians, secured the ascendancy of Austrasia, and united France as its mayor of the palace. Plectrude had a decidedly positive influence upon Pepin, but their marital relations were often troubled, because Pepin did not put away his concubine Alpaide (Chalpaida), who bore him a son, Charles Martel. Two sons issued from Pepin's marriage with Plectrude, Drogo and Grimoald, but both died as children. Plectrude was pious and very devoted to the Church, and in 697–698 she contributed much toward the founding of one abbey in Echternach (Luxemburg) and of another in Kaiserwerth.

After the death of her husband, Pepin, in the year 714, the widow Plectrude's regency passed to her stepson, Charles Martel. She herself withdrew to Cologne to the convent of canonesses she had founded, Saint Mary in the Capitol. There—no doubt with much prayer and penance—she concluded her earthly life on August 10, 725.

In the Church of Saint Mary in the Capitol at Cologne, the anniversary of Plectrude's death was especially celebrated from the very beginning as the *memoria Plectrudis reginae, fundatricis huius ecclesiae* [the memorial of Queen Plectrude, foundress of this church], and this noble woman was honored as a saint.[1]

---

[1] Cf. *Acta Sanctorum Augusti* 2:60; J. E. Gugumus, "Santa Plettrude", in *Bibliotheca Sanctorum* 10:968–69.

Saint
Vincent Madelgarius
and
Saint
Waldetrudis

Vincent:
  d. 677 in Soignies

Waldetrudis:
  d. April 9, 688, in Castrilocus

Parents of four children

Saint Vincent Madelgarius and his wife, Saint Waldetrudis,[1] were a saintly married couple who gave birth to four children who became saints.

Count Vincent's family was from Strépy (east of Mons in Belgium). He married Saint Waldetrudis (Waltrude, Waltraud), who was the daughter of a nobleman, Walbert, and his wife, Bertilia, and also the sister of Saint Aldegundis, the foundress of the convent at Maubeuge in Hainaut. She gave her husband, Vincent, four children, namely, Saint Adeltrudis, Saint Landericus (Landry), Saint Dentelinus, and Saint Madelberta. At the recommendation of their saintly parents, three of these four children entered religious life.

When the four children had grown up, the parents agreed to separate so as to lead lives consecrated to God in celibacy. Saint Vincent entered the monastery of Hautmont, which he had

---

[1] Cf. E. Brouette, "Vincenzo Madelgario", in *Bibliotheca Sanctorum* 12:1177–78; idem, "Valdetrude" in *Bibliotheca Sanctorum* 12:881–82; A. D. Haenens, "Aldetrude, santa badessa di Maubeuge", in *Bibliotheca Sanctorum* 1:750–51; G. Mathon, "Landerico, santo abate", in *Bibliotheca Sanctorum* 7:1092; A. Codaghengo, "Dentelino, santo fanciullo", in *Bibliotheca Sanctorum* 3:689–91; M. Devuyst, "Madalberta, santa vergine", in *Bibliotheca Sanctorum* 8:473–74.

founded. Later he withdrew to Soignies, where he founded another monastery in 653. He then served as abbot there until shortly before his death in 677. At the suggestion of the holy Abbot Gislenus (d. after 680), Saint Waldetrudis built a convent in Castrilocus (later known as Saint-Waudru in Mons, Belgian Hainaut). Saint Waldetrudis herself entered this convent; she received the veil from the holy Bishop Aubert of Cambrai. Eventually she became the abbess of this convent and died there on April 9, 688. She is portrayed shielding her four children under her mantle, almost like our Lady protecting those who fly to her patronage.

What became then of the four children of the saintly married couple Vincent Madelgarius and Waldetrudis?

1. Adeltrudis, while still a girl, was sent to live with her aunt, Saint Aldegundis, in the Abbey of Maubeuge (northern France), which the latter had founded. There she served for twelve years as abbess and died on February 25 in the year 696.

2. Landericus (Landry) first did military service and later became a monk. He succeeded his father, Vincent, as abbot and governed the two monasteries of Soignies (Flemish "Zinnik", in Belgian Hainaut) and Hautmont (in French Hainaut). It is said that before his death he also worked as a missionary in the vicinity of Brussels. He died on April 17 around the year 730.

3. Dentelinus died as a boy at the age of seven; he is honored throughout Hainaut as a saint, though, just like his parents and siblings, on account of the many miracles that occurred at his grave. He is considered the municipal patron of Rees (Cleve).

4. Madelberta became a Benedictine nun in the convent at Maubeuge and around 696 succeeded her sister Adeltrudis as abbess of this convent. She died on September 7 around the year 700.

Even though stories about the saintly couple Vincent Madelgarius and Waldetrudis and those of their four children have been overgrown and entwined with much that is legendary, the undoubtedly historical basis for these "lives of the saints" is that there was a couple who strove for perfection and raised their children so well that they, too, like their parents, matured in Christian perfection and holiness. In early Christian times there were saintly parents who had saintly children—the best example for this is Saint Gregory Nazianzen the Elder with his wife, Saint Nonna, and their children, Saints Gregory Nazianzen the Younger, Caesarius Nazianzen, and Gorgonia; so, too, even in the supposedly Dark Ages of the seventh and eighth centuries, there was such a holy couple with four saintly children.

Saint Bertha

and

Saint Gumbert

Bertha:
d. ca. 680

According to the chronicler Flodoard of Reims, Gumbert, the brother of Saint Nivard, a seventh-century archbishop of Reims, entered a second marriage with a woman named Bertha.[1] He was extremely charitable to the Church and used some of his fortune to found the monastery Saint Pierre-le-Bas (*S. Petrus inferior*) beside the Porta Basilicaria in Reims. Upon the death of his brother, Saint Nivard, he bequeathed all the possessions he had inherited from his mother to the churches in the city of Reims—what he had inherited from his father he left to his relatives. Then, with the consent of his wife, Bertha, he set out with a missionary zeal for souls to evangelize the still-pagan inhabitants of the northern coast of the Frankish kingdom; there he met his death and witnessed to Christ with his blood.

Bertha, too, followed the example of her noble husband, Gumbert. She left the city of Reims—it was about the year 660—and went to the village of Avenay, which is about sixteen miles distant from Reims. There she founded a convent, to which she bequeathed several estates from her inherited property. Then she entered this convent herself and became its first abbess. It is said that she was murdered by her stepsons toward the end of the seventh century, and she is revered—like her former husband, Gumbert—as a martyr. In the diocese of Reims the feast of Saint Bertha and of her husband, Saint Gumbert, is celebrated on May 1.

---

[1] Cf. G. Bataille, "S. Berta di Avenay", in *Bibliotheca Sanctorum* 3:89.

Saint
Aya

and

Saint
Hildulf

Aya:
>   d. April 18, 708/709

Hildulf:
>   d. June 23 or 27, 707

Saint Aya (Agia) and Saint Hildulf[1] are married saints from the end of the seventh and the beginning of the eighth century.

Aya was born to the count of Hainaut and to Uraia, a daughter of the count of Boulogne-sur-Mer. She married Hildulf, a Frankish nobleman. The couple lived for many years in a marriage that was pleasing to God but childless, and they performed many good deeds for the Church and for the poor.

Hildulf proved to be a great benefactor of the monasteries of Saint Gislenus and Mons. Having reached old age, each of these high-born, truly noble people withdrew to a monastery that followed the Benedictine rule and spirituality. Hildulf went to the monastery at Lobbes near Thuin (Hainaut), where in all humility he placed himself under the spiritual direction of the holy Abbot Ursmar and led a holy life until his death on June 23 or 27, 707. His wife, Aya, on the other hand, entered the Abbey of Castrilocus, also called Mons (Bergen, in Belgian Hainaut), where she likewise led a holy life until on April 18, 708/709, she was called to her eternal reward.

---

[1] Cf. A. D. Haenens, "S. Aia da Mons", in *Bibliotheca Sanctorum* 1:662; R. Van Doren, "S. Idulfo di Lobbes", in *Bibliotheca Sanctorum* 7:645.

Saint
Richard
and
Wunna

d. 720 in Lucca, near Pisa, Italy

Father of three children

A saintly English married couple who brought three saints into the world certainly deserve to be mentioned in a book about married saints and blesseds, even though almost nothing is known about them.[1] The title "King of the Anglo-Saxons" was incorrectly attributed to Saint Richard sometime in the tenth century; his wife, Wunna by name, is said to have died around 710. She was the mother of three children, namely, Saint Willibald, Saint Winebald, and Saint Walburga.

The father, Richard, was convinced by his son Willibald to go on a "pilgrimage for Christ". He set off in the year 720 with his two sons as pilgrims on a journey. Their first destination was to be Rome, and from there they would travel on to the Holy Land. Richard died, though, in the autumn of 722 in Lucca, near Pisa, and was buried there in the church of San Frediano. Around the year 1150 the remains of Richard were disinterred; one part of them was brought to Eichstätt. At both places people began to

---

[1] *Acta Sanctorum Februarii* 2:69–81; W. Grothe, *Der hl. Richard und seine Kinder* (Berlin, 1908).

honor Richard, the royal pilgrim, as a saint, surely on account of his saintly children, of whom Willibald is the most important.

After the death of his father, Willibald continued the pilgrimage and stayed for 2 1/2 years in Rome; from 723 to 727 he was a pilgrim in the Holy Land; from 727 to 729 he traveled in Byzantium; and from 730 to 739 he lived as a monk in Monte Cassino. On the trip back he returned to Rome in 739, and at the request of Saint Boniface he was sent by Pope Gregory III to the German missions. In 740 he received priestly ordination in Eichstätt. On October 21, 741, in Sulzenbrücken near Erfurt, Willibald was consecrated the first bishop of Eichstätt.

There he built the cathedral and a monastery and, supported by a rapidly growing number of co-workers, did mission work in Bavarian, Frankish, and Swabian territories. In the year 778 he dictated to the nun Hugeburc a report of the pilgrimage he had begun with his father, Richard. Saint Willibald died on July 7, 787.

The second son of the English couple Richard and Wunna is Saint Winebald, who was born around 701 in Wessex (southern England). He traveled with his father and brother to Italy in 720. In Rome he entered a monastery. On a journey to his English homeland (727–730), he recruited men to become itinerant missionaries. On his second journey to Rome (737–738), Saint Boniface called him to join the mission to Thuringia and in 739 ordained him a priest. Winebald cared for his mission territory from a base in Sulzenbrücken. Then from 744 to 747 he served in the Amberg basin in Oberpfalz; finally, he became a pastor in Mainz. Around 751 or 752 he rejoined his brother, Willibald, and together with him he founded Heidenheim Abbey in 752 as a missionary and cultural center in the midst of a population that to a large extent had reverted to heathen ways. He became the first abbot of the Benedictine monastery at Heidenheim. On December 18, 761, he died.

The third child of Saint Richard and his wife, Wunna, is Walburga, who was born around 710 in England. Together with Saint Lioba and Tatta, she was called by Saint Boniface to assist with the missions to Germany. At first she worked under Saint Lioba in

Bischofsheim; then, from 751 or 752 on, she was stationed at the double abbey of Heidenheim, which her brothers had founded near Treuchtlingen, south of Nuremberg. She died as the abbess on February 25, 779.

Surely both Richard and Wunna are in heaven, since they raised their two sons, Willibald and Winebald, and their daughter, Walburga, so well that they grew up to be saints. The writer J. Dirnbeck, in his "Modern Litany of the Saints", dedicated to them the following very contemporary invocation: "You knew how to create a family atmosphere in which your children matured into adults who not only were hearers of the Good News but also became its messengers. Richard and Wunna, pray for us, that we will be concerned about how best to hand on our faith to the children of tomorrow." [2]

---

[2] J. Dirnbeck, *Auf die man zählen kann* (Munich, 1987), p. 17.

Saint
Bertha of Blangy
and
Siegfried

d. 725

Mother of five children

Bertha, the daughter of Count Rigobert, married a certain Sieg-fried and became the mother of five children.

When her husband died, Bertha retreated with her two eldest daughters, Deotila and Gertrude, to the Abbey of Blangy-sur-Ternoise, which she had founded. Though she was elected abbess of the community, she declined that responsibility and lived there as a simple recluse.

In the year 725, after a holy life of self-sacrifice, she was called to her eternal reward.[1]

---

[1] Cf. *Acta Sanctorum Julii* 2:47–60; "S. Berta di Blangy", in *Bibliotheca Sanctorum* 3:90.

Saint Ida of Herzfeld and Egbert

b. ca. 766
d. September 4, 813 or 825

Mother of five children

Vision in a dream: Ida receives the commission to build a church in Herzfeld, in the diocese of Münster. (Stained-glass window in the Ida Chapel of the Church of Saint Ida, Herzfeld.)

Saint Ida of Herzfeld was an exemplary wife and mother.[1] She had been born into a Christian family herself around the year 766. All five of her brothers and sisters chose religious life, which would have been unthinkable had not a genuinely Christian spirit prevailed in their family. Two of Saint Ida's brothers, namely, Adalhard and Wala, became abbots of Corvey Abbey.

Ida herself, on the other hand, after a virtuous childhood and youth, married the Saxon duke Egbert, whom she tended very lovingly during a long and wearisome illness. Among the five children whom Saint Ida bore for her noble husband, we again find two religious vocations. Her son Warin became the abbot of Corvey, and her daughter Hedwig became the abbess of Herford. Both are considered to be blessed.

Together with her husband, Saint Ida of Herzfeld founded a church. After the death of her husband she led in Herzfeld (diocese of Münster, in Westphalia) a life of piety, penance, and love of neighbor. She died in Herzfeld on September 4, 813 (825?), and was laid to rest in the church that she and her husband had built.

---

[1] Cf. *Acta Sanctorum Septembris* 2:260–70; J. Baur, "Ida di Herzfeld", in *Bibliotheca Sanctorum* 7:637–38.

When her relics were disinterred for veneration on November 26, 980, more than 150 years after her death, the monk Uffing set about recording the miraculous life of Saint Ida of Herzfeld. She is revered by the women of Westphalia, who invoke her help especially in childbirth.

Saint
Bernard of Vienne
and
Spouse

b. ca. 778 in the vicinity of Lyons
d. January 23, 842, in the abbey of Romans (Département of Ain), France

St Bernard (Barnard) was a husband and father of a family who, during his wife's lifetime, became a Benedictine monk and subsequently the archbishop of Vienne. He was born around 778 in the vicinity of Lyons into a noble family.[1] At first he did military service in Charlemagne's army. Then he married, or—to put it more precisely—a marriage was arranged for him by his parents, even though he already sensed that he was called to religious life.

After his father's death and seven years of marriage, he made an agreement with his wife and separated from her and his children. He entered the abbey of Ambronay (Ambronianum) in Bugey, which he had founded, and became a Benedictine monk.

Four years later, the monk Bernard became the abbot of his monastery, and then in 810, after the death of Archbishop Vulferius of Vienne, he was elected to succeed him as archbishop.

This appointment to such high office, however, marked the beginning of a series of difficult trials and afflictions, in which Bernard's virtues were sorely tested.

When the emperor Louis the Pious divided his kingdom among his sons in 815 and a quarrel arose among them while they were rebelling against their father, Archbishop Bernard had to leave his episcopal see and flee to Italy. After returning to France, Saint Bernard stayed in the Abbey of Romans (in the Département of Ain), which he had founded. There the former husband and father died on January 23, 842.

---

[1] Cf. *Acta Sanctorum Januarii* 2:544–48; P. Villette, "San Bernardo (Barnardo), vescovo di Vienne", in *Bibliotheca Sanctorum* 3:68–69.

Saint Irmgard and Lothar I

b. ca. 800
d. March 20, 851, in Erstein in
Alsace, France

Married 821
Mother of four children

Little is known about this woman who is revered as a saint in Alsace.[1] She was born the daughter of Count Hugo of Tours and was a descendant of Duke Attich of Alsace. In the year 821 she was married to the emperor Lothar I. She must have been an exemplary, church-going wife and mother. Proof of this, besides the exemplary Christian education that her three sons, Louis II, Lothar II, and Charles, received, is the fact that the Empress Irmgard founded the abbey of nuns in Erstein in Alsace and that her daughter Rotrud became the first abbess of this abbey, which is located to the south of Strasbourg. Later emperors liked to make pilgrimages to this imperial abbey and to pray at the tomb of the saintly empress in the abbey church. Empress Irmgard died in Erstein on March 20, 851, four years before her imperial consort. In late summer of 855, the widowed Emperor Lothar I arranged the division of his dominions among his three sons, Louis II, Lothar II, and Charles. Then he entered the monastery of Prüme, where he died a few days later on September 29, 855.

---

[1] Cf. J. M. B. Clauss, *Die Heiligen des Elsass* (Düsseldorf, 1935), pp. 200f; A. M. Burg, *Le duché d'Alsace* (Wörth, 1959), p. 45.

Saint
Ludmila
and
Borivoy of Bohemia

b. ca. 860
d. September 15, 921, in Tetin, near
  Beraun

Mother of six children

Standing before us in the persons of Ludmila and Bori-voy are a pagan wife and husband who together found their way to the Christian faith, were baptized in one ceremony by Methodius, the Apostle to the Slavs, and—as it appears—lived an exemplary Christian married life. Thanks to both of them, Bohemia turned away from the pagan East and joined the Christian West.

A legend, which surely has a historical basis, tells us about the conversion of Saint Ludmila and her marriage with Borivoy of Melnik. In the county seat of the noble line from which Ludmila was descended, a statue of the pagan weather goddess Baba had been erected. The people gathered before it at certain times of the year. Once, as this was happening again, the Christian hermit Ivan appeared. In fiery language he condemned the worship of idols and praised the Catholic faith. As he was still speaking, he walked up to the image of the pagan goddess Baba and destroyed it right before the eyes of the people. Speechless and horrified, the crowd awaited the vengeance of the gods. The hermit, however, went back unperturbed to the woods from which he had come. Ludmila, who had witnessed all this with the crowd, was profoundly shaken. In her soul, for the first time, a spark of the Christian faith began to gleam. She followed the hermit Ivan to his cell and became his pupil. One day while she was there, she caught sight of the Bohemian duke Borivoy, of the Premyslid dynasty, who was hunting. He was delighted by Ludmila's charm and beauty and immediately asked for her hand in marriage. She demanded, however, that the duke convert to Christianity with her and follow her example. He agreed to this condition. So it came about that the two were baptized and married by Methodius in the church of Velehrad. The majority of the Bohemian people soon followed the example of the now-Christian duke and duchess and likewise professed the Christian faith.

It is said that the marriage of the duke and the duchess was blessed with three sons and three daughters. The couple, especially Ludmila, attached great importance to Christian education in their palace in Prague; this is evident in their grandson, Saint Wenceslaus. Together with her husband, Ludmila had several churches built. Besides this, she was very generous to the poor and earned the honorable title of "Mother of the poor".

Around 894, after both Duke Borivoy and his successors, Spytihinev and Ratislav I, died prematurely, Ludmila's daughter-in-law Drahomira took over as regent in the duchy of Bohemia. Because Drahomira was still a pagan, Duke Borivoy had instructed his wife, Ludmila to see to it that their oldest grandson, Wenceslaus, Drahomira's son, would have a Christian upbringing. Ludmila, virtuous woman that she was, carried out his instructions with great success. Ludmila's influence instilled in the young prince the beginnings of that profound Christian piety by virtue of which he later became a saint. Drahomira, though, who continued to cling to the old idols, harbored a venomous hatred for Ludmila, on account of the zeal with which the latter spread Christianity throughout the land. Drahomira succeeded in drawing part of the Bohemian nobility to her side, so that, as tradition tells us, at her behest two Bohemian nobles were willing to accost Ludmila at her widow's estate in Tetin, near Beraun, on September 15, 921, and strangle her with her own veil. Ludmila's body was buried at first in Tetin, but under Duke Wenceslaus it was transferred to the Church of Saint George at the castle in Prague.[1]

---

[1] Cf. F. Seibt, "Ludmilla" in *Lexikon für Theologie und Kirche* (LThK), 6:1179; E. and H. Melchers, *Das grosse Buch der Heiligen* (Munich, 1978), pp. 590–91; J. Olc, "Ludmilla", in *Bibliotheca Sanctorum* 8:293–96.

Saint Matilda and Henry I

b. ca. 895 in Engern, Saxony
d. March 14, 968

Married 909
Mother of five children

An especially noble figure among the wives of the German kings and emperors of the Middle Ages is Saint Matilda, the wife of King Henry I. She was born around 895 in Engern (Saxony), the daughter of the Saxon Count Dietrich, a great-grandson of Count Widukind, and the Danish-Frankish noblewoman Reinhild; she received the best possible education in the convent of Erfurt, where her grandmother Matilda was the abbess.

In the year 909 Matilda married Duke Heinrich der Vogler (Henry the Fowler), who was elected the German king in 919 and was crowned Henry I. She was an attractive, intelligent, loving, pious, and charitable wife; in the oldest documents, *Vita Mathildis prior*,[1] from the year 975, and *Vita Mathildis posterior*,[2] the title *sancta* (saint) is given to her, and she is described as "mirae sanctitatis femina" (a woman of marvelous holiness).

It has been said about her marriage:

She lived in concord with her husband; his love was the air she breathed. In converse with him she revealed all the treasures of

[1] MGH *Script.* 10:573–82.
[2] MGH *Script.* 4:282–302.

her soul, all of her tender, womanly qualities. She cheered and embellished his life, lightened his careworn spirits by her fresh and lively character and calmed his moods, which were often rather stormy. She never interfered in her royal husband's business of ruling; she never put herself forward with her opinion or her advice; but an unintentional, ingenuous word from her often showed him the way out of confusion and difficulties. She insisted on only one claim as queen: on the right to intercede for clemency and forgiveness. She exercised this right on every occasion, but when the king in his strict justice could not oblige her, she remained calm: she had satisfied the impulse of her heart, and then he could act according to the dictates of his heart.[3]

Five children were born into the marriage of Matilda and King Henry: (1) Otto, who later became King Otto I, the Great; (2) Gerberga, who married Duke Giselbert of Lorraine in 928 and King Louis IV of France in 940; (3) Hedwig; (4) Henry (d. 955), later the duke of Bavaria; and (5) Bruno (d. 965), later the saintly archbishop of Cologne. Matilda devoted herself to all of her children with tender, motherly care and sought to train their souls and their hearts in true reverence for God and good will toward their fellowmen. For twenty-three years Matilda was able to enjoy the happiness of untroubled married love. Then in 936 her husband died on a journey to Memleben, on the River Unstrut, at the age of sixty and was entombed in the cathedral of Quedlinburg.

The widowed queen gathered her children and fervently begged them to practice fear of the Lord and fidelity to the Commandments of God, but above all to maintain harmony and peace among themselves. That, unfortunately, did not happen, to some extent through Matilda's fault. She had always showed a preferential love for her second son, the handsome Henry, and this aroused the envy of the other children. Even now she wished her favorite

---

[3] Cf. J. Walterscheid, *Deutsche Heilige* (Munich, 1934), pp. 136f.; M. Lintzel, *Westfälische Lebensbilder* (Münster, 1937), 5:161–75; B. Kaul, *Die Strahlkraft der Heiligen* (Fribourg, 1989), pp. 32–35.

Duke Henry of Saxony makes a proposal of marriage to Matilda.
(Drawing by Ferdinand Loeke, nineteenth century.)

to become the successor to the German royal throne after the
death of her husband. The great leaders of the empire, however,
chose the older son, Otto, as king, as Henry I had wished, and they
brought him to Aachen for the coronation. Thereupon Henry
started an armed uprising against his brother Otto. King Otto I
was able to subdue it only after lengthy battles. The queen-mother
Matilda had to do a severe penance for favoring Henry; she offered
many prayers and shed many tears before she succeeded in reconciling the quarreling brothers.

Not long afterward, a new sorrow overtook Matilda. This time
the two brothers, Otto and Henry, turned against their mother and
accused her of wasting her possessions on unworthy individuals.
Matilda was forced to leave the royal court. She withdrew to a
convent. Only personal misfortune and much bitter experience
made the two sons realize that they had done their mother an
injustice; they made a public apology, and Matilda was allowed to

return to the royal court. From then on Matilda again devoted herself without restrictions to works of charity and piety.

On March 14, 968, the widowed queen mother Matilda died, after having been strengthened by the last sacraments brought to her by her grandson, Archbishop Wilhelm of Mainz. She found beside her husband, King Henry I, her final resting place in the cathedral of Quedlinburg.

Through her children and grandchildren Matilda became the ancestor of several ruling houses: the imperial descendants of Otto, according to the male line and according to the female line, the Salic Franks, the Hohenstaufens, and the French Capetians. Even more remarkable is the fact that Matilda is surrounded by saints from among her near relatives. Her youngest son, Bruno, Archbishop of Cologne, is revered as a saint. Her daughter-in-law Adelaide (Adelheid), the wife of her son Otto, who in 962 was crowned Emperor Otto I in Rome, is also revered as a saint. Matilda's great-grandson, Emperor Henry II, his wife Cunegund (Cunégonde), his sister Gisela and her husband, King Stephen of Hungary, and the latter's son Emeric likewise are considered to be saints.

Saint
Adelaide
and
Lothair

b. 931
d. December 16/17, 999, in the
   Benedictine Abbey in Seltz

Married 947
Mother of five children and two
   foster children
Canonized 1097

Saint Adelaide (Adelheid) is a saint who was married, not once, but twice—certainly a rare exception.[1] She was born in 931, the daughter of King Rudolph II of Burgundy and Bertha, the daughter of Duke Buchard of Swabia.

She shared the lot of many noble daughters and was betrothed while still a six-year-old child to King Lothair of Italy; in 947, having just turned sixteen, she was married to him. From this happy marriage sprang a daughter by the name of Emma, who eventually was married with Lothair II, the King of the Franks and the last of the Carolingians, and became the mother of King Louis V.

Adelaide's marriage with Lothair of Italy lasted only three years, for he died on November 22, 950, allegedly poisoned by his powerful opponent, the Margrave Berengar III of Ivrea. When Adelaide became a widow, she was only twenty years old. At that time she was considered to be particularly beautiful, clever, and pious, and soon her hand was requested by Berengar, the opponent of her

[1] Cf. J. C. Clauss, *Die Heiligen des Elsass* (Düsseldorf, 1935).

deceased husband—not for himself, but for his son, Adalbert. With this man she was supposed to enter a second marriage; Berengar wanted in this way to secure, and to a certain extent legitimize, the royal dignity that he had arrogated to himself. Adelaide, however, abhorred the idea of marrying the son of the man who may well have poisoned her husband, Lothair; she opposed this marriage, and for her opposition she was imprisoned in the fortress of Garda on the eastern shore of Lake Garda and was treated very badly. Adelaide's faithful chaplain Martin helped her to flee in secret; with the help of faithful friends of her deceased husband, she managed to reach the castle of Canossa, which Berengar then furiously but unsuccessfully besieged. This is because, from her refuge in Canossa, Adelaide called on the German King Otto I for help. The latter marched with an army over the Alps, vanquished Berengar, deposed him, and had himself crowned in Pavia as King of the Lombards.

To Pavia, then, came Adelaide as well, to thank her rescuer. King Otto I, whose first wife, Edith, had died in 946, was deeply impressed by Adelaide's beauty and noble character, and he requested her hand. On Christmas Day 951 King Otto I was joined in wedlock with Adelaide in Pavia. She lived now as the royal consort at the side of the German King Otto I; in 962, when he was crowned ruler of the Holy Roman Empire by Pope John XII in Rome, she was elevated to the rank of empress.

As empress and queen, Adelaide had abundant opportunities to promote all sorts of good and holy causes. She who once had been in need of protection herself had a motherly heart for all who were poor and oppressed, as Saint Odilo (Olon) of Cluny reports in his biography of Empress Adelaide around the year 1000, which he wrote "non modo auditu, sed visu et experimento", that is, on the basis of close, amicable acquaintance with the empress.[2] Adelaide, who is rightly called "one of the most noble and majestic female figures in German history",[3] led with Emperor Otto I an exemplary

[2] H. Paulhart, *Lebensbeschreibung der Kaiserin Adelheid, von Abt Odilo von Cluny: "Epitaphium domine Adelheid auguste"* (Graz, 1962).

[3] Cf. J. Weingartner, *Im Glanze der Heiligen* (Innsbruck, 1949), p. 10.

Christian married life, from which four children proceeded, namely, Henry (d. ca. 954), Bruno (d. 957), Otto—who would become Emperor Otto II—(d. December 7, 983), and Matilda, who subsequently became the abbess of Quedlinburg (d. 999). In addition to her own children, Empress Adelaide also brought to the imperial court two daughters of the hereditary foe of her deceased first husband and was a loving mother and protectress to them.

Above all she devoted herself very lovingly to her husband, Emperor Otto I, and showed an interest and an understanding for his duties as ruler. Saint Odilo, probably based on his own observation of Saint Adelaide's marriage and household, refers to the parable of the wise, loving and attentive wife in the Book of Proverbs (31:20–29). Besides her marital and familial concerns, Saint Adelaide looked with approval on the monastic reform movement that originated in Cluny. She supported the founding of monasteries, for example, in Peterlingen, San Salvatore in Pavia, and in Seltz (Alsace).

After the death of her husband, Emperor Otto I (d. May 7, 973), Adelaide's son acceded to the throne as Emperor Otto II. Unfortunately, his wife, Theophano, a Greek princess, was jealous of Adelaide's influence on her son and turned him against her mother-in-law, primarily with the argument that Adelaide was squandering the imperial wealth by her generosity. The empress mother was banished from the court. She returned to her homeland, yet she bore these humiliations with the same noble peace of mind and modest magnanimity with which she had previously borne the rank of empress at the side of her husband during her marriage.

Adelaide's son, Emperor Otto II, must have realized very soon how much he missed the advice of his experienced and reliable co-regent, his mother, for all his plans foundered and whatever he started failed. He repented and called his mother back. After the premature death of her son Otto II (d. December 7, 983, in Rome—his wife, Theophano, followed him to the grave on January 23/24, 1002), the now sixty-year-old empress mother had to take over the regency for her underage grandson, Otto III, in 983.

Then in 994, when Adelaide's grandson Otto III began to rule, Adelaide returned to private life. She devoted the last years of her life entirely to preparing herself for death. Her final undertaking was a journey to Burgundy, her homeland, where bitter dissension prevailed between the king, her nephew, and the people. She succeeded in restoring the peace. On this journey she also visited all of the foundations she had made and supported that were located along the way, to see whether everything was in order. On the return trip she then stayed for a while in Alsace, which she especially loved. She remained in the Benedictine Abbey of Seltz—her favorite foundation—until her death on December 16/17, 999.

In the introduction to the latest critical Latin edition of the *Life of Empress Adelaide by Abbot Odilo of Cluny*,[4] the editor and publisher H. Paulhart correctly states:

Mater regnorum [the mother of kingdoms] was the name that Gerbert d'Aurillac gave to Empress Adelaide in his letters, thus coining an expression that was meant to express the highest esteem and respect for her, whether she is considered as wife, mother, or regent. Adelaide, who in the course of half a century significantly helped to determine the destiny of the empire, first as the wife of the German king, then as empress, later as the mother and grandmother of two later emperors, was descended from the royal house of Burgundy. Widowed while still young, she was drawn into the tumultuous events in northern Italy around the middle of the tenth century, then overcame these difficulties through her second marriage with Otto I, and finally rose to the supreme rank in the empire. After the death of her second husband it was her lot on two further occasions to assume the responsibility for governing the empire, for her son after his death and then for her underage grandson. As a religious woman who was faithfully dedicated to the Church, she began to sense with the passage of years an inclination to the

---

[4] Paulhart, *Lebensbeschreibung*, p. 7.

contemplative life. Nevertheless she was not afraid, even in advanced years, of taking on political duties, when that was the need of the moment. When she passed away in the year 999, profound mourning prevailed in the circles in which she had moved.

Not even one hundred years would pass before Rome raised to the honors of the altar this empress, who already enjoyed universal respect, thereby sanctioning the cult that had arisen around her and her tomb. No less a figure than Odilo of Cluny, who was a trusted friend of Adelaide during her lifetime, felt impelled to extol her reputation. In order to keep her memory alive, he dedicated a written tribute to her that remains even today the most important foundation for all biographical works about Empress Adelaide.

In conclusion, we can only say that Pope Urban II, in canonizing Adelaide in the year 1097, wished to honor this exemplary wife, mother, and regent and to recommend her to married people of either sex as a model of good Christian married life.

Blessed
Ansfrid
and
Ilsunda

b. ca. 940
d. May 3, 1010

Father of one child

In much the same way that Saint Hilary of Poitiers was first a husband and the father of one daughter, then became the holy bishop and chief shepherd of his diocese, so too Blessed Ansfrid,[1] Count of Brabant, the scion of a noble Flemish line, was at first happily married to Ilsunda (Hilswind), who bore him a daughter named Benedicta. He was one of the most faithful friends of Emperor Otto III and was well regarded because of his integrity and wisdom; he sincerely strove to bring about order and peace in the territories that he ruled. Surely he was also an exemplary, faithful husband and father who—like his wife and his daughter—was very intent on leading a pious life as a believing Christian. Ansfrid probably practiced celibacy toward the end of his married life because he—like his wife—sensed within him the urge and the call to dedicate to God alone the remaining years that God would grant him. In the year 992 he founded a convent for his wife and his daughter in Thorn. Then he donated his county to the bishop of Lüttich and became a monk from then on.

After the death of Bishop Baldwin of Utrecht, Ansfrid was asked by Emperor Otto III to take charge of the episcopal see of Utrecht. At that time the emperor endowed the Church of Utrecht with large tracts of land. Ansfrid complied with the

---

[1] Cf. *Acta Sanctorum Maii* 1:428–32.

emperor's wish and took over the governance of the diocese of Utrecht as its chief shepherd. For this purpose he was also consecrated a bishop. For the emperor, Saint Henry II, Bishop Ansfrid was a much sought after advisor.

Unfortunately, the episcopal ministry of Bishop Ansfrid did not last very long, because he went blind. He withdrew to the hermitage at Hohorst and there went on living again as he had done before his elevation to the see of Utrecht, humbly and conscientiously following the Rule of Saint Benedict. In 1006 the hermitage in Hohorst was developed into a monastery by monks from Gladbach.

Bishop Ansfrid, who had been the husband of Ilsunda and the father of Benedicta, died around the year 1010. Ansfrid's remains rest in Saint Paul's Cathedral in Utrecht; in that diocese he is revered as a blessed, or even a saint, just like his wife, Ilsunda, and his daughter, Benedicta.

Saint
Henry II
and
Saint
Cunegund

Henry II:
*b. May 6, 973, probably in
  Hildesheim*
*d. July 13, 1024 in Grona, near
  Göttingen*

Canonized 1146

Cunegund:
d. March 3, 1033

Canonized 1200

Married 998/1000

*Queen Cunegund, by Albrecht Dürer,
Church of Saint Sebaldus,
sixteenth century*

The marriage of two saints that has most often become a topic of discussion by historians, theologians, and canonists is the marriage of the emperor Saint Henry II to Saint Cunegund. On the one hand, their marriage has been characterized as a Josephite marriage, in which the spouses, remarkably, vowed and practiced continence from beginning to end. On the other hand, some scholars have considered only the childlessness of the imperial couple, calling into question everything that might lend an exalted religious or supernatural character to their marriage as incredible, as a "silly fable" or a "meaningless legend". Perhaps some questions in this regard can be clarified by consulting contemporary sources.

First, however, let us look briefly at the essential facts about these august individuals.

1. Henry (the German king, later Emperor Henry II) was born on May 6, 973, probably in Hildesheim. He bore the same name as

his father and grandfather. For many years his grandfather Henry had caused his own brother, Emperor Otto I, the most unpleasant difficulties, often disputing the latter's supremacy. Henry the father is known in history with good reason by the nickname "the Wrangler". He, too, was involved in disputes with his cousin, King Otto II. After the death of Henry the Wrangler in 955, his son Henry II took the title of Duke of Bavaria. At that time Otto III ruled in Germany.

Due to the strained relations between his family (grandfather and father) and the royal house, it was assumed that the young Henry II would never take the throne, and so he was originally destined for the clerical state and educated accordingly—like his brother Bruno, who later became bishop of Augsburg. He received his education first with Bishop Abraham of Freising, then in the cathedral school in Hildesheim; his last teacher was Saint Wolfgang, the bishop of Regensburg.

When Henry II became the duke of Bavaria after all, he was bound by an oath of loyalty to his cousin, Emperor Otto III. When this emperor died in Rome at the early age of twenty, Henry II spoke with great respect about his cousin, "the great emperor". Henry II then became the successor to Otto III; in this capacity he was not quite so oriented toward Rome as was his predecessor, but rather tried first and foremost to rule well in the German lands. This has earned him the praise of modern historians; less so the fact that he was still, in the best sense, loyal to Rome and to the pope and felt that he shared responsibility for the Church and did much to reform and extend her. Therein, though, lies the principal reason for his canonization in 1146. Having rendered great service to Germany and the Church, Henry II died in his fifty-first year in Grona, near Göttingen, on July 13, 1024. Henry was not only happily married to a saint, Saint Cunegund, for about twenty-five years; through his saintly sister Gisela, he was also the brother-in-law of King Saint Stephen of Hungary.

2. Cunegund, who wedded Henry II around the year 998/ 1000, was born the sixth of the eleven children of Count Siegfried of Lützelburg (Luxemburg) and his wife, Hedwig.

Queen Cunegund was suspected of marital infidelity and was forced to undergo the ordeal of a so-called divine judgment. In order to prove her innocence, she walked over red-hot iron plates. Drawing by K. Weigand, nineteenth century.

Like Henry II, Cunegund, too, enjoyed the benefits of a meticulous education. Since she was, moreover, no less gifted than the future emperor, her marriage with him, aside from their childlessness, proved to be a happy one. Cunegund, in fact, was on many occasions a wise counselor for Henry II; several times she was even able to represent him worthily and wisely in carrying out the duties of the imperial administration.

When Duke Henry II of Bavaria was elected the king of the Germans and crowned in 1002 in Mainz by Archbishop Willigis, an identical ceremony was then conducted in Paderborn with Cunegund. Furthermore, on February 14, 1014, when Henry II was crowned emperor in Rome by Pope Benedict VIII, Cunegund was simultaneously crowned empress. In later life she, too, proved to be loyal to the pope and to the hierarchy and a great benefactress of the Church, especially in Bamberg. Since his childhood, Henry II had especially loved the castle of Bamberg in eastern Franconia and had patronized it more than any other.

Once he was married, however, he gave the castle of Bamberg to his wife, Cunegund, as a wedding gift.

The imperial couple built a church beside the castle in Bamberg; on Easter 1020 the same pope who had performed the imperial coronation of Henry and Cunegund then consecrated that church as the cathedral of the diocese of Bamberg, which the emperor had created.

In 1025, after the death of her imperial consort and one year of mourning, Cunegund entered the Benedictine convent of Kaufungen, which she had founded, as a nun. On March 3, 1033, she died there. On March 29, 1200, Cunegund, too, was declared a saint. Her remains were interred on September 9, 1202, beside those of her husband in the cathedral of Bamberg. Her feast day used to be celebrated on the day of her death, March 3; since the latest reform of the calendar and the liturgy, though, it is celebrated with that of Saint Henry on July 13, in order to emphasize that what God has joined in marriage should not be separated, even in the liturgy.

Let us now examine more closely the marriage of these two saints, Henry and Cunegund, and the controversial problems that have arisen concerning it.

Professor J. B. Sägmüller has dealt thoroughly with the subject, "Die Ehe Heinrich II., des Heiligen, mit Kunigunde" (The marriage of Saint Henry II with Cunegund),[1] and with the related controversy. From the twelfth century down to our day, the marriage of Saint Henry II and Saint Cunegund has been viewed by not a few authors as a "virginal marriage", in the sense that they ascribed to this couple, from the very beginning, perpetual abstinence from sexual relations. Besides this point of view, however, there have been authors from very early on, but especially in our time, who were of the opinion that Henry's marriage with Cunegund was childless for biological reasons; to make this fact harmonize better with the sanctity of the couple, it was then "transfigured" and understood in terms of a Josephite marriage.

[1] J. B. Sägmüller, "Die Ehe Heinrichs II., des Heiligen, mit Kunigunde", *Theol. Quartalsschrift*, Tübingen, 1905, pp. 78–95; 1907, pp. 563–77; 1911, pp. 90–126.

It is best to follow, with J. B. Sägemüller, what the monk Rodulfus Glaber[2] recounts about the marriage of Henry and Cunegund. Saint Odilo of Cluny (d. 1048) frequented the court of Henry II, and it was to this abbot that Rodulfus Glaber dedicated his chronicle, which was written before 1048. Therefore, his reports with regard to Henry II are completely trustworthy. Now, this monk reports that Henry II, even though he saw that he could not have any children by his wife, Cunegund, did not put her away on that account, but rather made over to the Church of Christ all of his possessions that otherwise would have gone to his children. From this it follows immediately—in the opinion of J. B. Sägmüller—that the circumstance in Saint Henry's marriage that prevented him from begetting heirs was impotency on the part of Cunegund. Whether this was sterility in the strict sense, or whether the incapability was prevenient or subsequent, cannot be determined from the report of the chronicler. Rodulfus Glaber goes on to report that Emperor Henry II did not divorce his wife, Cunegund, because of the aforementioned childlessness, the ulterior motive for which, of course, would be to marry another woman and to have children with her. Would Henry II simply have been able to do that? According to the German marital and ecclesiastical law of the day, he could have, for the law held that a marriage in which one of the parties was "unable to consummate the marriage with the other" (euphemistic translation) could be dissolved in such a way that the potent party could then marry someone else.

The German Church's practice of permitting the dissolution of a marriage in the case of impotency, however, was not in keeping with the custom of the Roman Church, which did not permit divorce on account of impotency but, rather, urged the couple to live together as brother and sister.

In his situation, Henry II was not obliged to follow the Roman usage; he could have adhered to the praxis of the German Church and sent Cunegund away so as to obtain heirs through another

[2] Rudolfus Glaber, *Historiarum sui temporis libri* V, NGSS 7:62.

marriage—something highly desirable for a German king and emperor. He did not do that, though, and from a certain point on he gave up all hope of having heirs. He made Christ the substitute heir. From the words spoken by Saint Henry at the foundation of [the diocese of] Bamberg, we can also infer that from a certain point on he abstained from marital relations with Cunegund and lived with her as a brother. That is a noble trait in the portrait of the saintly emperor; after all, Pope Gregory II once wrote in a letter to Saint Boniface that such self-control is possible only for truly magnanimous men.

Henry II acted toward his wife, Cunegund, in a much nobler and more generous way than Henry IV, who demanded at the gathering of the princes at Worms in 1069 a separation from his wife, Bertha, "quia non posset ei tam naturali quam maritali coitus foedere copulari", as it says in the letter from Archbishop Siegfried of Mainz to Pope Alexander II.[3]

As for the marriage of the saintly emperor, one should not overlook this magnanimous character trait of his. Even if a completely Josephite marriage, by reason of a vow of virginity taken by Saint Cunegund, is probably only a legend, nevertheless, the marriage of the saintly imperial couple was full of noble, mutual love; perhaps this marriage was actually a Josephite marriage in part, since Henry, after discovering Cunegund's sterility, remained faithful to her and from a certain point on deliberately practiced continence with her [within marriage].

Today many Christian married people who would like to have children but for biological reasons cannot could take the saintly imperial couple as their model. They should not insist on realizing their desires by artificial means—which are contrary to Divine Providence and against the regulations of the Church—but should submit in all humility and generosity to the will of God and show that much more love for each other and for others, especially for orphaned children.

---

[3] Cf. Jaffé, *Bibl[ia] rer[um] Germ[anorum]* 5:857.

Saint Emma and William

b. ca. 980
d. June 29, 1045

Married ca. 1010–1015
Mother of one son
Canonized January 4, 1938

Emma of Gurk. The illustration shows the foundress in Magyar-Croatian national garb as it was worn around the year 1500.

Emma, the only child of Count von Friesach-Zeltschach, was born around 980 and, because she became an orphan at an early age, was raised at the court of the emperor Henry II, to whom she was related on her mother's side. Around the year 1010 or 1015, she was married to Count William of Sanngau. Both of them had been trained in courtly manners and Christian morality, and accordingly they led an exemplary married life. God blessed their marriage with a son, who received his father's name, William. Through imperial grants of land, the already extensive property of the count and his wife was significantly enlarged. Emma stood faithfully beside her husband as a wise counselor and prudent assistant in managing the vast estate located in the Gurk and Sann valleys and extending far beyond. She also devoted herself to works of Christian charity and, by word and deed, came to the help of her subjects, especially the poor. Besides this, she was very much concerned about the religious and moral education of the vassals. That is the explanation for the numerous churches founded by Countess Emma.

In connection with a political dispute between Duke Adalbero and Count William, Emma's husband, the latter was murdered on March 20, 1036. So, after about twenty happy years of married life, Emma became a widow. Countess Emma had taken particular care in educating her son, William. He grew to maturity with the fear of God and chivalrous manners. As an adult he supervised, on his mother's behalf, the family's silver mines in Friesach and Zeltschach. According to some reports, he was murdered during a riot over food shortages. Thus the pious, charitable Countess Emma lost not only her husband but also her son through violence.

Now a childless widow, she retreated to the peaceful Gurk valley and, in her profound sorrow, sought consolation in good works and pious exercises. While secluded in this way, she arrived at the decision to use her considerable wealth for the glory of God, for repose of the souls of her husband and her son, for the salvation of her own soul, and for the benefit and edification of her fellowmen. For this purpose she founded in Gurk a Benedictine convent and, in Admont (Steiermark), a Benedictine monastery. She died on June 29, 1045; soon after her death the people revered her as one of the blessed. The canonization process of Countess Emma of Gurk began in 1466 and concluded on January 4, 1938, with the approval of the devotions to this noble wife and mother, who had to endure so much sorrow over the two men dearest to her.

The Austrian poet Guido Zernatto dedicated the following verses to this model for all widows who suffer tribulations:

Saint Emma, with rejoicing now the vales and skies are
    ringing.
Look down upon us graciously, and hear your children
    singing!
Our homeland's pride and ornament, a joyful flower
    blooming,
We praise you and salute you as the model of all women.
You were a mother kind and good, a faithful, godly wife,
A refuge for the poor and weak, a comforter in strife.

Faith gave you strength and courage to endure your heavy
    sorrow.
O guard our faith and help us bear the trials that come
    tomorrow!
The gold that God had given to you, you gave back to
    the Lord,
Exchanging wealth and fashion for a cloistered nun's
    reward.
Teach us, like you, to flee the world, despising idle
    pleasure,
To seek only what pleases God, to store up heavenly
    treasure.
Saint Emma, ready helper, lift your hands up to the
    Master,
That he may guard Carinthia from danger and disaster.
Prepare for us a blessed abode after our final battle,
That we with you eternally may praise our God and
    Father.

Saint Godeleva and Bertulf

b. near Boulogne, northern France
d. ca. 1070

Godeleva, portrayed in a fifteenth-century miniature by Arnaldo di Soissons, diocesan seminary in Brugge (Bruges)

The devout daughter of the noble couple Enfred and Ogiva was born on an unknown date in the vicinity of Boulogne, to the south of Calais in northern France, and was married while still very young to Bertulf, an uncouth, brutal Flemish count.

That was the beginning of an extremely unhappy marriage. For Godeleva (Godelève) was often cruelly mistreated by her husband and was finally driven away. Ultimately, the bishop of Tournai took the outcast woman into his care. It appeared that the two spouses were eventually reconciled. In reality, however, Bertulf's hatred for his wife was even greater. One night two serfs, his hirelings, forced their way into Godeleva's bedroom, strangled her with a shawl, and threw her body into a well. This allegedly happened in July 1070. The only certain date, however, is July 30, 1084. On that day Bishop Radbod of Noyon-Tournai had Godeleva's remains disinterred and reburied in the church of Ghistelles in West Flanders because of the great devotion shown to her throughout the region. Bertulf, who had instigated the murder of his wife, Godeleva, is said to have repented of his crime and become a monk in the abbey of Bergues-Saint-Winoc in Flanders.[1]

[1] Cf. Drogo, Monk of Saint-Winoc, *Vita sanctae Godelevae* (written before 1084), published by M. Coens, "La vie ancienne de Sainte Godelive de Ghistelles", in *Analecta Bollandiana* 44 (1926): 102–37.

Martyrdom of Saint Godeleva, Brugge (Bruges), Abbey of Saint Godeleva

Saint Margaret of Scotland and Malcolm III Canmore

*b. ca. 1046 in Reska, near
    Nadasad, Hungary*
d. November 16, 1093

*Married 1070
Mother of eight children
Canonized in the year 1251*

Born in Hungary of exiled noble parents, later a refugee in Scotland, where she was received quite hospitably and married her host, the king of Scotland, with whom she then lived happily and harmoniously and had a large family—this was the destiny of Margaret, the great-grandniece of Saint Edward the Confessor.[1] She was born around 1046 in Reska, near Nadasad, in Hungary, the daughter of the exiled successor to the English throne, Edward Atheling, and the Hungarian Princess Agatha; her siblings were Christine and Edgar Atheling.

During her youth, from her eleventh to her twentieth year (1057–1066), she lived at the court of her saintly great-granduncle, Edward the Confessor.

After the Battle of Hastings (October 14, 1066), Margaret had to flee again with her brother, Edgar, and they went to Scotland. There the refugees were received hospitably by King Malcolm III Canmore.

---

[1] Cf. David McRoberts, *St. Margaret, Queen of Scotland* (Glasgow, 1960); idem, "Margherita, regina di Scozia", in *Bibliotheca Sanctorum* 8:781–86.

Soon the king came to admire and love Margaret on account of her excellent virtues. The year 1070 saw the wedding of the two. Margaret, with her intelligence and virtuous character, managed to tame and direct the king's wild spirits; their marriage, which,

Margaret of Scotland embarking for Scotland (Edinburgh, Scottish National Gallery)

unfortunately, lasted only twenty-three years, was extremely harmonious and happy and was blessed with eight children, six sons and two daughters. The names of the six sons of Saint Margaret are Edward, Edmund, Ethelred, Edgar, Alexander, and David; the three last mentioned succeeded their royal father, Malcolm, one after the other on the throne as kings of Scotland. Margaret's daughters were Matilda (also called Maud), who was wedded to Henry I of England (d. 1135), the youngest son of William the Conqueror, and Mary, who married Count Eustachius of Boulogne.

In order to give her children a truly good and Christian education, Queen Margaret engaged excellent instructors. To her children she was an exemplary, loving, and caring mother; she was likewise a kindly and solicitous queen mother for all the Scottish people. The queen's efforts to please God by a life of prayer, penance, and works of mercy not only had a good influence on her husband, King Malcolm, but also impressed the people as an ongoing sermon in deeds. Margaret took pains to eradicate all injustice, to settle quarrels and disputes wherever they might arise, and to cultivate the Christian virtues of love of neighbor, moderation, and well-mannered chastity—not only at court, but among all her subjects. Those court officials who did not conduct themselves irreproachably were dismissed by the queen, with the approval of her royal consort. The queen and the king regularly visited the hospitals and the prisons. Often they personally brought food and drink to the poor and the sick.

In her forty-sixth year, Queen Margaret was afflicted with a very serious illness, which she endured with exemplary patience. While she lay deathly sick, an armed conflict broke out in which the king became involved. In the battle of Alnwick, King Malcolm and one of his sons fell. As she was dying, Queen Margaret heard the bitter news. The last words of Queen Margaret on the day she died, November 16, 1093, were, "Lord Jesus, who through thy death hast given life to the world, deliver me from all evil!" Her body was buried in Trinity Church in Dunfermline, which she had built. Pope Innocent IV canonized Queen Margaret as an exemplary wife and mother in 1251.

Blessed
Ida of Boulogne
and
Eustace II

b. ca. 1040 in Bouillon, Ardennes, South Belgium
d. April 13, 1113

Married 1057
Mother of three children

This blessed from the time of the Crusades was born around 1040 in Bouillon (Ardennes, South Belgium), the daughter of Duke Godfrey II the Bearded.

After a virtuous childhood and youth, Ida was married in 1057 to Count Eustace II of Boulogne and from then on lived an edifying Christian married life. Three sons issued from their union, who, during the First Crusade, proved to be exemplary knights, pious and brave; their names are Eustace III, Godfrey of Bouillon (born 1060) and Baldwin. While on the First Crusade, Godfrey was elected the first king of the Latin kingdom of Jerusalem, in 1099, and given the title *Advocatus sancti Sepulchri*. Old French epics and ballads associated Godfrey with the Swan Knight and, when he died in September of the year 1100, exalted him as the ideal of the Christian knight, imbued with humility, piety, and courage. This ideal surely has its origin in the excellent Christian education that Godfrey of Bouillon had received from his devout parents. The same is certainly true of his brother Baldwin also, who, after Godfrey's death, was crowned King of Jerusalem in Bethlehem on Christmas Day, 1100.

Blessed Ida of Boulogne, the mother of these two kings of Jerusalem, proved to be an extraordinarily pious woman who loved the Church, both during her marriage and then especially after the death of her husband in 1070. She founded various monasteries, for instance, Saint-Wulmer in Boulogne for Augustinian canons regular. Under the direction of Saint Anselm of Canterbury, with whom she corresponded until her death, she promoted the reform movement that had started at Cluny. She did not take the habit of a Benedictine nun, however, as some have claimed; from the holy abbot Saint Hugh of Cluny, however, she probably did obtain a spiritual "aggregation" with the monastery of Cluny, so that she can be regarded as an Oblate of the Benedictine Order. In any case, Ida of Boulogne was an edifying wife and mother who promoted Benedictine spirituality and who, in her personal life and in the education of her sons, adhered to the Benedictine motto *Ora et labora* [Pray and work]. Blessed Ida died on April 13, 1113, and was interred in the church of the monastery of Saint Vaast. A contemporary monk of the abbey of Saint Vaast wrote the life of this blessed, who was the mother of two kings of Jerusalem.[1]

---

[1] Cf. *Acta Sanctorum* 2:141–45; Rombaut van Doren, "Ida di Boulogne", in *Bibliotheca Sanctorum* 7:636–37.

The Servant of God
Pauline von Arnstadt

and

Ulrich von Schraplan

b. 1050 in Calw, Black Forest region
d. March 13, 1117, in Münsterschwarzach, near Würzburg

Mother of two children

The German Countess Pauline was a brave and at the same time pious woman. She was born probably around 1050 (as we can deduce from the *Life* of Pauline written by her confessor Sigeboto around 1150),[1] the daughter of the imperial lord high steward Moricho, who later became a lay brother in Hirsau Abbey, near Calw in the Black Forest.

After the death of her second husband, Ulrich von Schraplan, Pauline withdrew, together with several female companions, to the solitude of a remote, wooded valley between Rudolstadt and Arnstadt. Here she founded a chapel dedicated to Saint Mary Magdalen and a hermitage nearby for herself. Her daughter and her son, Werner, associated themselves with the pious little cloistered community, which gradually grew larger. The strict penitential practices and the women's diligent needlework and weaving made the modest establishment more and more renowned. Therefore, Countess Pauline wished to give her foundation an authentically monastic structure. She relinquished the place where she had been staying to the monks from Hirsau Abbey; the nuns would settle in a narrow gorge in the forest. Then began the laborious work of securing a livelihood for the residents of the two monasteries. The strength and resolve of this courageous woman were

---

[1] Cf. Sigeboto, "Vita beatae Paulinae", in *Monumenta Germaniae, Scriptores* 30, 2, pp. 909–38; J. Walterscheid, *Deutsche Heilige, eine Geschichte des Reiches im Leben deutscher Heiliger* (Munich, 1934), pp. 252f.

challenged also by many privations experienced on journeys and pilgrimages, for instance, to Rome and to Santiago de Compostela. In Rome she requested the pope's blessing upon her monastic foundation. On the journey home she fell from her horse and suffered an irremediably broken arm.

When the construction of the monks' cloisters was completed and the cornerstone for the church was laid at the place that henceforth was called "Paulinzelle", after the foundress, Countess Pauline and her son, Werner, wanted to bring over from Hirsau the monks who were to live at the monastery. She became seriously ill in the convent at Münsterschwarzach, however, and died there on March 13, 1117. In 1122 her remains were entombed in the basilica of Paulinzelle. In the Erfurt district of the diocese of Fulda this noblewoman, wife, mother, widow, and consecrated recluse, Pauline von Arnstadt was honored liturgically as well, each year on the day of her death, March 13.

Blessed
Aleth
and
Tescelin

b. ca. 1070
d. September 1 between 1105 and 1110

Married ca. 1085
Mother of seven children, among them Saint Bernard of Clairvaux

Blessed Aleth was a happy wife and mother who raised her seven children so well, and had such influence on her husband, that all of them became either priests or religious.[1] She was born around 1070, the daughter of the aristocratic nobleman Bernard de Montbard and Humbeline de Ricey. The parents dedicated the child to God even before her birth and raised her accordingly. Aleth affirmed the vow that her parents had made on her behalf and the call to religious life that they had in mind for her. As things developed, however, in the bloom of youth, at the age of fifteen, she married the young, brave, and virtuous Count Tescelin of Fontaines, a castle near Dijon. This was the beginning of an extraordinarily happy marriage and a large family. Her husband, Tescelin, however, because of his military duties, was often stationed for long periods of time far from his beloved wife and the children, who were born, year after year, one after the other. First there were three sons: Guy, Gerard, and Bernard; then, right in the middle, the one daughter, Humbeline; and, finally, the three remaining sons, Andrew, Bartholomew, and Nivard.

What did Aleth, a pious woman of faith, ask from God on her wedding day? For love and understanding in her marriage with her like-minded husband, of course; but, because her parents, even

---

[1] Cf. P. Sinz, *Das Leben des hl. Bernhard von Clairvaux* (Düsseldorf, 1962), pp. 35–40; L. André-Delastre, *La Bienheureuse Alethe, mère de Saint Bernard* (Lyon, 1952).

before her birth, had dedicated her in a special way to God for the religious life, she made an additional request. "O God, if you bless my marriage to Tescelin with children, I would like to give them all back to you, to serve you as my substitutes in religious life." God granted this request in a remarkable way, although at first it did not appear that way at all.

Indeed, Mother Aleth conscientiously raised all her children to be practicing Christians, and she set for them an example of genuine Christian life, not only by her piety but also through acts of charity done for the poor and the sick, whom she served by visiting their houses and performing even the lowliest tasks. In order to bring her sons into contact with priests, so that they might consider a vocation to the priesthood, Aleth invited all the priests from the village and the surrounding area to her castle year after year on the feast of Saint Ambrose, the patron of pastors, and regaled them with festivities. But five of her sons at first took after their military father: tournaments, fencing, and riding filled to the brim the days and years of their youth. Not one of these five sons felt drawn to monastic life, despite all the chivalrous spirit and attitude that could be found there as well. Bernard, however, the third son, was a quiet young man, rather timid and shy, awkward in everyday activities and much too serious for his age. He got along best with his mother. She died much too soon, on September 1 of one of the years between 1105 and 1110, not yet forty years old, while he was far from home at the school of the secular canons in Châtillon. Bernard deeply grieved her death. "The thought of his saintly mother pursued him. Often he seemed to see her before him, coming toward him, complaining and reprimanding him, that it was not for worldly trifles and pastimes that she had raised him so well." So it is written in the life of Saint Bernard of Clairvaux, which his friend, William of Saint-Thierry (d. 1148) composed. His mother in heaven would simply not leave Bernard in peace. This finally impelled the twenty-one-year-old young man to enter a monastery.

When this decision met with the vehement opposition of his father, Tescelin, and his brothers, it became apparent that Bernard was of a more chivalrous character than they. He managed to inflame his brothers and other young men from the vicinity with his ardent enthusiasm for Christ, so that ultimately not only he, but also his uncle Gaudrich, four of his brothers, and twenty young noblemen from neighboring castles were inspired by the ideal of religious life and entered the reformed Benedictine monastery of Cîteaux.

As Bernard and his four brothers took their leave of the ancestral castle, Guy, the oldest of the six sons of Tescelin and Aleth, said to Nivard, the youngest, "See, our entire inheritance now belongs to you." He replied, "Then heaven is to be yours and earth mine? That is not a fair division!" A few years later, Nivard, too, followed his brothers into the cloister. Their sister, Humbeline, after a period of worldliness and vanity, likewise entered a convent. Finally the aged father, Tescelin, too, the widower of blessed Aleth, joined his sons and became like them a monk.

Aleth led such an exemplary married life with her husband, Tescelin, and raised their seven children so well that she became, sevenfold, the mother of consecrated religious and the mother of saints, for her sons Gerard, Bernard, and Nivard, as well as her husband, Tescelin, are honored as blesseds in the Cistercian Order. Mother Aleth's greatest glory, however, is Saint Bernard of Clairvaux (d. August 20, 1153), the great preacher of the Crusades, Marian devotee, and Doctor of the Church.

In conclusion, let us quote what William of Saint-Thierry wrote in his life of Saint Bernard about Bernard's parents and their marriage.

Bernard was born in Burgundy at Fontaines, near Dijon, of parents who were highly esteemed on account of their worldly station but who were even more honorable and noble because of their Christian piety. His father, Tescelin, was a representative of the old, authentic knighthood, who feared God and defended justice. True to the instructions of the Precursor, he performed a military service that was in keeping with the Gospel: he oppressed no one, did not testify unjustly, and was content with his wages (cf. Lk 3:14), indeed, he had enough left over for every good work. He served his worldly commanders in word and deed and in arms in such a way that he never neglected to render also to the Lord God what he owed him.

His mother, Aleth, too, who was a descendant of the house of Montbard, in her station of life obeyed the command given by the Apostle: she was submissive to her husband and managed her household in the fear of God (cf. Eph 5:22). She zealously performed works of mercy and brought up her children to be thoroughly well-mannered. She bore seven children—not so much for her husband as for God: six sons and a daughter. The sons all would one day become monks, and the daughter would become a nun. . . . Though a noblewoman, she disdained to let her children nurse at someone else's breasts, as though she wanted her children to imbibe, together with their mother's milk, the goodness that this mother had within her. As they were growing up, as long as they were subject to her, she trained them for the wilderness rather than for the court. For she would not allow them to become accustomed to fancy dishes, but served very plain and simple food. By God's inspiration she designed the upbringing and instruction of her children as a kind of immediate preparation for their entrance into the cloister.

Let not the following things about Mother Aleth be passed over in silence. She lived a long time with her husband, complying with this world's code of honor and observing the laws of marriage. Then, a few years before her death, she surpassed all of her children in that endeavor for which she seems to have raised them, insofar as it is possible and permissible for a woman who is under the authority of her husband and does not rule over her own body (cf. 1 Cor 7:4). For in her home, in her married life, and in the midst of the world she seemed for a long time to emulate the life led by a hermit or a nun. She contented herself with meager food, dressed quite simply, and renounced the joys and glories of the world. She withdrew from worldly affairs and concerns whenever possible and devoted herself to fasting, watching, and praying. Whatever seemed to her to be lacking in this, her religious life, she made up for with alms and various works of mercy. In this way, by making greater progress from one day to the next, she reached her destination, so as to find in the next life her perfection in God, with whom she had walked through life and then crossed over. She fell asleep to the chanting of psalms by the clerics who had gathered and whom she had joined in their song. Indeed, even in her last moments, when her voice was scarcely audible, it seemed that her lips moved and that her tongue was still articulating the praise of God. Finally, while they were praying the invocation of the litany, "By your passion and cross, deliver us, O Lord", she lifted her hand, crossed herself and gave up her spirit so suddenly that she could no longer lower the hand that she had raised.

Saint
Leopold of Austria
and
Agnes

b. ca. 1075 in Melk, Lower Austria
d. November 15, 1136

Married 1106/1107
Father of eighteen children
Canonized January 6, 1485

From the genealogical tree of the
Babenbergers, Klosterneuburg

Saint Leopold, a descendant of the Babenberger line who was born around 1075 in Melk in Lower Austria,[1] was famous not only for his wise and peace-loving rule over the territory entrusted to him, but also for his marriage with Agnes, the daughter of the Emperor Henry IV, which was blessed with eighteen children. She was wedded to the thirty-one-year-old margrave in 1106 or 1107.

Agnes was at that time already a widow. Her first marriage had been to Duke Friedrich I of Schwabia. Their son from this marriage later became King Conrad III. It is suspected that Leopold, too, was a widower when he married Agnes. This supposition is based on two arguments. First, it is not very likely that a nobleman of that period would have remained unmarried for more than thirty years; second, there is convincing proof that Adalbert, the eldest son of Margrave Leopold, was born before the year 1106; therefore, he probably was the child of an earlier, less distinguished marriage of Leopold.

As for the children of Leopold's marriage with Agnes—the large number of them indicates that the saint's marriage with Agnes was

---

[1] Cf. F. Röhrig, "Der heilige Markgraf Leopold III von Österreich", in *Bavaria Sancta* (Regensburg, 1971), 2:130–43; K. Lechner, *Die Babenberger in Österreich* (Vienna, 1947).

harmonious and peaceful—two of those who reached adulthood became bishops, namely, Otto (who with fifteen companions became a Cistercian monk in 1132, then the abbot in the monastery of Morimond, and finally bishop of Freising and a very important church historian) and Conrad (who served first as bishop of Passay, then from 1164 to 1168 as archbishop of Salzburg). Two other sons succeeded Saint Leopold as ruler of Austria, Leopold IV and Heinrich Jasomirgott. Three daughters of Leopold and Agnes were married to well-born rulers, one to the duke of Poland,

During a hunt in the Danube meadows, the Mother of God appears to Margrave Leopold III and asks him to build a monastery on that spot.

another to the duke of Bohemia, and the third to the margrave of Montferrat.

At this point, while mentioning the marriage and the children of Saint Leopold, it must not be overlooked that there were also ugly quarrels among the margrave's children, for which, as it is supposed, their mother, Agnes, was not entirely without responsibility. Surely this caused Saint Leopold anxiety and grief. But bickering and disputes occur even in the best Christian families, and there is no guarantee that Christian married couples, even saints, will avoid all misunderstandings and will always have a positive influence on their adolescent children.

The legend about the founding of Klosterneuburg was first recorded in 1371. This charming story contains a grain of historical truth that may suggest, with delicacy and restraint, that there was, in spite of everything, a beautiful, peaceful marital love between the margrave Leopold and his wife, Agnes, the emperor's daughter. After his wedding with Agnes, Saint Leopold is supposed to have stood on the balcony of his castle on the Kahlenberg, a mountain near Vienna, surveying the territories he ruled. At that moment the bride's veil was snatched from her head and carried off by the wind. No matter how diligently they searched, it could not be found. Nine years later, though, as the margrave was hunting in the meadows along the Danube, the hounds suddenly began to bark, and Leopold found his wife's veil undamaged on an elderberry bush. Then the "Mother of Fair Love", Mary, appeared to him with the request that he build a monastery in her honor on that spot. He did so, surely on account of the great esteem and love he still felt for his wife, even in the tenth year of their marriage. This loving husband, this father and prince who dutifully cared for his family and the people of his land, this statesman who performed great services to the Church by founding and providing for monasteries, died on November 15, 1136—allegedly as the result of a hunting accident—in the sixty-first year of his life, in the forty-first year of his reign as margrave, and in the thirtieth year of his happy marriage. On January 6, 1485, Pope Innocent VIII declared this holy husband, father, and nobleman a saint.

Saint Isidore and Blessed Maria de la Cabeza

Isidore the farmer working in the field.
An angel helps him to plow.

Isidore:
  b. ca. 1080 in or around Madrid,
    Spain
  d. ca. 1130
  Canonized March 12, 1622

Maria:
  d. 1135
  Beatified 1697

Parents of one child

Isidore the Farmer was solemnly canonized by Pope Gregory XV on March 12, 1622, together with Ignatius of Loyola, Francis Xavier, Teresa of Avila, and Philip Neri. Saint Isidore and his wife, Toribia or Maria de la Cabeza, who is revered as blessed, were not of noble lineage and imperial rank like Henry II and Cunegund but, rather, of humble peasant stock. Nothing especially notable is reported about their marriage or about their life; tradition tells us only that they had one son, who died very young. It is said that after the death of their child, this farming couple agreed to continue their married life while observing strict continence and to devote themselves entirely to work, prayer, and the Mass.

We owe the first written accounts about Saint Isidore to a deacon named Johannes Aegidius of Zamora, who was stationed at the church of Saint Andrew in Madrid in the period from 1232 to 1275; almost 150 years after Isidore's death he recorded what he had heard about his way of life and the miracles that he himself

Isidore being observed by his master (drawing by Ludwig Seitz)

had witnessed at his grave.[1] According to this report, Isidore was born around 1080 in the city or in the vicinity of Madrid; he was an indefatigable worker and just as diligent about praying. Attending Holy Mass daily was something near and dear to his heart. Because of this, God blessed his labors even more abundantly, so that he was able to share his income generously with the poor without having to fear that he would go wanting. He married a young woman as rich as he in virtue and piety. As a tenant farmer he had won the complete confidence of the property owner, Juan de Vergas, but his envious co-workers went to their master and wrongfully accused him of neglecting his work by praying and going to church so much. Isidore, however, explained to his master that he had to serve God first of all and that God then took

[1] Cf. Z. Garcia Villada, "San Isidro labrador en la historia y en la literatura," in *Razón y Fe* 62 (1992): 37–53. *Acta Sanctorum Maii* 3:512–50.

care of him and helped him with his work through the ministry of the holy angels. It is said that Isidore's employer actually witnessed one day two angels tilling the fields with a plow drawn by white horses, thus doing the work while Isidore was in church hearing Mass.

One day Isidore's fellow laborers tried to harm him by bringing him false accusations about his pious wife. She customarily went each day to a little church in which the Blessed Virgin Mary was especially honored. There she carried out her devotions and made sure that the vigil lamp was always supplied with oil. The farmhands tried to make Isidore believe that his wife went to the little church each day to meet a shepherd and to have scandalous relations with him. Isidore, though, knew his wife too well and was certain that she was completely faithful to her marriage vows.

Both Isidore the farmer and his wife Toribia lived in such intimate union with God that it transformed their hard labor more and more into a yoke that is easy, a burden that is light. No one ever heard them scold or curse; the couple, who were poor themselves, never forgot those who were still poorer but, rather, demonstrated Christian love of neighbor by helping them and sharing their wages with them.

Isidore died in his fiftieth year on May 15, 1130, after he had predicted the hour of his death. Five years later his wife died, too, and followed him into eternal happiness. For a long time she has been honored as blessed. Devotion to Blessed Maria de la Cabeza (or Toribia) was solemnly approved by Pope Innocent XII in the year 1697. Saint Isidore, on the other hand—as mentioned already—was canonized in 1622, principally at the request of King Philip III of Spain. Once, when the king was dangerously ill and the doctors attending him had already given up all hope that he would ever recover, clerics in solemn procession carried the relics of the holy farmer Isidore into the king's chamber. Scarcely had the reliquary with Isidore's remains left the church of Saint Andrew in Madrid when the king's fever subsided. When the reliquary was placed in the king's sickroom, the king arose from his bed, fully cured.

Blessed
Erkenbert

and

Blessed
Richlinde

Erkenbert:
> b. ca. 1080 in Worms
>
> d. December 24, 1132, in Frankenthal

Richlinde:
> d. December 26, 1150, in Ormsheim

Parents of two children

Blessed Erkenbert, a husband and father of a family, was born around 1080 in Worms, the son of Reginmar, the bishop's chamberlain. When he was a very young boy, his education was entrusted to Abbot Stephan of Limburg. The superior noted that he was an outstanding pupil, especially because of his virtues. The anonymous biographer of Blessed Erkenbert was so impressed by him that he characterized him as follows: "Fuit enim fide catholicus, integritate, spei robustus, in caritate fundatus, in veritate radicatus" (For he was Catholic in his faith, strong in Christian hope, firmly anchored in charity, and rooted in truth).[1]

When, at age fifteen, he returned home to his family, he continued to lead a devout, almost priestly life. Only at his mother's insistence did he marry the pious Richlinde, who was equal to him in virtue; she gave him two sons, Wolfram and Kuno.

When Erkenbert became seriously ill on one occasion but then was miraculously healed, his zeal for religion increased even more, which his pious wife Richlinde understood very well. From then

[1] Cf. "Vita sancti Eckenberti", in *Monumenta Wormatiensia*, ed. H. Roos (Berlin, 1893), pp. 127–42.

on, with his wife's approval, he devoted himself exclusively to works of mercy for the poor. In the year 1119 he founded a chapter of Augustinian canons on his estate in Frankenthal, south of Worms, and eventually entered it himself. In 1129 he received Holy Orders and finally became the prior of the chapter that he had founded. His wife, Richlinde, followed his example and founded a convent for Augustinian nuns in nearby Ormsheim.

Prior Erkenbert died on Christmas Eve, December 24, 1132, in Frankenthal in the odor of sanctity. His wife, Richlinde, survived him by eighteen years. She died on December 26, 1150, as abbess of the convent she had founded.

Blessed Godfrey of Kappenberg

and

Jutta of Arnsberg

b. 1097 in the castle of the
    Count of Kappenberg,
    in Westphalia
d. January 13, 1127, in Ilbenstadt

*Godfrey of Kappenberg as a
Premonstratensian monk. In the
background are three monasteries
that he founded.*

Godfrey of Kappenberg was a saint whose happy marriage was dissolved for the sake of a higher calling. He was born in 1097 in the Kappenberg castle in Westphalia.[1] In this castle, situated on a promontory high above the green meadows on the banks of the Lippe river, the count lived with his wife, Jutta of Arnsberg, not only in peace and happiness, but also in the fear of God and piety. The life of both was based on the principles of the Christian religion. Everyone in the vicinity loved Count Godfrey and his wife, Jutta, because of their friendly hospitality and their good-hearted service to the sick and the poor.

Then one day Saint Norbert of Xanten, the founder of the Premonstratensian Order, came to Kappenberg Castle after preaching throughout the region of the Rheinland and Westphalia. For quite some time he was a guest at the castle. During this time

---

[1] Cf. *Acta Sanctorum Januarii* 1:834–63, containing three accounts of the life of Blessed Gottfried from the mid- and late twelfth century; H. Grundmann, "Gottfried von Cappenberg", in *Westfälische Lebensbilder* (1959), 8:1–115.

Count Godfrey experienced a difficult interior conflict. As a result of long conversations with the reformer Norbert, whose priestly zeal for souls knew no bounds, the count suddenly felt impelled to transform his castle into a monastery and to place himself at God's disposal in the religious state. But pride in his ancestral heritage, his great love for his noble wife, and, yes, a residual attachment to the passing things of this world would thwart his plans again and again. He wrestled with the dilemma, and finally his increasingly strong and mature love for God carried off the victory.

There was nothing left to do except to win his wife, Jutta, and his brother Otto over to his plan. He then met with the most obstinate resistance from his father-in-law, Count Friedrich of Arnsberg. After lengthy disputes, the persuasive eloquence of Saint Norbert nevertheless succeeded in clearing the way for Count Godfrey to carry out his plan. Kappenberg Castle actually became a Premonstratensian monastery, which Count Godfrey and his brother Otto then entered. When Count Friedrich of Arnsberg died in 1124, a convent following the Rule of Saint Norbert was founded for Jutta below the castle at the foot of the mountain. Here she began to live as a religious, together with Blessed Godfrey's two sisters, Beatrix and Gerberga. Similarly, other religious foundations were established on Godfrey's lands, for instance, in Ilbenstadt on the Main River and in Varlar.

Count Godfrey of Kappenberg became a humble monk who performed the lowliest tasks and willingly submitted to the strict provisions of his order's Rule. He died on January 13, 1127, only thirty years of age, in Ilbenstadt.

Counts Godfrey and Otto of Kappenberg. Monument to the founders, in the Collegiate Church of Kappenberg, ca. 1315.

Blessed
Wulfhildis

and

Rudolf of Bregenz

d. May 8, after 1180

In the Bavarian village of Wessobrunn, which is famous for the "Prayer of Wessobrunn", there used to be, before the [Napoleonic] secularization [of ecclesiastical states in 1803], not only a monastery, but also a convent, in which even the daughters of princes once led a life of the strictest mortification and penance. Among these was Wulfhildis, the pious daughter of Duke Heinrich IX of Bavaria and his wife, Wulfhildis of Saxony.[1]

Wulfhildis was married for only a short time to Rudolf, the last count of Bregenz and Pfullendorf. After her husband's death, she went first to Schongau, to stay with her brother Welf. There she experienced an ever greater longing to lead a life of complete union with God.

When she heard in Schongau about the flourishing double monastery in Wessobrunn and the profound sanctity of the venerable Abbot Walto, she decided to enter the cloister there. From the hand of Abbot Walto she received the veil, after renouncing all her inherited properties and bequeathing her expensive clothing and jewels to the convent. She entirely forgot her previous station in the world and performed the most menial household chores with genuine humility, together with her sisters in religion. She distinguished herself especially in her loving care for the sick. She was often a peacemaker and a consoler, too, in the family of her father, the duke, when they were afflicted with hardships.

On the eighth of May, sometime after the year 1180, Wulfhildis completed her life of devotion to God. The year of her departure

---

[1] Cf. L. Rosenberger, *Bavaria Sancta* (Munich, 1948), pp. 201–2.

cannot be determined exactly. In the convent in Wessobrunn she was revered as a blessed who had experienced married life, which soon ended because of her husband's death, and as a widow who had recognized that she was called to a life consecrated to God in the silence of a contemplative convent.

Saint Hildegund and Lothair

b. ca. 1130
d. February 6, 1183

Not much is known about this holy Countess and wife,[1] only that she was descended from the line of count von Mehre in Neuss (Cologne) and that she married Count Lothair. After his death, she made a pilgrimage to the tombs of the Princes of the Apostles, Peter and Paul, in Rome. There she prayed to know the will of God for her life, now that her marriage was over; she wanted to follow him unreservedly. She bequeathed her possessions to a Premonstratensian convent that she founded in her birthplace, Mehre. She became the first superior of this convent and distinguished herself by true humility and works of charity and mercy. She died on February 6, 1183.

---

[1] Cf. *Acta Sanctorum Februarii* 1:916–22; J. B. Valvekens, "Ildegonda", in *Bibliotheca Sanctorum* 7:766–67. [Butler's *Lives of the Saints* indicates that they had a son Herman who was called Blessed—ED.]

Saint Homobonus and Spouse

b. ca. 1130 in Cremona, Italy
d. November 13, 1197, in Cremona

Canonized January 12, 1199

Homobonus, a good man. By this name a tradesman who was born in Cremona before the middle of the twelfth century and worked there has gone down in the history of the saints. Only a year after his death, after various contemporary witnesses were interrogated, among them his confessor, Padre Osberto, and his bishop, the famous canonist Sicard of Cremona, he was canonized by Pope Innocent III on January 12, 1199, with a papal bull entitled *Quia pietas*.[1]

In the Cremonese Chronicle by Sicard (d. 1215), we find the following note:

> In these times [that is, the end of the twelfth century] there lived in Cremona a simple man [*vir simplex*] of great faith and piety [*fidelis plurimum et devotus*] by the name of Homobonus. Upon his death and by his intercession the Lord caused many miracles to happen as a confirmation [of his saintly life] in the

[1] Cf. R. Sacconi, *S. Omobono* (Cremona, 1938); G. D. Gordini, "Omobono di Cremona", in *Bibliotheca Sanctorum* 9:1173–75.

presence of all the people. That is why I [Sicard] made a pilgrimage to Rome, sought an audience with the pope, and asked him for the canonization of this man, which I did obtain.

Since that time the tradesman (cloth merchant, tailor) Homobonus has been very much revered in Cremona, and people diligently call upon his intercession in the crypt of the cathedral, where his relics are enshrined. His clients include not only his fellow tradesmen, but especially husbands who have marital difficulties. In fact, Saint Homobonus had them, too. His marriage remained childless; yet he did not put his wife away, but bestowed his fatherly love instead on abandoned children and saw to it that they received a good upbringing; he used his income to support the poor of the city and visited them in their miserable huts and helped in whatever way he could.

His wife at first showed no understanding whatsoever for these acts of charity; rather, she reacted to them with objections and animosity. He, nevertheless, tried, with unperturbed kindness, to win his wife over to his charitable projects, so that finally she became his willing assistant in them. Homobonus also mediated in situations where marital or family conflicts had broken out, seeking to bring about reconciliation and to restore peace; this he did so successfully that in the bull of canonization the Pope rightly gave him the honorific title *pacificus vir*, peacemaker.

Homobonus obtained the strength and perseverance that he needed for his good works from daily attendance at Mass and constant prayer; furthermore, he was fond of celebrating the Liturgy of the Hours with the clergy in the church of Cremona, and he even made it his custom to attend the nocturnal hour of Matins. The pious exercises of this exemplary layman also included various penitential acts and mortifications, as well as a fearless defense of the integral faith in disputes with sectarians and heretics. With good reason it has been written about him: "Homobonus is a representative of the widespread movement among the laity in the twelfth century that sought a spiritual and religious renewal in obedience to the Church; he distinguished himself by his piety, his penitential spirit, and especially by his love of neighbor."[2]

As he lived, so also did this exemplary Christian layman and husband die. On the morning of November 13, 1197, he had made his way, as usual, to the church of San Egidio in Cremona for Holy Mass. During the angelic hymn, *Gloria in excelsis Deo*, this good married man collapsed and fell down dead. He continued to glorify God in heaven, while the Lord approved his Christian life and death by many miracles, which are explicitly mentioned in the Roman Martyrology at the thirteenth of November: "In Cremona the holy confessor (and husband) Homobonus, famous for miracles, was numbered by Pope Innocent III among the host of the saints."

[2] Cf. P. Zerbi, "Homobonus", in LThK 5:466.

Saint
Raymond Zanfogni
and
Spouse

b. ca. 1140 in Piacenza
d. July 27, 1200, in Piacenza

Father of six children

Saint Raymond Zanfogni, also known as Palmerio, was a saintly husband and father from the second half of the twelfth century. We have much information about his life of piety and charity thanks to a contemporary *Vita* that was written by the canonist Rufinus de Piacenza at the request of Gerardo Zanfogni, the one son who survived his father.[1]

Raymond was born around 1140 in Piacenza to a humble family of artisans, and he learned the shoemaker's trade. After his father's death, at fifteen years of age, he set out with his mother on a pilgrimage to the Holy Land. There they devoutly visited the holy places, one after the other, with great emotion. On the journey home to Piacenza, the mother died, so that Raymond was now an orphan. With a palm branch in his hand he went to the bishop of Piacenza to report on his experiences in the Holy Land. Then he began to carry on the shoemaker's trade that he had learned. Because his relatives compelled him, he married. Five children, one after the other, sprang from his marriage.

When customers came to be measured for shoes or to have them repaired, Raymond liked to have religious discussions with them, based on his experiences in the Holy Land. Although he was illiterate, he displayed an astonishing grasp of his religion. Soon he was highly esteemed by his fellow townsmen. This helped

---

[1] Cf. *Acta Sanctorum Julii*, 6:638–63.

him to carry on a very effective apostolate. On feast days he went into the various workshops in Piacenza and gave the artisans instructions in faith and morals. He was so successful that he was urged to preach in the public squares, but he modestly and wisely declined, explaining that that was the duty of the clerics. He himself made every effort to deepen his religious formation; for this reason he diligently received the sacraments of Penance and Holy Communion.

After all five of Raymond's children died within the course of one year, he suggested to his wife that they practice complete continence from then on in their marriage. His wife, however, said that she was not ready to do that. They had a sixth child, a boy by the name of Gerardo, who was dedicated to God by his father. When his wife died, after a long and serious illness, Raymond found himself free to go on pilgrimage again. He journeyed first to Santiago de Compostela, then on the return trip to the church of Saint Madeleine in Provence, and finally to Pavia, to reverence the relics of Saint Augustine. After Pavia he traveled to Rome, where he had thoughts of visiting Jerusalem again. He had a vision of Christ, however, in which he was instructed to return to Piacenza and to dedicate himself to works of mercy in his hometown. Raymond obeyed the Lord's command. It was in 1178.

Then began the second phase of Saint Raymond's life, which was completely devoted to works of charity for the poor. He communicated his intention to the bishop of Piacenza, who approved it and gave him his blessing. From the canons regular at the church of the Twelve Apostles he received a building large enough to serve as a shelter for the homeless. He sought out poor and deserving souls and helped them. He collected alms for the care and medical treatment of the sick. Since public social welfare programs, such as we have today, did not yet exist at that time, Raymond's initiative caused a sensation; misunderstandings and suspicions followed. This only prompted him to appeal to the consciences of the rich and to take up the cause of the beggars, who were growing more and more numerous. Finally, Raymond placed himself at the head of a whole procession of beggars, who went through the town crying, "Help us, you cruel, greedy rich people, for we are starving while you live off the fat of the land!" Raymond, carrying a large cross on his shoulder, became the spokesman for the poor in the town of Piacenza, their official protector and defender, especially against powerful and unjust judges. He accompanied to court those who had fallen into debt through no fault of their own, stood up for them, and defended them against exploitation and injustice.

When Raymond saw that the works of mercy that he personally performed, day after day, were no longer sufficient, he started additional charitable institutions. For example, not far from his hospice he founded a women's shelter, as that is understood today: a refuge for battered women and repentant prostitutes. He would provide the necessary dowry for women without means who wanted to marry; for those who wished to enter the convent, he would make the arrangements for their admission. He also cared for abandoned children and for foreign pilgrims, visited the imprisoned, and obtained liberty for many of them by providing a guarantee for their good conduct in the future. Many of his interventions, though, caused misunderstandings on the part of the officials. Raymond also ventured into the political arena and sought to arbitrate between political parties. He did this especially when the quarrels between the towns of Piacenza and Cremona led to a war. The Cremonese took him prisoner during the conflict but soon released him when they became convinced of the man's sanctity and his upright intentions.

On July 27, 1200, Raymond Zanfogni died. The town of Piacenza, with the bishop in the lead, honored him with an extraordinary funeral. His remains were buried in a chapel near the church of the Twelve Apostles. Soon miracles began to take place through the intercession of the departed. More and more people revered Raymond as a saint, celebrating his feast on July 27. Several popes approved the legitimacy of these devotions, for example, Pope Martin V, in a papal bull, in the year 1422.

Saint Hedwig and Henry I of Silesia

b. ca. 1174 in Andechs Castle on the Ammersee, Upper Bavaria
d. October 15, 1243, in Trebnitz

Married 1186
Mother of seven children
Canonized March 26, 1267

Hedwig, who had the gift of prophecy, foretells her husband's imminent death.

Of all the marriages of women who have been declared saints, that of Saint Hedwig[1] with Duke Henry I of Silesia was doubtless one of the more blessed.

The bull of canonization dated March 26, 1267, declares that Hedwig, who was born around 1174 in Andechs Castle on the Ammersee in Upper Bavaria, "was descended from noble ancestors, such as had ruled nations and were famous for their great power. She sprang from them like a noble scion. She far surpassed the glory of her aristocratic origins, however, by the brilliance and greatness of her soul." Hedwig's father was Berthold VI, count of Andechs and duke of Meran; Hedwig's mother was Agnes of Wettin, the daughter of the margrave Dedo V of Niederlausitz. Hedwig's siblings, four brothers and three sisters, achieved high rank, as she did; let us mention here Hedwig's sister Gertrude, who was married to King Andrew II of Hungary sometime before 1203

[1] Cf. J. Gottschalk, *Hedwig von Schlesien, Botin des Friedens* (Freiburg im Breisgau, 1982).

and became the mother of Saint Elizabeth, the wife of Count Louis (Ludwig) IV of Thuringia.

The five-year-old Hedwig was entrusted to the nuns of the Benedictine convent at Kitzingen am Main for her education. Here she achieved a high degree of culture, including a knowledge of the Latin language, but especially a familiarity with Sacred Scripture. In the *Vita beatae Hedwigis quondam ducisse slesie*, a life of the saint completed around 1300, it says, "In her youth at Kitzingen Abbey she became acquainted with Sacred Scripture. She spent her youth profitably in the study of it. Sacred Scripture later became for her an abundant source of inner consolation and devotion."

Later, in faraway Silesia, Hedwig must have thought back with gratitude to her teachers in Kitzingen, especially the young nun Petrissa; two decades later she secured her as the first abbess for the cloister at Trebnitz.

One might suspect that the young Hedwig would gladly have entered Kitzingen Abbey, for in the *Vita* it says that "in contracting marriage she fulfilled the will of her parents more than her own." When Hedwig was only twelve, her parents, for reasons of familial and political expediency, gave her in marriage to the Silesian Piarist Prince Henry I, the eighteen-year-old son of Duke Boleslaus I.

No romantic love story brought Hedwig into her husband's embrace. Not one word is reported to the effect she found her spouse especially endearing or was extremely happy to be his beloved. Her parents had procured this husband for her, and Hedwig complied with the arrangement in childlike obedience. The young man took his betrothed with a very respectable dowry away from Bavaria, to distant Silesia, which at that time was settled almost exclusively by Poles. The young girl faced great challenges, for not only was she unacquainted with her husband, but the region, too, was completely foreign to her. She probably felt lonely at first in a strange land, but she did not complain about her fate. She courageously affirmed the change of circumstances, learned the Polish language, and began to love the still sparsely occupied land.[2]

Above all, she began to love her husband more and more, so that the author of the *Vita* could write that Hedwig "loved her husband, in God, as a virtuous man who was of service to the people". The bull of canonization, dated March 26, 1267, says,

> Because she [Hedwig] regarded the married state as a gift from heaven, she always kept it sacred. She never injured marital fidelity in the least. The children that God sent to her, she brought up in the fear of the Lord. She was lovingly submissive to the duke [Henry I] until his sudden death, yet not with the glow of sensual passion, but rather with prudent, cordial devotion.

J. Gottschalk[3] remarks that "Hedwig's influence upon her husband must have been strong, and his love for her very deep, since during the Christmas season of the year 1208, after the birth of their seventh child, the spouses agreed to take a vow of marital continence." Hedwig managed to accustom her husband, Duke Henry I, to the virtues that she herself practiced. The *Vita* records that

> he had even greater success then in ruling Poland, the more he not only fostered the sanctity of his wife but also emulated her virtues. In her footsteps he followed the humility and chastity that she had learned from Christ, so far as this was possible. Prompted by God and inspired by her spiritual exhortations, he became a man of almost monastic demeanor, not through vows and the wearing of a habit, but through his piety and lowliness of heart, which was manifest in his deeds. He even wore a round tonsure, and his beard was not free-flowing, but neatly trimmed to a moderate length. That is why history to this day has called him Duke Henry the Bearded. . . . There is no doubt

[2] Cf. W. Nigg, *Die Heiligen kommen wieder* (Freiburg im Breisgau, 1973), p. 90.
[3] Cf. J. Gottschalk, *Hedwig*, p. 31.

that the husband of such a woman was holy; even though she was subordinate to him according to the law [of marriage], she still was his leader on the path of virtue and piety.

Let us now consider also the seven children who issued from the marriage of Saint Hedwig and Duke Henry I of Silesia. Of the seven, only one survived the death of their mother, namely, Gertrude. She was born around 1200 and received the best possible education from the Cistercian nuns of the cloister at Trebnitz; she entered the community in 1212 and in 1232 became the abbess. Duke Henry I had founded the cloister at Trebnitz at the urgent request of his saintly wife, Hedwig. Upon arriving in Silesia, she had remarked with astonishment that there were no convents there yet in which she might eventually have her daughters educated, as she herself had been educated at Kitzingen Abbey. According to the *Vita*,

> By her recommendation and her request, Hedwig convinced her husband to use some of his means to found a cloister for Cistercian nuns. . . . The first abbess of this cloister [in Trebnitz], then, was Dame Petrissa, the schoolteacher of the young Hedwig, whom she summoned from Bamberg with other nuns from the aforementioned order.

The others sons and daughters from the marriage of Hedwig and Duke Henry I died very young: Boleslaus between 1206 and 1208, Conrad in 1213, Agnes sometime before 1214, and Sophie as well. Of the sons, only Henry II reached manhood. After his father's death he inherited the title Duke of Silesia, and between 1214 and 1218 he married Anna, the daughter of King Ottokar I of Bohemia and the older sister of Saint Agnes of Prague. Henry II fell while resisting the Mongol invasion on April 9, 1241. At that time Saint Hedwig remarked about her son, "He never gave me trouble. He always showed me the greatest respect and loved me from the heart, as a good child should." In the reports of the battle near Wahlstatt, the honorific title *Christianissimus dux Poloniae* [most Christian leader of Poland] was given to Duke Henry II, and he was nicknamed "the Pious", which proves how well he was raised in the Christian faith by his saintly mother and how well he lived out that faith.

How often, even in good Christian marriages, the relationship between mother-in-law and daughter-in-law is tense and troubled! As for the wife of Duke Henry II, the most wonderful harmony prevailed between her and her mother-in-law, Hedwig. They lived together for almost thirty years and encouraged one another in striving for sanctity. In the *Vita* it says, "Blessed Anna, after she set foot in Poland, was subject and obedient to Saint Hedwig in everything. . . . She was so intimate with her saintly mother-in-law that she became, as it were, the confidant in all the secrets of her sanctity."

It should also be mentioned that Duchess Hedwig, who had a keen interest in the missionary work among the Prussians, who were still pagans then, became the godmother of a Prussian girl who was baptized with the name Katharine and, with her husband's approval, raised this girl at her court.

Let us turn our attention again to the married life of Saint Hedwig and her husband, whom she cared for with great love and fidelity, in both joys and sorrows. "She strove to attain holiness, and not only through childbearing; she also observed continence within marriage." The *Vita* reports on this extensively.

She wished very much to please God through marital chastity and therefore, with her husband's consent, she pledged to practice continence, to the extent that the married state permitted. If she sensed that God had blessed her (with a child), then she reverently stayed away from her husband's chambers and from marital relations, persevering in this resolution until the birth of the child. . . . She not only strove to practice continence after each conception, as we have said, but through salutary advice and exhortation she also convinced her noble husband to observe holy continence together with her, indeed, every year throughout Advent and Lent, on all the Ember Days, on holy days, on the vigils and feasts of the saints and on Sundays. She was of the

178

opinion that her fasting would not be a pleasing offering to the saints or to God himself if it was accomplished amid worldly pleasures. Therefore she often lived continently with her husband for an entire month, occasionally six or even eight weeks at a time, even though they did not sleep in separate quarters.

The Lutheran theologian W. Nigg writes,[4]

It would be a mistake to conclude from this report that she was wanting in love for her husband. She was not filled with sensual passion, but neither was she a frigid woman, and through her continence she saved their marital union from sinking into an everyday routine carried out without any spiritual involvement; instead it always remained an intensely joyous celebration.

When the duke and the duchess were somewhere between the ages of thirty-one and thirty-five, they had a child again, their seventh, which was solemnly baptized on Christmas Day, 1208, in Glogau Castle in the presence of august personages. This child was a son, whose baptismal name, strangely enough, is nowhere recorded. It is emphasized, however, both in the bull of Hedwig's canonization and in the *Vita*, that from then on their marriage was governed by solemn vows of continence. The bull of canonization states that the duke and the duchess, "on the basis of a vow and in complete mutual agreement, renounced marital intercourse for many years"—"over the course of twenty-eight years", it says in the papal homily given at the canonization ceremony. On the other hand, we read in the *Vita*, "By mutual agreement they [Hedwig and Henry I] made a perpetual vow of chastity with the solemn blessing of the bishop [Lawrence of Breslau]. Strengthened by the Spirit of God, they then lived a virginal life for thirty years, which was distinguished by almost miraculous continence."

W. Nigg adds,

This vow of chastity taken by Hedwig and Henry, a married couple, is one of those deeds that modern man can hardly

[4] Cf. W. Nigg, *Heiligen*, pp. 90–92.

Saint Hedwig contented herself with the bare necessities of life so as to be able to help the poor and the sick more effectively; she gave to them whatever she could spare.

understand; he shakes his head in disapproval and feels that it is unnatural. Hedwig understood quite well the Sacrament of Marriage and the blessings of offspring, and in all likelihood she also had a correct opinion of the place of marital joys in human life. If the pleasures of marriage had meant nothing to her, then renouncing them would not have been a sacrifice. She did not pout and deny her husband his due, but rather with his approval took the vow together with him. Henry had reached the same conviction. Their vow cannot be compared with the melancholy resignation of an unconsummated marriage. Hedwig's decision had a much deeper significance: Her vow of continence was renunciation to the highest degree. She soared to this heroic decision because from now on a higher motherhood was demanded of her: instead of being merely a mother to her family, Hedwig was called to be the mother of the entire populace. Such a mission, which surpasses the natural realm, calls for reverence.[5]

Saint Hedwig was in fact an example of ready and willing service to the poor and the sick among the Silesian people. Because she wanted to remain free for works of charity on behalf of the poor and the sick, Hedwig did not enter the cloister in Trebnitz, either, as much as she valued and supported it, not even after the death of her husband, which occurred on March 19, 1238, in Krossen an der Oder.

Although Hedwig spent her five years as a widow in the vicinity of Trebnitz and in very close communication with the nuns, she herself never became a religious. The holy woman died in Trebnitz "on October 15 during Vespers in the year 1243", according to the *Vita*. On March 26, 1267, she was declared a saint by Pope Clement IV. She was an exemplary wife and mother of a family, moreover, a mother to the poor, and the mother of the entire Silesian people.

[5] Ibid., p. 97.

Blessed
Ingeborg
and
Philip II Augustus

b. 1176
d. 1236 in Corbeil

Ingeborg, the second wife of the French King Philip II Augustus, is honored in only a few isolated places as a blessed or a saint, but the case involving her marriage is so famous that it is worthwhile examining it in this book about married blesseds and saints.

Ingeborg—like her brother, Canute VI, king of the Danes—was a descendant of Valdemar I of Norway and his wife, Sophie, who in turn was the daughter of Prince Matislav of Novgorod. In 1193, when ambassadors from the French King Philip II Augustus arrived at the royal court in Denmark, the seventeen-year-old Ingeborg was noted not only for her beauty but also for her piety, high moral standards, and untarnished virginity.

Death had robbed the French King Philip, an extremely self-willed man, of his wife, Isabella, a daughter of Baldwin V of Hainaut and Countess Margaret of Flanders. He was looking for a new wife and believed that he had found her in the person of Ingeborg, the sister of King Canute VI of Denmark. Therefore he sent a legation, headed by Bishop Étienne of Noyon, to the Danish court. King Canute VI received the French legation amicably and, after obtaining the consent of the lords of the land, quickly agreed to the French king's request. The only difficulty concerned the dowry that Ingeborg, the sister of King Canute VI, was supposed to bring with her. King Philip wished the dowry to be the Danish king's ancient claim to the kingdom of England—and, in order to bring this about, the help of a Danish fleet and a Danish army as well.

When the French legation presented this demand to King Canute VI, he replied that King Philip II Augustus was demanding a bit too much; he would first have to take counsel with the lords of his land. They, however, had good reason to think that Denmark had enough to worry about, battling the neighboring pagan tribe, the Wends. Why should Denmark give up this battle now and attack the Christian people of England instead, which would put Denmark in danger on both fronts: on the one side, from the wild Wends, and on the other, from the mighty, freedom-loving English? The Danish king replied, therefore, that he could not endanger his own people on account of his sister Ingeborg's marriage, and therefore King Philip might demand something else for a dowry. The final agreement was that the dowry would consist of 10,000 marks in silver.

After providing her with the finest trousseau, King Canute VI gave his sister Ingeborg to be married to King Philip II Augustus. She was accompanied to France by Bishop Peter of Roskild and a suitable retinue. She was met by King Philip, together with the bishops and the lords of the French kingdom, who had come as far as Amiens. The marriage ceremony took place there. It is said, however, that even as his new wife was being crowned, King Philip was filled with revulsion and loathing for her.

Many authors depict the change in the French king's attitude toward his second wife and the motive for his separation from her as follows: King Philip II Augustus had hurried with great joy to meet his new wife in Amiens. In this happy mood he gave too little thought to political matters and did not immediately ask the legation that had been sent to the Danish royal court under what conditions the marriage contract had been concluded with regard to the dowry. When he heard, then, that his main purpose in arranging this new union—to obtain a claim to the English kingdom and to have a guarantee of Danish support for the conquest of England—had come to naught, the very thought of a marriage with Ingeborg vexed him. The king immediately made his retinue aware of his change of attitude, and he began right away to plan the dissolution of the marriage that he had just contracted.

In order to justify the intended divorce or declaration of nullity, the king's councillors tried to find a weighty reason that would be valid before a Church marriage tribunal. They thought that they had found one in a forbidden degree of consanguinity between the king's first wife and his second wife. A blood relationship between Isabella and Ingeborg was erroneously derived from Charles the Good, count of Flanders, a son of King Canute of Denmark.

King Philip II Augustus therefore wrote to Pope Celestine III, who charged the bishops of Beauvais and Chartres to render a judgment on this impediment to marriage. These bishops considered the alleged kinship of the two wives, Isabella and Ingeborg, as sufficient cause for dissolving the marriage.

A little more than two months after his marriage to Ingeborg, King Philip, encouraged by the opinion of the bishops of Beauvais and Chartres, convened a parliament in Compiègne, consisting of the bishops and the ranking noblemen ["estates"] of his kingdom, with the archbishop of Reims presiding. The alleged kinship between the two queens, Isabella and Ingeborg, was once again examined; witnesses were produced who testified under oath that the degree of consanguinity really existed. Thereupon the archbishop of Reims declared the king's marriage with Ingeborg to be invalid and null.

Queen Ingeborg, who was not conversant in French, understood nothing of what had been discussed and decided concerning her. When an interpreter informed her of the decision, she was seized with fear, and with tears in her eyes she cried out in broken French, "Woe to France, woe to France! Rome, Rome!" Thus she tried to indicate that she would appeal to the pope in Rome. The king, however, divorced Ingeborg as soon as the archbishop of Reims had pronounced the judgment that the marriage was null. He wanted to send her back to Denmark. She decided instead to remain in France to await the clarification of her case in a cloistered convent.

King Canute VI of Denmark had reason to be extremely bitter about King Philip's conduct toward Queen Ingeborg; he was not alone in his opinion that the marriage had been dissolved illegally.

He lodged a complaint with Pope Celestine III and proved that there was not the slightest degree of consanguinity between the late Queen Isabella and his sister Ingeborg.

In 1195 Pope Celestine III sent his legate, the cardinal-priest Melior, and the subdeacon Censius Cencio to France. They arrived in Paris and convoked a council of all the bishops and abbots in France in order to negotiate the reestablishment of the marital bond between King Philip II Augustus and his repudiated wife, Ingeborg. For fear of the king, however, the gathering of bishops and abbots reached no decision.

King Philip II Augustus did not heed the repeated admonitions of Pope Celestine III concerning the restoration of his marriage to Ingeborg; on the contrary, he went so far as to marry Agnes, the daughter of Bertold IV, duke of Istria and count of Méran. After several further but ultimately unsuccessful attempts of Pope Celestine III to bring about the reconciliation of King Philip of France with his repudiated wife, Ingeborg, the newly elected Pope Innocent III, through his legate, Peter of Capua, imposed an interdict on France on January 13, 1200. This ecclesiastical penalty affected the entire country, and because of the painful consequences, King Philip finally appeared to give in. He did not, however, send Agnes de Méran away; she died in August 1201. Only in the year 1213 did King Philip really take Ingeborg back graciously, after having humiliated her in the extreme for more than sixteen years.

There was great joy among the French people as a result. Ingeborg's marriage to King Philip II Augustus lasted until the death of the king in the year 1223; she remained childless, though. This circumstance, together with the king's long-lasting aversion to her, gave rise to the rumor that Ingeborg had some secret physical defect, which could scarcely have been true. After the king's death she lived a very secluded life for thirteen more years as a widow in various convents and died at the age of sixty in the year 1236 in Corbeil, where she was buried in the priory of Saint John.[1]

---

[1] Cf. F. Wachter, "Ingelburga", in *Allgemeine Encyklopädie der Wissenschaften und Künste* (Leipzig, 1840), 2, secs. H–N.

Blessed Mary of Oignies and Hans

b. 1177 in Nivelles (Brabant, Netherlands)
d. June 23, 1213, in Oignies

Blessed Mary of Oignies is one of the most striking figures from the early days of the Beguine movement [consisting of ascetic and philanthropic communities of women in the Netherlands], who spent her short life as a consecrated virgin while living in a noble, chaste Josephite marriage and who, together with her husband, selflessly served the lepers.[1]

The life of this blessed was conscientiously set down in writing by Jacques de Vitry, who was her spiritual director and confessor from 1207 until her death in 1213. He belonged to the austere priory of Augustinian Canons Regular that was founded in 1192; in 1216 he became a bishop and in 1229 a cardinal. He is considered an extremely reliable chronicler.

Mary was born in 1177 in Nivelles in Brabant (then part of the diocese of Liège, today in Mecheln), the daughter of a well-to-do family. Very early on, as a child, she was opposed to "the all-too-worldly, luxurious complacency and pride of wealth with which the citizens of the thriving cities enjoyed their prosperity."[2]

---

[1] Cf. L. Brede, "Maria Oignies", in P. Manns, *Die Heiligen in ihrer Zeit*, 2d ed. (Mainz, 1966), 2:44–46; J. de Vitry, "Vita B. Mariae Oigniacensis", in *Acta Sanctorum Junii* 5:542–72.

[2] Brede, "Maria".

Mary steadfastly refused to wear the expensive clothing and coiffures that would have befitted the wealth and prestige of her family. Her parents wanted to counteract this stubbornness, and, therefore, in 1191 they hastily found a suitable husband for their fourteen-year-old daughter, thinking that this would "bring her to her senses, since she was overly inclined to become a nun". The young groom, Hans by name, who had a brother Guido in Holy Orders, completely disappointed the expectations of his in-laws. Shortly after the wedding it was an open secret in Nivelles: Not only did he participate in the prayers and severe penitential practices of his young wife, Mary; the young couple, seized with the same ardent love for Christ, had even promised each other to practice continence within their marriage—to live as brother and sister! To the horror of their families, they turned their beautiful, well-furnished house into a sort of shelter for the homeless. In no time at all they had used up their wealth in the service of the poor and the sick, with such prodigal generosity that the citizens

Mary of Oignies lived the last years of her life as a Beguine hermitess in a cell near the Augustinian shrine near Oignies, southern Belgium. (Seventeenth-century engraving)

of Nivelles must have thought it was scandalous. The young husband and wife were therefore avoided as being anti-social or else ridiculed and insulted as madmen. The more the young couple sacrificed their earthly happiness, the more their deep spiritual communion grew. Their desire to imitate Christ impelled them to advance along their way of the cross, until they finally ended up in Willambroux, a leper colony at the city limits of Nivelles. That was the final station the two young spouses reached together. In breaking out of the narrow bounds of comfort and security, Mary was always the bolder, the more immoderate and ardent of the two; her husband stood to some extent in her shadow, and in his silent willingness to make sacrifices he was a vigilant protector and a never-failing support for his wife as they ran the gauntlet of bourgeois contempt. The couple moved into a little hut among the lepers and took care of these terribly suffering members of Christ's Mystical Body.

Husband and wife spent twelve years in the service of the lepers, obtaining the strength for this heroic life of sacrifice through meditating on the Passion of Christ, to whom they would often pray for hours in his eucharistic presence.

As time went on, the little hut in Willambroux was besieged by the needy and the curious. This was probably the reason why Mary sensed an interior prompting to withdraw to greater solitude. Her faithful husband, Hans, and her confessor at that time, her brother-in-law Father Guido, approved of Mary's decision. In 1207 she withdrew to the (then) remote village of Oignies in southern Belgium, which had a small shrine dedicated to the Mother of God, which was in the care of the Augustinian Canon Jacques de Vitry. This well-educated priest now became Mary's spiritual director and confessor for the rest of her life and her biographer after her death. The years spent in Oignies until her blessed return to her lasting home on June 23, 1213, were for Maria "a paradise of mystical graces, but at the same time an inferno of terrible sufferings".

Saint Ferdinand III and Beatrice

b. 1198
d. May 30, 1252, in Seville, Spain

Married 1219
Father of thirteen children
Canonized February 4, 1671

Saint Ferdinand stands before us as a saint who was married, not once, but twice and who lived a truly Christian married life and was a good father to his children and a prudent sovereign of his country.[1]

He was born in 1198, the oldest son of Alfonso IX, the King of León, and Berengaria (Berenguela) of Castile. Ferdinand's mother, Berengaria, was a very energetic, competent, and, above all, profoundly Christian woman who in these qualities closely resembled her sister Blanche of Castile, the mother of Saint Louis IX of France. Just as Blanche raised and trained her son to be not only an edifying Christian but also an exemplary ruler, indeed a saint, so, too, did Berengaria.

From his father, Alfonso IX, Ferdinand inherited the title of king and dominion over the kingdom of León, whereas from his mother, Berengaria, he received the same title and authority over

---

[1] Cf. *Acta Sanctorum Maii* 7:280–414; C. Fernández de Castro, *Vida del muy noble y santo rey Fernando III. de Castilla y León* (Cadice, 1948); D. Mansiolla, "*Ferdinando III.*", in *Bibliotheca Sanctorum* 5:624–27.

the kingdom of Castile. Ferdinand combined the two kingdoms on the Iberian Peninsula into an indivisible unit.

Berengaria awakened in her son Ferdinand his natural inclinations and valuable talents so that he became an eminent Christian ruler and an exceptionally brave hero in the battle to free Spain from Moorish-Islamic dominion. Propagating and strengthening the Christian faith and Christian life on the Iberian Peninsula was Saint Ferdinand's primary purpose; that is what his mother brought him up to do. Subordinate to this was his campaign against the Moors, which Ferdinand began successfully in 1224. The prayers he sent up to heaven before and after his battles, the decree that bishops and clergy were to accompany the army for the pastoral care of the soldiers, the reestablishment of Christian customs in the territories previously ruled by the Moors, the restoration of dioceses, churches, and monasteries—all these give witness to the purity of Ferdinand's intentions throughout his military campaigns.

Ferdinand's first marriage was to Beatrice, the daughter of the German King Philip of Swabia, the son of Frederick Barbarossa. This very happy marriage unfortunately lasted only fifteen years, from 1219 to 1234. From it issued ten children, among whom were: (1) Alfonso X (1220–1284), who became Ferdinand's successor as king of León and Castile; (2) Federigo (d. 1277); (3) Enrique (d. 1304); (4) Philip (d. 1262), who was a student of Albert the Great in Paris; (5) Sancho (d. 1261), who received Holy Orders and died as archbishop of Toledo; (6) Juan Manuel (d. 1283); (7) Berengaria, who entered the Cistercian convent in Las Huelgas (Burgos); and (8) Maria (d. 1234), after whose birth both the mother, Beatrice, and the child died. [Ferdinand then married Joan of Ponthieu, with whom he had three children, including Eleanor of Castile, wife of Edward I of England.—ED.]

King Ferdinand was strictly disciplined, pious, and upright; he ruled according to the precepts of the Gospel. He was clement toward his subordinates and extremely generous to monasteries, especially to those of the newly established orders of Franciscans, Dominicans, and Trinitarians. He was a loyal son of the pope in

Rome. His mother, Berengaria, had instilled in him a Catholic spirit that was faithful in every respect.

Ferdinand lived peacefully and happily with each of his wives; he especially loved Beatrice and was absolutely faithful to her. Together with his wife he raised his children to be good Christians and always gave them good example. He rejoiced that two of his children responded to the call to a consecrated life: His son Sancho became a priest, indeed, later the archbishop of Toledo, and his daughter Berengaria became a nun. Several of his other sons, having reached manhood, stood bravely by their father in the wars of liberation; they responsibly carried out their royal father's commands, especially in the year 1243, when Ferdinand became sick.

Southern Spain was freed from Islamic dominion, but Ferdinand's dream of driving the Moors out of North Africa as well and of liberating the many Christian slaves who toiled and suffered there as forced laborers was never fulfilled. In Seville, while he was making final preparations for the North African expedition, he came down again with an illness, this time a fatal one. He called together the members of his family and gave them his final instructions for leading a genuinely Christian life and maintaining a peaceful and harmonious coexistence. Then, with sincere remorse, he made a public confession of his sins and—despite his serious illness—received the Viaticum kneeling. Lastly he conferred upon his heir and successor, Alfonso X, together with his paternal blessing, the responsibility for the kingdoms of León and Castile, with the command that he be kind and just toward all men. Facing the crucifix that had been set up before him, which he reverenced again with great emotion, King Ferdinand died during the hymn *Te Deum*, which he had commanded the clergy in attendance to sing. This was on May 30, 1252. According to his own instructions he was buried in the Cathedral of Seville in the habit of a tertiary of the third order Franciscans, to which he belonged. Pope Clement X canonized him on February 4, 1671, expressing the wish that this truly Christian ruler, husband, and father might be in every age an example and an intercessor, especially for Spanish Catholics.

Blessed
Jutta of Sangerhausen
and
Johannes Konopacki of Bielcza

b. ca. 1200 in Sangerhausen, Thuringia
d. May 5, 1260

Mother of four children

Today, after many sorrowful events, there is talk of a newly established friendship between the German and Polish peoples; an additional motivation for this development could be found in the happy marital relationships experienced by German and Polish blesseds and saints. The best example of this, to be sure, is the marriage of Saint Hedwig. We would also be justified in pointing out the happy marriage of Blessed Jutta of Sangerhausen.[1] Jutta, who was born around 1200 in the vicinity of Sangerhausen, in Thuringia, married the Polish Baron Johannes Konopacki of Bielcza. She was for him an ideal wife and the mother of four children. All four of them, thanks to the Christian upbringing that they received from their staunchly Catholic parents, chose to enter religious life.

After the death of her husband, the widow Jutta spent herself in caring for the sick and then lived for four years as a hermit near Chełmża (in German "Kulmsee", north of Torun, Poland). She led a life of evangelical poverty and complete union with God, prudently guided by her confessor, the Franciscan friar Blessed John Lobedau (d. October 9, 1264, in Chełmża).

Devotion to her sprang up immediately after her holy death on May 5, 1260.

[1] Cf. *Acta Sanctorum Maii* 7:602–13; H. Westphal, *Jutta von Sangerhausen* (Meitingen, 1938); idem, "Untersuchungen über Jutta von Sangerhausen", in *Zeitschrift für Geschichte und Altertumskunde Ermlands*, no. 27 (Braunsberg, 1938): 515–96; W. Lampen, "Jutta di Sangerhausen", in *Bibliotheca Sanctorum* 7:1033–36.

Saint
Elizabeth of Hungary
and
Louis

*b. 1207 in Saros Patak Castle in
    northern Hungary*
d. November 17, 1231, in Marburg

Married 1221
Mother of three children
Canonized May 27, 1235

Saint Elizabeth of Hungary had an exemplary Christian marriage that, aside from being painfully short, was extraordinarily happy.

She was born in the year 1207 in the castle of Saros Patak, south of Kosice in northern Hungary. Her father later became King Andrew II of Hungary; his wife, Elizabeth's mother, was Gertrude of Andechs, a sister of Saint Hedwig. King Andrew II, after bloody conflicts with his brother, ascended to the Hungarian royal throne in 1205. His wife, Gertrude, exerted a great influence over her husband and favored her Bavarian relatives and the Germans who had been invited to settle in the land; being power-hungry and avaricious as well, she was hated by the Hungarian nobility, and she was murdered on September 28, 1213, when her daughter, who resided in Wartburg in Thuringia, was only six years old.

In the year 1211, the four-year-old Elizabeth had been engaged to the eleven-year-old Louis (later Landgrave Louis [Ludwig] IV of Thuringia) for political reasons and had been brought to the splendid court in Thuringia. She was transported there in a silver cradle lined with silk sheets, together with a sumptuous dowry.

Far from her Hungarian homeland, Elizabeth grew up among foreigners. She was brought up under the care of Countess Sophia, who was now her foster parent and ten years later became her mother-in-law. Countess [or Landgravine] Sophia, a descendant of the Wittelsbacher house, had had difficult experiences in her marriage with Landgrave Hermann, who was anything but a "fearless, blameless knight", and as a result she was quite mature in the religious sense. Four years after the death of her husband she would enter the Cistercian convent in Eisenach. She raised her future daughter-in-law Elizabeth in a religious spirit and instructed her in the etiquette necessary for a person of her rank. Very early on, however, Elizabeth felt compelled by the ostentation and intrigue at the court at Wartburg to take an opposing stance.

In 1221 Elizabeth, now fourteen years old, was wedded to Landgrave Louis IV. The young couple traveled to Hungary for their honeymoon. There Elizabeth learned the particulars about the dreadful murder of her mother, Gertrude. After their return to German soil, the two newlyweds took up residence in Wartburg.

W. Nigg[1] comments as follows on the married life that Saint Elizabeth was beginning.

She [Elizabeth] lived her married life affectionately, with every fiber of her being, and revealed to her husband a sweet womanly charm full of tenderness. Elizabeth's marriage was contracted for dynastic reasons and not on the basis of a personal inclination; nevertheless, the marital union was happy beyond all expectations. . . . Elizabeth was not the sort of wife who is cool and aloof, who draws back like a mimosa at every tender approach or pleads a headache as an excuse; no, she was an extremely warm, affectionate person who hungered for love and intimacy. The spouses had been acquainted since their childhood; the same mother had reared them; and even after their wedding they still called each other brother and sister. From a

[1] Cf. W. Nigg, *Die heilige Elisabeth* (Düsseldorf, 1963), pp. 161ff.

very early date there was between them a love more intimate than that experienced by many couples who have been married for a long time.

"Their two hearts had become so united in sweet love for one another that they could no longer be separated", it says in Chaplain Berthold's chronicle. . . . Elizabeth wished at all times to please her husband by wearing well-fitting garments. When Louis returned home [to Wartburg from business in the territories that he ruled], Elizabeth would run to meet him, embrace him with great joy, and, with her passionate Hungarian blood, "kiss him affectionately more than a thousand times on the mouth"; tenderly and warm-heartedly she would clasp Louis, giving herself to him completely and making her great capacity for love the basis of her life. Thanks to the union of their souls, the erotic love between Elizabeth and Louis only served to increase the sympathy and harmony between them. This was an intimate unfolding of the sacramental character of married love: sweet and fragrant, endearing and charming.

Louis' contribution to this marital bliss was essential. . . . Louis was a man completely unlike his irresponsible father; he was of a serious character and would not allow himself to be misled by the whisperings and intrigues at court, but instead remained faithful to Elizabeth. Whenever other knights suggested infidelity against Elizabeth, Louis decisively rejected the very thought of it, for he was unwilling "to sadden his dear wife".

Louis once declared, "Let people say what they will, but I say it clearly: Elizabeth is very dear to me, and I have nothing more precious on this earth."

Besides his great love for his wife, Elizabeth, Landgrave Louis possessed an unusually good understanding of her character, especially for her profound piety. In this regard he never placed any obstacles in her way; he allowed her that freedom. For example, when Elizabeth would arise at night and devote herself to prayer, Louis might pretend to be asleep; often, though, he would clasp

Elizabeth bids farewell to her husband as he departs for the Holy Land.

her hands and say, "Dear Sister, spare yourself; lie down and get some rest!"

As for Elizabeth, a small shadow sometimes clouded her marriage, when she experienced mixed feelings and wondered uneasily whether she might be devoting herself to her husband with a love that was too intense, whereas her heart ought to belong to God alone. Once she said to her maidservants that she needed nocturnal prayer "so as to withstand an excessive love for my husband". Often there were moments when Elizabeth even regretted that she had married at all and could not die a virgin.

W. Nigg concludes his comments on the marriage of Saint Elizabeth with the remark,

The two spouses were in agreement with respect to the most profound things that can unite human beings, that is, the things of God, and, thanks to their common perspective, "the holy angel was often a messenger between them". This mysterious expression profoundly illumines the experience of the spouses and suddenly clarifies the underlying principles by which they lived. A marriage can be successful only when an angel serves as a messenger between those united in marriage; this does a hundred times more good than all the modern marriage counseling services put together. An angel going back and forth between a husband and a wife—indeed, you could scarcely say anything more beautiful about a married couple.

The Dominican Dietrich von Apolda (d. after 1297) writes in his life of Saint Elizabeth, which he began in 1289, about the sanctity of her marriage.

Blessed with the delights of a chaste love and an intimate union, they [Elizabeth and Louis] could not stand to be separated from each other either for a long time or by a great distance. Therefore Elizabeth frequently followed her husband along rough roads, on lengthy journeys, and in bad weather, led more by the ardor of pure love than by carnal desire. For the chaste presence of her modest husband did not hinder this most pious wife either from watching and praying or from other good works. The pious man rejoiced in the Lord over her holy practices and supported her by his fidelity and his encouragement.

In her husband's absence, Elizabeth spent many a night in watching and prayer. During this time she did not wear magnificent clothing but went about dressed as a widow. Next to the skin she wore wool or a hair shirt. She did this even when she was clothed in garments embroidered in gold or in purple robes. When she knew that her husband would soon return, she adorned herself splendidly. She explained,

> I want to adorn myself, not out of worldly pride, but for the love of God alone—in a fitting manner, however, so as to give my husband no cause to sin, if something about me were to displease him. Only let him love me in the Lord, with a chaste, marital affection, so that we, in the same way, might hope for the reward of eternal life from him who has sanctified the law of marriage.

Dietrich von Apolda briefly summarizes the way Elizabeth acted toward her husband: "In his absence she conducted herself in a blameless, God-fearing manner; in his presence she was all affection, love, and goodness. God made her womb fruitful with the most noble offspring, so that she was spared the shame of sterility and experienced the consolation of children."

Three children were sent into the blessed marital union of Elizabeth and Louis. In 1222, at the age of fifteen, Elizabeth bore her first child, Hermann, who later became landgrave of Thuringia. Then, in 1224, she gave birth to Sophia, later the duchess of Brabant and ancestral mother of the Hessian landgraves. Finally, in 1227, she had Gertrude, later the abbess of Altenburg.

Conscious of her responsibilities, Elizabeth had a great love not only for her husband and children, but also for all her fellow men and women in need. She lovingly served the sick and helped all who were in difficulties so generously that many people around her lodged complaints about it with the landgrave. He, though, understood the munificence of his beloved wife and said, "Let her do good and give whatever she can for God!"

Only six years after Elizabeth's wedding to Landgrave Louis IV of Thuringia, a painful separation of the two occurred. At the behest of the pope, a crusade was preached in 1227. Inspired with a holy zeal, many agreed to wear the cross as a symbol of their promise to fight against the enemies of Christ in the Holy Land.

Saint Elizabeth cares for the sick.

After mature deliberation with Bishop Conrad of Hildesheim, Landgrave Louis also, who was a Christian through and through, asked the bishop to clothe him with the sign of the cross in the name of Christ. He wished it to remain hidden, however. Therefore he did not fasten the cross to his garment, as was the custom, so that his wife, whom he loved tenderly, would not see it and become anxious about his impending departure. Once, though, when she was looking for something in his pocket, as often happens, she found the cross and was, so to speak, shattered by terrible dismay.

The melancholy day of their leave-taking arrived. A few weeks later, Elizabeth's dark foreboding became a reality—Landgrave Louis IV was carried off by plague in southern Italy; he died in Otranto on September 11, 1227. When the news of his death was brought to Elizabeth, the saint was deeply shaken and cried out, "Now the world and everything in it that I loved is dead." She had to experience the hardest lot that can befall a wife in a good marriage: the death of the husband whom she loved so intimately. The body of her departed husband was brought back home; the following words escaped Elizabeth's lips while she was in its presence. "If I could have him alive again, even though it cost the entire world, I would take him and then go begging with him forever." What great love is expressed in these words of that nineteen-year-old wife who, after six years of being happily married, was now a widow!

After the death of her husband, Elizabeth was deprived of the freedom to dispose of her widow's pension, on the pretext that she was wasting all her property on the poor.

To escape such unjust and patronizing treatment, Elizabeth left Wartburg at night, alone, taking with her nothing but her children. At first she had to live on the alms that she begged. But from the Franciscans, who had come to Eisenach in 1225, Elizabeth had heard about Saint Francis of Assisi and had learned to love voluntary poverty. Her husband's counselor, the austere Franciscan Conrad of Marburg, who had also become Elizabeth's spiritual director in 1226, had encouraged her progress in the virtue of mortification. Thus Elizabeth, despite all her misery, was happy that she had the privilege of suffering and renouncing everything for God. In thanksgiving for this grace that had been bestowed on her, she even had the Franciscans in Eisenach sing a *Te Deum*.

As time went on, influential relatives took up her cause again, and the men who had returned home after staying in the company of her husband in southern Italy now conducted her back to Wartburg.

Yet Elizabeth no longer felt at home in the castle of Wartburg. After a short time the widow moved to the property that had been left to her in Marburg, and she founded there a large hospital, which she funded with her income. Every day she visited those entrusted to her protection there and devoted herself to caring for them.

In the year 1231 this great lover, Elizabeth, on the night before the seventeenth of November, died at the age of only twenty-four. On May 27, 1235, she was canonized as an exemplary young wife who had masterfully achieved a unity and harmony between her love for God and her love for both her husband and her children, as well as for the sick and the poor. With good reason this young saint is characterized in the Preface of the Mass for her feast day on November 19 as follows:

It is truly fitting and right, always and everywhere to give you thanks, Lord, God our Father, and to glorify your grace on the feast of Saint Elizabeth. For you have endowed her with a great love. She loved her husband with all the ardor of her heart. When she lost him in death, she followed the call of the Gospel. She sold what she had and joyfully gave everything to the poor, who honored her as their mother. In them she saw Christ, and she wanted to serve him in the poorest of the poor. Happy in spite of difficulties, she suffered calumny and injustice; made perfect at a young age, she attained the joys of heaven.

Saint
Zdislava of Lemberk
and
Havel of Lemberk

b. ca. 1220
d. ca. 1252

Married ca. 1227
Mother of four children
Beatified August 28, 1907
Canonized May 21, 1995, during the Holy Father's pastoral visit to the Czech Republic

Zdislava, a wife and mother,[1] became the patroness of Bohemia when her cult was approved by the Holy See on August 28, 1907. She was born around 1220, the daughter of the Baron of Brünn, Pribislav Berka of Krlzanov, and Sibyl (who, some say, was a daughter of the Count Palatine, Otto of Wittelsbach, while others record that she came from Sicily).

Throughout her childhood and youth, Zdislava persevered in genuine, deep piety and magnanimous love of neighbor. At the age of seven she ran away to lead a solitary life; her parents brought her back, however.

At the age of seventeen—against her will, since she longed to live a life of consecrated virginity—she was married to Count Havel of Lemberk. With infinite patience Zdislava endured her husband's quick temper and rudeness during the years of their marriage. She gave birth to four children and gave them an ideal Christian education. Of these four children, only two are known by name: Havel, who died young, and Margarita. The husband

---

[1] Cf. I. Taurisano, *La Beata Zdislava dei Berka* (Florence, 1909); W. Wostry, "Die selige Zdislava von Gabel", in *Deutsch-Gabel in tausendjähriger Vergangenheit* (Deutsch-Gabel, 1926), pp. 15–29.

of Saint Zdislava played a leading role in the political events of Bohemia and, in that arena at least, proved himself to be a loyal knight of Christ. At his wife's recommendation he founded two Dominican friaries, located in Jablonné and Turnov.

Zdislava became a secular tertiary in the Dominican Order, the first to do so in Bohemia. She dwelled especially on the Passion of Christ and repeatedly experienced ecstasies. A chronicle from the late fourteenth century ascribes several miracles to Saint Zdislava after her death, which took place in 1252.

Besides the help that Saint Zdislava afforded the Dominican friars in propagating their order, she is noted for her generosity to the poor and for her profound devotion. Saint Zdislava was buried in the Dominican church of Saint Lawrence, adjoining Lemberk Castle.

Blessed Gherardesca of Pisa and Alferio di Bandino

b. ca. 1212
d. soon after 1269

Married ca. 1231/1232

Cecco di Pietro, image of Gherardesca of Pisa, Pisa, Museo Nazionale di San Matteo, fourteenth century

Against her will, Gherardesca, who was born around 1212, the daughter of a count, was married to a nobleman, Alferio di Bandino, around 1231 or 1232.[1] The marriage did not turn out to be a happy one, not only because the couple remained childless, but particularly because, in the midst of her cares and suffering, the young wife, Gherardesca, became more and more conscious of being called, not to marriage, but to dedicate herself completely to God in religious life. Again and again she wondered: Was there a possibility after all that her marriage could be legitimately dissolved? How would it be if both she and her husband joined a religious order? Her longing for such a resolution of her marital problems gradually matured into an answer to her question: She asked the opinion of her husband, who was a man of faith. Very soon he realized that he, too, was called to the religious rather than the married state. Finally, he consented to a dissolution of the marriage, if that was possible according to the laws of the Church.

[1] Cf. *Acta Sanctorum Maii* 6:516–32; Valfredo della Gherardesca, "I Santi camaldolensi della famiglia dei Conti della Gherardesca", in *Rivista Camaldolense* (1927), 4:351.

Such marital separations have, in fact, always been feasible within the Church—down to the present day—if both spouses consecrate themselves entirely and unreservedly to God and enter religious life.

In the year 1234—after a marriage of at most three years—Alferio di Bandino became a monk in the very strict Camaldolese monastery of San Savino in Pisa. Gherardesca did the same: a small cell was built for her, attached to that monastery.

History is silent from then on about the Camaldolese monk Alferio. A *Life* of Gherardesca has come down to us, however, probably composed by her confessor, the monk Padre Paolo, from San Savino.

The life of nun and former wife—as we can read in this *Vita*—was distinguished more and more by extraordinary charisms; she possessed, for example, the gift of reading hearts. Rapturous visions concerning Christ, his Mother, the Blessed Virgin Mary, the disciple whom Jesus loved, the Apostle John, and the poor souls in Purgatory were granted to her with increasing frequency. She also had the gift of healing and brought about ever greater numbers of remarkable conversions among hardened sinners, to whom she announced their most secret offenses.

These extraordinary phenomena in the life of Sister Gherardesca, however, awakened mistrust and envy in many of the monks in the monastery of San Savino in Pisa. Gherardesca was reported to the superiors of the order; she was subjected to severe trials, and finally she was even excommunicated. But her father confessor stood by her faithfully through it all and defended her innocence, so that ultimately the severe punishment of excommunication was lifted. Everything was in order again, and she who had been calumniated carried off the victory.

Shortly after 1269 Gherardesca died and was laid to rest in the church of San Savino in Pisa. Her feast day is observed in the Camaldolese Order on June 9.

Saint Louis IX of France and Margaret of Provence

b. April 25, 1214, in Poissy, west of Paris
d. August 25, 1270, in Tunis

Married May 27, 1234
Father of eleven children
Canonized 1297

Saint Louis IX

Among the personages who ruled during the Middle Ages and have been raised to the honors of the altar, no doubt Saint Louis IX of France is one of the most attractive figures, for he can be considered also as a husband and the father of a family.[1] Furthermore, his life, including his moral and religious life, is singularly well attested by four contemporary biographers, who set down in writing the life of this saint almost immediately after his death: (1) the Dominican priest-friar Godefroi de Beaulieu, who was the confessor of Louis IX for twenty years and who wrote his biography in 1272–1273, that is, two to three years after the king's death; (2) Guillaume de Chartres, likewise a Dominican friar and priest, who merely wished to supplement the work of his confrère Godefroi; (3) Guillaume de Saint-Pathus, O.F.M., the confessor of Queen Margaret of Provence, the king's widow, who wrote a life

---

[1] Cf. *Acta Sanctorum Augusti* 5:275–758, including: "Vita Sancti Ludovici auctore Gaudefrido de Bello Loco, regis confessario", pp. 541–58; "Appendix vitae primar, auctore Guillelmo Carnotensi", pp. 559–69; "Vita Secunda, auctore anonymo reginae Margaritae confessario", pp. 571–672; "Vita tertia, auctore Joanne Joivillio, regis familiari", pp. 672–750.

of Louis IX sometime after 1297; and (4) Jean de Joinville, an intimate friend of the ruler, who composed his biography of Saint Louis IX between 1298 and 1309.

Louis was born in 1214 in Poissy, the son of King Louis VIII and his wife, Blanche of Castile. The most important influence in the education of the future king of France was no doubt his mother, who inculcated in him a sense of his Christian duties and a very vivid horror of sin. When the young King Louis IX was still underage, Blanche of Castille told him, "You know, my child, how much I love you, but I would rather see you dead than commit a mortal sin!"

Louis lost his father at the age of twelve—King Louis VIII died in 1226—and therefore the boy was crowned king in Reims on November 26, 1226; because he was still underage, however, his mother acted as regent for ten years.

Louis IX was married on May 27, 1234, at the age of nineteen to the thirteen-year-old Margaret of Provence. That was the beginning of an extraordinarily happy Christian marriage and a family blessed with many children. At the outset, it is true, the young king's mother controlled the life of the young couple excessively and kept the spouses separated from each other for another six years. After that time, Blanche of Castile continued to interfere in the young couple's marital life, even in the most intimate matters, so that both husband and wife were forced to put up a fight against the importunity of the mother or mother-in-law. This was not always easy for Louis; either he disappointed his jealous mother, who was filled with a morbid envy of her pretty daughter-in-law, or else his young wife sensed that her husband, Louis, was not loyal to her, whereas she stood by him faithfully, sharing everything with him. She wanted to be with him always and therefore even accompanied him on his Crusades and bravely endured with him the associated toils and hardships.

Saint Francis de Sales has left us a moving description of the marital fidelity of Margaret of Provence:

If someone had asked this brave princess where she was traveling, she surely would have replied, "I am traveling to the same place where the King is traveling." And if he had inquired further, "But do you know exactly where the King is traveling?" she would have answered, "Of course he told me in general, but it is not my concern where he is traveling; I care only that I am traveling with him." If someone had then exclaimed, "You have, then, no plan during this journey?" she would have said, "No, I have no other plan than to be with my dear lord and husband."[2]

If one were to pass judgment on the marital life of Louis IX, one could say without reservation that it fulfilled all the requirements made by Pope Pius XI in his encyclical on marriage, *Casti connubii*. It was a chaste marriage, in which there was no misuse of the marriage right. If the Pill had existed then, these two spouses would certainly never have been tempted to use it; for ever since their youth they had faithfully practiced marital continence, as is often required by the precepts of the Church. The biographers explicitly report that they observed continence during the so-called "days of abstinence" in the liturgical year, in Advent and Lent, also on Friday and Saturday of each week, and, furthermore, for one day before and one day after the reception of Holy Communion, which Louis IX and his wife, Margaret, according to the custom of that time, received only six times a year, at Easter, Pentecost, on the Feast of the Assumption of the Blessed Virgin Mary, on All Saints Day, Christmas, and the Feast of the Presentation. It goes without saying that sexual abstinence was also practiced in this marriage whenever the wife was pregnant, and that was the case at least eleven times during the thirty-six years of this marriage. For Margaret gave her husband eleven children, of whom nine reached adulthood.

This chaste marriage was an exceptionally harmonious, peaceful, and happy one; throughout the course of it, Louis and his wife drew strength from their religion by fervent prayer, daily attendance at Holy Mass, and participation in the Divine Office chanted by the monks.

[2] Francis de Sales, *Treatise on the Love of God*, bk. 9, chap. 13.

Moreover King Louis IX led a very frugal, contented, and disciplined life, for which he gave a regular accounting, week after week, to his father confessor.

In Louis' case, a simple modest way of life meant doing without splendid clothing. That was perhaps the one source of disagreements and quarreling in this marriage. For the idea that Louis, the king of France, should dress so very simply was displeasing to his wife. She would have preferred to see him in luxurious garments—which is understandable, since most married people want their partner to be well dressed; at any rate, this was the case with Margaret, the queen of France. King Louis IX, though, for all his devotion to his charming wife, whom he loved tenderly, was unwilling to oblige her in this point. The upshot was that one day, as Louis' friend Joinville recounts, they had a little marital dispute, which is amusing to overhear. In a debonair tone, Louis said to his dear Margaret, "Well, then, you want me to dress more expensively? Good, it shall be so; I must comply with your wishes, and you with mine. Therefore I wish that you would be so kind as to dispense with all of your cosmetics. You will adjust to my way, and I will adjust to yours!" "We do not know how Queen Margaret reacted to her husband's facetious suggestion; evidently Louis wanted to play a little joke on his wife."[3]

As an exemplary Christian husband and the father of a family, King Louis IX, together with his wife, was also quite concerned about the proper Christian upbringing of his nine growing children. Evidence for this is found in the instructions he left behind for them all, specifically for his daughter Isabel (later the wife of Thibaut V, count of Champagne and king of Navarre) and for his son Philip.

For the son who would inherit his throne, he dictated on his deathbed in Tunis the following instructions as a testament:

My dearest son, my first instruction is that you should love the Lord your God with all your heart and all your strength. Without this there is no salvation. Keep yourself, my son, from

---

[3] Cf. W. Nigg, *Heilige im Alltag* (Olten, 1974), pp. 59f.

everything that you know displeases God, that is to say, from every mortal sin. You should permit yourself to be tormented by every kind of martyrdom before you would allow yourself to commit a mortal sin.

If the Lord has permitted you to have some trial, bear it willingly and with gratitude, considering that it has happened for your good and that perhaps you well deserved it. If the Lord bestows upon you any kind of prosperity, thank him humbly and see that you become no worse for it, either through vain pride or anything else, because you ought not to oppose God or offend him in the matter of his gifts.

Listen to the divine office with pleasure and devotion. As long as you are in church, be careful not to let your eyes wander and not to speak empty words, but pray to the Lord devoutly, either aloud or with the interior prayer of the heart.

Be kindhearted to the poor, the unfortunate, and the afflicted. Give them as much help and consolation as you can. Thank God for all the benefits he has bestowed upon you, that you may be worthy to receive greater. Be just to your subjects, swaying neither to right nor left, but holding the line of justice. Always side with the poor rather than with the rich, until you are certain of the truth. See that all your subjects live in justice and peace, but especially those who have ecclesiastical rank and who belong to religious orders.

Be devout and obedient to our mother the Church of Rome and the Supreme Pontiff as your spiritual father. Work to remove all sin from your land, particularly blasphemies and heresies.

In conclusion, dearest son, I give you every blessing that a loving father can give a son. May the three Persons of the Holy Trinity and all the saints protect you from every evil. And may the Lord give you the grace to do his will so that he may be served and honored through you, that in the next life we may together come to see him, love him, and praise him unceasingly.[4]

[4] Louis IX, "Testamentum spirituale ad filium", in *Acta Sanctorum Augusti* 5:546. English translation by ICEL in *The Liturgy of the Hours according to the Roman Rite*, 4:1347–48, Office of Readings for the memorial of St. Louis, August 25.

King Lewis IX.
Reliquary bust in the treasury/vault, Notre Dame Cathedral, Paris

In these moving documents the profound piety of Louis IX and his ideal of the Christian ruler are beautifully expressed. This saintly king would have been happy to see one of his children grow up enthusiastic about the priestly or religious state, especially about the Dominican, Franciscan, or Cistercian Order, which he esteemed so highly. In particular he had such hopes for his son Jean Tristan, to whom his regal consort, Margaret, gave birth three days after Louis was captured by the Saracens and whom she called Tristan on account of her sorrow. The king would have been glad to see this son as a religious priest and his daughter Blanche as a nun; yet these hopes were not realized. Louis IX refrained, however, from forcing anyone into a priestly or religious vocation.

He raised his children to be not only genuinely pious but also generous to the poor and to the mendicant friars. King Louis IX felt completely at home in the Cistercian abbey of Royaumont that he founded; he used to withdraw to that place as though to a "temporary cloister" and observe all the ascetical practices and participate in the liturgical functions with the monks; he would even serve the one hundred monks at table.

Under the prudent and absolutely just rule of Louis IX, France experienced a period of peace and prosperity. It was pure idealism that prompted this regent to venture abroad on the Crusades. In the year 1244, during an illness, he had made a vow to take part in a crusade to liberate Jerusalem, which had fallen again into the hands of the Muslims. In Egypt he succeeded in taking Damietta by storm in June of 1249. Yet a few months later Louis suffered a serious defeat by al-Mansurah; he and his knights were taken captive. Gravely sick with dysentery, he had to set Damietta free and pay a ransom. Thereupon a great number of his companions returned to France, while he himself remained for more than three years in Palestine. After receiving news of his mother's death—Blanche had carried on the business of governing during his absence—King Louis IX returned to France at the end of November 1252 and attended directly to the affairs of his realm. In his private life from then on he resembled a monk rather than a king. His way of life had always been very simple, but after returning from the Crusade his life-style was even more plain and austere. He did away with all forms of luxury at court and, furthermore, performed corporal penances, observing a strict fast on certain days and wearing a rough belt beneath his clothing; he even took the discipline on occasion.

In 1267, when the Sultan Baybars of Egypt had taken possession of a large part of Palestine, King Louis IX decided once more to organize a crusade. With a fighting force of 60,000 men the king set sail from Aigues-Mortes. The first destination was Tunis. There they intended to wait for Charles d'Anjou, who would help them in their battle with the Islamic foe. While they were waiting, however, cholera broke out among Louis' troops. Louis himself fell sick, as did several thousand of his soldiers. He felt that the end was near, and so he dictated his final words of counsel for his successor to the throne, Philip the Bold. He had himself placed upon a bed of ashes and died on August 25, 1270, with his arms stretched out in the form of a cross; the final words upon his lips were "Nous irons à Jérusalem." Instead of the earthly Jerusalem, this pious king, who was an ideal husband and father, attained the heavenly Jerusalem.

Pope Boniface VIII declared King Louis IX a saint on August 11, 1297.

Blessed
Umiliana Cerchi
and
X. Bonaguisi

b. ca. 1219
d. May 12, 1246

Mother of two children

Blessed Umiliana[1] was born in the year 1219, the daughter of the nobleman Ulivieri dei Cerchi, a descendant of the d'Acone family of Val di Sieve, which is mentioned by Dante Alighieri in the *Divine Comedy*, Paradiso 16, verse 65.

At a tender age Umiliana lost her mother and was then raised by a stepmother, Ermellina di Cambio dei Benizi, a relative of Saint Philip Benizi. Not yet sixteen years old, Umiliana was married to an invalid banker from the house of Bonaguisi. Two girls issued from their marriage. Although this marriage was the result of her relatives' very materialistic motives, her first biographer, the Franciscan friar Vito da Cortona, emphasizes in his biography of Blessed Umiliana Cerchi, written in 1248, that she conducted herself as a model wife. She was a good housekeeper; she loved her children and cared for her sick husband. As the beautiful young wife of an influential man, she had to wear jewels and fancy clothes and attend parties, and so on, which she did only with reluctance. On the other hand, she devotedly cared for the sick and the poor and distributed among them her finest clothing and best linens. As her husband lay on his deathbed, she tried in vain to convince him to give back all that he had gained by usury.

In 1239, after five years of marriage, she became a widow at the age of twenty. She renounced a great part of her inheritance for

---

[1] Cf. *Acta Sanctorum Maii* 4:385–418; R. Sciamannini, "Cerchi Umiliana", in *Bibliotheca Sanctorum* 3:1132–34.

the benefit of the poor and devoted herself with love and magnanimity to raising her two daughters. After one year of mourning, she returned to her parents' house, according to the custom of the time. She had to leave her two children in the care of her deceased husband's relations. She vowed perpetual chastity, and—after her repeated requests for admission to the Poor Clares in Monticelli were turned down—she lived from then on in a tower beside her parents' house, in the so-called Torre dei Cerchi, under the spiritual direction of the Franciscan friar Blessed Michele degli Alberti. The aforementioned biographer of Blessed Umiliana described her pious ascetical life as a model for women who become Franciscan tertiaries. Umiliana Cerchi died in the odor of sanctity on May 12, 1246, only twenty-seven years of age. Pope Innocent XII approved her cult.

Saint
Kinga
and
Boleslaus V of Kraków

b. 1234 in Hungary
d. July 24, 1292, in Stary Sącz

Married ca. 1248
Beatified 1690
Canonized by Pope John Paul II on June 16, 1999, in Stary Sącz, Poland

The Hungarian royal family in the thirteenth century was a family of saints. Among them was Saint Kinga (Cunegund), who was born in 1234, the daughter of Bela IV, king of Hungary, and Maria Laskaris. Saint Elizabeth of Hungary was an aunt of Saint Kinga and a sister of her father, Bela IV. Other saintly relatives of Saint Kinga are Saint Hedwig and Saint Agnes of Prague; Blessed Jolenta (Yolanda) and Blessed Margaret were sisters of Saint Kinga; Saint Elizabeth (Isabella) of Portugal and Blessed Salomea were nieces of Saint Kinga, who was also the aunt of the holy bishop Louis.

At about the age of fourteen, Kinga[1] was wedded to Boleslaus V, prince of Kraków and later of Poland. The spouses decided to practice continence within a Josephite marriage. Tradition testifies that they lived together for forty years as chaste virgins. Prince Boleslaus V has gone down in history with the epithet "the Chaste", while the Church has bestowed the honorific title of "Virgin" upon Princess Kinga.

As the mother of her people, Kinga cared especially for the poor, the sick, and the oppressed.

---

[1] Cf. *Acta Sanctorum Julii* 5:669–747; P. A. Bierbaum, *Heilige Vorbilder aus der Familie des hl. Franziskus* (Werl i. W., 1933), pp. 455–57. [See also the biography and homily for the canonization of Saint Kinga published in *L'Osservatore romano*, July 7, 1999, pp. 5, 11.]

After the death of her royal consort, which occurred in 1279, the court importuned Kinga to take over the regency, but she refused. In 1280, she founded a Poor Clare monastery in Stary Sącz, living there as a guest for eight years before entering it in 1288. At that time, the pious princess said to the sisters, "Forget what I have been; I come only to be of service as the least among you." In fact, she carried out the lowliest tasks in the convent, sweeping the paths, washing the bowls, and performing the most menial services for the sick. Later on, she yielded to the insistent and unanimous requests of her sisters in religion and—very much against her personal wishes—accepted the position of abbess. She continued to behave as though she were subordinate of all and gave a moving example of humility.

Her cloistered life lasted thirteen years. Her many mortifications finally exhausted her strength. As she was dying, on July 24, 1292, she was fortified by a vision of Saint Francis of Assisi. In ecstasy she cried to her sisters, "Make room! See, our holy father Francis is coming to stand by me!"

The beatification process for Princess Kinga was begun in the year 1628. In 1690 Pope Alexander VIII approved the cult of the virginal Princess Kinga, who became a humble Poor Clare. Pope Clement XI declared Blessed Kinga the Patroness of the Polish and Lithuanian peoples in 1715. During a pastoral visit to Poland in June 1999, Pope John Paul II canonized Saint Kinga at a liturgy celebrated in Stary Sącz.

Saint
Humility
and
Ugoletto dei Caccianemici

b. ca. 1226 in Faenza, Italy
d. May 22, 1310, in Florence, Italy

Married 1242
Mother of two children
Cult approved by Pope Clement XI in 1721

Saint Humility was a wife and mother of a family who, after the death of her two children and with the consent of her husband, became a Benedictine religious of the Vallombrosan congregation[1] and the mother of many spiritual daughters.

She was born in 1226 in Faenza, the daughter of the nobleman Elimonte and his wife, Richelda Negusanti, and was baptized with the name Rosana. At the age of fifteen, in the year 1241, she lost her father. In 1242, at sixteen, she married the patrician Ugoletto dei Caccianemici. The couple had two children in quick succession, but both died shortly after they were baptized. The twenty-four-year-old wife did not abandon herself pessimistically to sadness and frustration or, on the other hand, to senseless worldly pleasures; instead Rosana, together with her husband of nine years, Ugoletto, considered turning their lives over to God and entering religious life in the double monastery of Saint Perpetua in Faenza. Her husband consented. So began for Rosana the life of a nun with the religious name of Humility, which completely corresponded to the reality.

Sister Humility was soon afflicted with a very serious illness, but in 1254 she was miraculously cured. Thereupon she left the

[1] Cf. G. Cantagalli, "S. Umiltà, abbadessa vallombrosana", in *Bibliotheca Sanctorum* 12:818–22.

grounds of the convent with permission in order to withdraw to a cell adjoining the Vallombrosan convent of Saint Apollinare; she lived the rest of her life as a strictly cloistered recluse.

Through contact with Sister Humility there, young Christian women from Faenza came to acquire a true taste for consecrated life in complete union with God. Several young women constructed beside the cell of Sister Humility an additional cell, so as to begin living a spiritual life under her direction. Thus it came about that in 1266, from this group of young Christian women under the direction of Sister Humility, developed a convent in Santa Maria Novella, in which the now forty-year-old Sister Humility could be a mother again, this time with respect to spiritual daughters. With much kindness, wisdom, and energy she strove to lead them to the pinnacle of sanctity, and in many cases she succeeded in doing so.

The fifteen years that followed passed in meditation and silence and the faithful practice of those virtues demanded by the Rule of Saint Benedict and the ordinances of Saint John Gualbert for the Vallombrosan Congregation.

At the age of fifty-five, Sister Humility prepared to found a new spiritual refuge for young Florentine women. By her inspiring talks and her instructions, but especially by her saintly example in living as a religious, Sister Humility remained, for the members of both convents she had founded, a constant incentive to strive for holiness. On May 22, 1310, after six months of painful suffering, the earthly life of Sister Humility came to an end during her eighty-fifth year.

The burial of the departed nun in Florence was a veritable triumph of devotion to this holy woman who had once been a wife and mother of two children, who had become the mother of many spiritual daughters in two convents that she herself founded—a saintly woman who had led her daughters heavenward in a profound spirituality that can still be discerned in the few conferences of hers that have been handed down, talks that are stylistically quite modest but which have been compared by experts to the writings of Saint Catherine of Siena, a Doctor of the Church.

Pope Clement XI approved the cult of devotion to Saint Humility in 1721 as something existing *ab immemorabili tempore* [from time immemorial]; her incorrupt body rests today in the church of the Holy Spirit in Varlungo, near Florence.

Blessed
Jacopone of Todi
and
Vanna di Bernardino
di Guidone

b. ca. 1230 in Todi in Umbria, Italy
d. December 25, 1306, in
Collazzone

Married between 1265 and 1267

A fifteenth-century painting of
Jacopone of Todi by Paolo di Dono

Jacopone of Todi was a frivolous man of the world, a lawyer by profession and a songwriter by inclination, who received the grace of conversion after the tragic death of his beautiful young wife and became a Franciscan lay brother.[1]

Around the year 1230 he was born in the city of Todi in Umbria, the son of the aristocratic Benedetti family. Jacopone studied law in Bologna and then began a legal practice, more or less, in his hometown. He must have been more of a playboy at first, however, composing songs to be performed at festivals. Many of his fellow citizens in Todi and his relatives hoped that, once he was married and had started a family, he would give up his irresponsible, frivolous ways. Eventually he chose a particularly noble, chaste, and pious young woman from the best family, namely, the beautiful Vanna di Bernardino di Guidone, from the

---

[1] Cf. F. Holböck, "Der selige Jacopone da Todi", in *Geführt von Maria* (Stein am Rhein, 1987), pp. 310–15; W. Nigg, *Der christliche Narr* (Zurich, 1956), pp. 63–111; F. Casolini, "Beato Jacopone da Todi", in *Bibliotheca Sanctorum* 7:618–23.

house of the count of Coldimezzo, and he married her between 1265 and 1267.

Jacopone was nothing if not experienced; he knew all the tricks of the legal trade and continued to indulge in great extravagance and worldly amusements. Yet he was proud of his beautiful wife. He loved Vanna ardently and sang her praises in verse. "The fairest lady owns my thought:/ Her mouth and rosy cheek,/ So dear, so soft, so finely wrought,/ No eloquence can speak./ Her tender glance holds me enchained,/ Her gently curving brow:/ If I could court her not in vain,/ 'Twould be a heaven now."

Vanna was noble, pious, and generous, but she had to conceal many a good deed from the shrewd eyes of her worldly minded spouse. To all appearances she adapted to the mundane ways of the noble ladies in the town of Todi, in order to comply with her husband's wishes. Hidden from the whole world, however, she performed penitential acts and thus made reparation for the misdeeds of her husband and of many an adulterer in Todi.

It flattered Jacopone's vanity when the beauty of his attractive wife aroused admiration on all sides. The fact that she turned the heads of people, especially of lewd men on the street, catered to Jacopone's need to make an impression. He was struck all the harder, therefore, by her completely unexpected and tragic death in 1268, after only one year of marriage. It came about as follows: One day Vanna was to attend a raucous festival performance that her husband had organized. On the platform for the honored guests, among the other aristocratic ladies of the town of Todi, at Jacopone's command, she had to sit, dressed up like a beauty queen. In the midst of the festive exuberance, the platform suddenly collapsed and came crashing down, burying the guests of honor—among them Vanna—in the ruins.

When Jacopone drew his beloved wife from the wreckage, she was dying. He opened her belt and bodice so as to give her some relief and found beneath the gorgeous gown a girdle made of goat's hair against the tender young body of his badly injured wife. The dying woman whispered haltingly into her husband's ear, "That was for you!"

The sudden death of his wife had already shaken the high-spirited attorney profoundly; the additional realization that she had been concealing from him a life of penance left him entirely speechless. He had not had the faintest idea of his wife's real character and intentions! What deep conviction his wife had, with her chaste and hidden purity and piety, in contrast to his superficial striving for effect. Completely caught up in his foolish ostentation and zest for life, he had not even been aware of what was going on within the person closest to him. He had thrust upon Vanna a life of luxury and had required her to parade about beside him in conspicuously expensive clothing, while she had longed passionately for a modest Christian way of life and had worn a hair shirt in reparation for the vainglory that had been imposed on her. This violation of Vanna's soul that he had committed caused Jacopone the most bitter pangs of conscience as he knelt beside her coffin.

Until that hour, Jacopone the attorney had been a money-hungry lawyer who greedily stirred up the disputes of his clients instead of settling them. When he had to face the corpse of his beloved wife, however, everything went black. The inconsolable husband found consolation only when someone reminded him of the Mother of Sorrows beneath the Cross on Golgotha. With each of the seven sorrows piercing her heart, she seems to cry out to all sinners, "That was for you!" Jacopone underwent a conversion, gave up his brilliant career, divided all his wealth among the poor, and from then on thought of nothing but doing penance.

After ten years had passed, Jacopone decided to become a lay brother in the order of the Seraphic Saint. Humility prevented him from seeking Holy Orders; for his whole life he remained a simple lay brother. He performed the most menial tasks in the friary and glowed with an ardent love for Jesus Christ and his sorrowful Virgin Mother. The greatest sorrow he experienced as a friar was caused by his recognition that God is loved so little or not at all and is much offended instead, particularly by married couples, whose life together is so often without love and frequently marred by shameful abuses that disregard the real purpose of marriage.

Impelled by such insights, Jacopone began to censure the sins and vices of his day with reckless candor and to criticize wickedness and corruption in the various stations and classes of society, lamenting even abuses within the Church. In doing so he also railed against the power-hungry machinations of Pope Boniface VIII and was not afraid to employ the harshest terms: "Pope Boniface, you took possession of your office like a fox; you rule like a wolf; and you will end like a dog!" Pope Boniface was ruthless in dealing with his enemies, and Jacopone's boldness so infuriated him that he not only excommunicated him but also sentenced him to life imprisonment on bread and water.

Jacopone endured this with perfect humility, but he appealed to the pope in a moving poem with the request that he at least lift the excommunication. This request, which he repeated in the Jubilee Year of 1300, was not granted. Only through the general amnesty proclaimed by Pope Benedict XI, who was elected in 1303, were Jacopone's prison doors opened. He went then to the Franciscan friary at Collazzone, where he continued his austere life of penance, until his death on Christmas night in 1306.

While on his deathbed the former playboy continued to compose moving songs ("Laudi") in praise of Christ and his Virgin Mother. His most beautiful and touching hymn—which is said to be worth a whole volume of poetry—is the sequence *Stabat mater*, which originated in his bitter suffering after the tragic death of his beautiful and beloved young wife, Vanna.

Blessed
Raymund Lull
and
Blanca Picany

b. ca. 1233 at Palma de Mallorca, Spain
d. between December 1315 and March 25, 1316, while returning from Tunis to
Majorca

Married 1256
Father of two children

Raymund (Ramón) Lull[1] was born in 1232 or 1233 in Palma de Mallorca to a noble family originally from Barcelona; at the age of fourteen he became a page at the court of King James I of Aragon and then the tutor and seneschal (steward in charge of the kitchen and dining hall) of the king's third son, Prince James II of Majorca.

In 1256 this extremely high-spirited young man married Blanca Picany, who bore him two children, Dominicus and Magdalena. When he was thirty-one years old—this was in June 1263— Raymund Lull was composing a rather questionable *canzone* for a lady "with whom he was foolishly in love," as he himself wrote, when suddenly the crucified Lord Jesus Christ appeared to him; this happened again several times afterward. On October 4, 1263, in the Church of the Friars Minor in Palma, after the bishop preached a fiery sermon portraying Saint Francis' total devotion to God, Raymund decided to begin a new life. He made a lengthy pilgrimage through France and Spain. In 1264, on the advice of Saint Raymund of Peñafort, he returned to his home and family on the island of Majorca. He began to study intensively and deepened his knowledge of religion. After nine years of studies, most

---

[1] Cf. *Acta Sanctorum Junii* 7:581–676; C. da Langasco, "Beato martire Raimondo Lullo", in *Bibliotheca Sanctorum* 8:372–75; E. W. Platzek, *Raimund Lull* (Düsseldorf, 1962/63), 2 vols.

of them spent in solitude on Mount Randa, a miraculous intuition into the coherence of religious truths was granted to him, together with a clear understanding of the purpose of his life henceforth: to be a missionary for the conversion of the Jews and Muslims. Nothing could keep him at home now, neither wife nor children nor property. Obsessed by the idea of starting to win back the dechristianized areas in Africa and Asia Minor, Raymund Lull spent the following years traveling repeatedly through a large part of the lands bordering the Mediterranean. Despite stonings, beatings, and imprisonment, he did not cease preaching boldly, in season and out of season, to the Jews and Muslims, proclaiming God as one and triune and Jesus Christ as the incarnate Son of God. With clairvoyance he called for a concerted effort of Christians for the conversion of nonbelievers and those of different beliefs; he worked out plans for crusades, complete with the economic, political, and military details, and likewise plans for reorganizing the Church's universal missionary activity.

He was not content with developing plans for the conversion of Jews and Muslims, however; he himself set about attempting it in the course of various missionary journeys. At intervals he continued to apply his first-rate knowledge of philosophy and theology to the task of writing, and in almost innumerable works he demonstrated, in theory as well, how the Jews and the Muslims can and must be won over to the Christian faith.

During the last missionary journey that the then eighty-year-old Franciscan tertiary made to Tunis, the people stoned him. Half-dead, he set out on the return trip to Majorca. He died along the way some time between December 1315 and March 25, 1316.

One thing about the life of Blessed Raymund Lull that would be of particular interest in this book about married saints is the question of how this blessed dealt with his marriage and his family. Yet he himself is silent about this, as are without exception the authors who have written about the life and work of this important missionary to the Muslims in the Middle Ages and profoundly mystical writer. When the hour of his conversion struck and he realized that God was calling him to be a confessor and to lead other men out of Judaism and Islam to the true faith, did he simply leave his wife and his two children behind, convinced that God was calling him away from them? That is to say, is the case of Raymund Lull similar to that of Saint Nicholas von Flüe? Or did Raymund's wife and his two daughters voluntarily stay behind, or had death already carried them off before Raymund Lull devoted himself definitively to his missionary work? In any case, in examining the life of this missionary, one senses that celibacy and not marriage is probably the life-style more suitable for such a task, according to the words of the Apostle to the Gentiles, Saint Paul, in the First Letter to the Corinthians (1 Cor 7:32–34).

Blessed
Alda
and
Bindo Bellanti

b. February 28, 1245, in Siena, Tuscany, Italy
d. April 26, 1309, in Siena

In Siena (Tuscany, Italy) during the first half of the thirteenth century lived an exemplary couple: the merchant Pietro-Francesco Ponzi, who lived by the motto "Honest in business, Christian in conduct", and his wife, Agnes, née Bulgarini. They yearned to have a child, but for a long time their marriage remained childless. Then one night Agnes had a remarkable dream: Her bedroom was brightly illuminated, and she gave birth to a baby girl who was immediately surrounded by many people; from heaven the woman heard a voice that said to her, "Raise this child very carefully, for God has chosen her for himself!"

As it happened, Signora Agnes soon became pregnant, and she did indeed give birth to a dear daughter. After the Baptism, during which the child received the name Aldobrandesca (Alda for short), the woman told her husband for the first time about the dream she had had and asked him to cooperate in raising the child to be a good girl for God's sake. Both mother and father conscientiously made every effort to provide their child with an excellent Christian upbringing and education.[1] Alda matured into a pretty, intelligent, and pious young lady, who soon attracted the longing glances of the young men of Siena.

One day the young nobleman Bindo Bellanti asked Alda's parents for their daughter's hand in marriage. They soon consented, because the young man was not only from an aristocratic family

---

[1] Cf. *Acta Sanctorum Aprilis* 3:466–72; P. Burchi, "B. Aldobrandesca", in *Bibliotheca Sanctorum* 1:751–52.

but also had an ideal character and a good education. They forgot what had been said to them even before the birth of their child.

Alda herself, to be sure, told the young man that she really wanted and ought to enter religious life, but that in obedience to her parents she would agree to marry him.

The wedding took place. The young couple at first followed the biblical example of Tobias and Sarah. After a certain period of time, though, they decided after all to make use of their marital rights so as to bring children into the world. But this did not come about, because Bindo Bellanti suddenly became very sick with a strange, extremely unpleasant illness. Alda cared for her husband with fervent love and hoped to be able to nurse him back to health. Death, however, overtook him rather quickly. It really appeared as though this marriage was not in keeping with God's plan. He had placed his hand upon her, even before she was born, and said, "You are mine."

After the death of her husband, Alda entered the third order of the Humiliati, a thriving religious community at that time, and led a stirring life of penance and love of God and neighbor. With increasing frequency the young widow experienced extraordinary phenomena, which indicated God's predilection for her. In ecstasies and visions the Lord drew his bride closer and closer to himself and mystically gave her a share in his Passion; he also gave her the charism of performing dramatic cures and miracles even during her lifetime.

Blessed Alda spent the final years of her life in Saint Andrew's Hospital in Siena, where she devoted herself to the poor patients with extraordinary generosity and self-sacrifice. She died on April 26, 1309, at the age of sixty-four.

Blessed
Angela of Foligno
and
Spouse

b. 1248 in Foligno, Umbria, Italy
d. January 4, 1309

Mother of several children

After a woodcut dated 1521

This saintly wife and mother has been described as a mystic who contemplated the mysteries of the Trinity and the Holy Eucharist, but there is good reason to include her also among the great devotees of the Sacred Heart of Jesus.[1] In this book, she may also be considered one of those married saints who can serve as an example to Christian couples, if only as regards her profound remorse over the errors and sins she committed during her marriage.

Angela was born in 1248, the child of noble parents, in Foligno in the province of Umbria. On account of her extraordinary beauty, even as a girl, many young men were infatuated with her. While still very young, she was married to a wealthy young land-owner who allowed her to indulge her inclinations to idle pleasures, luxurious clothing, and amusing society. Although the marriage was blessed with several children, Angela did not change her life-style one bit. In all probability she neglected the care and education of her children and was not very punctilious about marital fidelity.

At the age of thirty-seven, however, Angela suddenly and quite

---

[1] Cf. *Angela von Foligno: Gesichte und Tröstungen* (Stein am Rhein, 1975); F. Holböck, *Das Allerheiligste und die Heiligen*, 2d ed. (Stein am Rhein, 1986), pp. 135–43; F. Holböck, *Aufblick zum Durchbohrten* (Stein am Rhein, 1990), pp. 124–28.

unexpectedly was overcome with disgust for her superficial and sinful way of life, which evidently involved serious sins. All at once Angela was tortured, day and night, by unbearable spiritual pangs.

In her autobiography (*Memoriale*), Angela admitted in these words:

> Indeed, I began to be ashamed of my sins, but this shame hindered me from making a complete confession. So it happened that I frequently received Holy Communion without having made a good confession beforehand. Thus I received the Body of the Lord in a state of mortal sin. Because of this I was now disturbed by pangs of conscience by day and by night. One day I prayed to Saint Francis to help me find an experienced father confessor, who would be able to understand my state of soul and to whom I could confess everything with complete sincerity.

She soon found such a confessor in Brother Arnold, a Friar Minor who was distantly related to her. To him she made an honest confession of all the sins that she had ever committed—this was in the year 1285. This priest now became her spiritual director and also her secretary, who recorded both her autobiographical notes and also her mystical visions and the other revelations that were granted to her. After her conversion, Angela began to perform severe penances for the sins of her married life. At the same time, God himself admitted her to a hard school of suffering, for in quick succession her mother, her husband, and all of her children, too, were snatched away from her by death.

The widowed penitent now bound herself by vows of perpetual chastity and strict poverty and designated that her great wealth should be used to support the poor and the sick in her town. In 1291 she asked to join the third order of Saint Francis and was admitted. From then on Angela's desire to please only the crucified Savior grew ever stronger. She made his Passion and death the constant theme of her meditation. The Cross—as she emphasized on several occasions—now became her resting place. She loved ever more fervently the Lord on the Cross, with his five wounds, especially the wound in his side and his pierced heart; he was the Bridegroom of her soul, who claimed all her love. From then on Angela received special graces with increasing frequency: the ecstasies and visions began. In her autobiography she says, "I received the special grace and privilege of looking upon the Cross, upon which I saw, both in the flesh and with the eyes of my soul, Christ, who died for us. At the same time, to my great sorrow, I became aware of all of my sins; indeed, I felt that *I* was the one who had crucified Him."

In the time after her conversion, the widow Angela became the mother and instructor of many spiritual sons and daughters in the town of Foligno and far beyond; from the lips of this mystically gifted woman they could hear very practical and effective lessons in asceticism and mystical doctrine that was preeminently sound. From her humble cell she sent to her disciples messages and admonishments concerning the proper manner of loving God and following after the crucified Christ.

On January 4, 1309, this wife and mother died, after twenty-four years of striving, through penitential practices and love for the Crucified, to make reparation for all of the failings of her married life.

Saint Elizabeth of Portugal and Denis

b. 1271 in Barcelona or Zaragoza
d. July 4, 1336, between Portugal and Castile

Married June 24, 1288
Mother of two children
Canonized May 25, 1625

Elizabeth of Portugal with Two Crowns (Jan Provoost, Genoa, Galeria di Palazzo Bianco, 15th–16th century)

Saint Elizabeth (Isabella) of Portugal was a saint who succeeded brilliantly in making peace and mediating disputes, in her family and in her marriage.[1] Christian married couples experiencing disagreements and conflict in their marriage and family could take this saintly wife and mother as an example and, of course, call upon her as a powerful intercessor. Before the great reform of the liturgy, the fourth reading of the second nocturn at the hour of Matins on her feast day (July 8) said: "At her birth it immediately became apparent what a happy peacemaker between kings and countries this saint would become; for joy over her birth transformed the calamitous feud between her father and her grandfather into a cordial harmony." And the Church used to pray: "Most gracious God, thou hast endowed the holy queen Elizabeth with many noble gifts, among them the privilege of putting an end to terrible wars; grant to us by her intercession, after the peace for

[1] Cf. S. A. Rodriguez, *Reinha Santa* (Coimbra, 1958; *Acta Sanctorum Julii* 2:169–213; L. Chierotti, "Elisabetta, regina del Portogallo", in *Bibliotheca Sanctorum* 4:1096–98.

which we humbly pray in this passing life, the grace of obtaining eternal happiness."

This noble aristocratic woman was born in the year 1271 (some say in Barcelona, others say in Zaragoza), the daughter of Peter III of Aragon (d. 1285) and Constance, daughter of Manfred, the Hohenstaufen king of Sicily. She was the granddaughter of Emperor Frederick II and the great-niece of Saint Elizabeth of Hungary, whose name she received at her Baptism, only forty years after the holy countess had been declared a saint by Pope Gregory IX in 1235.

In 1283, at the age of twelve, Elizabeth was engaged, for dynastic reasons, to Denis, the king of Portugal, and on June 24, 1288, they were married. The seventeen-year-old queen would give her husband two children: in 1290 a daughter, Constance, who later married Ferdinand IV (d. 1342), the king of Castile, and in 1291 a son, Alfonso, who then succeeded his father on the royal throne as Alfonso IV of Portugal.

Elizabeth's marriage with King Denis turned out to be not very happy at first, because of her royal consort's easy-going life-style. But Elizabeth endured all the insults and slights on account of the king's mistresses with great patience and forgiving love. To atone for the adulterous escapades of the king, Elizabeth undertook austere penitential practices and lived a life of renunciation and prayer as though she belonged to a religious order. She prayed, sacrificed, and made reparation in order to obtain the conversion of her husband. In doing so, she thought nothing of herself and did not weep for the many wrongs that had been done to her, but rather lamented that God was so much offended. Indeed, she even accepted lovingly the children of her husband's mistresses and raised them as her own children in Christian discipline and piety.

Finally, after a long and sorrowful time of trials, the queen managed to convince the king to give up his immoral way of life; she guided him to a serious conversion, so that afterward he even became an example for Christian husbands and princes.

Enraged that she had obtained the king's conversion, the wicked foe tried to take revenge on the queen through base calumnies. A jealous page slandered the queen, accusing her of having an immoral relationship with another page. But God himself defended the innocence of Queen Elizabeth against all the insinuations of the jealous page. Through a mistake that was probably providential, the slanderer himself, instead of the falsely accused page, met his death in a fiery limekiln. Friedrich Schiller dramatized this episode in the poem "Der Gang zum Eisenhammer".

Again and again Queen Elizabeth negotiated peace within the royal family through her serious admonishments and insistent pleas: in 1299 at Portalegre between King Denis and his rebellious brother Alfonso; in 1321 at Coimbra and then once more in 1323 between King Denis and his son, Alfonso. The queen intervened in this quarrel between father and son like an angel of peace; she placed herself between the adherents of the two men as they were fighting and convinced them to lay down their weapons. Then, when she was accused of partiality toward her son, Alfonso, and was therefore supposed to be confined to Alemquer until she had admitted her error, King Denis demonstrated his unconditional esteem for his wife and commanded that she be set free. Soon after the death of her husband, the queen mediated between her son, Alfonso, and his half-brother Sanchez.

While King Denis was seriously ill, Queen Elizabeth cared for him with tremendous love and selfless devotion; she considered not only his sick body, but also his sick soul, and she prepared her husband to die completely reconciled with God. The former adulterer ultimately died a holy and truly edifying death on January 6, 1325, at Santarem.

Now a widow, Queen Elizabeth devoted herself exclusively to works of charity. She sold her belongings, especially her costly jewelry, and gave the proceeds to the poor and to the convents she had founded, and from then on she dressed like a Franciscan tertiary. In that garb she made a pilgrimage to Santiago de Compostela. Upon returning home to Coimbra, she withdrew to the convent of Poor Clares that she had founded; nevertheless, in order to have the freedom to perform her works of charity, she put off taking the vows of that order until shortly before her death.

In this final period of her life, too, Queen Elizabeth repeatedly made her influence felt for the common good and the restoration of peace. She left the convent one last time in order to make peace again between her son, Alfonso, and her son-in-law, Ferdinand IV, during the war between Portugal and Castile. The sixty-five-year-old queen hastened to the battlefield, despite the oppressive heat in the summer of 1336. The mere news that she was approaching brought about a cessation of the military conflict. When the queen arrived in Estremoz on the Portuguese border, however, she came down with a high fever that would lead to her death. She died in the arms of her son and daughter-in-law on July 4, 1336. Her body was brought to Coimbra and buried there in the church of the Poor Clares. On May 25, 1625, Pope Urban VIII solemnly canonized this great noblewoman, who managed so magnificently to make peace in her marriage, in her family, and among the peoples of the Iberian Peninsula.

Saint Elzear
and
Blessed Delphina

Elzear:
> b. ca. 1285 in Ansouis, Provence,
> France
> d. September 27, 1323, in Paris

Canonized 1369

Delphina:
> b. ca. 1282 in Puy-Michel
> d. November 26, 1360, in Apt

Married 1299

Picture of Delphina, Stampa populare,
nineteenth century

Saint Elzear of Sabran and his wife, Blessed Delphina of Glandèves,[1] were a truly Christian married couple who practiced continence and lived as virgins for the entire duration of their marriage.

Elzear de Sabran was born in 1285 in the castle of Ansouis, a village in Provence situated between the towns of Apt and Aix. He was the son of Ermangaus, who was lord of Sabran and count of Ariano Irpino (Avelino, in the kingdom of Naples, Italy) as well as count of Lauduna d'Albe de Roquemartine, and his pious wife, the countess of Lauduna. This saintly mother took little Elzear in her arms after his Baptism and asked God to take the child back immediately if he foresaw that otherwise Elzear would someday stain his soul with mortal sin. The count's young son was diligent and pious and loved the poor, and these traits were reinforced by the excellent education bestowed on him by his uncle William of

---

[1] Cf. *Acta Sanctorum Septembris* 7:494–555; G. Duhamelet, *S. Eléazar de Sabran et la B. Delphine* (Paris, 1944).

Sabran, the abbot of the famous Benedictine abbey of Saint Victor in Marseilles.

Around 1282, at any rate three years before the birth of Elzear of Sabran, Delphina (Dauphine) was born in Puy-Michel in the Lubéron mountains. She was a descendant of the noble family of Glandèves. She was betrothed to Elzear at the age of fourteen. At first she was opposed to the wedding, but she finally gave in when Elzear assured her that for the time being he would not make use of his marital rights. Two years after their engagement, in 1299, the wedding took place. It was Delphina's ardent desire, by all means, to remain a virgin, despite the marriage. Elzear respected his wife's intention, and they finally vowed to live together as brother and sister in a virginal marriage.

After his father's death, Elzear inherited various titles and estates, including the county of Ariano in Italy. He traveled there but received at first a hostile reception from the populace. Nevertheless, Elzear managed to win the hearts of the people in his county through his kindly, modest manners and his generosity. Every day he hosted twelve poor people at his table. With remarkable calm and self-control, he bore the affronts that occurred now and then, saying, "They said even more malicious things about Christ."

As a member of the third order of Saint Francis of Assisi, he prayed the Church's Liturgy of the Hours, performed strict penances, and cared selflessly and lovingly for the sick. Elzear also proved to be an excellent government minister and colonel in the army of King Robert of Naples. When Emperor Henry VII of Luxembourg besieged Rome in 1312, King Robert of Naples gave Elzear command over all the soldiers loyal to the pope and fighting to defend him. He succeeded in forcing the imperial troops to withdraw from the beleaguered city.

Elzear was commissioned by King Robert to lead a delegation to the French court in Paris, so as to arrange a marriage between the king's son Charles and Princess Marie of Valois. During this stay in Paris, Elzear became so seriously ill that he died, on September 27, 1323, at the age of only thirty-eight. He was buried in Apt in the Franciscan church there as a member of the third order who had been particularly faithful in keeping the Rule. The notable Franciscan theologian François de Maironis, who may well have been Elzear's confessor, gave the funeral oration. In the year 1369 Elzear was declared a saint by his godchild, Pope Urban V, whose ascent to the papal throne he had predicted.

Elzear's like-minded wife, Delphina, also led a life that was very pleasing to God. She, too, was a Franciscan tertiary. After her husband's death she left Ariano and the kingdom of Naples, where Elzear had rendered such salutary service at the royal court. She disposed of her large estates and then retired to Apt, north of Marseilles, to live a life of prayer, penance, and beneficence. After she died on November 26, 1360, in Apt, she was buried at the side of her saintly husband. Pope Innocent XII declared Delphina blessed.

Devotion to these holy spouses, Elzear and Delphina, is very popular, both in France and in southern Italy. They demonstrate quite forcefully to married couples that marriage is much more than just a matter of satisfying one's sexual urges.

Blessed
Michelina of Pesaro
and
Spouse

b. 1300–1316 in Pesaro, central
Italy
d. June 19, 1356, in Pesaro

Married ca. 1312–1328
Mother of one son
Cult approved on April 24, 1737

Michelina[1] was born sometime between 1300 and 1316 in Pesaro, the daughter of the wealthy nobleman Antonio dei Pardi Metelli and his wife.

When she was only twelve, the girl's parents gave her to a man from the house of Malatesta to be his wife. Michelina's marriage to this husband was in keeping with their noble station, but by no means did they lead an edifying Christian life together. One child was enough already for the young parents; having more children would have required too many sacrifices. Was it a case of exhausting their resources too soon on a life of excessive comfort and missing out on an honest search for a deeper meaning in life? At any rate, the husband died during the eighth year of their marriage.

The twenty-year-old widow became acquainted with a woman named Sira, or Soriana, who had come from Syria to Pesaro and whose exemplary Christian way of life made a deep impression on her. Michelina took this woman into her home. As a result, she herself gradually changed her way of living. Then, when her only

---

[1] *Acta Sanctorum Junii* 3:927–29; P. A. Bierbaum, O.F.M., *Heilige Vorbilder aus der Familie des hl. Franziskus* (Werl, 1933), pp. 379–81.

child, her son, Pardino, suddenly died, Michelina began a completely new life with Soriana: she renounced her wealth and lived in extreme poverty and seclusion, dedicating herself single-mindedly to works of mercy. She continually strove to live according to the evangelical counsels, in poverty, penance, and piety, as a tertiary in the third order of Saint Francis. Her fervent devotion to the sufferings of Christ awoke in her the desire to see for herself the places in the Holy Land where our Lord underwent his Passion. She did in fact set out on a pilgrimage to the Holy Land. There she took care of lepers for a time. On Mount Calvary in Jerusalem the grace of a consoling vision was granted to her.

After returning home to Pesaro, Michelina performed austere penances to make reparation for her sins, failings, and negligence during her marriage. On June 19, 1356, she died. Her cult as a blessed received the official approval of the Church on April 24, 1737.

Saint Bridget of Sweden

and

Ulf Gudmarsson

*b. June 1303, in Finta Manor in
    the village of Skederik,
    Uppland, Sweden*
d. July 23, 1373, in Rome

Married September 1316
Mother of eight children
Canonized 1391

In Saint Bridget (Birgitta) of Sweden we find a truly extraordinary woman who set an excellent example in various states of life, as a virgin, as a wife and the mother of a family, as a widow, and then as the foundress of a religious order. Here we will describe her only as a Christian wife and mother during the years of her married life.[1]

Bridget's father, Birger Persson, was *lagman* (chieftain) of the Uppland region in Sweden. After the death of his first wife, Kristina Johannsdotter, in 1295, he married Ingeborg Bengtsdotter. His second marriage was blessed by God with seven children: three sons (Peter, Bengt, and Israel) and four daughters (Ingrid, Margaret, Bridget, and Catherine).

Bridget was born in June 1303 in Finta Manor in the village of Skederik (province of Uppland). When she was thirteen years old, she thought of dedicating her whole life to God as a consecrated virgin. Her father, though, had other plans for her. For political reasons he sought closer ties between his family and the family of his colleague Gudmar, the *lagman* of Närke. The latter had two

---

[1] Cf. F. Holböck, *Gottes Nordlicht: Birgitta von Schweden und ihre Offenbarungen*, 2d ed. (Stein am Rhein, 1988).

eligible sons, Ulf and Magnus; Birger, on the other hand, had two eligible daughters, Catherine and Bridget. Now, Catherine was supposed to marry Magnus Gudmarsson, and Bridget was to wed Ulf Gudmarsson. Accordingly, Bridget married, as one of the oldest accounts of the saint's life puts it, "non voluptatis, sed paternae voluntatis causa" (not because of carnal desire, but on account of her father's will).

The double wedding took place in September 1316. The wedding day was not a happy day for Bridget, since she "had desired and longed only to serve the Lord in the virginal state". Later, Saint Bridget would often tell her saintly daughter Catherine that she would have preferred then to die rather than to marry.

Nevertheless, that wedding day was the start of a relatively happy married life that, in any case, was led according to Christian principles and was blessed with eight children; the marriage lasted twenty-eight years, through joys and sorrows, from 1316 to 1344, the year of Ulf's death.

On her wedding night, when Bridget was alone with her husband, Ulf, for the first time, she reminded him of the example given in the Old Testament book of Tobit, in which that young man and his bride, Sarah, promised each other that at first they would exercise a tactful, dignified restraint with regard to sexual relations in marriage. For this reason Bridget and Ulf followed the biblical example and lived together as brother and sister for more than a year, as the bull of canonization and the oldest account of Saint Bridget's life both emphasize. The continence they practiced for one to two years is in marked contrast to the sexual conduct of young people in our time!

Let us take a closer look, now, at this young married couple, who lived in Sweden, which had become Christian only two hundred years previously.

Ulf Gudmarsson, the son of Gudmar Magnusson, the *lagman* of Västergötland, was eighteen years old in September 1316 when he married the thirteen-year-old Bridget. The chronicle of Abbess Margareta Clausdotter portrays him as "a very good, pious, upright and God-fearing young man, who was, moreover, quite

The following text appears within the illustration border:

ORATE · PRO · NOBIS · ET · EIVS · VXOR

DOMINA · INGEBVRGIS · CVM · FILIIS · EORVM · QVORVM · ANIME · REQVI

ESCANT · IN · PACE · hIC · IACET · NOBIL

VIROR · DNS · DOMINVS · BIRGERVS · PETRI · FILIVS · LEGIFER · VPLANDIARVM

The parents of Saint Bridget (Cathedral of Upsala)

243

experienced in everything". He probably had not had extensive schooling at that time, for he is described further as *simplex*, which probably means here "uneducated". It was his young wife, Bridget, who taught Ulf to read and write. Under her direction, though, he made great strides, both in learning and in piety. He progressed to the point where he could pray the *Little Office of the Blessed Virgin Mary*, the "layman's breviary" of that era, and, together with Bridget, he became a tertiary in the third order of Saint Francis. The young man also diligently pursued his studies in law, so that by 1330 he was capable of assuming the important office of *lagman* of Närke in central Sweden.

After their wedding, Ulf settled with his young wife in Ulvåsa, which is about five miles distant from the town of Motala. There he lived—whenever he was not away on business—for the twenty-eight years of his marriage with Bridget, on an extensive farm. As *lagman*, Ulf had to attend to duties in his territory or at the royal court, but he always loved to return to his estate. No doubt he was drawn there by unshakable fidelity and by his tender love for his wife, Bridget, and by their common care for the growing number of children God sent into their marriage.

We have mentioned that the marriage of Saint Bridget and her pious husband, Ulf, was blessed with eight children. Their married life, however, did not consist exclusively of begetting, carrying, bearing, feeding, and rearing children. Rather, from a perspective of faith, Bridget and Ulf knew the significance that marriage must have for spouses. Each one was a support for the other and, at the same time, a sweet burden; together they journeyed and rested on their way to the kingdom of heaven. In the married state Bridget proved to be that "strong woman" who is portrayed so vividly in the Old Testament book of Proverbs 31:10–30.

The oldest *Life* of Saint Bridget says,

> She loved God and watched over her conduct so that no one could accuse her of wrongdoing. She fled all frivolity and irresponsible persons and had only respectable maids in her house. She was careful to lead her domestics, too, in the way of serving

God and being of assistance to their neighbors. She revered Jesus Christ with her prayers and her tears, to such an extent that, when her husband was away, she would keep watch for the entire night, striving to discipline her body through many genuflections and mortifications.

This description of Bridget is noteworthy, inasmuch as it emphasizes what she did as a wife, during the frequent absences of her husband for business reasons, in order to observe continence as necessary within her marriage. She was able to put into practice what Pope Pius XI expresses even in the title of his encyclical on marriage, *Casti connubii*:

In order that marital fidelity might shine forth in its full glory, even the familiar intercourse of the spouses with one another must bear the mark of chastity. Married couples, therefore, must conduct themselves in everything according to the norms of divine law and natural law and always strive to obey the will of the all-wise and all-holy Creator, with the greatest reverence for the work of God.

Through prayer, vigils, and ascetical sacrifices, Bridget succeeded in preserving marital fidelity and chastity (in the sense of occasional continence as needed). It has already been mentioned that the newlyweds, who were still quite young, decided at the beginning of their marriage to renounce sexual relations entirely at first. Then they did so year after year throughout the season of Lent, as well as on major feasts and on the Friday of each week, as the old *Lives* of Saint Bridget and the bull of canonization by Pope Boniface IX explicitly mention. In the period immediately before or after their pilgrimage together to Santiago de Compostela in Spain, Bridget and her husband, Ulf, decided to observe complete continence for the rest of their married life. They even agreed to set each other free of their marital obligations so that they could enter religious life; this actually took place in the Cistercian monastery at Alvastra.

The bull of canonization by Pope Boniface IX says,

Bridget looked well to the ways of her household and did not eat the bread of idleness [cf. Prov 31:27]. She opened her hand to the poor and reached out her hands to the needy [cf. Prov 31:20], because for God's sake she untiringly performed the duties of an inexhaustible charity toward the needy, the sick, and the despised. Even while her husband was still alive, she invited twelve poor people to dine at her house each day, waited on them herself and gave them all they needed; every Thursday she washed their feet in memory of the Lord's Last Supper. Using her own income, she restored ruined hospitals in several regions of her native land; she visited the poor and the sick there most diligently as a loving, merciful, and industrious servant. . . . She touched, washed, bandaged, and tended their wounds without horror or loathing. She was animated by a marvelous patience, so that she bore the infirmities of her own body, the insults of others, as well as all the contradictions of life, with touching humility and resignation to the will of God. She praised the Lord and became more and more steadfast in faith, firm in hope, and ardent in charity. She loved above all else justice and righteousness and despised the lusts of the flesh with its various temptations. Being noble-minded, she looked down on the vainglory of empty show and reputation. Whose wisdom could compare with the superior understanding of this woman, which was evident from earliest childhood until her final hour? As far as human frailty permitted, she was able to employ correctly in all matters the gift of discerning spirits, and she never called good evil or evil good; nor did she make light out of darkness or darkness out of light.

It is a magnificent tribute that Pope Boniface IX paid to the housewife Bridget of Sweden in his bull of canonization, and it is a well-founded one, since the cause of this Swedish woman had been investigated very thoroughly.

Given the times in which this noble couple lived their Christian

Bas-relief of Saint Bridget
(school of Bernini, Casa Santa Birgitta, Rome, 17th century)

married life, it goes without saying that they experienced cares and sorrows as well. Civil war raged throughout the land. Ulf and his men had to go to war. Bridget, however, who in her husband's absence had to manage the entire estate at Ulvåsa, accompanied him in spirit with her prayers and good wishes. The bloody events weighed heavily on Bridget's soul.

After peace was restored in the Swedish kingdom, the joyful day came in 1328 when Bridget's husband, Ulf, was dubbed a knight. The ideal of Swedish manhood, in Lady Bridget's eyes, was that of the Christian knight, who considers it his highest honor, and swears by God, the Blessed Virgin Mary, and Saint Eric "to defend, to the best of my ability, the Church and the Kingdom, orphans, virgins, and widows". In one passage of her *Revelations*, Saint Bridget cries out, "There is no harder life than the life of Christian knighthood, which is dedicated to spreading the true faith." She explains, "The monk has a white habit; the knight a breastplate and a shield of iron. The monk has his own bed, hard though it may be, but the knight must lie down in his armor. And although monastic self-denial is difficult, it is yet harder to be in constant danger of death while facing a heavily armed foe."

Bridget's husband, Ulf, who was named *Lagman* of Närke in

1330, owned mansions, mines, and iron-works in his province. Through inheritances and purchases the couple's property, which was already quite extensive, grew considerably. As a result of these circumstances, Ulf gradually became one of the most influential men in the entire land. Despite this, Bridget remained simply a helpful mother, at the service of her family and her people. She not only cared for her growing family, but also prudently supervised the conduct of her maids. Every evening she gathered her domestics in the spinning room, as is the Nordic custom, and read to them from Sacred Scripture or from the lives of the Saints. She did not like to scold and punished only when necessary. Later on, she accused herself of having committed sins of omission by being insufficiently strict. Her motherly care for the corporal and spiritual welfare of the people on the estate at Ulvåsa allowed her no leisure. "Bridget hated idleness", one of her contemporaries assures us. Yet this woman had a critical attitude toward wealth and comfortable living because she knew how dangerous they could be. Bridget viewed her property merely as a loan that God had entrusted to her stewardship, and she said, "Everything that a man owns over and above his personal needs is excess and should be shared compassionately with others." That is why her generosity often knew no bounds.

To conclude this portrait of Saint Bridget's life as a spouse, mother, and housewife, we can only add and affirm what Pope Paul VI wrote in a letter to Bishop John Taylor of Stockholm on September 29, 1973:

As wife and mother, [Bridget] was a shining example; she lived united to her husband by the bond of Christian love, and she reared her eight children with discerning wisdom, that is to say, she wished them to grow up to be not only good citizens of their fatherland, but also servants and children of God. And so it came about that the seeds of religious vocation came to flower among her offspring. Indeed, her second daughter, Catherine, with the aid of divine grace, reached the heights of sanctity. Nor may we neglect to mention the charity of St. Bridget lavished on the members of Christ suffering from poverty or other distress.[2]

Since the marriage of Saint Bridget with her noble husband, Ulf, was blessed by God with eight children, we might also note what happened in the lives of these children.

1. The first child, named Marta, was born in 1319 or 1320. As an adult she married a rich but stern man named Siwid Ribbing. Bridget suspected that this would be the beginning of an unhappy marriage. From this marriage issued one son, Peter Ribbing, who lost his life on a pilgrimage to the Holy Land. After the death of her first husband, Marta married Knut Algotsson, a wealthy man with properties in Sweden, Norway, and Halland. From this marriage she had two daughters, Catherine and Ingegerda Knudsdotter; the latter became the abbess of the convent of Saint Bridget in Vadstena.

2. Charles, born 1321, the lively, vain, rather superficial eldest son of Saint Bridget, caused her many cares. His irresponsibility and high spirits drew him into various adventures and led him into many sins. Charles was married three times. As to his political position, he succeeded his father, Ulf, as *lagman* of Närke. Charles died on March 12, 1372, in Naples, as he was setting out with his mother and his brother Birger on a pilgrimage to the Holy Land.

3. Birger, born in 1323, was, in contrast to his older brother, Charles, very serious and thoughtful and never gave his mother any trouble. When he went on pilgrimage to the Holy Land with his mother, he was already widowed once; soon afterward he married a second time. He died on August 27, 1391, as the guardian and custodian of the cloisters in Vadstena. His mother sent him a letter with fifteen valuable rules of life, which he followed conscientiously. It should also be mentioned that, from his first marriage to Benedicta Glysingsdotter, Birger had two sons, named Ulf and Gudmar, who both died young. Ulf, who had joined the monks of Vadstena, died before he made profession; Gudmar, who

[2] *L'Osservatore romano*, October 25, 1973, p. 5.

lived with his father, Birger, in Vadstena, but outside the monastery, died soon afterward. Birger's second marriage to Martha Siggesdotter remained childless.

4. Bengt (Benedict), born in 1326, wanted to enter the Cistercian monastery in Alvastra but died there before he received the habit.

5. Gudmar, born in 1327, died at the age of 11, during the time when he was going to school in Stockholm.

6. Catherine (Karin), born about 1331, Bridget's favorite daughter, was the co-worker and companion of her holy mother in Rome and on the Holy Land pilgrimage, and she herself matured in sanctity. She longed for religious life, yet at her father's behest she married the nobleman Eggard Lydersson von Kürnen (Kyren). On their wedding day, as she entered the bridal chamber with her husband, she spoke so enthusiastically of the virtues of temperance and chastity that the two newlyweds vowed perpetual continence. In the Jubilee Year 1350, Catherine, with her husband's consent, followed her saintly mother to Rome and then lived together with her there for twenty-three years as her most faithful disciple.

7. Ingeborg, born in 1332, was admitted to the Cistercian convent in Risaberg; she lived a holy life and died young, around the year 1350.

8. Cecilia was born in 1334; when she reached school age she was commended to the Dominican nuns in Skännige in Östergötland for her education, maybe in the hope that she would enter there someday. Cecilia had no inclination toward religious life, however. She decided to get married to the young knight Bengt Philippson. When he died in 1363, Cecilia married the physician at the royal court, Lars Johannsson.

As diverse as these eight children of Saint Bridget and her husband, Ulf, were in their natural gifts and temperaments, Bridget managed in each case to fulfill the command of the Mother of God, who once appeared to her and said, "Take care that these children of yours become my children also!" Even about the irresponsible son Charles we read in a contemporary chronicle that he had a special love for the Virgin Mary, the Mother of God, and often said that he would "rather languish in hell than allow Mary to be deprived of any of her honor".

Saint Bridget raised her children to be true children of Mary and genuine Christians, and she was anxious to keep all pernicious influences away from them. With her husband's approval, moreover, she urged her children from a tender age to perform works of charity for the needy and the sick. She deliberately brought them along on her visits to the sick in their homes or in hospitals, so that her children would witness her splendid example of willing, humble service. She also entrusted her growing children to wise instructors and tutors.

We should now turn again to the separation of Saint Bridget from her husband, Ulf, which at first was voluntary and then became definitive at his death. After the great pilgrimage to Santiago de Compostela that he made together with Bridget, Ulf wanted to dedicate himself entirely to God as a monk in the Cistercian abbey of Alvastra. As a novice he submitted eagerly and joyfully—to the extent that his health allowed—to the strict rule of the reformed branch of the Benedictine order. He died—before he made solemn profession—in the odor of sanctity on February 12, 1344. The same man who at the beginning of his marriage with Saint Bridget was a "typical Swedish knight who liked loud festivals and was an enthusiastic connoisseur of horses", with personal failings and weaknesses besides, matured under Bridget's influence in nobility and virtue until, at age forty-six, in the prime of life, he intended to serve God faithfully in religious life. God, however, had other plans.

Many biographers think that on the journey back from Santiago de Compostela, when her husband, Ulf, lay deathly ill in Arras, Bridget received her first illuminations concerning the order she was to found. She spent a few years as a guest in Alvastra. Here she was prepared by many mystical graces for her task of founding a religious order. So as to work more effectively for the foundation, Bridget went to Rome in 1349 and then in 1372–1373 made a pilgrimage to the Holy Land. The last twenty-four years of her life were spent in Rome, where she exerted a strong influence on the ecclesiastical and secular leaders of the day for the genuine renewal of the Church. Bridget died in Rome on July 23, 1373. In the year 1391 she was declared a saint.

Blessed
John Colombini

and

Biagia Cerretani

b. 1305 in Siena, Italy
d. July 31, 1367, in the Abbey
*   Santissimo Salvatore, near*
*   Acquapendente, Italy*

Father of two children

Painting by C. Incisione, Antwerp,
1634

During the years in which Saint Catherine, that uniquely gifted virgin and Doctor of the Church, made her hometown of Siena famous, a married man, John Colombini,[1] was carrying out an extremely effective apostolate in this same Tuscan town. He was born in Siena in the year 1305. He was apprenticed as a textile merchant, and in that trade he earned enough that he was able to marry and start a family. He married a woman by the name of Biagia Cerretani, who bore him two children; nothing is known of any other children. The "woe" that Jesus declared with respect to the rich, for whom it is difficult to enter the kingdom of heaven, may have had its effect upon this well-to-do, very worldly minded businessman. The hour of conversion suddenly struck for him when he was fifty years old. While he was waiting for his midday meal, which his wife was preparing for him as usual, he was seized with impatience because the food was not on the table at the proper time. To calm him down, his wife gave him the story

[1] Cf. *Acta Sanctorum Julii* 7:333–408; F. Belcari, *Vita del b. Giovanni Colombini da Siena* (Parma, 1839).

of Saint Mary of Egypt to read. The book made a profound impression on the merchant. He began to share his wealth with the poor. The many churches in Siena, which until then he probably knew only from the outside, became places where he spent more and more time in silent prayer. Often he stayed for hours on end in one of these churches, immersed in contemplative prayer. His was a continual conversion, and he combined his newfound spirituality with an active charity on behalf of all the needy people in Siena.

John Colombini's good example was infectious. A man by the name of Francis Vincenti came into contact with the converted merchant. The two began to live in extreme poverty and austerity. Finally, John Colombini made a vow of chastity, with his wife's consent. He placed his daughter in the convent of Saints Abundio and Abundanzio ("Santa Bonda"). With the exception of one portion for his wife, he made his entire fortune over to this convent. Then he began to lead a life very similar to that of Saint Francis of Assisi. As was the case with this Seraphic Saint, like-minded disciples joined John Colombini. Attracted by his virtues and the miracles that he was said to have worked, they, too, wanted to strive for perfection and sanctity.

Because of several idiosyncrasies in their way of life, John Colombini and his companions were suspected of heresy, and as a result they were reported to the Inquisition. This was a source of trouble and annoyance for the town officials. Consequently, the men were expelled from Siena. In this way, though, other towns in the vicinity of Siena, for example, Arezzo, Città di Castello, Lucca, Montalcino, Pisa, Florence, and Pistoia, came to hear about John Colombini. More and more people marveled at the example of poverty and penance set by Colombini and his disciples, who were soon nicknamed *Gesuati* (not "Jesuits"), because in their sermons and prayers they particularly loved to pronounce the name of Jesus and called on their listeners to follow Jesus. They always began and ended their prayers with the formula *"Viva Gesù* [Praised be Jesus]!"

When Pope Urban V returned from Avignon to Rome, he landed in the small harbor of Corneto on June 4, 1367, so as to stop along the way in Viterbo and spend some time there. The *Gesuati* were present at the welcome given to the Pope, and they paid him homage. He in turn granted them an audience and spoke at length with them. He approved their way of life and then even clothed them at his own expense in new habits: an alb worn under a dark mantle. Finally, he commended them to his brother, the cardinal bishop of Avignon, as their protector.

After this momentous event in the development of his community, John Colombini and his companions set out again on the way to Siena. In Bolsena, however, the blessed was stricken with a fever that soon was running very high. The sick man was brought to the monastery near Acquapendente named Santissimo Salvatore. There he died on July 31, 1367. The body was brought to the convent of Santa Bonda. The funeral ceremonies were held there in the convent church, attended by throngs of people and the local authorities.

Although John Colombini was never officially declared blessed, Pope Gregory XIII arranged for him to be included in the Roman Martyrology. Pope Paul V approved the readings for the Mass and the Divine Office in honor of this blessed, for use in the diocese of Siena and by the *Gesuati*. Their order flourished remarkably in Italy and Spain. In 1668, however, it was dissolved by Pope Clement IX because the members, who were supposed to work for the salvation of souls through prayer, works of penance and charity, and especially through the care of the sick, had strayed from the proper charism of their order.

Blessed John Colombini, husband and founder, wrote many informative letters, 140 of which are extant and have been edited and published by D. Fantozzi (Lanziano, 1925), as well as many lyrics (*laude*), among them a poem to Jesus Christ that begins with the words "Diletto Jesu Christo, chi ben t'ama [Dear Jesus, how much I love thee]."

Blessed
Joan Mary de Maillé
and
Robert de Sillé

b. April 14, 1331, Roche-Saint-Quentin, Touraine, France
d. March 28, 1414, in Tours

Married 1347
Cult approved on April 28, 1871

Born at Roche-Saint-Quentin (Touraine), Joan Mary,[1] while still an eleven-year-old girl, experienced the first of many visions granted to her: the Blessed Mother appeared to her with the Christ Child. Afterward the girl spontaneously consecrated herself to God, promising to contemplate our Lord's Passion in a special way. She received a good Christian upbringing, in which the influence of her family's Franciscan father confessor was especially important.

Against her will but in obedience, the sixteen-year-old Joan Mary married Baron Robert de Sillé in 1347. The couple decided to live their married life with their virginity intact and to forgo the joys of marital sex in order to devote themselves entirely to caring for the pitiable victims of the Black Plague (1346–1353). During fifteen years of marriage, the couple, in fact, radically renounced legitimate sexual relations, so as to place themselves in charity at the service of those who were sick with the plague. Is such resolve at all possible in young adulthood? By one's own power, certainly not, but it is possible with the grace of God.

Joan Mary's husband, Robert, was taken prisoner by the English and died in 1362, after 15 years of practicing continence within marriage. The widow was forced by the family of her departed

---

[1] Cf. M. de Crisenoy, *La bienheureuse Jeanne Marie de Maillé, la mystique des temps de misère* (Paris, 1948).

husband to leave the castle. She went to Tours and cared for the poor and the sick of the city. As a result of wrongful accusations, she had to hide for a time in the hermitage of Planche-de-Vaux. There she lived a contemplative life in poverty and penance. For reasons of health she returned to Tours in 1386, lived next door to the Franciscan monastery, and placed herself under the spiritual direction of the Franciscan Father Martin de Bois-Gaultier. Her reputation as a woman with gifts of understanding and prophecy spread far and wide, and soon people were coming to her for counsel. Filled with zeal for the restoration of religious and moral life in France, she traveled several times to the court of King Charles VI.

Joan Mary de Maillé died in Tours on March 28, 1414. Pope Pius IX declared on April 28, 1871, that the veneration of Blessed Joan Mary was justified.

Saint
Catherine of Vadstena
and
Eggard von Kürnen

b. ca. 1331 in Ulvåsa, Uppland, Sweden
d. March 24, 1381, at Vadstena, Sweden

Married ca. 1345
Cult approved in 1484

Catherine (Karin) was born in 1331 or 1332, the second daughter of Saint Bridget and Ulf Gudmarsson. (She is also called by her patronymic, Karin Ulfsdotter.)

At about the age of fourteen she was married to the nobleman Eggard von Kürnen. The couple agreed to take a vow of perpetual continence and planned to have a virginal Josephite marriage. The marriage did not last long, though, because in 1349 or 1350 Cath-

Jesus and Mary appear to Saint Bridget, at whose side is her daughter Catherine (oil painting, unknown artist, ca. 1600; Brigittine Convent, Piazza Farnese, Rome).

erine went to Rome to visit her mother. There she learned of the sudden death of her husband in 1351. So Catherine remained at her saintly mother's side, performed with her all of her pious exercises, and was her faithful companion on her various pilgrimages, particularly the one to the Holy Land in 1372–1373. At her holy mother's side Catherine, too, attained sanctity.

After Catherine stood by her mother again at her death on July 23, 1373, in their common lodgings on the Piazza Farnese in Rome, she brought the body of Saint Bridget back to their Swedish homeland. Then Catherine entered the convent that her mother had founded at Vadstena, on the Vättersee, in southern Sweden. The cause for her mother's beatification and canonization was a particular concern of hers, and so she soon went again to Rome in order to advance the process. For five more years Catherine remained in Rome. In 1380 she returned to Sweden and soon afterward became the abbess of the convent at Vadstena. She died an early death there on March 24, 1381.

Her reputation for sanctity developed very quickly as a result of miracles that occurred. The cause for her canonization was conducted between 1466 and 1489 but has not yet been concluded. She is commemorated on August 2, because on this day in the year 1848, with the permission granted by Pope Innocent VIII, her relics were transferred to a new resting place in a ceremony attended by the Swedish King Sten Sture.

At the conclusion of this brief biography of the holy daughter of Saint Bridget, the question once again arises as to the meaning and justification of a Josephite marriage. People today view this sort of marriage with great skepticism, but in the Middle Ages it was not very unusual. It would be unfair to dismiss it in all reported cases, to presume that the couples did not really keep their courageous resolution from start to finish, or to explain the phenomenon away as a pious legend invented to disguise the fact of sterility of one or the other partner, whether of psychological or physical origin.[1]

[1] Cf. *Acta Sanctorum Martii* 3:503–31; H. Jägerstadt, "Katharina von Schweden", in LThK 6:62–63.

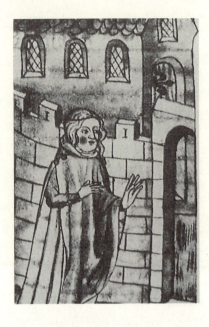

Blessed
Dorothy of Montau

and

Albert Schwertfeger

*b. February 6, 1347, in Montau an
der Weichsel*

d. June 25, 1394, in Marienwerder

Married 1363
Mother of nine children

*Miniature from the Staatsbibliothek,
Munich*

In Blessed Dorothy of Montau we have before us a German woman
about whom her confessor, spiritual director, and biographer Meis-
ter Johannes von Marienwerder (d. 1417)—former professor at the
University of Prague and subsequently a canon—expressly wrote
several revealing chapters (27–31) concerning her marriage in book
two of his account of her life.[1] He introduces these chapters from
the *Vita* dealing with her marriage with the words:

> Not only those who are virgins or who practice continence, but
> also married people who please God by their faith and good
> works deserve to attain eternal happiness. Hence it was surely
> not chance but Divine Providence that united this bride (Dor-
> othy of Montau) beloved by God with a husband as *his* bride, so
> that the married state, as it has been approved by the Church,
> might be confirmed also by holiness of life, and so that she who
> would be brought low by the hardships she was to endure in her

[1] Cf. H. Westphahl, *Vita Dorotheae Montoviensis Magistri Johannis Marienwerder*
(Cologne-Graz, 1964), pp. 90–95.

married life might glorify the Lord all the more in her children. In each successive state of life (as a virgin, as a wife, and as a widow) she would be tested more and more thoroughly for the praise and glory of God.

Dorothy was born on January 25, 1347, the seventh of nine children of Willem Swarcze (d. 1359), a dike expert and farmer who had moved from the Netherlands to Montau an der Weichsel with his wife, Agatha. On February 6, 1347, the child was baptized in the parish church in Montau and then raised a Christian. In the year 1352, as a five-year-old child, Dorothy experienced for the first time special proofs of God's grace. Subsequently she began at a very tender age a life of severe penances, watching at night, fasting, and mortifications.

In the bloom of her youth, Dorothy refused all the lads who asked for her hand. Finally, however, after her father died in 1359, she was compelled by her older brother to marry Albert, a wealthy man from the Schwertfeger family in Danzig. The wedding took place in mid-August 1363—she was only sixteen—in Montau, with the pastor, Father Otto, presiding. The husband selected for Dorothy must have been a good deal older; by trade he was a skilled master craftsman, but he was quick-tempered. The rather unusual, for him incomprehensible, asceticism of his young wife bewildered and embittered him. The couple took up lodgings in a fine house in Danzig, at Langgasse 64.

As far as sexual relations in their marriage were concerned, Albert at first exercised a very noble and considerate restraint, to the joy of his pious young wife: so much so that the biographer of Blessed Dorothy speaks of a "castum et honorabile connubium", that is, a chaste and honorable marriage, and of an "unspotted marriage bed" ("thorus immaculatus"). He speaks also of a marital union in which "fides, prolis et sacramentum" were respected, according to the saying of Saint Augustine that the essential characteristics of a marriage are fidelity, the willingness to receive the blessing of children, and the sacramental seal and dignity of marriage.

In October 1366 Dorothy gave birth to her first child at age nineteen, and eight more followed. In the years between 1367 and 1378 four of them died in childhood. On December 8, 1378, four were still living, having been rescued by their mother from a fire, but these children, too, died young, in 1383, of the plague that was raging at that time in East Prussia. Only the last child, Gertrude, who was born in March 1380, survived the disastrous plague. She later became a Benedictine nun in Kulm. To her Blessed Dorothy dedicated a treatise on the spiritual life (*Die geistliche Lehre*).

Can we really call Blessed Dorothy's marriage "praiseworthy", as her biographer does when he entitles book two, chapter 27: "De laudabili ejus matrimonio"? The marriage was prolific, but aside from that it was quite troublesome. It should not be overlooked that, because of Dorothy's mystical experiences, the marriage became quite difficult for her husband, also. One Italian author[2] in his portrayal of Dorothy's life calls her husband, Albert, "ricco e pio, ma di pessimo carattere", that is, rich and pious, but having a very bad disposition, probably because he would lose his temper and start to beat his wife when she did not keep up with the household chores. This was a consequence of her mystical states, especially when she found herself again, as she herself put it, in the state of "ardent love". Albert tried to drive this strange enthusiasm out of her by alternating between rough mistreatment and uncouth tenderness. His efforts were useless, because again and again, ever more compellingly, the supernatural burst in upon Dorothy's cramped bourgeois existence. So it had been ever since 1364, shortly after their wedding, when her initial vision of the Crucifixion tore down the curtain between the visible and the invisible and her heart, in her own words, "had become inflamed with an ardent love". She felt racked beyond human endurance, as though on a cross, by the twofold, almost irreconcilable duties with respect to her family and her mystical vocation. Marriage became for her a martyrdom. Only gradually did Dorothy's patient suffering transform to some extent her husband's obstinate character.

[2] Cf. A. Romeo, "Dorothea", in *Bibliotheca Sanctorum* 4:817.

After the death of the children, the couple decided to go on a long journey together as pilgrims. They traveled south via Aachen to "Vinsterwald" (today Einsiedeln, in Switzerland), as the sources tell us. As winter set in, they appeared again in Danzig on November 11, 1384, but only to make preparations for a much more decisive departure. On April 5, 1385, Albert sold the house and the workshop. The townspeople saw the little family set out again on the country road. This time they rode in a covered wagon, and their five-year-old daughter, Gertrude, came along. During their travels highwaymen robbed them of the few belongings they had brought with them, which were supposed to enable them to start a new household. When they arrived again in Einsiedeln on October 11, 1385, the tension that tore Dorothy's heart grew unbearable. It was probably the worst temptation of her life, to which she gave in for a moment, in that she coaxed her husband, who wanted to return to Danzig, to travel alone and to leave her behind at the hermitage in "Vinsterwald". Albert agreed to do so. Having finally won her freedom, Dorothy's exultation was indescribable. When the couple went before the curate in Einsiedeln, however, to have the separation approved, the husband regretted the consent he had just given, and the priest ordered Dorothy to accompany her husband back to Danzig. Without a word of complaint she took up her cross again.

What happened after that was like a nightmare. They started out on the trip home in winter, at the end of January 1387, at great danger to their lives. On March 25, 1387, the couple arrived by ship—via Lübeck—in Danzig. A troublesome search for lodgings followed, a miserable shelter in a hut beside the church of Saint Catherine, then the mockery of the neighbors, which gradually turned vicious when Dorothy was denounced as a witch and a heretic. From then on Albert was constantly sick and responded to Dorothy's selfless, faithful, and patient care with grumbling and worse. The two were so poor that Dorothy had to go begging from time to time. "Apparently independent from their external misfortune and yet mysteriously related to it, Dorothy's interior life unfolded in an increasingly more profound union with the crucified

Lord, and in utter openness and resignation to the stream of triune love." Thus L. Brede[3] describes Dorothy's spiritual development.

In one of his rare impulses of generosity, Albert, who had recovered his health, sent his wife, Dorothy, along with a group of pilgrims from Danzig who went to Rome in late August 1389, so that she could celebrate the Jubilee Year there. She had unique mystical experiences, and by the time she returned to Danzig, on May 15, 1390, her husband had died and been buried (around February 16, 1390).

Dorothy then entrusted her little daughter, Gertrude, to a convent in Kulm, gave away the rest of her belongings in Danzig, and resettled in Marienwerder. There she found a kindly, high-minded priest in the person of the cathedral rector, Johannes von Marienwerder, who took her under his spiritual direction. He tested Dorothy severely, was convinced of the authenticity of her piety and of her special charisms, and relieved her of the tormenting fear that she had perhaps deceived herself and might be the plaything of demonic suggestion. On May 2, 1393, he cloistered her as a recluse in a cell that had been added on to the cathedral in Marienwerder.

Here the blessed received many revelations and extraordinary graces. Our Lord himself once called her "a martyr", and finally, before sunset on June 25, 1394, she died of "heartbreaking love". From then on, as the crucified and risen Lord had announced to her, she beheld "the glory and the joy of the martyrs". Is Dorothy of Montau perhaps a martyr, a "witness" to the indissolubility of marriage, which is selflessly and faithfully affirmed and lived, even in the midst of great difficulties? If so, then she is an example for many married couples, who may find it difficult to affirm the permanence of their marriage, despite many temptations, until finally they are separated by death.

In the "Acts of the Process for the Canonization of Dorothy of Montau, 1394–1521,"[4] we find the following summary statement about the marriage of Blessed Dorothy of Montau: "Prefata Doro-

---

[3] Cf. L. Brede, in P. Manns, *Die Heiligen in ihrer Zeit*, 2d ed. (Mainz, 1966), 2:155.

[4] Cf. R. Stachnik, *Akten des Kanonisationsprozesses Dorotheas von Montau 1394 bis 1521* (Cologne and Vienna, 1978), p. 1403.

thea post contractum matrimonium in ipso matrimonio persev-
eravit honestissime et castissime usque ad annum Domini 1390,
quo anno dictus Adalbertus, vir ejus, diem vite sue clausit extre-
mum [The aforesaid Dorothy, after she had married, persevered in
marriage with the utmost honor and chastity until the year of the
Lord 1390, in which her husband Albert concluded the last day of
his life]."

Blessed
Hedwig
and
Jagiello

b. ca. 1374 in Hungary
d. July 17, 1399, in Kraków

Married 1386
Beatified 1979

Church of the Holy Cross, Kraków,
16th century

In the case of Blessed Hedwig (Jadwiga),[1] Queen of Poland, problems arise, not only concerning the betrothal of children, a practice that was once common in noble families, but also with regard to the legitimacy of marriage between children.

Hedwig was born around 1374, the third and youngest daughter of Louis I of Anjou, the king of Hungary, Poland, and Croatia, and Princess Elizabeth, the daughter of Duke Stephen II of Bosnia. While still a four-year-old child she was not only betrothed to Wilhelm, the eight-year-old son of Margrave Leopold III of Austria, but was also married to him on June 15, 1378, in Hainburg.

The children, who were validly married per se, were raised together, alternately in Vienna and in Budapest. From the age of six onward Hedwig remained in Hungary year-round, because her father, King Louis, intended to have her placed upon the royal throne of Hungary after his demise. After the death of King Louis,

---

[1] Cf. S. Dal Pozzo, *Regina e santa* (Rome, 1950); P. Naruszewicz, "Beata Edvige, regina di Polonia", in *Bibliotheca Sanctorum* 4:929–33; H. Quillus, *Königin Hedwig von Polen* (Leipzig, 1938).

however, the matter was decided differently: Hedwig's eldest sister, Maria, was to become queen of Hungary, while Hedwig would be queen of Poland. The ten-year-old Hedwig was in fact crowned queen of Poland on October 15, 1384, by Bodzanta, the archbishop of Gnesen.

The Habsburgs now wanted Queen Hedwig to have at her side, as consort and king of Poland, Wilhelm von Habsburg, with whom she had been married since she was four years of age. The Polish nobility, however, were clever enough to prevent that; they had proposed another consort for Queen Hedwig, namely, the Lithuanian grand duke Jagiello. For Hedwig this new marriage contract entailed a great personal sacrifice, but she was willing to make it in the best interests of Poland and for the conversion of the Lithuanian people. Therefore, she agreed to the marriage contract with Jagiello only on the condition that he would be baptized and would lead his people to the Christian faith. On February 12, 1386, the grand duke Jagiello came to Kraków. Three days later, on February 15, 1386, he was baptized, together with his brothers, and took the name Ladislaus. Now, in the cathedral of Kraków, in the presence of Archbishop Bodzanta and of many members of the clergy, Hedwig publicly revoked the marriage with Wilhelm von Habsburg that she had been compelled to enter as a four-year-old child.

On the occasion of Hedwig's new wedding to Jagiello-Ladislaus, Pope Urban VI called for a careful examination of Hedwig's first marriage. Convinced that the accusations that Wilhelm von Habsburg made against Hedwig were unjust—indeed, the young Austrian margrave did not even bother to appear in Rome to testify at the Church tribunal in which he himself had brought legal action—Pope Urban VI finally sent a bull to Jagiello-Ladislaus on April 18, 1388, in which he praised the latter's conversion prior to marrying Queen Hedwig and explained that there was nothing objectionable about his marriage with her, which had been celebrated on February 18, 1386. The successor of Pope Urban VI, Pope Boniface IX, even approved the request that he stand as godfather for the eventual firstborn son of the royal couple. That would have been impossible had any doubt remained as to the validity of Hedwig's marriage with Jagiello-Ladislaus.

Hedwig subsequently developed into an exemplary ruler who spared no pains in fostering the development of the Polish and Lithuanian peoples. Queen Hedwig became, so to speak, a godmother for Lithuania, for she had a deliberate plan for leading the people there out of paganism into the light of Christian faith and morals.

For Poland, Queen Hedwig obtained from Pope Boniface IX the establishment of a theological faculty at the University of Kraków on February 11, 1399, so that men in priestly formation could receive a good theological education. Queen Hedwig also cared lovingly for the poor and the sick and founded hospitals in several localities (in Sandomierz, Biecz, Sącz, and Kraków). She often visited the sick who were sheltered in them.

In Lithuania Queen Hedwig erected the diocese of Vilnius. There, as well as in Poland, she had numerous churches built, and she saw to it that zealous pastors began to work in these newly constructed churches. She also provided them with the necessary liturgical books and altar furnishings. She even worked to promote the use of the vernacular in the liturgy and to this end founded a Benedictine monastery in Kraków, in which Polish was used as the liturgical language.

After an all-too-short but very beneficial reign over Poland and Lithuania, Queen Hedwig died on July 17, 1399, in Kraków. Pope John Paul II, during his pastoral visit to Poland June 2–10, 1979, brought as a gift for his former archdiocese of Kraków the decree of the Congregation of Rites declaring that Queen Hedwig was blessed and that her feast could be celebrated on July 17.

Saint
Rita of Cascia
and
Paolo Mancini

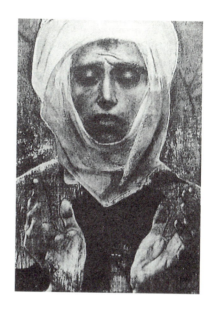

b. ca. 1381 in Roccaporena,
    province of Spoleto, Umbria,
    Italy
d. May 22, 1457

Mother of two children
Canonized May 24, 1900

Basilica of San Lorenzo, Florence

Saint Rita[1] has been revered throughout the world as the "saint of the impossible" since her canonization on May 24, 1900, by Leo XIII; surely she can be of assistance to those who are experiencing serious marital problems, since she was married to an unpredictable man, endured his brutal ways with the utmost patience, and sacrificed much for the salvation of his soul.

This great saint was the long-expected object of her parents' hopes and prayers. For years Antonio and Amata Lotti had looked forward to having children, but to no avail. At last Rita—the name is a shortened form of Margarita—was born in May 1381 in Roccaporena near Cascia (province of Spoleto, Umbria, Italy). This only child had the advantages of loving parents and a very happy home life. The strong faith of the parents was passed on to Rita. As she blossomed into a beautiful young woman, she sensed in her heart a growing desire to consecrate herself to God in the convent of Santa Maria Maddalena in Cascia.

---

[1] Cf. B. Schneider and H. Martin, *Die heilige Rita von Cascia, Helferin in aussichtslosen Anliegen* (Stein am Rhein, 1989). The depiction of Rita's marriage was taken almost word for word from this beautiful illustrated volume.

Rita asked her parents for permission to take this step. Despite their strong faith, they were horrified by their daughter's intention, thinking that God could not possibly deprive them of their only child, who was a miraculous answer to prayer after so many years of childlessness. That would leave them with no support in their old age! Therefore, after Rita had explained to her parents her decision to enter the convent, her father tried to reason with her and dissuade her, while the mother listened, speechless, with tears in her eyes. What was Rita to do? She made a pilgrimage to the nearby hermitage of Santa Croce; there she attended a Mass celebrated by the pious Augustinian monk Padre Ugolino and afterward asked to talk with him. The priest agreed with her that it is truly an exalted vocation to serve God and the Church as a bride of Christ and that a calling to live according to the three evangelical counsels is a great grace. In her case, however, in spite of all the good indications and her unquestionable suitability for the cloistered life, God was demanding that she renounce this prospect.

Rita's parents were extremely grateful when they heard their daughter say that she would consider their situation, give up her own plans for the future, and for their sake offer to join her life with that of a man in matrimony. It pained the parents to see their only daughter suffer, but they hoped that a solicitous husband and the joys of marriage would heal the wound with time.

Young Rita's charm had not gone unnoticed by the youths in the village. Quite a few of them would gladly have asked for her hand in marriage. Although Rita usually had a friendly, amiable manner, she was nevertheless very reserved in dealing with the opposite sex. Therefore, none of the young men in the village dared to court her. Only one was bold enough: Paolo Mancini.

Several years before that he had left the village of Roccaporena and gone abroad; he wanted to see the world and get some experience. So he served for a few years as a mercenary in the army of Cascia. Under the command of Captain Lorenzo da Collegiacone, Paolo Mancini had taken part in a series of successful military campaigns. Proud of his unit's victories over various Italian cities, he then returned to his village of Roccaporena. He had many stories to tell; he enjoyed boasting of his heroic deeds. There was no overlooking the fact that his mercenary service had brought him a certain affluence: one could tell from his appearance. This earned Paolo Mancini a certain reputation in the village, although it was rather shady. Then, too, despite his conviviality and garrulousness, his true character shone through: Paolo Mancini was quick-tempered. Little things would often throw him into a towering rage. Once he was angry, he did not hesitate to make his displeasure felt.

When it happened that the celebrated war hero asked Rita's parents for her hand in marriage, they found themselves in a spiritual dilemma. They saw that Paolo Mancini would be able to offer their daughter security and prosperity . . . but that anger, that uncontrolled, contentious character of his! How could their beloved child, their only daughter, Rita, live with that? Their sentiments thus divided, Signore and Signora Lotti tried to console and reassure each other. "The Paolo we knew was a good boy, and smart. It's just that this soldiering has left its mark on him, made him restless and combative. But when he is married and has to take on responsibility for a wife and later for his own children, his equilibrium will return—at least we hope so. Besides, a loving, caring wife, the kind our Rita will surely be, can really work miracles."

Finally the parents managed to convince themselves. Our daughter, who can be so clever, good-natured, and yet firm, will be able to deal with that Paolo Mancini. She will have a good influence on him and his rebellious nature. Mother Amata, who did not want to lose her daughter to the Augustinian nuns, was quite confident that the basic goodness of Paolo Mancini they had once known would reemerge; with a good Christian wife at his side, his restlessness would disappear automatically, and Rita in turn would be well cared for by Paolo. With a somewhat heavy heart Rita's parents finally gave the former mercenary their consent and their blessing upon the wedding.

Of course, it was not such an easy thing for Paolo Mancini to court Rita. To be sure, she found his imposing figure not unattractive, but interiorly she still longed to become a bride of Christ in the religious state, not to give herself to a man. Finally, Rita recalled the admonitions of Padre Ugolino at the hermitage of Santa Croce: Obedience to God can also be practiced by submitting to the will of your parents. So eventually she gave her parents her consent to become Paolo's wife. Profound gratitude for her daughter's obedience filled the motherly heart of Signora Amata.

No one in the village of Roccaporena was surprised by the news that Rita had been promised to Paolo Mancini, the mercenary who had come back home. Soon everyone agreed that the two would make a handsome and happy couple.

Was this marriage really happy? At the start, everything went well. Infatuated and flattered to have won for himself the most beautiful girl in the village, Paolo treated his wife, Rita, with kid gloves. At first, the pair were actually happy together. During the early years of their marriage, they were blessed with two healthy children, Giovanni and Paolo, who became their father's pride and joy. For Rita, the boys were the fulfillment of her love. Her parents, too, were able to enjoy the two grandchildren. Moreover, alongside their daily work, peace and harmony prevailed in the family.

Gradually, though, Paolo Mancini's adventuresome side and his wanderlust rose to the surface again. More and more often he would stay out for the evening so as to meet secretly with his friends from the Ghibelline party, which was hated in Roccaporena. Then, when he came back from these gatherings upset and infuriated, Rita was not spared angry outbursts if she asked him why he was so late or even if she showed that she was anxious about him. Nor did Paolo Mancini hesitate to raise a hand against his young wife. Soon everyone in the village knew what Rita had to put up with, even though she never complained to third parties about her marital woes. Furthermore, Rita suffered because of her husband's partisan allegiance, for he was an enthusiastic adherent of the Ghibellines, while most of the residents in Roccaporena favored the Guelf party.

Gradually things became very difficult for Rita as a wife and mother. She managed to follow the advice of the Augustinian Father Ugolino, though, and to unite her abandonment with that of the crucified Lord. Rita experienced how power flowed to her from the Cross, a strength that did not permit her to go to pieces, even in situations where other wives would have been shattered. However much her husband raged and fumed, Rita always remained quiet and was constantly filled with a strange inner calm. Since she had no help in this world and could not speak with anyone about her marital concerns, she commended everything to the bitter but redemptive Passion of our Lord on the Cross. As she walked along the difficult, thorny paths of her married life, she united herself ever more fervently with the Sacred Heart of the Suffering Servant. From him she drew strength, consolation, and courage; with him she also found, again and again, an answer to her question as to the meaning of her marital cross.

Rita lived to see her faithful love prevail. After years of painful humiliations, her silent sacrifices, prayers, and sufferings brought her husband to his senses, so that he made a sincere resolution to control his unruly passions. Through humility and patience Rita was able to accomplish what could never have been brought about by getting up in arms or losing her temper with her volatile, quarrelsome husband.

It happened one night when Paolo Mancini returned home late, exasperated. The meeting with his partisan friends must not have gone according to his wishes this time. Enraged, he was about to enter the house and unleash his fury and frustration on his innocent wife. Inside, however, he found his wife in the parlor— immersed in sorrow—kneeling before the image of the Crucified and weeping bitterly. Fernando's first thought was: There had been an accident. Had something happened to one of his sons, who were his pride and joy? Suddenly, it was clear to him: he himself was the cause of his wife's sorrow, her anguish, and her cares. Pictures from the past appeared before his eyes: his rudeness and cruelty toward Rita during all those years. He was overcome with remorse, which was accompanied by the realization: Something has to change in my marriage. I have to change myself! For the first time he saw Rita with the eyes of true love. Look at all the pain and sorrow he had caused such a noble soul during the years of their marriage through his quarreling and unkindness! He begged his wife to forgive him for everything. This time Rita sensed her husband's sincerity and goodwill. They were reconciled, and it did not take much to convince him to make his peace with God as well, by means of a contrite confession.

After he was reconciled with God in the Sacrament of Penance, a new life began, not only for the husband, but for the entire family. Without Rita having to urge him, Paolo now gave up his political activities with the Ghibelline party and put an end to other quarrels and enmities.

After sixteen years of married life together, peace and harmony had finally entered the Mancini household. Rita thanked God for this with all her heart.

In her happiness, which had been achieved with such difficulty, the saint did not suspect that an even more difficult calamity would befall her and her family. One day, Paolo told his wife that he absolutely had to ride to Collegiacone; he had learned that, as a result of partisan disputes that had just erupted, some men were planning to ambush his former captain, Lorenzo. Rita implored her husband to stay out of the argument. Her memory of earlier days was still too vivid. Paolo must not become a backslider. He, however, justified his course of action as coming to the aid of a friend. Although he could understand Rita's fears, he had made his decision; he felt obliged to stand by his old commander and friend, to warn him and defend him. Thus Paolo finally left the house with Rita's consent; she was unwilling and unable to keep him from helping his friend. Nevertheless, while staying at home, she anxiously accompanied him with her prayers.

That evening Rita waited a long time for her husband, for he had promised her that he would be home before dark. Fears and worries eventually became an almost unbearable burden on her soul as night fell and Paolo had still not returned. Then, suddenly, there was a muffled knocking at the door to the house. Rita opened it. A stranger stood outside. In the darkness she could make out the silhouettes of several other figures. They were carrying a bier with someone lying on it.

After Paolo had warned his friend, he set out in haste on the way home. To be sure, Captain Lorenzo had invited him to stay a while. Paolo, though, wanted to keep his promise to Rita and arrive home before dark. Along the way, however, he was surprised by a powerful thunderstorm and had to take refuge in a sheltered spot. When he was finally able to set out again, several armed men were lying in wait for him. They attacked Paolo, who was unarmed, and dealt him several serious wounds with daggers. Thinking that he was dead, the murderers fled. A man from the village who was walking along the way, unaware, found the mortally wounded man on the road. He saw immediately that it was too late to offer any sort of help. All he could do was listen to a few words spoken by the dying man: words of farewell to Rita and to their two sons, along with the request that both sons and the other relatives forgive the murderers, as he had forgiven them.

Faced with the corpse of her beloved husband, Rita pondered in her heart what she had just heard. How painful this loss was now! After so many difficult years of marriage she had been able at last to live together in love and harmony with her husband—and now he had met a violent end!

The ray of light falling in the darkness of her mourning was the knowledge that Paolo had forgiven his murderers as he was dying. She could not thank God enough that he had given her husband the opportunity to realize the petition from the Our Father: "Forgive us our trespasses as we forgive those who trespass against us." Rita was convinced that God had granted her husband pardon for all his sins, because he himself had magnanimously forgiven his murderers.

Full of gratitude for what God had wisely ordained and permitted, and half consoled by her pious belief that her husband had died in the state of sanctifying grace, Rita finally returned to her daily household chores. Rita could have continued leading a widow's life in silence and peace. Now, though, the two growing sons began to be a source of worry. For both of them—Rita sensed it and recognized it in their strange behavior—were plotting revenge. No sooner had their father been buried than they were uttering evil threats against the murderers. Rita begged her sons to give up such unchristian thoughts. But all of the mother's warnings and pleadings were in vain; they were greeted only with icy silence. When her sons did say something, it was always: They will pay for the death of our father; his memory demands vengeance.

As for the mother, she was ready to make any sacrifice in order to keep her sons from becoming murderers. Her own life, her health, her belongings . . . Rita offered everything to God. Better that both her sons should die than sin by taking the lives of other men. Ultimately Rita's prayer was answered in a strange and very painful way.

The plague arrived one day in Roccaporena and demanded tribute of the inhabitants. In most households there were sick people. Fresh graves lined up in the village cemetery. Mourning called on the Mancini house as well: Paolo, Rita's father-in-law, and his wife were carried off by the plague within a short interval. Finally, both of Rita's sons, too, came down with the terrible sickness. They were long and bitter hours that Rita spent at the bedside of her dying sons; their hearts were poisoned by thoughts of revenge, and she sought to purge and cleanse them by her exhortations. Eventually she succeeded, with God's help. Both sons, Giovanni and Paolo Maria, renounced all thoughts of revenge before they died and explicitly forgave their father's murderers.

Death passed Rita by at this time. God willed to offer her the opportunity to realize the dream of her youth, her longing to consecrate herself to God in religious life. After sixteen years of marriage and six years of widowhood, Rita was permitted to enter the Augustinian convent in Cascia, after having been turned away several times. There, until her death on May 22, 1457, she led a heroic life of penance, atonement, and stirring devotion to the divine Bridegroom, Jesus Christ, and practiced works of charity on behalf of her sisters in the community and the inhabitants of Cascia. Fifteen years before her death, Rita received the stigmata of the crown of thorns imprinted on her forehead as a sign of her constant devotion to the humble, redemptive sufferings of our Lord.

Blessed
Margaret of Savoy

and

Theodore Palaeologus of Montferrat

b. 1382 in Pinerolo, near Turin, Italy
d. November 23, 1464

Married 1403
Mother of two stepchildren
Cult approved in 1566

In the year 1382 in Pinerolo, near Turin, Margaret, the daughter of Prince Amadeus of Savoy and Catherine of Geneva, was born.[1] The girl spent her childhood and youth at her father's castle in Pinerolo, where the progress that she made in faith and kindliness was evident in her earnest conduct.

When Margaret's father died, in 1402, her uncle Louis, who was her guardian, betrothed her to Theodore Palaeologus, marquis of Montferrat. In 1403 she agreed to this marriage, which was planned as a way of ending the rivalry between the two noble houses of Savoy and Montferrat. Margaret was well aware of the difficulties that awaited her in this marriage. Theodore Palaeologus of Montferrat was considerably older and had, besides, a demanding character and a rough military manner. Furthermore, from his first marriage he had two children, named Giangiacomo and Sofia.

Margaret lovingly devoted herself to bringing up her two stepchildren and was just as concerned about the welfare of the needy people in the duchy. In 1411, when Genoa was struck by famine and plague and her husband was summoned there to help rout the French, Margaret showed remarkable foresight by organizing every possible form of social and charitable assistance for the needs of the

[1] Cf. E. Schepisi, *La beata Margherita di Savoia* (Alba, 1964); A. Ferrua, "Beata Margherita di Savoia", in *Bibliotheca Sanctorum* 8:793–96.

populace. After she had returned to Montferrat, her interest turned to the Council of Constance, and she worked for its success; she wanted to do her part to resolve the painful Western Schism, to which her cousin Amedeus VIII had contributed as the anti-pope Felix V.

In the year 1418 Theodore of Montferrat died, and Margaret became a widow. She served as regent for the duchy until her stepson, Giangiacomo, attained majority. Then she withdrew, with several ladies from the local court, to the castle in the quarter of the city called Santa Maria Maddalena, on the border of Alba (Cuneo). These former ladies in waiting did not leave the castle except to care for the sick and the poor. This association of ladies eventually became a cloistered community of regular tertiaries of the Dominican Order. This community was canonically erected by Pope Eugene IV in a bull of July 13, 1445.

It should also be mentioned that Duke Philip Visconti of Milan repeatedly asked Margaret to renounce the widowed state so as to marry him. She, however, remained faithful to her new vocation. The last years of her life were marked by sickness, persecution, and misunderstanding, those three "arrows" which, according to a vision, were to pierce her heart. Margaret of Savoy died on November 23, 1464, and was immediately revered as blessed by the populace of Alba. Her cult was approved in 1566 by Pope Pius V, the former vicar of the Dominican convent in Alba, and again in 1670 by Pope Clement X.

Saint
Frances of Rome
and
Lorenzo dei Ponziani

b. 1384 in Rome
d. March 9, 1440, in Monte
Oliveto

Married 1396
Mother of six children
Canonized May 29, 1608

Lüttich, Abbaye de la Paix Notre
Dame, 17th century

Frances of Rome is a saint who lived as an exemplary wife in a
marriage lasting forty years and conscientiously fulfilled her duties
as the mother of a family.[1] She was born at the beginning of the
year 1384 in Rome, the daughter of the nobleman Paolo Busso
(who was related to the most important noble houses, such as the
Orsini and the Savelli) and the noblewoman Jacobella dei Roffre-
deschi. Frances had a sister, named Perna, and a brother, named
Simeon.

Frances' mother raised her to be an extraordinarily pious girl. As
an eleven-year-old, she gladly would have dedicated herself to
God as a religious, but her father was opposed. He married her to
Lorenzo dei Ponziani in the year 1396.

The young couple began to live in the Palazzo Ponziani, in
the vicinity of the church of Saint Cecilia, in the Trastevere quarter of Rome, together with Lorenzo's brother Paluzzo and his
wife, Vannozza. Frances struck up an intimate friendship with her

---

[1] Cf. Johannes Matiotti, *De vita et miraculis S. Francescae Romanae*, ed. M. P. Rivaldi,
(Rome: Stampa Francesca Romana, 1964).

sister-in-law, because she, too, had been more or less compelled to marry, even though she, like Frances, had felt called to religious life. The two young women often consulted with one another as to the proper means of seeking perfection within marriage and of glorifying God through works of charity.

Frances survived her husband by five years; during her long marriage she was a faithful, self-sacrificing wife. She managed to provide the proper social setting for Lorenzo's life, while leading him gradually toward the glorification of God.

Frances had the privilege of bringing six children into the world during her marriage. Three of them died soon after birth; two died in childhood; and only one son survived his parents, namely, Battista, who lived to be forty-four years old. He married Mabilia Papazunni, a very arrogant daughter-in-law who used to insult and offend Frances deliberately. Through her heroic patience and touching humility, but also through many prayers and sacrifices, Frances finally succeeded in converting her daughter-in-law completely.

The names and dates of the three children of Saint Frances who survived infancy are: Battista (b. 1400; d. 1444), Evangelista (b. 1403; d. 1410), and Agnes (b. 1404; d. 1410). Evangelista and Agnes were victims of the plague that raged in Rome in 1410.

Frances was devoted to her husband, Lorenzo, and with the same unselfish love she cared for her children and, furthermore, for the poor and the sick, whom she would visit in their homes or in the hospitals of the city, generously rendering them service.

Despite her noble lineage, Frances liked to dress in an extremely modest fashion. In shabby attire she would gather alms and firewood for the poor in the city of Rome. She fasted frequently and prayed much, both at home and in the churches of Rome. She always managed, however, to harmonize her prayer life with her duties as a housewife, spouse, and mother. As soon as her husband needed her or the household required her attention, she did not hesitate a moment to interrupt her pious exercises. She used to say, "A married woman must leave all her devotions when the household demands it." Frances spent herself almost completely in the service of the poor and the sick, yet she led a remarkably interior life. God granted her special graces in visions and ecstasies, and she became a mystic enjoying intimate converse with Christ, his Virgin Mother, and her own guardian angel.

This exemplary wife and mother was not spared trials and sufferings. In the same year she lost two children, aged six and seven, during the plague of 1410. Her husband, Lorenzo, was commander of the papal armies in the campaign against King Ladislaus of Naples, who succeeded twice in conquering and plundering Rome, leaving it almost in ruins. In this military conflict Lorenzo received a serious stab wound. Though he was near death, Frances nursed her husband back to health with steadfast loving care. In exchange, however, their son Battista was taken hostage.

During the hostilities, the palace of the Ponziani family went up in flames. The family was now in dire need. Nevertheless, Frances continued to look after the sick, the poor, and the homeless. To help her in her charitable work, she began in 1425 to gather around her like-minded women and girls from the noble families in Rome. Eventually this developed into an association whose members remained in the world but renounced the spirit of the world and resolved to live a consecrated life according to the Rule of Saint Benedict. Lorenzo, Frances' husband, his soul refined by sorrowful trials and tribulations, gave his saintly wife free rein to pursue her pious works of mercy.

The association of Benedictine oblates, known as the Oblates of Mary and affiliated with the Benedictines of Monte Oliveto, which Frances had founded, was approved by Pope Eugene IV on July 14, 1433. Frances lovingly and selflessly cared for her husband to the end. After his death, in 1435, she herself entered the community of oblates, on March 21, 1436. For four more years, until her death on March 9, 1440, she was a shining example to her spiritual daughters. Her last words were, "The heavens are open, the angels are descending, the archangel has accomplished his task. He stands before me and beckons to me to follow him."

Pope Paul V canonized this exemplary wife, mother, and foundress on May 29, 1608. In the breviary of the Olivetan Benedictine

Order there is a poignant phrase describing the marriage of Saint Frances: "She did not cease to be mindful of the things of God during her marriage, so that she pleased God in her husband and her husband in God."

Blessed
Helen of Udine

and

Antony die Cavalcanti

b. ca. 1396/1397 in Udine, Italy
d. April 23, 1458

Married 1414
Mother of six children

Not much is known about the childhood and youth of this wife, mother, and widow from the Venetian town of Udine. She was born in 1396 or 1397, the daughter of the nobleman Carlo dei Valentini and Elisabetta di Maniago.[1] Almost nothing is known either about her married life with the nobleman Antony dei Cavalcante, also born in Udine, whom Helen married in 1414 at about the age of 18—only that the marriage was very prolific. Helen bore her husband six children: three sons (Carlo, Speranzio, and Antonio) and three daughters (Elisabetta, Caterina, and Allegrina, who was called Lirina).

As a widow, Helen consciously strove to imitate Christ and, contrary to her rather worldly conduct as a married woman, led a very strict and penitential life. From this fact it can perhaps be inferred that this woman, once she became a widow, began to realize that during her marriage she had not always lived in accordance with the commandments of God and the precepts of the Church.

When her husband died, after twenty-seven years of marriage, Helen decided—probably at the recommendation of Padre Angelo di San Severino, a powerful mission preacher from the Hermits of Saint Augustine (Augustinians)—to withdraw as much as possible

---

[1] Cf. G. Biasutti, *Profilo spirituale della beata Elena Valentini* (Udine, 1958); N. Del Re, "Valentini, Elena", in *Bibliotheca Sanctorum* 12:886f.

from the world and from all mundane concerns and to become a tertiary in the order of her spiritual director. At first she kept living in the house she had inherited from her husband, namely, in the Borgo Mercato-vecchio in Udine. In 1446, though, she moved to the house of her sister Perfecta, who likewise had joined the Hermits of Saint Augustine as a tertiary. She remained there until her death on April 23, 1458, and led a life of penance, piety, and love of neighbor.

From 1455 on she was quite crippled as a result of an accident and was confined to her bed, but God conferred upon her various charisms, including the gifts of working miracles and of reading hearts, and granted her visions and ecstasies. Pope Pius IX approved devotions to Blessed Helen of Udine in 1848. The relics of this blessed wife, mother, and widow were kept at first in the church of Santa Lucia in Udine, where she had been buried after her death. Since 1845 the relics of Blessed Helen of Udine have been revered in a worthy place in the cathedral of Udine.

Blessed
Antonia of Florence

and

Spouse

b. 1401 in Florence, Italy
d. February 28, 1472, in Aquila, central Italy

Mother of one child

Antonia (whose family name is unknown, which is why she is named after her place of birth) was born into an aristocratic family in the city of Florence in 1401. She was to become the wife of a Florentine nobleman and the mother of one son.[1]

Antonia's marriage—whether it was happy or unhappy is likewise unknown—lasted only a very short time.

After her husband's early death, Antonia entered the third order Franciscan convent in Florence that had been founded in 1429 by Blessed Angelina of Marsciano. Soon she was sent to the convent of the same community in Foligno, where she lived as a very holy religious from 1430 to 1433. Then she prayed and sacrificed for thirteen years as the superior of a convent in Aquila in the Abruzzi region (central Italy). Seeking a life of greater austerity and counseled by Saint John of Capistrano, she founded there in 1447 a convent of Poor Clares, "Corpus Christi". She served as its superior for seven years and by her teaching and example drew numerous followers to the community.

God favored with many singular graces this humble nun who had once been a married woman, who endured with heroic patience the difficulties of the married state, the faults of her sisters in community, and the daily pains and unpleasantness of a long-lasting illness. At the age of seventy-one, on February 29, 1472, she went to her eternal reward in the heavenly homeland. Pope Pius IX approved the cult venerating her as blessed on September 17, 1847.

---

[1] Cf. D. Lupinetti, *Beata Antonia da Firenze* (Lanciano, 1953).

Blessed
Galeotto Roberto Malatesta

and

Margherita d'Este

b. February 3, 1411
d. October 10, 1432, in Sant'Arcangelo

Blessed Galeotto Roberto Malatesta was born on February 3, 1411, the natural son of Pandolfo, Lord of Brescia, and Caterina Castellano. He received a pious upbringing from Elisabetta Gonzaga, the wife of his uncle Carlo, who later adopted him. The uncle arranged for the sixteen-year-old youth to be married against his will to Margherita d'Este, the daughter of Margrave Nicolo III of Ferrara, on November 26, 1427. Galeotto had two brothers, named Sigismondo Pandolfo and Domenico. When their uncle Carlo died in 1429, Galeotto, as the firstborn of the three brothers, succeeded him as master of the house. He made over the property he had inherited to the Church, left the wife he had been forced to marry, and became a third order Franciscan. Until his death, on October 10, 1432, at the early age of twenty-one, he led a life of penance and mortification in Sant'Arcangelo.[1]

---

[1] G. Giovanardi, "Il beato Galeotto Roberto Malatesta", in *Miscellanea Francescana* 35:4 (1936): 287–97. G. Pecci, "Malatesta, Galeotto Roberto", in *Bibliotheca Sanctorum* 8:582–84.

Saint
Nicholas von Flüe
and
Dorothea Wissling

b. 1417 in Flüeli bei Sachseln,
    Canton Unterwalden (now
    Obwalden), Switzerland
d. March 21, 1487, in Ranft

Married 1447
Father of ten children
Canonized May 15, 1947

A saintly farmer composed the profoundly moving prayer, "My Lord and my God . . .", which points toward radical renunciation for the sake of greater union with God; yet if he had taken this prayer quite seriously at an earlier date, he would not have married at all. "My Lord and my God, take from me everything that separates me from you. Give me everything that brings me closer to you. Take me from myself and give me to yourself to be entirely yours!" Or is a sacramental marriage a means of abiding with God and in no way a separation from him? In deciding to separate from his wife and children—a step that to many people is baffling— Nicholas von Flüe, at any rate, must have felt that to continue living a married life would be an obstacle to intimate union with God. Was he right or wrong?

In any case, Nicholas [Klaus] von Flüe[1]—born in 1417 in Flüeli bei Sachseln (Canton Unterwalden, now Obwalden, Switzerland), the son of the farmer Henry von Flüe and Emma Robert of Wolfenschiessen (Canton Unterwalden, now Nidwalden)—did get

---

[1] W. Nigg, *Niklaus von Flüe* (Olten 1980); R. Durrer, *Dokumente über Bruder Klaus* (Luzerne, 1947).

married in 1447 at age thirty to Dorothea Wissling, the oldest daughter in "Neuhof", high up on Mount Schändi, on the sunny side of the Sarner Valley, where the highly regarded Wiss clan had lived since time immemorial. Was he compelled to do it? Did he do it freely and lovingly? In those days marriage was assumed to be part of a healthy farmboy's plans, unless he thought God was calling him to the priesthood or the religious life. In the case of Nicholas von Flüe, though, there seems to be no mention of any such vocation, even though he must have been very pious already in his childhood and youth. He probably heard many attractive things about the "Friends of God", a religious movement in Alsace, from the hermit Matthias von Bolsheim, then prior of the Benedictine Abbey of Engelberg.

After his wedding to Dorothea, of course, the farmer Nicholas von Flüe conscientiously led a normal Christian married life, consisting of work and prayer and, no doubt, a healthy attitude toward sex, as the fruitfulness of their marriage demonstrates. The couple was blessed with ten children, five boys and five girls. In this marriage, certainly, children were accepted from God willingly and gratefully and were then brought up to be capable men and women and good Christians. On account of their intelligence and competence, two of the five sons were elected, one after the other, to serve as *landammann*, the highest office in the canton. The youngest son, Nicholas, studied in Basel, Paris, and Pavia. On March 18, 1491, he became the chaplain in Ranft. In 1496 he was recommended for the University of Pavia by the duke of Milan. In 1502 he became a pastor in Sachseln. He died in Sachseln on October 7, 1503, at thirty-six years of age. The oldest daughter, Verena, married Hensli Scheuber of Wolfenschiessen and became the mother of Konrad Scheuber, who as the *landammann* of Nidwalden was highly esteemed but then, like his grandfather on his mother's side, became a hermit and died in the odor of sanctity.

The line of "Brother Klaus [Nicholas]" has not been extinguished to this day, and among his descendants, besides the saint's youngest son, there have been over thirty priests who served the Church.

In the "Litany of Brother Klaus", Saint Nicholas von Flüe is called, among other things, a "loving husband" and a "faithful father and provider". Surely he was an edifying example of both until he was "called by God to be a hermit".

It happened on October 16, 1467. After twenty years of marriage, the farmer Nicholas von Flüe left his wife, Dorothea, and his children and became a hermit. After initial attempts as a wandering pilgrim, then as a recluse on Mount Klisterli in the Alps, he finally settled in Ranft, in the Melch valley, not far from his property.

There he devoted himself entirely to prayer and penance. He lived for more than nineteen years on the Holy Eucharist, taking no earthly food, until he died on March 21, 1497, in his seventieth year, after a life of almost continual prayer and severe penances. He was renowned as a counselor and peacemaker.

How can we explain the fact that this husband and father left his wife and children, considering that he was canonized on May 15, 1947, and thus is supposed to be an example for those in our time who enter a Christian, indissoluble marriage?

For many people, even pious Christian couples, the fact that Brother Klaus left his wife and his children is a "stumbling block" that is extremely difficult to put aside.

Nevertheless, the following important circumstances must not be overlooked.

1. Saint Nicholas von Flüe did not leave his wife and children frivolously and unthinkingly, but rather after a difficult interior struggle.

2. He did so only after conferring seriously and conscientiously with his spiritual director and confessor, Father Heimo Amgrund from Kerns.

3. He was obeying God's call, which he clearly discerned only after much prayer.

4. He sought solitude with God not out of selfishness, personal preference, or laziness, but for the love of God alone, and he knew that the Lord wanted to be loved "with all your heart and with all your strength".

5. Finally, he made this painful decision only after discussing it

Nicholas von Flüe at the Diet of Stans, where he united the factions of the Swiss Confederation in 1481 (engraving by C. Bosshard)

for several days with his wife and only after she had agreed to a "separation from bed and board". Even then, neither one found the separation easy to accept.

The Benedictine monk Father Michael Jungo, in his book *Verborgene Krone: Lebensgeschichte der Dorothea von Flüe* [Hidden crown: Biography of Dorothea von Flüe],[2] portrays the separation of the two spouses with sympathy and good psychological insight, as follows:

> Dorothea had just nursed her son Nicholas, who was only a few weeks old, and put her youngest to bed. Still a bit pale, she then sat down quietly at her spinning wheel. Then her husband, Klaus, came in. He paced up and down the room a few times,

---

[2] M. Jungo, *Verborgene Krone: Lebensgeschichte der Dorothea von Flüe*, 4th ed. (Stein am Rhein, 1984), pp. 47ff.

then sat down opposite her at the far end of the bench along the wall. For a long time he wordlessly watched the swift play of the spindle. Then he got up quickly, went to the window, and gazed at the evening light as it grew dim. Without turning around and without warning he broke the heavy silence. "Wife," he said, almost gruffly, "I must go away; God wants me to!" She became deathly pale, got up with effort while continuing to stare at him, took a step backward, and leaned against the wall. He had turned around and now came slowly toward her, his eyes fixed upon her lips as though seeking help. . . . Her voice sounded brittle: "It can't be, Klaus! It just can't be!"

The following days were like a pitch black night for Klaus and Dorothea. . . . "What will become of our children, if you leave?" Dorothea spoke up as though continuing an inner dialogue with Klaus. "God, who is taking their father away, will himself be a Father to them", he answered. "And this little puppy here?" she said, as the youngest child started to whimper. "God has chosen him to enter his service." Thus Klaus uttered a prophecy. She retorted, however, "Are not we two united for all eternity through the Blood of Christ?" He replied, "Yes, that we are; and only your free consent can let me go—to live alone with God. . . ." Dorothea fell silent, lost in thought. Then it erupted: "Woe is me! I cannot do it! . . . You took me from my father's house. . . . Brother, father, husband, you became everything for me. . . . Wherever I look I see only you. . . . My sorrow becomes joy when you share it, and my joy is bliss when it shines from your eyes. . . ." He buried his face in his hands and then said, emphasizing each word, "God will be everything for you, too, child!" "Ah, God is far away and you are so near. . . . It is more than I can bear!"

That same evening Dorothea found her husband kneeling before the cradle. He was motionless, with his hands folded at his lips. As though spellbound she stood at the threshold. Yet she could not control herself for long, her tears overflowed, and sobbing she exclaimed, "Klaus!" He started, looked around timidly but remained kneeling. "Klaus! If it is necessary for you to be happy and at peace—I don't want to stand in the way of your happiness. . . . If only you will be happy, then I don't matter." "Ah, wife," said Klaus, "it is not a question of my happiness—but of his, of God's will! He has bound me; I am his prisoner, and he is taking me where I do not want to go." "How can I believe that he, who has joined us forever, wants to take you from me and bind you to himself?"—"I don't understand it either. I only know that he is the Lord and that his love is calling me irresistibly into solitude. . . . Where and why, he alone knows. . . . Oh, if I only knew!" "What more can I say?" she said after an oppressive silence. "Go, then. Go! And God help me!" Then, as though she were having second thoughts: "Am I doing it for God; am I doing it for you? I no longer know my own mind. I only know that I love you more than ever and that it is only for love of you that I give my consent. . . ." Her face had reddened slightly, and her eyes shone the way they did the time she had given that other, first, sweet consent.

Klaus had stood up slowly and, without taking his eyes off her, raised his callused hand, as though he wanted to caress her head—but he stopped midway through the gesture and let his hand drop. . . . She had noticed the movement and offered her freckled neck. The warm touch that she yearned for did not come. The farewell had begun. She threw herself down on her knees beside the bed, hid her head in the covers and sobbed. . . .

The next three days weighed upon the von Flüe house like a nightmare.

The father confided his plan to his eldest son. The mother cut and sewed away at a strange long garment. On the day before the feast of Saint Gall—it was a clear, mild autumn day— Klaus took his son Walter on a final tour of his properties. Dorothea stood at the threshold and watched them. She saw how he stroked the foreheads of the cows at the drinking trough, how he measured off the meadows in a firm gait. Finally, the woods concealed him from her sight.

That last night, Klaus and Dorothea prayed together the whole night through. As the morning star slowly rose in the space between Mount Pilate and the Stanserjoch, the husband and wife took leave of each other forever.

It was a harrowing moment on October 16, 1467, the feast of Saint Gall, as father Klaus, dressed in a poor hermit's cowl, head uncovered, and barefoot, with his rosary and pilgrim's staff, stood before his family to bid them farewell. Once again he blessed each of his children. Then he took the youngest, named Nicholas after him and only sixteen weeks old, out of the cradle and put him in the arms of his wife, thanking her again for everything.

The sacrifice that father Klaus was offering recalled the one that God had once demanded of the patriarch Abraham, who was to lay his beloved son as a sacrificial lamb upon the altar on Mount Moriah. In order to make the sacrifice complete, Klaus planned to leave his Swiss homeland and go to the Friends of God in Alsace. Before he crossed the border of the confederacy, however, the Holy Spirit announced to him, through the advice of a farmer and interiorly through a vision and a special illumination, that he must

Nicholas von Flüe takes leave of his family
(engraving, 1712, after an earlier engraving by G. Nolmar)

293

not go abroad, where he might be viewed as a spy, but should remain in his Swiss homeland. A further revelation finally directed him to the wooded Ranft gorge. The cell there in which Brother Klaus lived for twenty years was small: 2½ paces long, 1½ paces wide, and so low that the crown of his head touched the ceiling.

Many people knocked on the door of the hermit's cell, asking for counsel and prayers, for help and consolation. Not only compatriots of the saint came—townspeople and farmers from all the cantons; visitors from abroad appeared as well, scholars and professors, ecclesiastical officials and laymen with famous names. The husband and father, who had sacrificed to God what was dearest to him, became the father of his country and a peacemaker, because God was with him in a special way.

Brother Klaus died in his lowly cell on March 21, 1487. His cult was approved as early as 1669; his canonization, however, did not take place until May 15, 1947. His separation from his wife and children at God's bidding is still widely misunderstood today. Nevertheless, this great and mystically gifted man was truly an exemplary and loving husband and father who became the care-worn father and protector of the entire Swiss confederacy. He found in his grandson, the Servant of God Konrad Scheuber, an imitator in his bold decision to separate from his wife and children.[3] Let us note also a few details about the latter man.

Konrad Scheuber[4] was born in 1481, during the lifetime of Saint Nicholas of Flüe, in Altzellen, parish of Wolfenschiessen, canton of Nidwalden, the son of pious, upright farming folk. His mother, Verena, was the oldest daughter of the saintly Brother Klaus.

Konrad was conscripted as a soldier and took part in the wars of religion during the Reformation period. Among other campaigns, he fought in the battle of Kappel, in which the Swiss reformer Huldrych Zwingli lost his life on October 11, 1531, while serving as a field chaplain. Afterward Konrad Scheuber was nominated to

[3] M. Dutli, *Der Hüter des Vaterlandes*, 14th ed. (Stein am Rhein, 1991).

[4] O. Wimmer and H. Melzer, *Lexikon der Namen und Heiligen*, 4th ed. (Innsbruck, 1982), p. 494.

the town council in his native place and then in 1543 was elected *landammann* for the canton of Nidwalden. He yearned for solitude, though. As soon as he had permission, he resigned from his official posts. With his wife's consent, he bade her and their two daughters farewell and went to Ranft in Flüeli bei Sachsen. There, in his grandfather's hut, he spent three years in prayer and penance. Disturbed by the constant stream of visitors, he then settled on his own land in Bettelruiti ob Wolfenschiessen and built for himself there a hut together with a chapel. Here, too, many came to him seeking advice; even departed souls visited him and asked for his prayers.

Konrad Scheuber died on March 5, 1559. Because of the many prayers that were answered at his grave, his remains were disinterred on July 12, 1602, and laid to rest in the church.

Brother Klaus (Nicholas von Flüe), engraving, 1712

Blessed
Mark of Montegallo
and
Chiara dei Tibaldeschi

b. 1425 in Fonditore, near Montegallo, Italy
d. March 19, 1496, in Vicenza, Italy

Married 1451
Cult approved 1839

Mark, the son of the wealthy Chiaro de Marchio, was born in 1425 in Fonditore, near Montegallo.[1] He studied medicine at the universities of Perugia and Bologna and then practiced as a physician in Ascoli. Acceding to his father's wishes, in 1451 he married Chiara dei Tibaldeschi, a descendant of a noble family. They both practiced continence, never consummating the valid marriage they had entered. When Mark's father died, one year later, the spouses decided by mutual agreement to separate, each one leaving the other free to answer a call to religious life. The wife entered the Poor Clare convent of Santa Maria "delle donne" in Ascoli, while the husband became a member of the Franciscan Friars of the Observance (*Fratres de Observantia*).

In this case, then, two people who were more or less forced to get married dissolved their marriage, which they had never consummated—with the approval of the ecclesiastical authorities, of course—and entered religious life in the conviction that God was calling them to that state. This proved true for the husband, at any rate, for he now became an extraordinarily zealous friar, priest, and mission preacher who guided many souls who were striving for perfection and attained this ideal himself.

After his novitiate in Fabriano and the requisite theological

---

[1] Cf. *Acta Sanctorum Martii* 3:71–74; G. Fabiani, "Beato Marco da Montegallo", in *Bibliotheca Sanctorum* 8:739–40.

studies, Padre Mark became superior in San Severino. Then he began his apostolate as a mission preacher under the direction of an experienced confrère, the saintly Giacomo della Marca (d. 1476). Together with him, and later on his own, Padre Mark sought to heal the two great abuses that at that time wounded and burdened society in the southern regions of Italy: extremely hostile political disputes, on the one hand, and usury, on the other. Padre Mark, the saintly doctor, proved now to be a successful physician of souls who preached peace and reconciliation and repeatedly brought them about. Furthermore, in many places he countered usury by founding a so-called *monte di pietà*, a fraternal financial association where needy people could borrow money practically interest-free.

Even with his exhausting preaching schedule, Padre Mark found time to write several edifying books and to have them published, for instance, *La tabula della salute* (The table of salvation), which appeared in 1494 in Florence.

In Vicenza, where Padre Mark had preached several times with great success, he became deathly ill and died on March 19, 1496. To this mission preacher, who was buried in the church of San Biagio Vecchio in Vicenza, the faithful soon were paying the tribute of a fervent devotion. In 1839 this cult was approved by Pope Gregory XVI.

Blessed
Seraphina
and
Alexander Sforza

b. 1434 in Urbino
d. September 8, 1478, in Pesaro

Married 1448
Cult approved 1754

Sueva of Montefeltro,[1] the daughter of a count, later Princess Sforza by marriage, eventually joined the Poor Clares, taking the religious name Seraphina, and became an abbess. Of all the married blesseds and saints, her story is a particularly interesting case because her extremely unhappy marriage is involved in the history of the Church's marriage law, as several available studies show. Her marriage, nevertheless, proved to be a source of blessings both for her and for her profligate husband, as was their separation through a papal dispensation so that she could profess solemn vows in a religious order.

Sueva was born in Urbino in the first half of the year 1434, the last child of Count Guidantonio of Montefeltro and Catherine Colonna, a niece of Pope Martin V (Colonna).

In 1438, at the age of four, Sueva lost her mother and, five years later, her father, too. Her eldest brother, Oddantonio, was placed as guardian over her, and then her stepbrother Federico. In March 1446 she left her native town of Urbino and went to live with her uncle, Cardinal Prospero Colonna, who sought to marry the four-

---

[1] Cf. N. Del Re, "Sforza, Serafina", in *Bibliotheca Sanctorum* 11:1010–12; B. Feliciangeli, *Sulla monacazione di Sveva Montefeltro-Sforza, signora di Pesaro* (Pistoia, 1903); F. Madiai, "Sulla monacazione di Sveva Montefeltro-Sforza, signora di Pesaro", in *Le Marche* 3 (1903): 269–76; idem, "Nuovi documenti su Sveva di Pontefeltro-Sforza", in *Le Marche* 9 (1909): 94–142.

teen-year-old with the forty-year-old Alexander Sforza, lord of Pesaro. The wedding actually took place *per procura* [by proxy] on January 9, 1448. On September 1, 1448, Sueva went to Pesaro to live with her husband. He, however, departed very soon afterward to perform six years of military service for his brother Francesco in the campaign to conquer Milan.

Princess Sueva then, with astonishing success, substituted for her husband, the lord of Pesaro, in the daily business of ruling. She received good advice from her aunt Vittoria Colonna and her cousin Elisabetta Malatesta Varano. For her stepsons, Battista and Costanzo, Prince Alexander Sforza's two children from his first marriage, the young princess was an amiable stepmother beyond reproach.

Her husband's long absence from Pesaro and his complete lack of concern for his youthful wife caused her serious problems and put her marital fidelity to the test. During these six years did she yield to the flatteries of a courtier, so that Alexander Sforza had some justification in accusing her of adultery? He even reproached her for having attempted to poison him. It is certain, nevertheless, that Alexander Sforza wanted to divorce his young wife so as to be able to continue a life of vice, particularly with a mistress whom he brought along to his castle in Pesaro. The prince mistreated his wife, attempted several times to poison her, and once tried to strangle her. The protection to which she was entitled from her relatives was of no help to Princess Sueva against all the unjust accusations. Finally Sueva was compelled by her husband, Alexander, and her brother-in-law Francesco Sforza, the duke of Milan, to retire to Corpus Christi, the Poor Clare convent in Pesaro. This humiliation served, however, to purify and mature the prisoner. Eventually she adapted in every way to convent life. At the end of August 1457, on the basis of the dispensation granted by Pope Callistus III, Princess Sueva made her solemn profession and vowed perpetual poverty, chastity, and obedience. On that occasion she took the religious name of Seraphina.

This older but wiser Poor Clare became an apostle of penance and prayer; she prayed especially for the conversion of her dissolute husband. After a considerable length of time she ultimately experienced the great joy of seeing Prince Alexander Sforza repent and become a new man. He came to the Poor Clare convent of Corpus Christi, fell on his knees in remorse, and begged his wife for forgiveness. He returned several times and was consoled and strengthened by the spiritual conversations that he was able to conduct with his wife, who had become an exemplary religious. Alexander lived for nine years after his conversion and, like his wife, led a life of penance, self-sacrifice, and atonement.

Seraphina spent eighteen years as a worthy daughter of Saint Clare in the Corpus Christi convent in Pesaro. Then in 1475 she was unanimously elected abbess on account of her exemplary conduct. She survived her husband by five years. On September 8, 1478, she was called to her eternal reward, where she surely met her former husband again.

The believers in Pesaro began devotions to Blessed Seraphina soon after her death, and Pope Benedict XIV approved them on July 17, 1754. The former Princess Sforza had endured her spouse's moods and vices with heroic patience, had given outstanding service as a stepmother and a regent, and then as a nun had prayed and done much reparation for the conversion of her profligate husband. The incorrupt body of this seraphic blessed rests in the cathedral of Pesaro.

Saint
Catherine of Genoa
and
Julian Adorno

b. April 15, 1447
d. September 15, 1510

Married January 13, 1463
Beatified 1675
Canonized 1737

Saint Catherine of Genoa had to go through the "purgatory" of an extremely difficult and unhappy marriage in order to attain personal sanctity and to bring about the conversion of her irresponsible husband.

Catherine[1] was a descendant of the house of Fieschi, one of the most famous noble families in Genoa. She was born there on April 15, 1447, after her brothers, Giacomo, Giovanni, and Lorenzo, and her sister, Limbania, as the youngest daughter of the wealthy business magnate James Fieschi and Francesca di Negro. Her father had already died half a year before she was born. She was probably baptized soon afterward with the name Catherine in the cathedral of San Lorenzo in Genoa, which is practically next door to her birthplace. From childhood on the girl displayed singular gifts, and her pious mother gave her a good upbringing. Her older sister, Limbania, who had consecrated her life to God and become an Augustinian nun at the convent of Santa Maria delle Grazie in Genoa, was also a very positive influence. As a member of an

[1] Cf. F. Holböck, *Die Theologin des Fegefeuers Katharina von Genua* (Stein am Rhein, 1980).

aristocratic Genovese family, the youngest of the Fieschi children surely received a fine education, not only with respect to religion and morals, but also with regard to schooling and manners.

When Catherine had reached the age of thirteen, she wanted to imitate her older sister, Limbania, and enter religious life at the convent of Santa Maria delle Grazie. This wish cannot be dismissed as youthful enthusiasm, for as a thirteen-year-old Catherine proved to be extraordinarily mature, not only physically, but also intellectually and spiritually. Long before that she had shown herself to be remarkably devoted to prayer and penance. Catherine's request for admission to the convent was refused by the prioress, however, who said, "We don't want any children in our convent; it wouldn't be good, either, for too many women from the mighty, terrible house of Fieschi to be staying in our house."

Catherine was very sad that her application was refused. She then sought to make up for the grace of religious life, which had been denied her, by even greater zeal in performing works of piety, penance, and love of neighbor in the lay state.

When she turned sixteen she became the victim of the political plans of her eldest brother, Giacomo, who had become the head of the family after the death of their father.

In the year 1453 Constantinople had fallen into the hands of the Turks, which turned out to be a shattering event for all of Christendom, especially for the city of Genoa. At that time Genoa lost control of its foreign territories. As a result, the former sources of income and prosperity for the Genovese aristocracy dried up. Now, instead of wresting from the Turks the territories they had lost, the noble families of Genoa tore themselves to pieces in a period of internal political disputes. These battles, which resembled a civil war, were especially fierce between the powerful old Fieschi and Adorno families, on the one side, and the leading family of the Fregosos on the other.

In opposition to the Fregoso family and the Sforza family of the duke of Milan, whom the former had called in to rule Genoa, the Fieschi and Adorno families—who otherwise were constantly feuding among themselves—formed a close alliance. This friendly compact between the Fieschi family, which favored the Guelf party, and the Adornos, who favored the Ghibellines, was supposed to be consummated and sealed by a marital union, namely, the marriage of the sixteen-year-old Catherine Fieschi with Julian Adorno.

This representative of the Adorno family had distinguished himself during the conquest of Ascio and was the governor of this island, but subsequently he was imprisoned by the doge—a Fregoso. When Julian Adorno finally regained his freedom in 1460, he returned to Genoa. On January 13, 1463, in the palace of the Fieschi family in Genoa, he was wedded to the sixteen-year-old Catherine.

Julian Adorno was a violent, brutal, morally dissolute, and uncontrollable man who already had to care for three illegitimate children—maybe five, as it was rumored. Furthermore, he was an ostentatious spendthrift and a playboy. During the first ten years of his marriage, he managed to squander almost entirely, not only his own considerable wealth, but also that of his young wife, Catherine. In other ways, too, this marriage proved to be extremely unhappy. Julian Adorno completely neglected his young wife, both in the house where Catherine had grown up and where the couple lived for the first two years of their marriage, and also in the palace of the Adornos, to which they moved in 1466.

These were bitter, sorrowful years that the young noblewoman had to spend, almost like a prisoner, within the cold stone walls of the Adorno family palace: alone, neglected, and forgotten, all too often offended and slighted, and even betrayed by her husband's adultery.

The tangled political situation in the republic of Genoa at that time aggravated the young woman's unhappiness. For the doge then in power, Paolo Fregoso, became more and more of a tyrant. Hence the prospects for the Adorno and Fieschi families, which were in opposition to him, had become hopeless. Consequently, Julian Adorno, Catherine's husband, would take out on his household his rage over the political situation; since his ambition was totally frustrated, he would turn to dice and card games and to loose women. In that way he gambled away or dissipated enormous sums. When he then returned home, he had nothing left for his young wife but a sinister, disdainful glare.

Thus Catherine spent the first five years of her marriage, to which she had consented only at her oldest brother's insistence, which bordered on compulsion, and also that of her mother so as to keep the peace: years marked by sadness, increasing melancholy, and almost total seclusion.

In the summer, Catherine would live alone in the country house of the Adorno family in Prà, in the vicinity of Genoa. Here she was a bit better off, inasmuch as she could go on pilgrimage now and then to the shrine cared for by the Benedictines at the abbey of San Nicolò del Boschetto. There she could discuss her plight with an experienced monk-confessor and relieve her spiritual sufferings by tearfully pouring out her heart in prayer to the all-holy Lord.

Her marriage itself brought her no joy. The sexual consummation of the marriage, the advantage of being the wife of a prominent man, the honor of having many subordinates at her bidding as lady of the house, the flatteries with which people tried to cheer her—all of that held no attraction and no real meaning for Catherine, whose love had belonged to Christ in a special way since her childhood. Still, she realized that an indissoluble marital bond chained her to a man who cared for nothing except boasting and ostentation, leading a life of abandon, and running up expenses as though their combined wealth had no limits at all.

Catherine probably remonstrated with her husband kindly and tactfully at first. Then, when these efforts came to naught, she may have used a more severe tone of voice. She soon noticed, however, that it was of no use with this husband—on the contrary, it just made matters worse.

Divorce, though, was out of the question. Catherine's marriage had been arranged in the interests of reconciling the feuding Fieschi and Adorno families. Her religious sense suggested to her the idea of accepting and affirming her marriage as a form of reparation that God himself had destined her to make: on behalf of her husband, for the two noble houses, for the entire republic of Genoa, and also for the Church and all mankind, which at that time were experiencing conflicts of many sorts.

Thus Catherine began to suffer silently, in a spirit of penance and atonement, all the sorrows that afflicted her and to offer everything up. The misunderstood young wife found the strength to do so in prayer and in the Holy Sacrifice of the Altar. The only time the "recluse" would leave her house each day was to go to one of the churches in Genoa to attend Mass.

It is certain that during this period Catherine's mother, her brothers, her relatives, and acquaintances often urged her to give up her secluded way of life. No doubt they argued that, considering the high station of her husband and of her family, she was obliged to appear in society; that way she might even regain some influence over her husband. If she continued as she had been doing, she would fall prey to melancholy and depression, get sick, and shorten her life. If, on the other hand, she began again to attend festivals and entertainments—with the clothing and manners that would show off her beauty, which was still remarkable— surely she would soon be the talk of the town. She could then arouse her husband's jealousy and thus reclaim his affections. That was why it was silly to lead such a solitary life as she had done in the first five years of her marriage, even for religious reasons.

They continued to importune the young married woman in this way, until she gradually began to have doubts about her way of life until then. She wondered whether it might be better not to stay completely aloof in the future so as not to be entirely excluded from the usual social life of the Genovese ladies of rank and high station.

So, at the beginning of her sixth year of marriage, Catherine actually started to give up her solitary way of life, to receive visits and to return them, to appear again more and more often in society, and to participate in public events, all the while conforming in her dress, her jewelry, and her entire demeanor to the ways of the other ladies in society, and eventually surpassing them. The next five years in the world, however, did not make Catherine happy at all. On the contrary, in the eighth year of her marriage she suddenly felt enormously unhappy; she was beset by sadness that became ever more intense. Suddenly it seemed impossible for her to continue farther down the worldly path on which she had set out. She was aware of an oppressive feeling of being dependent upon the world and its sensual pleasures, which still leave the heart empty. Furthermore, she was horrified by her husband's dissolute ways, which had already consumed the greater part of their combined wealth. Extremely despondent and thirsting for human sympathy, she went on March 22, 1473, to see her sister, Limbania, at the convent of Santa Maria delle Grazie.

In the parlor of the convent, the Augustinian nun tried to console her disheartened sister, Catherine; she advised her to have a good thorough talk with her father confessor. Catherine took this advice. Her heart was instantaneously struck by the arrow of God's immeasurable love. At the same time, she had a deeply disturbing glimpse of the pitiable state of her soul, which was deformed by sins and failings. In a moment of clairvoyance she recognized all the graces the Lord was offering to her, out of sheer love, in order to draw her away from the world and to himself. Simultaneously, an unbounded love for God and deep remorse filled her soul. She began a profound conversion that transformed her completely and culminated in 1477, after a four-year period of penance and purification.

After her conversion, Catherine of Genoa did not fall into a one-sided routine of pious exercises. She now devoted herself with equal zeal to works of mercy in caring for the poor and the sick. She attended to these people with unspeakable kindness and great love, washed the threadbare clothing and undergarments of the poor and the sick and mended them, insofar as that was still possible, or else replaced them. The places where sickness and frailty dwelled—in the physical and the moral sense—where there were fears and sorrows, tears and laments, and where others only glanced quickly so as to run away as fast as possible: this was Catherine's field of activity. She also made her way into places where she was greeted only by desperate complaints and the hateful slogans of feuding factions; there, too, Catherine offered consolation and strove to heal body and soul. In all these charitable works she did not forget the lost sheep that had been especially entrusted to her through the Sacrament of Matrimony.

Soon after Catherine's conversion, her husband, Julian Adorno, experienced financial ruin. He had dissipated so much of their wealth that in 1473 he had to sell his country house in Prà and rent the Adorno palace in Genoa. The nobleman who once had been rolling in wealth was now a poor wretch. But the misfortune that had befallen him, and the heroic patience and silent equanimity with which his wife, Catherine, always faced it, gradually softened this hard-hearted man and conquered his pride. Finally, thanks to Catherine's many prayers and sacrifices, her irresponsible husband was brought to the point of conversion. He came to his senses, repented of his former dissolute life, and resolved to live henceforth with Catherine as brother and sister in a chaste, continent marriage.

In order to turn his back on the seductions of the world and to avoid succumbing again to its enticements, Julian Adorno humbly took the penitential garment worn by members of the third order of Saint Francis. From 1479 on, he was a faithful assistant to his saintly wife in her service to the needy and the sick. Eventually, this transformed his stern, quick-tempered character. Finally, his holy death (sometime after January 10, 1497) seemed to his beloved wife, Catherine, like the answer to the prayer she had repeatedly sent up to God, her great Love: "O my Love, I ask thee for this soul! Give it to me, I beg thee! Thou canst give it to me."

About Catherine it should also be mentioned that, on account of her generous service to the sick, the magistrate of the republic of Genoa appointed her the manager of Pammatone Hospital. In that position she spent herself entirely for the sick, especially during the five plague epidemics that afflicted Genoa. Catherine died in the night, between September 14 and 15, 1510, in her sixty-third year. She had suffered an extremely painful purgatory during thirty-four years of married life. After receiving the grace of conversion, she and her husband together had served the sick for the last twenty-two years of their marriage. As a widow she had continued for thirteen more years to care for the poorest of the poor with generosity and charity.

Blessed
Louisa of Savoy

and

Hugh de Châlons

b. December 28, 1462, in Geneva
d. July 24, 1503

Married 1479
Cult approved in 1839

Louisa (Ludovica) was born on December 28, 1462, in Geneva, the daughter of Duke Amadeus IX and Yolande of France (the sister of the French King Louis XI); she was married in 1479 at the age of seventeen to Hugh de Châlons, lord of Nozeroy.[1]

Louisa's life, from her youth, during her betrothal, and as a wife, was always characterized by great austerity and profound piety. After the death of her husband, in the year 1490, only two years passed before the princess, who had already been leading a life of prayer and charitable works, entered the Poor Clare convent in Orbe (Canton Vaud, Switzerland), which had been reformed by Saint Colette Boillet. There Louisa was outstanding for her sanctity of life. She donated all of her wealth to the church in Orbe; she wanted to live and die in Franciscan poverty. On July 24, 1503, the unassuming former wife and princess died poor, but rich in merits for eternity. In 1839 Pope Gregory XVI approved the invocation of and devotion to Louisa of Savoy as a blessed.

---

[1] Cf. P. Durio, *Vita della beata Ludovica di Savoia* (Rome, 1840).

Blessed
Margaret of Lorraine
and
René of Alençon

b. 1463 in Château Vaudémont in Lorraine
d. November 2, 1521, in Argentan

Married 1488
Mother of three children
Cult approved on March 20, 1921

Blessed Margaret (Marguérite) of Lorraine was born in Vaudémont, Lorraine, in 1463, the daughter of Duke Ferri of Lorraine
and Yolande of Anjou. On account of her charm and virtuous
character she attracted the notice of extended social circles at an
early age. At the age of twelve she was brought to the court of
"good King" René of Anjou. Here, through reading the *Legenda
aurea*, she acquired a zeal to imitate the saints; she wanted more
than anything to become a recluse. In 1480 she returned to Lorraine; in the bloom of youthful beauty, she was also noted for her
purity and profound piety. On May 14, 1488, Margaret married
Duke René of Alençon, but after only four years she was widowed. During these four years of marriage she bore her husband
three children, namely, Charles, Frances [Françoise], and Anne;
she was also very open-minded and, with the duke's support,
looked after the living standards of the subjects in the duchy. On
November 1, 1492, Duke René died. Now Margaret not only had
to see to the care and education of her three children; she also
reigned with wisdom and justice for twenty years in the place of
her deceased husband. Suitable marriages were arranged for the
three children. The son, Charles, married Margaret of Angoulême

[1] *Acta Sanctorum Nov[orum]* 1:418f.; M.-O. Garrigues, "Beata Margherita di Lorena,
duchesse d'Alençon", in *Bibliotheca Sanctorum* 8:777–78.

and thus became the brother-in-law of King Francis I. One daughter, Frances, became the duchess of Bourbon, and Anne, the second daughter, became the duchess of Montfort.

Under the direction of Saint Francis of Paola (d. April 2, 1507), Margaret of Lorraine led during this period a strictly regimented spiritual life of asceticism. The widowed duchess particularly enjoyed caring for the poor and the sick. With great zeal she oversaw the founding of schools and the formation of God-fearing teachers. She dealt very severely with hard-hearted landlords and selfish officials. For all that, she always remained modest in her demeanor. With genuine devotion she spent a large part of each day in meditating on the Passion of Jesus Christ and in attending Holy Mass, during which the Redeemer's sacrifice on the Cross is made present in the Holy Eucharist. After conferring the rule of the duchy to her son, Charles, she devoted herself exclusively to her personal sanctification. In 1513 she became a tertiary in the third order of Saint Francis and, using her own financial resources, founded a Poor Clare convent in Argentan. Eventually, she entered this convent, made solemn profession there in 1520, and then, until her death on November 2, 1521, led an exemplary religious life according to the Rule.

Public devotions to this pious duchess—who gave good example for four years as a Christian spouse and as a mother cared lovingly for her three children; who ruled prudently over her subjects in the duchy, and then was a humble, kindly sister in religion to the Poor Clares of the convent in Argentan—were approved on March 20, 1921, by Pope Benedict XIV.[1]

Saint
Joan of France
and
Louis of Orleans

b. April 23, 1464, in Nogent-le-
  Roy, France
d. February 4, 1505

Married September 8, 1476
Canonized May 28, 1950

S. Johanna Valesia

Joan of France (or of Valois) was a saint who, twenty-two years
after her church wedding, had to watch as Church officials declared her marriage null.[1] She was the daughter, the sister, and the
wife of three kings of France. Her grandfather was King Charles
VII, who—thanks to the providential intervention of Saint Joan of
Arc, the Maid of Orleans—was crowned king in Reims in 1429;
his son Louis XI of France (d. 1483), who married Charlotte of
Savoy, was the father of Saint Joan of France, who was born on
April 23, 1464, in Nogent-le-Roy. King Louis XI was sorely
disappointed at her birth, not only because he had hoped for a
successor to the throne instead of a daughter, but especially because the child was deformed and ugly.

King Louis XI betrothed his unloved daughter when she was
twenty-six days old to her two-year-old cousin, Louis of Orleans.
This betrothal was taken seriously, for it resulted in a church

---

[1] Cf. A. Girard, *Sainte Jeanne de France, duchesse de Berry* (Bourges, 1950); R. M.
Gabriel-Marie, *La Spiritualité de sainte Jeanne de France* (Paris, 1950).

wedding on September 8, 1476, in Montrichard, when the bride, Joan of France, was twelve and the groom, Louis or Orleans, was fourteen. The marriage contract was signed on August 11, 1476, by the father of the bride, King Louis XI, and on August 28, 1476, by the mother of the groom, Marie de Clèves.

Louis of Orleans had nothing but distaste for his wife, Joan; she, on the other hand, bore everything patiently and kindly and responded to his neglect with good deeds and love.

In the year 1483, the father of Joan of France, King Louis XI, died. His son and successor to the throne of the French kingdom, King Charles VIII, the brother of Joan of France, was then still a minor and therefore needed a guardian. The defunct King Louis XI, however, had not designated the nearest male relative, namely, Louis of Orleans, Joan's husband, to be the guardian, but rather the older sister of the underage king, who was married to Pierre de Bourbon. Louis of Orleans was furious about this. He led a rebellion but was conquered and taken prisoner; it appeared that he had forfeited his life. His noble-minded wife, Joan of France, however, managed to intercede so earnestly for her husband, Louis of Orleans, that he was finally pardoned. During the two years that Louis of Orleans was imprisoned, his wife, Joan of France, repaid him with goodness for everything he had done to her thus far in their marriage: she visited and consoled him as often as possible.

After the premature death of King Charles VIII, the brother of Saint Joan of France, Louis of Orleans became king in the year 1498 and as Louis XII ascended to the throne of the French kingdom.

With this new title he had no business more urgent than to have recourse to the reigning pope, Alexander VI, with the demand that his marriage to Joan of France be declared invalid. He gave three reasons: (1) twenty-two years previously he had contracted marriage against his will, under duress, compelled by King Louis XI; (2) on the very day of the wedding he had made a notarized deposition on the matter; and (3) his wife was incapable of child-bearing.

Pope Alexander VI authorized a commission to investigate the case. On August 10, 1498, the Queen was summoned to appear before the marriage tribunal that was in session in the church of Saint-Gatien in Tours. She solemnly protested against the declaration of nullity. There were contradictory testimonies from the two spouses concerning the consummation of their marriage. Thereupon the queen demanded that King Louis XII take the *juramentum veritatis*; he unscrupulously swore that he told the truth in alleging that his marriage had not been consummated.

Then the queen yielded and acknowledged the commission's declaration that her marriage was null. The question remains whether the Church terminated a putative marriage on the grounds of invalidity or whether it dissolved a valid marriage that had not been consummated. The queen simply declared, "This does me a great injustice, but may God be praised for everything. I know that he allows all this, so that I can serve him better than before and carry out my wish (that I had expressed even as a child) to found an order in honor of the Blessed Virgin Mary." Let it be noted that not a few theologians of the day questioned the commission's judgment of nullity.

King Louis XII was happy to have achieved what he wanted with relative ease, and he married the widow of the defunct King Charles VIII, the sister-in-law of the repudiated Queen Joan of France. To the latter King Louis XII assigned the duchy of Berry, with its seat in the city of Bourges.

On March 15, 1499, Joan of France made her entrance there. She ruled her duchy with great wisdom and kindness and restored justice everywhere to a place of honor. In the years 1499–1500, during which the plague was raging in the duchy of Berry, there were no limits to the willingness of Duchess Joan of France to help the needy. For all her motherly care for her duchy, she still did not forget the task that had been assigned to her in her childhood. At the age of seven she had had a vision of the Blessed Virgin, who said to her, "Before your death you will found an order in my honor, which will be a cause of great joy for me and my Son." After becoming sick and having premonitions of her death, the duchess—on the advice of her confessor, the Franciscan priest Blessed Gabriel Mary Nicolas—set about founding the Order of the Annuntiata (*L'Annonciade*). This strictly contemplative order spread rapidly.

The foundress of the order survived the day of the foundation, February 12, 1502, by only a few months. On that date Pope Alexander VI had approved the Rule of the Annonciades of Bourges (Annunciation Sisters) in the bull *Ea quae*. On January 22, 1505, the duchess, who edified all by her piety and humility, came down with a serious illness, which led to her death on February 4, 1505. Pope Benedict XIV declared Joan of France blessed on April 21, 1742, and Pope Pius XII canonized her on May 28, 1950.

Blessed Helena of Bologna

and

Benedict dall' Oglio

b. 1472 in Bologna, Italy
d. September 23, 1520, in Bologna

Married 1489
Cult approved 1828

This blessed wife and widow, after going home to God in her forty-eighth year, unfortunately had biographers who were not entirely objective and hence not to be taken very seriously. In the attempt to exalt her as much as possible above average people, they invented fantastic details about her life that could not possibly have been true. For instance, they made her into the daughter of the Turkish ruler Muhammad II. At the age of five she is said to have come to Italy from the Near East. In Bologna she supposedly led a holy, virginal life and was therefore rewarded by God with special charisms (visions, the gift of prophesy, and so on).

In fact, Blessed Helen (Lena, Elena)[1] was born in Bologna in the year 1472, the daughter of the respected notary Silverio Duglioli and his wife, Penesilea Boccaferri. She received from her parents a first-rate Christian upbringing. Even as a girl she exhibited a desire to consecrate herself to God in perpetual virginity. At her parents' wishes, however, she married at age seventeen, in 1489, the forty-year-old Benedict dall' Oglio. For thirty years she led together with him an exemplary and harmonious married life, allegedly while practicing complete continence. There are no proofs whatsoever for this, though; presumably the marriage remained childless for some biological reason or other, so that the couple

---

[1] *Acta Sanctorum* 6:655–59; G. D. Gordini, "Beata vedova Duglioli", in *Bibliotheca Sanctorum* 4:853–55.

eventually decided to renounce the expression of their marital love in sexual relations. The fact is that the course of this marriage was uncommonly harmonious, peaceful, and happy.

After the death of her husband, the widow devoted herself even more zealously to works of piety and self-denial. She was called by God from this life in her forty-eighth year, on September 23, 1520, and her body was buried in the church of San Giovanni in Monte in Bologna. Soon afterward, the departed wife and widow was the object of great reverence and devotion on account of her edifying Christian life. People called on her for help in various needs, as the numerous *ex voto* tablets at her gravesite testify, on which Helen dall' Oglio, née Duglioli, was already described as a blessed or even a saint. In the year 1828 Pope Leo XII confirmed and declared that devotions to this noble woman were authorized.

Blessed Helen of Bologna and Andrea Giustiniani (Pinakothek, Bologna)

Blessed
Louisa Albertoni
and
James de Cithara

b. 1474, in Rome
d. January 31, 1533, in Rome

Married 1494
Mother of three children
Cult approved on January 28, 1671

This blessed[1] was born in 1474 in Rome, a descendant of the noble house of the Albertoni. Because Louisa (Ludovica) lost her father while she was still a very small child and her mother remarried, the little girl was entrusted to her grandmother on her mother's side and then to an uncle on her father's side.

The girl grew up to be a beautiful young woman of extraordinary character. At the age of twenty, Louisa was married against her wishes to the nobleman James de Cithara, who loved her dearly. She gave him three children.

After only twelve years of marriage, Louisa's husband died in 1506. She determined to structure her life as a widow according to the description in the fifth chapter of the First Letter to Timothy: she became a member of the third order of Saint Francis and from then on consecrated her life entirely to prayer, penance, and works of charity. With great discretion she set about assisting the poor in their need; she visited the destitute in their miserable huts and consoled and encouraged them in word and deed, above all through generous almsgiving.

Similarly, Louisa looked after needy girls, instructed them in the true faith and proper Christian morality, and sought to guard them

---

[1] N. Del Re, "Ludovica degli Albertoni", in *Bibliotheca Sanctorum* 1:717–19.

from temptations. She obtained honest work for them and gave them the dowry they needed in order to enter a good Christian marriage.

Because Louisa continued to help others by making generous gifts from the vast wealth she had inherited, she finally became poor herself. Her relatives were horrified. God, however, rewarded her liberality and her Franciscan poverty, which she had chosen quite deliberately, by granting her extraordinary graces, among them the gifts of prophecy and miracle-working.

Devotions to this noble woman, who died on January 31, 1533, in Rome, her birthplace, began very soon after her death. Pope Clement X, who was related to the Albertoni family by marriage, sanctioned the devotions to Louisa and approved her cult on January 28, 1671. Over the tomb of this blessed Roman wife, mother, and widow in the church of San Francesco a Ripa in Rome stands the beautiful and impressive statue of this blessed that was sculpted by the famous Giovanni Lorenzo Bernini.

Louisa Albertoni. Marble statue by Giovanni Lorenzo Bernini.
Church of San Francesco a Ripa, Rome.

Saint
Thomas More

and

Jane Colt

b. February 7, 1478, in London
d. July 6, 1535, executed

Married 1505; remarried 1511
Father of four children
Canonized May 19, 1935

One saint who is especially preeminent in the company of married saints is the English Lord Chancellor Thomas More. He married twice and was an exemplary husband and father. Furthermore, particularly when it was a question of the illegitimate divorce and remarriage of the English King Henry VIII, he was a courageous defender of the indissolubility of a valid, consummated marriage, and for this stance he suffered much, even martyrdom.

Thomas More was born in February 7, 1478, in London, the second of the six children of Judge John Moore (d. 1530 at age seventy-nine) and his wife, Agnes, who died sometime between 1482 and 1499, when Thomas was still young.

He attended the renowned Saint Anthony's School in London and as a twelve-year-old became the page of the then Lord Chancellor (later Cardinal) John Morton. At the age of fourteen, Thomas More went to Oxford University (1492–1494) and then studied law and theology in London.

Between 1499 and 1503, Thomas More lived in the guest house of the London Carthusians. During this time he was discerning whether he had a vocation to the religious life. The young man, indeed, longed to love God and to dedicate himself entirely to him, but he realized that he was not capable of renouncing marriage and family. Therefore he ultimately decided on marriage. In January 1505, after having been admitted to the bar as a lawyer in 1501 and elected as a burgess in the newly established Parliament, the twenty-seven-year-old Thomas More married Jane Colt, who was ten years younger. She bore him four children.

This extremely happy but unfortunately short-lived marriage came about in a rather unusual way. The nobleman John Colt had invited the young Thomas More to his estate, Netherhall, in the county of Essex. Thomas accepted the invitation. During his visit he found in the household of John Colt—among seventeen brothers and sisters by two marriages—three eligible daughters, who had received a "virtuous upbringing" and were noted for their respectable conduct. Thomas fell in love with the second of these three daughters. He realized, though, that it would be very painful and also somewhat shameful for the eldest of the three daughters if the younger sister was preferred and betrothed first.

Therefore, out of a certain pity for the older sister, he turned his affections to her and married her soon afterward.[1] The sixteen-year-old Jane Colt had lived until then exclusively in the country with her parents and her siblings and was rather uneducated and inexperienced. How much Thomas More loved his young wife in the course of their six and a half years of marriage can be inferred from the fact that, more than twenty years later, he still called Jane Colt his *"cara uxorcula"*, his "dear little wife", and wistfully reminisced about their all-too-short period of marital happiness.

In the summer of 1511 his beloved wife Jane died, having completed only twenty-two years, leaving the young widower, Thomas More, with four children, who ranged in age from two to six years. What else could he do but remarry as soon as possible, after a few weeks, "for the sake of his family rather than for

[1] Cf. P. Berglar, *Die Stunde des Thomas Morus* (Olten, 1978), pp. 160–61.

Thomas More as a young nobleman. Painting by his friend Hans Holbein from the year 1527. Uffizi, Florence. (Photo: Alinari, Florence.)

pleasure", as Thomas More's friend Erasmus of Rotterdam wrote in a letter to Hutten. In that letter, More's second wife, the silk merchant Alice Middleton, is described as "not especially beautiful and no longer a little maid, either" ("nec bella nec puella", as Thomas himself used to joke).

Nevertheless, she was a hard-working and enterprising house-wife. He lived with her as lovingly and pleasantly as if she were a maiden of the most charming beauty. It is a rare husband who elicits from his wife as much compliance by commands and sternness as he does through compliments and jokes. What else might he not achieve, after he succeeded in teaching his wife, who was no longer the youngest of women and had a character that was by no means sensitive but rather intent on material possessions, how to play the zither, the lute, the monochord, and the flute, and in having her practice each of them daily for a certain amount of time?[2]

The second wife of Thomas More, Lady Alice, who remained childless, has sometimes been compared with the classical Xanthippe, mainly because she could accommodate herself only with difficulty to his combative stance toward the adulterous King Henry VIII. Instead of in prison, she would have preferred to see her husband in freedom at her side, living in good bourgeois prosperity. After Thomas More had already spent a long time in incarceration, Alice More finally received permission to visit him. On that occasion she greeted him unceremoniously in the following words (according to the so-called "Ro Ba" biography of Thomas More, published in the year 1599).[3]

What the good year, Master More . . . I marvel that you, that have been always hitherto taken for so wise a man, will now so play the fool to lie here in this close, filthy prison, and be content thus to be shut up amongst mice and rats, when you might be abroad at your liberty, and with the favour and good will both of the King and his Council, if you would but do as all the Bishops and best learned of this realm have done. And seeing you have at Chelsea a right fair house, your library, your books, your gallery, your garden, your orchard, and all other necessaries so handsome about you, where you might in the company of me your wife, your children, and household be merry, I muse what a God's name you mean here still thus fondly to tarry.

[2] Cf. W. P. Eckert, *Erasmus von Rotterdam, Werk und Wirkung* (Cologne, 1967), 2:447.

[3] Edited by E. V. Hitchcock, *The Life and Death of Sir Thomas More* (London, 1950), quoted by James Monti, *The King's Good Servant but God's First* (San Francisco: Ignatius Press, 1999), p. 412.

And still Thomas More loved his second wife, too, with all his heart. In his autobiographical epitaph, which he composed [in Latin] in 1532, he has left her a stirring memorial. It reads:

Here lies Jane the well-beloved wife of me, Thomas More, who have appointed this tomb for Alice, my wife, and me also, the one, being coupled with me in matrimony, in my youth, brought me forth three daughters and one son, the other has been so good to my children (which is rare praise in mothers-in-law [stepmothers]) as scant any could be better to her own. The one so lived with me, and the other now so liveth, that it is doubtful whether this or the other were dearer to me. Oh, how well could we three have lived together in matrimony if fortune and religion would have suffered it. But I beseech our Lord that his tomb and heaven may join us together. So death shall give that thing that life could not.[4]

Why, then, did Thomas More love his second wife, too, despite her pronounced resemblance to Xanthippe? Surely because she fulfilled in exemplary fashion her duties as a mother in raising the children from his first marriage and also kept up with the household chores. Thomas More was often away from house and family because of the great demands that his work made upon him; he was grateful to know that he could rely completely on Lady Alice. As one author has rightly emphasized,

In this marriage—whatever may have been lacking in beauty—there was at no time a lack of mutual respect or of a clear understanding as to the competence of each spouse. . . . In a curious sentence, a sort of marble postscript in the Old Church at Chelsea, Thomas More described the happiness of an earthly "triple alliance", which only fortune and religion prevented from occurring, but which, beyond the common grave, heaven might be able to grant. This sentence proves that Thomas More

---

[4] Cf. Berglar, *Stunde*, p. 160.

loved both of his wives, truly and sincerely loved them, each in the appropriate manner and degree—according to the age at the time, the circumstances, and the personalities of all three who were involved. A secret that lies hidden in the soul of Thomas More remains a mystery even when we reflect that the young man's saying, "Because I love you, you are my wife," is supposed to become the mature man's saying, "Because you are my wife, I love you." Only in this way does a marriage succeed. In going from Jane Colt to Alice Middleton, it would seem, Thomas More traveled this very path; he went through a development that would otherwise have to take place within one marriage.[5]

Thomas More was not only a husband inspired by genuine marital love and fidelity, but also a loving, caring father. It is remarkable, though, that among his four children, all of them from his first marriage, his firstborn, Margaret, was closest to him. Nevertheless, he dearly loved all four, and also their foster-sister Margaret Giggs (or Gyge), a nurse's child who was the same age as his own Margaret, as well as Alice, the daughter of his second wife from her first marriage. Here, briefly, are the most important facts about the lives of Thomas More's four children.

1. Margaret: The favorite daughter of Thomas More, this gifted and highly educated young woman was born in October 1505 and at the age of sixteen, on July 2, 1521, married the twenty-three-year-old William Roper, who came from a prominent family of lawyers. He lived for several years in the household of his father-in-law. For More, the marriage of his darling daughter remained under a cloud, because his son-in-law was an adherent of Martin Luther's teachings. To make matters worse, he was independent to the point of obstinacy and had such a vehement temperament that discussing anything with him, especially theological questions, was a hopeless exercise; the only thing that could help was prayer. William Roper did, in fact, return to the Catholic Church before 1535; he then became a zealous champion of the faith and—

[5] Ibid., p. 169.

continuing More's charitable works—made magnanimous endowments, especially for the poorhouse that Thomas More had founded in Chelsea. With prudence, steadfastness, and courage, he helped oppressed Catholics and took up the cause of fellow believers who had been impoverished or imprisoned. In 1542 he was incarcerated in the Tower of London for a time and was brought to trial for supporting Catholic refugees. In 1578 he died, almost eighty years old, thirty-four years after his wife, Margaret, who had died in 1544.[6]

About Margaret it should be mentioned that she—especially during Thomas More's imprisonment—held the first place in her father's heart. "The correspondence of the two that was written between More's arrest and his death furnishes not only the most moving but also the most revealing insights into the soul of Thomas More."[7]

2. Elizabeth: She was born in 1506 and at age nineteen, on September 29, 1525, married the court official William Dauncey.

3. Cecily: She was born in 1507 and at age eighteen, on September 29, 1525, married Giles Heron, the son of the treasurer of the royal household, Sir John Heron. During the lifetime of his father-in-law, Giles Heron was a rather rebellious young man, but in 1540, five years after Thomas More's death, he followed him when, like his father-in-law, he was executed, the victim of false accusations.

4. John: Thomas More's only son was born in 1509; he married Anne Cresacre, who bore him eight children. John died in 1547. The descendants of Thomas More—and they are quite numerous even today—can all be traced back to Thomas More's son, John, and his wife, Anne.

Thomas More, whose professional duties often obliged him to be away from his wife and family, saw to it that his children were brought up properly. His letters to them and to their tutor, William Gonell, show that he thought about them with tender care. Conscious of his responsibility for their temporal well-being and

---

[6] Cf. E. Reynolds, *Margaret Roper* (London, 1960).
[7] Cf. Berglar, *Stunde*, p. 130.

FAMILIA THOMÆ MORI ANGL. CANCELL.

Thomas Morus A°.50. Alicia Thomæ Mori uxor A°.57. Iohannes Morus pater A°.76. Iohannes Morus Thomæ filius A°.19. Anna Grisacria Iohannis Mori sponsa A°.15. Margareta Ropera Thomæ Mori filia A°.22.
Elisabeta Dauncia Thomæ Mori filia A°.21. Cæcilia Heronia Thomæ Mori filia A°.20. Margareta Giga Clementis uxor Mori filialiqus Condiscipula et cognata A°.22. Henricus Patensonus Thomæ Mori morio A°.40.

The Family of Thomas More, 1526, by Hans Holbein the Younger.
Pen and brush drawing over a crayoned sketch. Kunstmuseum, Basel, Switzerland
(Kupferstichkabinett, Inv. 1662.31).

326

eternal salvation, he often reflected on the correct priority of values that should be communicated to the children. He set great store on educating his children in genuine piety, so that they would follow Christ's example of loving God and neighbor. He wanted his children

> . . . to put virtue in the first place among goods, learning in the second; and in their studies to esteem most whatever may teach them piety towards God, charity to all, and modesty and Christian humility in themselves. By such means they will receive from God the reward of an innocent life, and in the assured expectation of it will view death without dread, and meanwhile possessing solid joy will neither be puffed up by the empty praise of men, nor dejected by evil tongues.[8]

Such is the gist of a letter that Thomas More sent to William Gonell, the tutor of his household. This was also in keeping with his personal conduct, for he was in all respects a practicing Catholic who prayed much, received the sacraments often, and was extraordinarily charitable to the poor and the needy.

As for the witness of Sir Thomas More to the indissolubility of marriage, the following should be said.[9]

In the year 1509 King Henry VIII ascended the throne of England. He seemed to be a good ruler and a true son of the Catholic Church. His treatise against Martin Luther earned him the papal title of *Defensor fidei*, Defender of the Faith. In 1522 the king, who was married to Catherine of Aragon, the widow of his deceased brother, fell in love with a lady-in-waiting, Anne Boleyn. Henry VIII attempted to have his previous marriage declared invalid in Rome. The reason he offered was that until then it had been considered an impediment to marriage if the prospective bride was the widow of the groom's deceased brother. In his particular case, though, the pope had granted a dispensation from

[8] Elizabeth Frances Rogers, ed., *St. Thomas More: Selected Letters* (New Haven and London: Yale University Press, 1961), p. 105.

[9] Cf. G. Kranz, *Politische Heilige* (Augsburg, 1958), 1:176–99.

this impediment. The real reason King Henry VIII wanted his marriage to be declared invalid was a different one altogether: his wife, Catherine of Aragon, had given birth to one son after another, but they were either stillborn or died soon after birth. King Henry VIII needed an heir to the throne. Catherine, evidently, could not give him one. In 1527 the king asked the highly esteemed lawyer Thomas More to counsel him in this marital matter of his. More, however, replied that the question of whether the king's previous marriage was valid or not was a theological and canonical question, which he was not competent to decide. The king still insisted on hearing More's opinion. So Thomas More asked for time, consulted with various bishops, thoroughly studied the particular case, and finally came to a conclusion, which he communicated to the king. The pope had legitimately granted a dispensation; therefore, the marriage was valid.

In 1529 the attempt made by Cardinal Wolsey, in his capacity as papal legate, to settle "the Great Matter" of Henry's marriage according to His Highness' wishes foundered. The pope's refusal and the failure of Cardinal Wolsey threw the king into a rage. He deposed Cardinal Wolsey as lord chancellor and in his place appointed Thomas More to be lord chancellor. More, of all people—so the king thought—would finally support him now that he was intent on opposing Rome and settling his marital affairs on his own.

How could Thomas More, a loyal son of the Church, accept the office of chancellor, when he had already objected to the king's divorce from his wife, Catherine of Aragon? More's nephew Rastell later explained that More had at first declined; thereupon the king became furious and finally compelled Thomas More to accept the office. Once in the king's service as lord chancellor, Thomas More was a free man no more. It is true that he explained several times to Henry VIII that he was not on His Majesty's side with regard to the marriage question and therefore could not be of service to him in the Great Matter. Thereupon the king solemnly promised him that he did not want to force him to act against his conscience in any way. In 1530 King Henry VIII tried once again to obtain from the pope a declaration of nullity for his marriage, hinting this time that the pope was obliged for political reasons to do so for him out of gratitude. Yet the pope stood firm.

In 1531 the leading lords among the king's adherents sent a joint letter to the pope, in which they declared that many European universities considered the king's marriage to be invalid; surely the pope could concur with the judgment of so many scholars. In the list of noble signatories appended to this letter to the pope, the name of Thomas More was missing.

Various intrigues and political pressures had rendered the English Parliament pliant, and in 1532 they decided that the "annates" (that is, the tribute that each newly elected bishop paid to Rome, consisting of his income from his first year in office) henceforth would belong to the crown. On May 15, 1532, the bishops renounced the right to enact canonical decrees without the king's assent. That signaled the break with Rome. The next day Thomas More resigned from the chancellorship. In stepping down he lost all sources of income. Subsequently, when his house was searched by the police, the officials were astounded to find that Thomas More had no hoard of treasures.

The attempt to demonstrate that the former lord chancellor had been derelict in his duties proved his righteousness beyond a shadow of a doubt. With utmost composure, Thomas More made clear to his children that his ascent to prosperity was now at an end, and that the course would proceed in reverse. "Then may we yet, with bags and wallets, go a begging together and hoping that for pity some good folk will give us their charity, at every man's door to sing *Salve Regina*, and so still keep company and be merry together." [10] Knowing well the king's rancor, More prepared his family for what was to come. As William Roper, Margaret's husband, wrote in his biography of his father-in-law,

Somewhat before his trouble [More] would talk unto his wife and children of the joys of heaven and the pains of hell, of the

[10] W. Roper, *Life of Thomas More* (London: R. Triphook, 1822), p. 52.

lives of holy martyrs, of their grievous martyrdoms, of their marvellous patience and of their passions and deaths, that they suffered rather than they would offend God, and what a happy and blessed thing it was, for the love of God to suffer the loss of goods, imprisonment, loss of lands, and life also. He would further say to them that upon his faith, if he might perceive his wife and his children would encourage him to die in a good cause, it would so comfort him that for very joy thereof it would make him merrily run to meet death.[11]

In the year 1533, Archbishop Cranmer, the king's creature and docile instrument, declared the royal marriage to Catherine of Aragon to be annulled. A few days afterward, Anne Boleyn, as the wife of Henry VIII, was crowned queen in Westminster Abbey. Thomas More was invited to the ceremony but stayed home. When friends challenged him about this, he explained, "It lieth not in my power but that they may devour me; but God being my good Lord, I will provide that they shall never deflower me."[12]

On Christmas Day, 1533, the King's Council published a book that justified the marriage of Henry VIII with Anne Boleyn. Thomas More, however, was accused of having written a pamphlet against the marriage and of arranging for its publication. More defended himself vigorously against this accusation. He had always expressed himself plainly whenever the king asked his opinion, but he had never engaged in public polemics against His Majesty. At that, the king's minions let the matter rest, only to discover a much more serious accusation against More, namely, that he was in agreement with the high treason of the Maid of Kent. This nun, who was supposedly favored with divine revelations, prophesied that if Henry VIII married another woman, he would cease to be king within the month. Opponents of the king spread the prediction abroad. A month passed, and Henry VIII was still on the throne. The false prophetess and her disciples were arrested, charged with high treason, and condemned to death by a law of

[11] Ibid., 53.
[12] Quoted in Monti, *King's Good Servant*, p. 312.

Parliament. Thomas More's name and that of John Fisher, the only bishop who remained loyal to the pope, were expressly inserted into the law. They allegedly had known about the high treason of the Maid of Kent and her disciples but had not reported it; the penalty was expropriation and imprisonment. Thomas More, however, vindicated himself brilliantly.

In March 1534 a law was passed limiting potential heirs to the throne to the descendants of Henry VIII and Anne Boleyn. Every English subject now could be compelled to take the "succession oath"; anyone who refused could be punished with prison and the loss of property. Thomas More had no legal objection to the Succession Act per se; rather, he objected to the preamble to this law, in which Henry's first marriage was declared invalid, and to the formula of the oath, which contained a rejection of papal authority. Thomas More was summoned to appear on April 13, 1534, before the new lord chancellor and the archbishop of Canterbury to take the mandatory oath. Before he complied with the summons, he went to Confession and attended Holy Mass, during which he received Holy Communion. Then he took leave of his family.

In the presence of the lords, Thomas More refused to take the required oath. He said that he could not swear to it without placing his soul in danger of eternal damnation. For this he ended up a prisoner in the Tower of London.

As a lawyer, Thomas More knew very well that his incarceration was illegal. Parliament, however, hastened to close the lacuna in the law discovered by More so as to legalize any proceedings against him.

In 1535 the Supremacy Act was passed, which declared the king the sovereign head of the Church of England. Parliament likewise approved the Treasons Act, which forbade every malicious statement against the king's supremacy under pain of disembowelment.

Every conceivable method was used to try to elicit a statement against the king's supremacy from Thomas More while he was imprisoned, so as to prove him guilty of high treason and subject to the death penalty. All attempts were unsuccessful. Ultimately, the judges had to have recourse to false testimony. A certain Master Rich stated under oath that Thomas More, in speaking to him, had expressly denied that the king was the head of the Church of England. More contested this statement. Two persons who were present with Rich at the conversation in question could not recall anything of the sort. Nevertheless, Rich's perjured testimony was enough for the judges to declare Thomas More guilty. Despite More's brilliant speech in his own defense, the judges condemned him to the punishment provided in the law: He was to be hanged, cut down while still alive, then drawn and quartered. Henry VIII "magnanimously" commuted this punishment to beheading. Thomas More, however, stood firm to the last.

On July 6, 1535, this valiant defender of the indissolubility of a valid, consummated marriage and of the papal primacy was beheaded. In 1835 the exemplary husband and father was declared blessed, and on May 19, 1935, he was declared a saint.

Saint
Francis Borgia
and
Eleonor de Castro

b. October 28, 1510, in Gandía, Spain
d. September 30, 1572, in Rome

Married 1529
Father of eight children
Canonized April 12, 1671

Painting by Leo Samberger

A happily married husband, eight times a father, viceroy, duke, Jesuit, priest, and father general of the Society of Jesus—Saint Francis Borgia was all this. He used to sign his name "Francis, the sinner", not so much on account of his own sins—throughout his whole life these were hardly serious or numerous—but rather humbly acknowledging that he was a descendant of the infamous Borgia family. He was atoning for them, seeking to make reparation for the crimes of that branch of the Spanish nobility, including those personally committed by Pope Alexander VI, who was his great-grandfather.[1]

Francis Borgia was born on October 28, 1510, in the ducal palace in Gandía, Spain, the first child of the third duke of Gandía, John Borgia, and his wife, Joan of Aragon; on his father's side he was the great-grandson of Pope Alexander VI, while on his mother's side he was the great-grandson of the Catholic king of Spain, Ferdinand II.

---

[1] Cf. O. Karrer, *Der hl. Franz von Borja, General der Gesellschaft Jesu* (Freiburg im Breisgau, 1921).

333

Two brothers and four sisters followed Francis, the firstborn, who as the prospective fourth duke of Gandía received an especially careful education. From his seventh birthday on, Francis was trained by a private tutor; grammar, arithmetic, and music were the major subjects, while instructions in military service and riding were the minor subjects.

In the year 1520 the ten-year-old Francis lost his mother, who died at the age of twenty-eight. His father married again, this time with Francisca de Castro. New additions to the duke's family arrived, until there were seventeen children in all. The family was soon torn apart, though, by disturbances in the duchy. The brother of Francis' mother, John of Aragon, the archbishop of Saragossa, took in two of the duke's children, the eleven-year-old Francis and his little sister Luisa. The archbishop maintained a brilliant court in Saragossa and surrounded the young heirs of the duchy of Gandía with princely pomp. Francis went to Mass every day and received the sacraments on major feast days, but other than that his stay in the archiepiscopal palace contributed little to his education.

During the year 1522, the duke's family conferred about a plan that was to be for Francis, the future heir of the duchy of Gandía, the first step in the career for which he was destined. For many years the palace of Tordesillas in the vicinity of Valladolid hosted two royal majesties: the unfortunate mother of Emperor Charles V, Joan the Mad, the widow of Philip the Fair, who required special custody on account of her mental state, and her daughter Catherine, later queen of Portugal, who was obliged to live with her afflicted mother to console her. A suitable entourage was provided to preserve the emperor's sister from melancholy. The honor of belonging to this entourage as a page was granted to Francis Borgia, among others, and he spent two of his developmental years in these surroundings. He then returned to Saragossa and his uncle the archbishop for another two years. Here he completed his general education.

At the instigation of his father, Francis then went to the imperial court; there, during the years of 1528–1539, he became a confidant of the emperor Charles V, whose star was in the ascendant

over Europe. Both Francis Borgia and the emperor were aficiona-
dos of hunting and horsemanship. They had a propensity for
splendid processions on festive occasions and were passionately
devoted to jousting, falconry, and elegant sports like fencing and
riding. For all that, the two were religiously inclined, but hardly
enthusiasts. They attended Holy Mass daily and received the sacraments several times a year. Both were distinguished for their strength
of will and high moral caliber. Charles V was already married,
while Francis was still single. He manifested a certain reserve toward the ladies and tended to be rather strict in this regard. This
did not prevent him, however, from bestowing his attentions
upon a lady-in-waiting of the empress Isabella, namely, Eleonor de
Castro. When this was confided to the empress, evidently by
Eleonor, who had been Isabella's companion since their youth
together in their Portuguese homeland, she interceded with the
emperor Charles V as a marriage broker. He sent a messenger at
once with a letter written in his own hand to Gandía, to Francis'
father, to obtain his consent to the marriage of his son Francis with
Eleonor de Castro. It is to be suspected that the duke of Gandía
had already made plans of his own for a suitable match for his
firstborn son from among the daughters of the nobility. Hence the
duke of Gandía thanked the emperor but at first refused his request; he preferred to make arrangements himself for his son
Francis, when the time was right. At Francis' suggestion, the
emperor then invited the duke of Gandía to the imperial court.
Now the father gave in and consented to the betrothal of his son
with Eleonor de Castro. On July 27, 1529, the marriage contract
was signed. On this occasion the duke ceded to his son half of the
barony of Lombay. The emperor, for his part, attached to these
lands the title of marquis; the empress appointed the new marquis
as her equerry (chief stallmaster), while his young wife, Eleonor,
became chief stewardess of the imperial household.

Francis Borgia's relations with the court became even more
intimate through his marriage, if that is possible; the empress
Isabella's goodwill toward her "first lady of the palace" carried over
to her husband. The marquis of Lombay, Francis Borgia, seemed

to have a dispensation from the strict Spanish etiquette in the palace of the empress. He was admitted at all times, which was highly exceptional for a twenty-year-old. Yet the emperor, who was often away, relied completely on his conscientious friend.

Francis Borgia and Eleonor de Castro had an exemplary marriage and family life, full of tender love and absolute fidelity. Having a similar aristocratic background and education, the two spouses were also well-matched in their inclinations, especially in their faith. Their common reverence for the emperor and the empress could only strengthen the bond of their mutual love.

It was a great joy for the couple when God sent them their first child. The little son and heir was baptized Carlos at the request of Emperor Charles V; the child was in many respects raised together with the emperor's son, Prince Philip, later King Philip II. Soon after Carlos a daughter followed, who received the name of the empress Isabella at her Baptism. After these two children came other sons, Juan, Alvaro, Fernando, and Alonso, and also two daughters, Juana and Dorothea. The sons all chose the married state in later life and continued the noble line of Borgia both in Spain and in Latin America. Two of the three daughters married, namely, Isabella and Juana; the youngest daughter, Dorothea, died in 1552 at the age of fourteen in the Poor Clare convent in Gandía, where one of the grandmothers, an aunt, three sisters, and two half-sisters of Francis Borgia had already entered and where three of his granddaughters would eventually enter religion.

In the spring of 1539, as Emperor Charles V stood at the height of his good fortune and renown, his wife, Isabella, suddenly took sick and died, after a short illness, on May 1, 1539, in the bloom of her youthful beauty. In her will Empress Isabella had forbidden any embalming of her body; only the marquise Eleonor, Francis' wife, was allowed to prepare the body, since she was the principal chambermaid of the empress. She also stipulated that she be buried in Granada. The duty of leading the funeral procession on the journey fell to the marquis Francis Borgia. Immediately before the interment he had to open the casket to certify the remains; when he caught sight of the already completely disfigured countenance of the empress, Francis Borgia was profoundly shaken by the transience of human life. This was the beginning of the famous "conversion" of Francis Borgia. The death of Empress Isabella and the sight of her corpse had revealed to the young marquis with unusual severity the transitoriness and relative futility of earthly things. After this experience he resolved to lead his life henceforth *sub specie aeternitatis*, in the light of eternity, and to redirect his spiritual life, not from bad to good—for Francis Borgia was never bad—but rather from superficiality to deeper concerns.

Francis was already at that time the head of a large family, with eight children who were not yet grown. He needed a post with an income so as to provide a future for his children in keeping with their station. For all his striving for perfection, Francis wanted to remain a good father. Appraising his situation in this way, he accepted the title of viceroy of Catalonia offered him by the emperor. He conscientiously discharged this office from 1539 to 1543 with justice and great prudence. As viceroy Francis Borgia also came to know and esteem the first great Jesuit fathers, Blessed Peter Faber and Antonio Araoz.

On January 7, 1543, Francis' father, the third duke of Gandía, John II, died at the age of only forty-eight. Through his death Francis Borgia, formerly the marquis of Lombay, automatically became the fourth duke of Gandía and the head of the Borgia family.

To his troubles in ruling the duchy were added all too soon a concern for the health of his wife, the duchess Eleonor. In April 1544 she began experiencing severe pains in the chest, together with a persistent fever and fainting spells, which sapped her strength. After a brief improvement and a relapse, the duchess died on March 27, 1546. Duke Francis Borgia overcame his bitter sorrow over the all too early departure of his wife, after seventeen extremely happy years of marriage, thanks to his deep faith, which offered him consolation and strength, especially through the sacraments.

The role of mother in raising the children was now taken over by the sister of the deceased duchess, Joan of Meneses, who for many years had been an inseparable part of the family.

At thirty-six years of age, Francis Borgia was in the prime of life; he still had time to make a fresh start. What was it to be? To reside in the quiet little country town of Gandía in peace and comfort as his deceased father had once done—Francis was incapable of that. Even while the duchess was still alive, a close relationship had started between Duke Francis Borgia and the Society of Jesus and its founder. It was even said of the duke, "He is devoted, body and soul, to the interests of the Society, and [in Gandía] they say that, if he were free, he would enter [the Society of Jesus]." That did in fact come to pass. As far as marital ties were concerned, the death of his wife had freed him to enter the order; with regard to his duties as the father of a family, most of his children were already approaching the age at which they could manage on their own.

Francis made the Spiritual Exercises with the founder of the Jesuits, Ignatius of Loyola. The latter admitted him on October 9, 1546, into the Society of Jesus. His admission, however, was to remain secret until all eight of his children were provided for and all the affairs of governing the duchy of Gandía had been settled. Thus Francis Borgia lived from 1546 until 1550 as the duke of Gandía, to all outward appearances, while secretly he had renounced his worldly titles and was already in religious life. He had founded a Jesuit college in Gandía, which on November 4, 1547, was raised to the status of a university; there the duke studied theology, receiving the title of *Doctor theologiae* on August 20, 1550.

On August 26, 1550, Francis Borgia made his last will and testament and entrusted to his firstborn son, Carlos, the government of the duchy. Five days later he set out for Rome, so as to be admitted publicly now to the Society of Jesus. On May 26, 1551, he was ordained a priest in Oñate; on August 1, 1551, he celebrated a private first Mass in the Loyola castle; and on November 15, a well-attended public first Mass at Vergara. He then went on to benefit the Society greatly while serving at various posts.

At the second general congregation of the Jesuits, Padre Francis Borgia was elected father general of the Society of Jesus on July 2, 1565. In that important position he continued to be a source of blessings for his order. Pope Saint Pius V entrusted further important tasks to him. In the night of September 30—October 1, 1572, Francis Borgia died in Rome in the odor of sanctity. His sanctity was solemnly confirmed by Pope Urban VIII on November 24, 1624, at his beatification and by Pope Clement X on April 12, 1671, at his canonization.

Blessed
Thomas Percy
and
Anne Somerset

b. 1528
d. August 22, 1572

Father of four children
Beatified May 13, 1895

Besides Thomas More, another English confessor and martyr named Thomas should be mentioned among the married blesseds and saints: Thomas Percy the younger, who was born in 1528, the son of Thomas Percy senior, the count of Northumberland. When he was nine years old, he lost his father, who was executed on June 2, 1537 because of his participation in the "Pilgrimage of Grace", a religious and social uprising against King Henry VIII. This tragic turn of events had strong repercussions in the soul of the count's young son. When he reached the age of eligibility, he married a like-minded noblewoman, Anne Somerset, from the line of the count of Worcester. Their marriage produced four children.

When Queen Elizabeth I in turn began to persecute Catholics, Count Thomas Percy the younger fearlessly followed his father's heroic example. Together with the count of Westmorland, he led the 1569 uprising for the reestablishment of Catholicism in England. The uprising failed, and Count Thomas Percy the younger fled to Scotland. A price was put on his head, and he was betrayed to the English and arrested. He spent 2½ hard, painful years in prison. Especially grievous to him during this time was the separation from his beloved wife, Anne, and from their little children. He probably never saw their youngest daughter, named Mary. He was executed on August 22, 1572, because, despite demands that he abjure the Catholic faith, he remained steadfastly loyal to the successor of Peter and to the Catholic Church. Twenty-four years after the martyrdom of her husband, Anne Somerset died in exile in France. Their daughter Mary founded in Brussels a Benedictine convent, which was later moved to Haslemere (diocese of Southwaek, England). Pope Leo XIII beatified the courageous husband and father Thomas Percy the younger on May 13, 1895.

Saint Alphonsus Rodriguez

and

Mary Suarez

*b. July 25, 1532, in Segovia,
northwest of Madrid*
*d. October 31, 1617, in Palma
(Majorca)*

Married around 1558
Father of two children
Beatified June 12, 1825
Canonized January 15, 1888

Alphonsus (Alonso) Rodriguez[1] is a saint for whom marriage was only the response to a dilemma and for whom the death of his wife and children appeared to be a blessing that allowed him to strive for and attain his true vocation as a consecrated religious. He was born the son of a textile merchant on July 25, 1532, in Segovia (Spain). The ten-year-old boy was prepared for his First Holy Communion by the Jesuit priest Blessed Peter Faber, and at the age of fifteen he was sent to Alcalá to study at the Jesuit College. Unfortunately, his father died in 1545, leaving Alphonsus' mother with eleven children. As a result, Alphonsus had to interrupt his studies, which he had scarcely begun, so as to take over his father's business and, as the firstborn son, to support his widowed mother and his ten siblings.

Neither he nor his mother had any commercial aptitude whatsoever, so the business was soon headed for bankruptcy. Around 1558, he married Mary Suarez, who did not have a sizable dowry, and

[1] Cf. M. Dietz, S.J., *Der hl. Alfons Rodriguez, Laienbruder aus der Gesellschaft Jesu, eine Blüte spanischer Mystik* (Freiburg im Breisgau, 1925); I. Behm, "Alfons Rodriguez", in *Spanische Mystik* (Düsseldorf, 1957), pp. 232–43; C. Testore, "Alfonso Rodriguez", in *Bibliotheca Sanctorum* 1:861–63.

from the beginning the marriage was ill-starred. For their worries about the business did not diminish. Furthermore, Alphonsus' wife soon bore a child and then a second. Both proved to be sickly. Then his wife and his mother as well fell seriously ill. Within a short period of time Alphonsus lost, one after the other, his wife, his two children and his mother.

These were heavy blows to Alphonsus, but later on, looking back over his life, he described these fateful events as his greatest good fortune. Why? Surely because he was now free to devote himself entirely to God. At first Alphonsus retreated from the world and led in strictest solitude a life of prayer and penance. He had been married for six years; he described the first three years after becoming a widower as his purgative way and the second three years his illuminative way. God began to prepare his soul gradually, through profound insights and many illuminations, for the third period of his life, which would be the unitive way. On January 31, 1571, Alphonsus was admitted to the Society of Jesus as a lay brother. After a six-month novitiate in Valencia, he was sent in July 1571 to the newly erected college called "Montesione" in Palma on the island of Majorca, where he remained uninterruptedly until his death on October 31, 1617. From 1580 on he was assigned to serve as porter for the Jesuit community. To all outward appearances he led a quiet, inconspicuous life. His spiritual life, on the other hand, by the grace of God was extremely rich and deep, as is evident from the autobiographical, ascetical, and mystical writings he left behind. As doorkeeper he carried on an invaluable apostolate directed toward all who came into conversation with him or asked his advice. For instance, he awakened in Peter Claver, later to be the apostle to the blacks, an enthusiasm for the missions in Latin America and effectively spurred him on to strive for holiness.

The former husband and father who, after the death of his wife and two children, had become a Jesuit lay brother, a porter, and a mystic, was beatified on June 12, 1825. On January 15, 1888, Pope Leo XIII solemnly canonized him, together with the Jesuit cleric John Berchmans, in Saint Peter's Basilica in Rome and established October 30 as his feast day.

The Servant of God Renata of Bavaria

and

Wilhelm V of Bavaria

b. April 20, 1544, in Nancy, in Lorraine, France
d. May 22, 1602, in Altötting

Married 1568
Mother of ten children

Contemporary engraving

Renata[1] was an ideal wife, animated by a profound faith and always willing to serve others. Her husband, Duke Wilhelm V (known as "the Pious"), loved her as his wife and the mother of his children, while the Bavarian people honored her as the mother of their land; both viewed her more and more as a saint.

Renata was born on April 20, 1544, in Nancy, in the province of Lorraine, the daughter of Duke Francis I of Lorraine. As a child she was always sickly. Later, when she was seriously ill and the attendant physicians had already given up all hope of recovery, the sick girl had recourse to the Virgin Mother of God and vowed to make a pilgrimage to Loreto in Central Italy. At that she fell into a death-like sleep, from which she awoke completely cured, pronouncing the words "Gloria tibi, Domine [Glory be to you, O Lord]." The sickness had suddenly disappeared. Renata was well again and remained healthy throughout her later life. She now decided that the life that God had so wondrously granted her should be entirely employed to his greater glory. She never deviated from

[1] J. Walterscheid, *Deutsche Heilige* (Munich, 1934), pp. 244–45; L. Beer, *Heiligenlegende* (Regensburg, 1928), 2:505–8.

this purpose, but always allowed herself to be guided by the Spirit of God.

She did this in a very special way in the year 1568, when she married the Bavarian crown prince Wilhelm V, the Pious, in the *Liebfrauenkirche* [Church of our Lady] in Munich, during a solemn ceremony presided over by the renowned bishop of Augsburg, Cardinal Otto von Truchses. Five years later Wilhelm V began to rule Bavaria as duke. The couple led an exemplary Christian married life. Their marriage produced ten children, who received a strict, disciplined upbringing in the fear of the Lord.

Besides their large family, Renata and Duke Wilhelm V also cared for the sick and the poor in their land. Just as the duke personally served twelve poor men at table, so, too, did Renata serve twelve poor women; and just as the duke provided clothing and shelter for seventy-two needy men each year, so too did the duchess provide for seventy-two poor women. Furthermore, she went into the most miserable hovels in order to offer assistance to crippled poor and sick people.

After eighteen years of beneficent rule in Bavaria, Duke Wilhelm V voluntarily abdicated the throne in 1597, then retired with his wife, Renata, to Maxburg castle, where the couple spent the final years of their life with no other thought than to strive for perfection and holiness. They renounced all sexual relations, practiced continence, and lived in strict seclusion like the Carthusians. For their own physical needs they provided only what was most essential, while there was no limit to their generosity toward the poor and the sick. While her husband, Wilhelm, was still reigning as duke, Renata had founded a hospital in Munich in honor of Saint Elizabeth of Hungary and had also assisted her husband in founding the *Herzogspital* [duke's hospital] and the hostel at Rochusberg. From her seclusion in Maxburg, Duchess Renata selflessly practiced active charity toward all those who were suffering and in need.

As this pious woman had been in life, so she was in death. Although at the beginning of 1602 the doctors had determined that the fifty-eight-year-old duchess Renata was in good health, she often spoke of her imminent death. In order to prepare herself for it, she made a pilgrimage with Duke Wilhelm V to Ebersberg in honor of Saint Sebastian and then farther to Altötting to the shrine of Mary, the Mother of God, to pray to the dear Blessed Virgin for safe passage home. While praying fervently in the Chapel of Grace, Renata was struck down by a fever. Soon afterward, on Mary 22, 1602, death appeared at the side of Renata's sickbed. Wilhelm V had his beloved wife buried in the church of Saint Michael in Munich, which he had built. With him the entire Bavarian people mourned the death of this kind and saintly duchess. The duke kept the heart of the deceased noblewoman as a precious relic. As one author has written, "It was, after all, like one half of his own heart, since the pair, Duke Wilhelm V the Pious and Renata, his exemplary wife, had been one in heart and soul during the thirty-four years of their married life, until death separated them."

As for the ten children of this noble couple, it should be emphasized that two of them followed the example of their saintly parents in every respect. Of the firstborn son, later the elector Maximilian I, it has been said that he, like his father before him, possessed the virtue of piety to a preeminent degree. Magdalena, the lastborn child of the duke and the duchess, became the duchess of Pfalz-Neuburg by marriage. Through her incessant prayers and her own edifying spiritual life, reflecting the upbringing that she received from her pious parents, she finally brought about the return of her Protestant husband, Duke Wolfgang Wilhelm of Pfalz-Neuburg, and his conversion. When the Lord called Duchess Magdalena to her eternal reward on September 25, 1628, she had the consolation of seeing that, besides her husband, many of their subjects had returned to the Catholic faith, especially in and around Düsseldorf in the Rhineland, which at that time belonged to Pfalz-Bavaria. About Duchess Magdalena, the daughter of the Servant of God Renata of Bavaria, a Protestant nobleman is quoted as saying, "This princess could very well justify the custom among the Catholics of invoking the saints; for to her, who is so full of mercy, I could take refuge and be certain that she would not refuse a single one of my requests."

Saint
Joan de Lestonnac
and
Gaston de Montferrant

b. 1556 in Bordeaux
d. February 2, 1640, in Bordeaux

Married 1573
Mother of seven children
Canonized May 15, 1949

In the French Baroness Joan (Jeanne) de Lestonnac[1] we find a saint who lived for twenty-four years in a happy marriage and bore her husband seven children. She was born in 1556 in Bordeaux, the first child of the Catholic baron Richard de Lestonnac and the Calvinist Joan Eyquem de Montaigne, the sister of the famous philosopher Michael de Montaigne (1533–1592). Her famous uncle used to say of young Joan, "It is difficult to tell which is greater, the beauty of my niece's body or that of her soul. It can truly be said, however, that nature has created in her a masterpiece by uniting a beautiful soul with a beautiful body."

Joan had to fight hard to preserve her Catholic faith, since her mother and her instructresses were inclined to Calvinism. While she was young, she sensed a desire to give herself entirely to God as a religious. At her father's bidding, however, she was married at age seventeen in 1573 to Baron Gaston de Montferrant, the lord of Landiras and La Mothe. In this marriage she brought seven children into the world; two of her daughters became nuns.

In the year 1596 the baroness de Montferrant was bereaved of her husband and almost simultaneously of her twenty-year-old

---

[1] P. Hoels, *Au service de la jeunesse: Sainte Jeanne de Lestonnac* (Paris, 1949); F. Baumann, "Im Dienste unserer Lieben Frau: Die heilige Mutter Johanna de Lestonnac", in *Pius XII. erhob sie auf die Altäre* (Würzburg, 1960).

son. From then on the widow again used her maiden name, Joan de Lestonnac, not so as to efface the memory of twenty-four happy years of marriage, but to emphasize that she was free again to make a new start in life. She saw to it that her children were brought up correctly, and she dedicated her remaining hours to prayer and good works.

After six years of being a widow, Joan de Lestonnac believed that the moment had arrived for her to realize her youthful plan and to consecrate herself to God in the religious state. At first she planned to enter the order of the Annonciades of Saint Joan of France—the unfortunate daughter of Louis XI and the repudiated wife of King Louis XII—to which two of her daughters already belonged. In her estimation, though, this order was not strict enough. So in 1603 she entered the "Feuillantines", the Reformed Cistercian convent in Toulouse. The severe penances demanded of the nuns in this order rapidly threatened the weak health of the widow, who was then already forty-seven years old. So, after six months in the novitiate, she was forced to leave the convent. By a special supernatural inspiration, Madame de Lestonnac finally received a commission from the Lord to found a religious community herself, under the protection of the Virgin Mother of God, for the salvation of young girls, whose faith was greatly endangered at that time by the intrigues of the Calvinists. This she did in the year 1605. The founding of this order was accompanied by difficulties of all sorts and by hostility toward the foundress. Nevertheless, during the years between 1608 and 1622, she succeeded in establishing thirty convents of the new religious community under the mantle and protection of their heavenly Mother.

In the year 1620 the two daughters of Saint Joan de Lestonnac received a papal dispensation to transfer from the Annonciades to the community of their mother. It was not long before they were being considered prospective successors to the foundress and first general superior; yet both died before their mother did. In the years that followed, she had to suffer much through misunderstandings about her best intentions and through slander and vindictive treatment. Mother Joan de Lestonnac, however, withstood these trials with impressive humility. She said, "I stay with the Mother of God at the foot of the Cross. Then it is always a joy and an honor for me to suffer for God." On February 2, 1640, Joan de Lestonnac, this edifying wife and mother, charitable widow and humble foundress, who became a saintly nun and the mother of many spiritual daughters, ended her holy life at the age of eighty-four in Bordeaux. In 1890 she was beatified, and on May 15, 1949, she was canonized.

Blessed Mary of the Incarnation

and

Peter Acarie

b. February 1, 1566, in Paris
d. April 18, 1618, in the Carmel
at Pontoise

Married 1582
Mother of six children
Beatified June 5, 1791

Statue by Germain Jacquet, Paris,
Carmelite convent of Créteil

A wife of a count and mother of six children who becomes a nun in the strict order of the Discalced Carmelites is surely an exceptional person. She was special for other reasons as well.

Barbara Avrillot[1] was born on February 1, 1566, in Paris, the daughter of Nicholas Avrillot, lord of Champlâtreux, and Marie L'Huilier. At the age of fourteen this precocious, clever, and beautiful girl wanted to enter the convent. Her parents would not permit it. As a sixteen-year-old she was compelled by her parents to marry Peter Acarie, the viscount of Villemor and lord of Montbrost and Roncenay. The beautiful, wealthy, and attractive young wife, however, had no other thought than to love God with her whole heart and to strive to please him—now, of course, by fulfilling her marital duties with the highest possible degree of

---

[1] Bruno de Jesus Maria, *La belle Acarie: Bienheureuse Marie de l'Incarnation* (Lille, 1942); Giovanni di Jesu Maria, "Beata Maria dell'Incarnazione Barbara Avrillot", in *Bibliotheca Sanctorum* 8:1013–15.

perfection. She wanted to be a conscientious, faithful, and loving wife to her husband and a loving, caring mother to their six children and to her husband's subjects. As a result of the ideal education that they received from their parents, the three daughters became nuns; one of the three sons, Peter, became a priest. During the thirty years of her married life, Barbara Acarie deliberately made every effort to demonstrate that Christian married couples can attain sanctity and perfection, not in spite of their marriage, but precisely through their marriage.

Madame Acarie was distinguished, not only for her love of God and love of neighbor, but also for her faith. Her adherence to the teachings of the Church was unshakable at a time when apostasy was becoming widespread even in France. Madame Acarie was outstanding for her works of mercy as well, especially during the siege of Paris in 1590; she also showed great zeal in caring for the eternal salvation of people who had been led astray into error. God rewarded her for her edifying life of charity based on faith by granting her many graces, including extraordinary gifts; he also tested her with various interior and exterior trials.

A period of harmony and peace in Barbara's marriage and family was followed by a period of affliction and misfortune, when her husband fell into disfavor with King Henry IV and was banished from Paris; this happened after a defeat suffered by the league to which Peter Acarie belonged

In this sorrowful time Madame Acarie cared for her husband and her children by night and by day. Finally, she obtained the complete rehabilitation of her husband. After four years of serious trials, the family was reunited and regained possession of their house in Paris and all their belongings. Madame Acarie again enjoyed the high esteem of society, including the royal family. The most renowned personages used to meet in her salon in Paris, especially the leaders of the French school of spirituality, such as Cardinal Pierre de Bérulle and Saint Francis de Sales.

In autumn 1601, the writings of Saint Teresa of Avila came into her hands. She read them and was profoundly impressed by them and was inspired to bring the Reformed Carmelites to France. After overcoming enormous difficulties she succeeded. Thus she helped to found Carmelite convents in Paris (1604), Pontoise (1605), Dijon (1605), and Amiens (1606). While achieving this, Madame Acarie had the great joy of seeing her three daughters enter the Carmelites; her fifteen-year-old daughter Marguerite was the first.

In 1613 the noblewoman's husband, Peter Acarie, became seriously ill. For nine days she did not leave his sickbed, neither by day nor by night, until she saw him die the death of a righteous man, consoled and strengthened by the Last Rites. The tears and prayers of the widow won her heavenly consolation, for she was assured—beyond all doubt—that her pious husband had attained eternal happiness.

Now that Madame Acarie was freed of marital and familial duties, she broke off all ties with this passing world and resolved to become a Carmelite nun, just like her three daughters. To this end she sought out the Carmel that was the poorest and the farthest away from Paris, namely, the convent in Amiens. There she requested admission as a lay sister. On April 7, 1614, she was clothed in the habit and received the name Mary of the Incarnation (Marie de l'Incarnation). As a religious, she edified her sisters in community by the impressive meekness with which she performed the most menial tasks in the convent. She distinguished herself by her great love of poverty and showed a special and tender devotion for her sisters who were sick and suffering.

On April 8, 1615, Sister Mary of the Incarnation was allowed to make perpetual vows. On December 7, 1616, the new prioress, who was not particularly well-disposed toward her, sent her away from Amiens to the Carmel in Pontoise—allegedly for reasons of health. There, after a long illness—fortified by the repeated reception of Viaticum and consoled by several visions and ecstasies—she gave her noble soul back to the triune God on April 18, 1618.

On June 5, 1791, this strong-willed woman, who was distinguished more for her noble soul than for her noble blood, and who lived as an exemplary Christian wife and mother, founded the Carmelite Order in France, and finally became a Carmelite nun and mystic herself, was beatified by Pope Pius VI.

Saint Jane Frances de Chantal

and

Christopher de Rabutin

b. January 1572 in Dijon
d. December 13, 1641, in the
    Visitandine Convent in
    Moulins

Married December 29, 1592
Mother of six children

Portrait from 1636, preserved in the
Visitandine Convent in Turin

The *Introduction to the Devout Life* by Saint Francis de Sales, addressed to "Philothea", first appeared in print in 1609, when Jane Frances (Jeanne Françoise) Frémyot de Chantal[1] had already been widowed for eight years after a nine-year marriage. Therefore, what the holy bishop of Geneva wrote about married love in part three of his book no longer applied to his saintly friend and co-founder of the Congregation of the Blessed Virgin Mother of God of the Visitation. Nevertheless, looking back on her short but happy married life, the countess de Chantal could honestly say that during those nine years she constantly took to heart what her present spiritual director and great spiritual friend wrote about charity in the life of husband and wife, parents and children.

We quote at length from this chapter, "Instructions for Married Persons", from the *Introduction to the Devout Life*.

---

[1] H. Waach, *Johanna Franziska von Chantal* (Eichstätt, 1957).

"Matrimony is a great sacrament; but I speak in Christ, and in the Church." It is "honorable to all" persons, in all persons, and in all things, . . . It is the nursery of Christianity. . . . Hence the preservation of holy marriage is of the highest importance to the state, for it is the origin and source of all its streams.

. . . Above all things, I exhort married people to that mutual love which the Holy Spirit in Scripture so much recommends to them. O you that are married! It means nothing to say: Love one another with a natural love: two turtle doves make such love. Nor does it mean anything to say: Love one another with a human love: the heathens have well practiced such love. I say to you with the great apostle, "Husbands, love your wives, as Christ also loved the Church." And you wives, love your husbands as the Church loveth her Savior. It was God who . . . with His invisible hand has knotted the holy bond of your marriage and has given you to one another. Why then do you not cherish each other with a most holy, most sacred, and most divine love?

The first effect of this love is an indissoluble union of your hearts. . . . The soul must sooner separate from the body of the one or the other than the husband from the wife. This union is not understood principally of the body, but of the heart, of the affections, and of love.

The second effect of this love must be the inviolable fidelity of one party to the other. [This fidelity is symbolized by the ring that the Church blesses for the couple. Never should your hearts admit any affection for any other man, for any other woman.]

The third fruit of marriage is the birth and lawful rearing of children. It is a great honor to you who are married that God, in His design to multiply souls who may bless and praise Him for all eternity, causes you to co-operate with Him in so noble a work. . . . Preserve, O husbands, a tender, constant and heartfelt love for your wives. . . . The weakness and infirmity of your wives, whether in body or in mind, ought never to provoke you to any kind of disdain, but rather to a mild and affectionate compassion. God has created them such, to the end that they should depend upon you and that you should have them for your companions in such manner that you should still be their heads and superiors. And you, O wives, love tenderly and cordially the husbands whom God has given you, but with a love respectful and full of reverence. God indeed created them of a sex more vigorous and commanding and was pleased to ordain that the woman should depend upon the man. . . . All Holy Scripture strictly recommends to you this submission. Yet the same Holy Scripture renders it agreeable as well, . . . by commanding your husbands to exercise [authority] over you with a great charity, tenderness, and mildness. "Ye husbands," says Saint Peter [1 Peter 3:7], "likewise dwelling with your wives according to knowledge, giving honor to the woman as to the weaker vessel." While I exhort you to advance more and more in this mutual love, which you owe one another, take care that it does not degenerate into jealousy of any sort. It often happens that just as the worm is bred in the most delicate and ripest apple, so jealousy grows in that love of married people which is the most ardent and affectionate. Nevertheless, it spoils and corrupts the substance of such a love, for little by little it breeds strife, dissension, and divorce. Indeed, jealousy never enters where friendship is grounded on true virtue in both persons. Jealousy, therefore, is an infallible mark that the love is in some degree sensual and gross, and that it has met with a virtue imperfect, inconstant, and subject to distrust. It is a foolish boast of friendship to strive to exalt itself by jealousy. Jealousy is in truth a sign of the height and bulk of the friendship, but never of its goodness, purity, and perfection. The perfection of friendship presupposes an assurance of the virtue of those whom we love, and jealousy presupposes a doubt of it.

If you married men desire that your wives should be faithful to you, give them a lesson by your example. . . . O wives, . . . never suffer any wanton addresses to approach you. Whoever presumes to praise your beauty and your grace must be suspected. . . . If to praise you he adds the dispraise of your husband, he offers you a heinous injury. . . .

Love and fidelity joined together always produce familiarity and confidence. This is why the saints have used many reciprocal caresses in their married life, caresses truly affectionate, but chaste, tender, and sincere. Thus, Isaac and Rebecca, the most chaste married couple of antiquity, were seen through a window caressing one another in such a manner that, though there was no immodesty, Abimelech was convinced that they must be man and wife. The great St. Louis, equally rigorous to his own flesh and tender in the love of his wife, was almost blamed for the abundance of such caresses. Actually, he rather deserved praise for being able to bring his martial and courageous spirit to stoop to these little duties so requisite for the preservation of conjugal love. Although these demonstrations of pure and free affection do not bind hearts, yet they tend to unite them and serve for an agreeable help to their life in common. . . .

[Christian couples should realize] that the raising of a house, or family, consists not in building up a fine residence and in storing up a great quantity of worldly possessions, but in the good education of children in the fear of God and in virtue. In this no pains or labor should be spared, for children are the crown of their father and mother. . . .

Saint Paul leaves to wives, as their portion, the care of the household. For this reason many think with truth that their devotion is more profitable to the family than that of the husband, who does not reside so much at home and cannot, as a consequence, so easily form it in virtue. Because of this consideration Solomon in his Proverbs makes the happiness of the whole family depend on the care and industry of the valiant woman whom he describes. . . .

[Husband and wife . . . ought mutually to encourage each other in holy devotion. Thus every wife ought to count herself fortunate who has a religious husband, for] a man without devotion is a creature severe, harsh, and rough. Husbands ought to wish that their wives should be devout. Without devotion a woman is very frail and is inclined to weaken or to lose her

virtue. Saint Paul says that "the unbelieving husband is sanctified by the believing wife; and the unbelieving wife is sanctified
by the believing husband," because, in this strict alliance of
marriage, the one may easily draw the other to virtue. But what
a blessing is it when man and wife, being both believers, sanctify
each other in the true fear of the Lord!

As to the rest, their mutual forbearance with each other must
be so great that both will never be angry with each other at the
same time, so that a dissension or dispute may never be seen
between them. . . . The Holy Spirit cannot remain in a house in
which there are disputes, recriminations, and the re-echoings of
scolding and strife.[2]

Let us now look more closely at the marriage of Saint Jane
Frances Frémyot de Chantal. It should not be overlooked that her
character was marked by a repressed sadness, which is understandable, considering the things that she experienced during her childhood and youth. Jane Frances was born in January 1572 in Dijon,
the daughter of the president of the parliament in Burgundy,
Bénigne Frémyot, and the noblewoman Margaret Berbisy. A few
months after her birth Paris trembled at the atrocities of the Saint
Bartholomew's Massacre, and the bloody disturbances of the
Huguenot wars overshadowed her youth. During that period, her
father, as the president of parliament, her husband, as a high-
ranking officer, and her brother, as a hostage, were all involved in
the political and religious conflicts. A dominant factor in forming
her temperament was the awareness that the faith was under attack.
From her second year on, after she lost her mother, the young girl
was exposed to the torments of a governess who has been described
as a "female Satan".[3]

On December 29, 1592, the twenty-one-year-old Jane Frances
was married to Christopher II, the baron de Chantal and seigneur
[lord] de Bourbilly. The couple settled in the latter locality. A

[2] Francis de Sales, *Introduction to the Devout Life*, trans. John Ryan (New York:
Harper and Brothers, 1950), pp. 162–68.
[3] G. Kranz, *Politische Heilige* (Augsburg, 1958), 2:294.

witness in the process of canonization years later made the following statement about the Chantals:

> Together, these two spouses provided a model of a genuinely holy marriage. They had between them one heart and one soul. Jane Frances surrounded her young husband with honor and obedience and loved him with a touching tenderness, with ardor and reverence. At the same time she in turn was loved and respected just as much and surrounded by the most tender confidence of her husband. All of this was quite evident.

Unfortunately, Jane Frances quite often had to endure her husband's absence for months at a time on account of his service at the royal court. She was then entrusted with administering the estate and its employees and showed herself to be a very prudent lady of the manor and housewife, who was concerned, above all, about maintaining a pure, religious atmosphere in the castle and in the court. She arose early in the morning, said morning prayer together with the hired help, and then went to work herself with diligence.

Her happy and harmonious marriage was blessed with six children, of whom only four survived infancy. These four are as follows:

1. Celsus Benignus. He became an officer, lived at the French court, and fell in battle in 1607.

2. Marianne. She was married at the age of twelve to the sixteen-year-old baron de Thorens, a brother of Saint Francis de Sales; after a few short years of marriage she was widowed.

3. Françoise. She married and became a happy mother.

4. Charlotte. She died unexpectedly at the age of ten, just as her widowed mother was beginning to found the Visitation Order.

The happy married life of Jane Frances and Baron Christopher de Chantal at Château Bourbilly unfortunately lasted only nine years. It was shattered by a tragic accident: the Baron de Chantal was inadvertently shot while hunting, immediately after the final confinement of his good wife. Suddenly the husband was torn from his loving wife, the attentive father from his children.

The twenty-eight-year-old widow at first took her children back to Dijon to live with her father. When her quick-tempered father-in-law threatened to disown her children, though, unless she and her children moved in with him, the widow was forced to go to Château Monthélon with her children. There, for seven long, bitter years, she experienced all the helplessness of being a widow. She had to endure terrible humiliations from her father-in-law. The old baron de Chantal, in fact, had become a slave to one of his maids.

This wretch tyrannized the entire household, incited the baron against his daughter-in-law, and sought by a thousand torments to drive the widow away from the manor. Jane Frances, who was very sensitive, suffered untold grief as a result of this chicanery.

Yet, instead of protesting against such treatment, she kept her peace with astonishing patience. She even took charge of the four illegitimate children that the hateful maid had by the elder de Chantal, raised them together with her own children, and taught them their lessons. She also forgave that unfortunate marksman who had mortally wounded her husband and, as a sign of reconciliation, stood as godmother for his child. She drew the strength to overcome self in this way from her profound faith.[4]

Then in 1604, in Dijon, the countess met the celebrated preacher and bishop Francis de Sales, who was delivering a series of Lenten sermons. As the widow became better acquainted with the bishop, she felt more and more drawn to him by a completely pure and noble attraction. This developed into an extraordinarily beautiful, holy friendship that was full of blessings for them both, as well as for others. Francis de Sales became for the widow, who

[4] Ibid., p. 295.

had been so sorely tried, a spiritual director who led her to perfection and holiness. He also looked after her children. Above all, he showed her the way to a new purpose in life—the founding of the Visitation Order. Jane Frances de Chantal saw how her widowhood would take on a new meaning through the religious foundation. That is why she enthusiastically agreed to the bishop's plans.

After her eldest daughter, Marianne, was married to the baron de Thorens, a brother of Bishop Francis de Sales, and her brother, the archbishop of Bourges had taken charge of her fourteen-year-old son, she intended to put her friend's idea into action and, with her two other daughters, to found the first convent of the new order. The plans of the two saints seemed to be thwarted, however, when President Frémyot, the father of Saint Jane Frances, decided that he would again give her away in marriage. Her whole family was opposed to her going into the convent. As she was saying goodbye, her son put his arms around her neck and begged her to stay. When all his pleading had no effect on his mother, he made one last desperate attempt. He threw himself down full length at the threshold and tearfully exclaimed, "Mother, if I cannot make you stay, then you will have to leave over the body of your son." Jane Frances de Chantal hesitated for a moment, then thought of Jesus' words: "He who loves son or daughter more than me is not worthy of me."

It was in the year 1610 that Francis de Sales founded in Annecy the first convent of the Visitation. Jane Frances de Chantal led her nuns by her shining example, and she always had good counsel from her spiritual friend, the bishop of Geneva, whose see was in Annecy. She survived him by almost twenty years. The order soon became one of the most flourishing in France and radiated a good influence by the edifying life of its sisters. Twenty-six convents had sprung up from these humble beginnings in the course of thirty years, when Jane Frances—formerly a wife and mother, then the mother of many daughters in the religious family that she and her saintly friend Francis de Sales had founded—was called home by God to her eternal reward on December 13, 1641, while making a visit as general superior to the Visitandine convent in Moulins.

Blessed
Virginia Centurione
and
Gasparo Bracelli

b. April 2, 1587
d. December 15, 1651

Beatified September 22, 1985

The aristocratic daughter of one of the doges of Genoa, who lived and worked in that famous Italian port during the second part of the sixteenth and the first half of the seventeenth century, became an evangelist of charity worthy of the honors of the altar, as Pope John Paul II solemnly declared at the beatification of Virginia Centurione.[1]

This blessed from the city of Genoa was born on April 2, 1587, the daughter of the doge Giorgio Centurione and Leila, née Spinola, who likewise belonged to the Genovese nobility.

Obeying her father's will, Virginia was married at the age of fifteen to the young son of a renowned family, Gasparo Bracelli by name. He indulged altogether too much in gambling and pleasure and shortened his earthly existence by a life of vice. The unfaithful husband gave Virginia two daughters but abandoned his family. Virginia Centurione Bracelli lovingly pursued him with patience and humility until she succeeded at least in bringing him back to the fold before he died and reconciling him with God.

---

[1] N. Ferrante, "Centurione, Virginia, vedova Bracelli", in *Bibliotheca Sanctorum*, appendix pp. 304–5; see *L'Osservatore romano*, October 7, 1985, pp. 5, 8.

After a few short, unhappy years of married life, Virginia became a widow in 1607. Her father wanted to give her away in marriage a second time. The daughter vehemently refused, however, and devoted herself at first to solitary prayer and penance. Then she began to serve as a dedicated lay apostle. First, she looked after abandoned and ruined country churches and had them renovated. Then, gradually, she started to care for abandoned youngsters, founding four schools for them. After providing for her own two children, with the help of her mother-in-law, Maddalena Lomellini, and the Capuchin priest Padre Mattia Bovoni, she began to spend the entire day serving the poor and the sick. Her work could be called a full-time apostolate, especially around the year 1630, when plague, famine, and war left Genoa and all of northern Italy in dire need.

In 1626 Virginia gave up her remaining wealth for the sake of the poor. She opened wide her motherly heart in leading the association of the Hundred Ladies of Mercy (*Cento Signore della Misericordia*), who had consecrated themselves to the patronage for the poor of Jesus Christ. Together with these women, Virginia helped wherever she could and brought comfort by her ardent words, which burned with a magnanimous love of God.

The apostolate that she had begun eventually developed into the "Work of Refuge" (*Opera del Rifugio*), which was designed as a place to shelter and assist abandoned and endangered youngsters. Virginia took such young people into her own house, and when this became too small, she rented a vacant convent in that quarter of the city of Genoa known as "Monte Calvario". Here she sheltered forty youngsters, whom she placed under the protection of Our Lady of Refuge. It was the thirteenth day of April, 1631. From then on this date was considered the anniversary of the founding of two religious orders that originated in the work of Virginia Centurione Bracelli: the Sisters of Our Lady of the Refuge of Mount Calvary (*Suore di Nostra Signora del Rifugio in Monte Calvario*) and the Daughters of Mount Calvary (*Figlie di Nostra Signora al Monte Calvario*).

Virginia knew how to interest Church officials and the civil authorities in her work. Furthermore, at her insistence the Virgin Mother of God was proclaimed the Queen of Genoa. She petitioned the cardinal-archbishop of Genoa for the introduction of the Forty Hours devotion in the city of Genoa; she also requested the preaching of missions, and for this purpose the congregation of the Missionaries of Saint Charles was founded. Besides this, she performed a great service as a peacemaker between the feuding factions in the city and saw to it that a serious dispute between the doge and the cardinal-archbishop of Genoa was settled.

On December 15, 1651, this highly meritorious woman died and was deeply mourned by the inhabitants of the republic of Genoa. Unfortunately, with the passage of time she was entirely forgotten, so that not even her spiritual daughters knew that Virginia Centurione Bracelli was the foundress of their religious community. Instead of calling themselves the Bracelli Sisters after her, they used the name of one of their early patrons, Emmanuele Brignole and were known as the Brignolines. On September 20, 1801, however, on the occasion of the 150th anniversary of her death, her grave was opened, and her body was found to be completely incorrupt; then people remembered again this great woman and apostle of charity of the seventeenth century, at a time of great distress in Genoa. In 1931 the cause for beatification was begun, and on July 6, 1985, it was successfully concluded by a decree promulgating a miracle attributed to the intercession of Virginia. On September 22, 1985, Pope John Paul II beatified her in Genoa.

Blessed
Mary of the
Incarnation (Guyart)
and
Claude Martin

*b. October 28, 1599, in Tours,
France*
*d. April 30, 1672, in Quebec,
Canada*

Married 1617
Mother of one son
Beatified June 22, 1980

Engraving by L. Edelinck

Wife, mother, widow, nun, missionary, and mystic—the charismatic French woman Marie Guyart Martin was all this. She was born on October 28, 1599, in Tours in western France, the fourth of eight children of Florentius Guyart and his wife, Jeanne Michelet, who worked as bakers. At the age of fourteen, she sensed quite strongly that she was called to religious life and not to marriage. In her autobiography she speaks of the "cross of being married" and of the fact that, through the death of her husband, the silk manufacturer Claude Martin, whom she married in 1617 and by whom she had one son with the same name, the Lord "freed her from the fetters of marriage".

An excerpt from the autobiography of Blessed Mary of the Incarnation follows:

At the age of fourteen or fifteen I felt a great longing for the cloistered life. In Tours at that time there was only Beaumont Abbey, which followed the Rule of Saint Benedict. I was acquainted with it because I sometimes prayed there. When I presented my wish to my mother, she did not dismiss my plan; rather, she kindly encouraged me and said that if Madame de Beaumont, a cousin of ours [who was a nun] knew about it, it was quite possible they would admit me. The plan went no farther, though. Since I was very shy, I did not insist upon this wish that I had once expressed. I assumed that my mother thought me unsuitable for the religious state on account of my cheerful and high-spirited personality, which probably seemed to her incompatible with a religious vocation. It is clear to me, however, that God in his goodness did not want to have me in this convent or some other, at least not just then. I must conclude this, when I reflect on the workings of Divine Providence in the time that followed: I was supposed to carry the cross of the married state. If I had had a guide or a spiritual director, I would never have given my consent. But I knew nothing at all about spiritual directors and even less about the use that one should make of one's spiritual director. So I blindly followed the guidance of my parents. God's Providence prevented them from making their selection from among the young men who were courting me. Otherwise, all of the graces and proofs of God's goodness that I received after my husband's death might have been denied me. . . .

Our Lord let my parents put me in a situation where the pastimes which had been denied me in their house became available to me. At the same time he removed all my desire for them and, instead, filled me with a desire for seclusion. Thus I was preoccupied with the love of a good which I did not yet understand, shunning the companionship of my peers in order to remain at home reading books of devotion. I gave up entirely those books which dealt with frivolous matters to which I had been attached simply for the sake of amusement.

Our whole neighborhood was amazed, bewildered by my withdrawal and by the attraction I had to go to church every day, as well as by my inclination for the practice of virtue, especially the virtue of patience; for they could not see what I was experiencing interiorly and how the goodness of God was working in me. Even I myself did not understand how this happened, except that I followed his lead in prayer and obeyed him in practicing those virtues for which he provided the opportunity.

For almost two years his divine goodness allowed me to endure great suffering, for it was during this period that he tried my soul. Yet he never abandoned me, for this interior support of which I have spoken gave me both strength and great patience and gentleness in the most painful assaults. Prayer was my recourse, for it seemed to me that in these sufferings God wished to prepare my soul and purify it through tribulation. . . .

The Divine Majesty, not satisfied with having given me a distaste for worldly things and the strength to carry the crosses which he had permitted, strengthened me interiorly and gave me a profound desire for the reception of the sacraments. I was about eighteen years old at this time. This frequent reception gave me great courage and gentleness and a very lively faith that confirmed my belief in the divine mysteries. . . .

I was nineteen years old when the Lord freed me from the fetters of marriage by taking my husband home to himself. As soon as I became free I felt a great repugnance for marriage. The disposition that God had given me and also the guidance of the Holy Spirit were incompatible with any other love. . . .

Although I had loved my husband and was deeply grieved to lose him at first, my soul immediately dissolved and overflowed with thanksgiving when it was separated from him. Now all that I had left was God, in whom my heart with its sentiments could find fulfillment. Various business matters connected with this separation then caused me new sorrows. On a natural plane they far surpassed the strength and abilities of a young woman my age. But an abundance of God's goodness provided such strength and courage for my mind and my heart that I was able to bear everything. Relying on the blessed words, "I am with those who suffer affliction," I sensed that I was miraculously supported. I believed firmly that the Lord was with me, because he said so. So neither the loss of temporal goods, nor lawsuits nor poverty, not even my little son, who was only six months old, could dismay me, even though I knew that both he and I were deprived of everything. I had no experience at all in worldly, temporal concerns. But the Spirit, who supported me interiorly, gave success to everything that I undertook.

My mother-in-law died one month after the death of her son, for fear that I would leave her. I would not have done that, for I was determined to remain with her so as to assist her, insofar as that was God's will. I also considered raising my child. But God's goodness arranged things for the best in a different way for me and my child. Such a decision would have involved me in business interests and put me in danger of leaving the path along which the Lord wanted to lead him and me. . . .[1]

Marie Guyart, the widow of Claude Martin, had difficulty separating herself from her son, Claude, who was born on April 2, 1619, a few months before the death of her husband. It was even more difficult for the boy to separate himself from his mother, when, after more than ten years of employment in the transport business of her brother-in-law Paul Buisson, she finally began to pursue her vocation and joined the Ursuline nuns in Tours on January 21, 1631.

She writes,

I had a great, great love for my son; it was a sacrifice for me to leave him. Since God willed it, though, I did not want to do anything on my own; instead I commended it all to Divine Providence. . . .[2] Everyone blamed me for leaving a child who was not yet twelve years old, especially leaving him without any

[1] F. Holböck, *Ergriffen vom dreieinigen Gott* (Stein am Rhein, 1981), pp. 275–89; Mary of the Incarnation, *Zeugnis bin ich Dir: Autobiographie* (Stein am Rhein, 1981), pp. 35–42. See also *Marie of the Incarnation: Selected Writings*, ed. Irene Mahoney, O.S.U. (New York—Mahway: Paulist Press, 1989), pp. 43–44 and 186–87, from which all but the first paragraph of this translated quotation has been taken.

[2] Mary of the Incarnation, *Zeugnis*, pp. 138ff.

secure support, as well as leaving my father who was very old and who was deeply moved at not having me with him any more. All this hurt me deeply, but I had graven on my memory those words of our Lord from the Gospel: "He who loves father and mother more than me is not worthy of me; and he who loves son and daughter more than me is not worthy of me" (Mt 10:37). This strengthened me so much that I grieved for no one, and holding our Lord's will dear, I wanted only to obey it. . . .[3] My brother and sister[-in-law] promised to take care of my child and to provide for whatever he would need."[4]

Claude Martin junior had the benefit of a good education and ultimately, by the grace of God and certainly with the help of his mother's prayers, became a Benedictine monk and priest in the Maurist Congregation. He compiled a biography of his mother from the letters she wrote to him, together with her two autobiographies from 1633 and 1654 and her other spiritual writings.

On February 22, 1639, Sister Mary of the Incarnation—for that was the name the widowed Marie Guyart Martin took as an Ursuline nun—set sail for Canada. There she worked as a missionary with a tremendous zeal for souls and, at the same time, while undergoing long, difficult mystical trials in the period from 1639 to 1647, became a great mystic enraptured by the triune God. On April 30, 1672, Sister Mary of the Incarnation Guyart Martin died. Pope John Paul II beatified her on June 22, 1980.

[3] Mahoney, *Marie*, 186.
[4] Ibid.

Saint
Marguerite Dufrost de Lajemmerais

and

François d'Youville

*b. October 15, 1701, in Varennes,
    northeast of Montreal,
    Canada*
d. December 23, 1771, in Montreal

Married 1719
Mother of six children
Beatified May 3, 1959
Canonized December 9, 1990

Saint Marguerite Dufrost de Lajemmerais [d'Youville] was a Canadian wife and mother of six children, two of whom became priests. By founding her own congregation of nuns, which is still very active today, she became the resourceful mother, not only of her own offspring, but also of numerous sisters in religion.[1]

Marguerite was born on October 15, 1701, in Varennes, northeast of Montreal, in Canada, the daughter of Christophe Dufrost, the wealthy captain of the French colonial army in Canada, and Marie-Renée Gaultier. The father died when the girl was only seven years old. Her mother's remarriage caused the child many sorrows, for her stepfather was very stubborn and had his peculiarities, which the young Marguerite did not like.

At the age of twelve, she went to school for two years with the Ursuline nuns in Quebec. After returning home, she helped her mother with the chores and led a relatively secluded life. She was

---

[1] Margherita d'Youville, *Cenni biografici scritti dal figlio* (Rome 1958); S. Mattei, "Beata Maria Margherita Dufrost de Lajemmerais", in *Bibliotheca Sanctorum* 4:852–53; F. Holböck, *Neue Heilige der katholischen Kirche* (Stein am Rhein, 1994), vol. 3.

happy, though, when a young man asked for her hand and freed her from the oppressive restrictions of living with her parents. When she was twenty-one she married François d'Youville, a man of humble origins who, nevertheless, was relatively well-to-do. Marguerite d'Youville, as she was now called, gave this man six children. Her husband had no concept of thrift; instead, he dissipated in a short time the wealth that he brought with him and often was lacking in the love that is due to a spouse; he did not even hesitate to mistreat his wife. Thus marriage became for her, not a source of joy and contentment as she had expected, but rather a sorrowful way of the cross. By following this way, however, according to the plan of Divine Providence, she matured and was prepared for her later activity in the service of the sick, the poor, and the needy, as well as for her work as a foundress.

When François d'Youville died, Marguerite was left completely destitute, with five children and a sixth one on the way. Four of the young widow's children died in childhood; only two sons reached adulthood. With the help of benefactors they were able to study; they became priests and brought much consolation and joy to their careworn mother.

After the priestly ordination of her two sons, the widow was freed from all familial cares, and so she employed all of her time and energy in the service of the sick and the poor. In 1738 she established an infirmary in a rented house. This gradually developed into an actual hospital. In order to care for the sick, Marguerite gathered helpers, who eventually became associated as a religious community, the Congregation of the Sisters of Charity [of Montreal]. The sisters were called the Grey Nuns (*les grises*) after the color of their habit. In the same year that it was founded, this religious congregation was approved by the competent bishop of Montreal. The congregation grew and established houses in several provinces of Canada and in the United States. As for Marguerite, she governed the congregation wisely as general superior and attained thereby an intimate union with God. At all times—even in difficult trials, when fate dealt heavy blows—she had an unshakable trust in Divine Providence, which always guides everything for the good of those who love God with all their heart [cf. Rom 8:28].

Marguerite, the courageous wife, mother, widow, and foundress who had withstood so many trials, died completely resigned to God's will in her seventieth year on December 23, 1771. Pope John XXIII beatified her on May 3, 1959, and Pope John Paul II canonized her on December 9, 1990. Her religious congregation, which Pius IX approved, is still active today in Canada and in the United States.

Blessed
Anne Mary (Gianetti) Taigi
and
Dominic Taigi

b. May 29, 1769, in Siena
d. June 9, 1837, in Rome

Married January 7, 1790
Mother of seven children
Beatified May 30, 1920

Blessed Anne Mary Taigi, née Gianetti,[1] was a saintly wife and mother of seven; during her process of beatification, her husband and two of her children, Maria and Sofia, testified to her exemplary conduct as a wife and mother.

She was born in Siena on May 29, 1769, the daughter of Luigi Gianetti and Santa Masi. Because of financial difficulties, the couple moved to Rome soon after Anne Mary's birth, in the hope that the family would be better off there. They survived in the Eternal City only because the mother was able to take in work occasionally.

Anne Mary went to school with the school sisters (*Maestre Pie*) of Santa Agata dei Goti, but because of a severe case of smallpox she was not able to finish elementary school. This meant that she received very little formal education, although at home she had already had a solid religious upbringing, which was reinforced by the nuns.

On January 7, 1790, the twenty-one-year-old virgin was married in the Roman church of San Marcello al Corso to the twenty-eight-year-old Dominic Taigi, who was employed as a servant in

---

[1] Cf. C. Salotti, *La beata Anna Maria Taigi secondo la storia e la critica* (Roma, 1922); A. Bessière, *Anna Maria Taigi, Seherin und Prophetin* (Wiesbaden, 1961); F. Holböck, *Ergriffen vom dreieinigen Gott* (Stein am Rhein, 1981), pp. 315–19.

the princely house of Chigi. As a young wife, Anne Mary was in danger at first of becoming too attached to worldly vanity. She could not get very far, of course, since her husband did not earn all that much—only six scudi a month; what Anne Mary earned above and beyond that as a servant girl with the Marini family and through occasional sewing, knitting, and embroidering was hardly worth mentioning. Nevertheless, on account of the trifles that the young wife indulged in at first, she was severely upbraided one day by a Servite priest to whom she made her confession in Saint Peter's Basilica. In her great remorse she promised to change her life and was completely converted to God. Subsequently, she was enrolled in the third order Trinitarians and truly began to lead a profoundly religious life.

Anne Mary's marriage was blessed with seven children: Anne was born in 1790, Camillo in 1793, Alessandro in 1795, Luigi in 1797, Sofia in 1802, Luisa in 1806, and Maria in 1810. Three children (Maria Serafina, Luigi, and Luisa) died in infancy. The other four had excellent training from their mother and received their First Holy Communion at a relatively early age. The family prayed together every morning after rising and also before and after meals. All the family members had to be home in the evening for dinner, and afterward they prayed the Rosary together; following this there was a reading from the lives of the saints and occasionally a suitable religious song. Then the children received a blessing from their parents and were sent to bed. On Sundays and feast days—and whenever possible on work days as well—they attended Holy Mass in one of the churches in Rome. Often Mother Taigi would go to a Roman hospital, accompanied by her daughters, who in this way received early training in an important corporal work of mercy, namely, visiting the sick.

All of the children of the Taigi family who reached maturity were raised in the faith as good, practicing Catholics. They all remained members of the working class, though, because their mother, despite tempting offers from highly placed intercessors, never gave permission for one of her children to grow up in a higher social class. Each of the grown children of Blessed Anne

Mary Taigi learned and practiced a trade: hairdresser, hatter, stocking weaver. Besides true faith and piety, one thing that Mother Taigi particularly emphasized in raising her children was a solid preparation for marriage; all of her grown children would follow their mother's example, receive the Sacrament of Matrimony, and live a genuinely Christian married life.

Sofia, one of the daughters of Blessed Anne Mary, was widowed at an early age, after a marriage that was blessed with six children, and was in dire need. Mother Taigi lovingly welcomed this daughter and her six children into her household and cared for them, together with her own children who were not yet married. Of course, in this household there were, despite a modest degree of comfort, many cares and worries. Many of these were caused by the inconstancy and the unrefined manners of the head of the family. Nevertheless, Anne Mary was always faithfully devoted to her husband throughout the forty-eight years of their marriage until her death. She never vexed him, so that during the beatification process Dominic Taigi declared, "During the lifetime of my wife, Anne Mary, my house always seemed to me like a paradise."

There was never a loud argument between the two spouses, which is astonishing, given two such contrasting characters as the kindly, calm, and even-tempered Anne Mary and the impulsive Dominic Taigi. Very often Dominic returned home from his service in the household of Prince Chigi weary and sullen, downcast or angry. Anne Mary, though, intuitively understood her husband's situation; instead of reacting over-sensitively and impatiently to her husband's unkind behavior, she demonstrated patient sympathy and the greatest consideration. As Dominic himself admitted during the beatification process:

Often I came home tired because of the work that was demanded of me, and I was upset and irritable. Anyone who serves someone of high rank knows very well how often you just have to take things and swallow them. My wife, though, had such a kind and gentle way that I would quickly find that my mood had improved; not only that, but I was able to get over all those irritations and be glad that I was home again. That is why, whenever I felt uneasy and put-down, I used to hurry home and would soon be happy again. . . . Where are you going to find wives like that today?

And Dominic's reply to a question about his family's financial situation: "At our house we never lacked the necessities. Why? Because my wife always prayed and worked."

Even sixteen years after the death of his wife, Anne Mary, Dominic Taigi was still deeply impressed, indeed fascinated, by the virtues she had practiced so heroically. Remembering her gratefully and joyfully, he went on to meet her again in eternal happiness at the venerable age of ninety-two years.

Among the virtues of Anne Mary Taigi, wife and mother—besides piety, faith-filled resignation to the will of God, industriousness, and her willingness to make sacrifices and reparation—we should also mention her impressive love of helping others and her hospitality. She not only accepted the seven children that God gave her joyfully and with gratitude; she had room in her small, modestly furnished lodgings for her frail mother as well, and for the six children of her widowed daughter, Sofia. She also welcomed a priest, Don Raffaele Natali, who later became her first biographer, into her household and took care of him. In the course of her married life, God granted to Anne Mary Taigi more and more mystical gifts and charisms, for instance, the gifts of healing, of prophesy, and of reading hearts. Many people came to her in their doubts and difficulties to ask for her advice. More and more visitors arrived in the home of the blessed, among them priests and religious, indeed even a Prince of the Church, Carlo Cardinal Pedicini, and the former queen of Etruria, Marie-Louise de Bourbon. Moreover, the Blessed was in regular contact, one could say on friendly terms, with Saint Vincent Pallotti, with Saint Caspar del Bufalo, with Blessed Vincent Strambi, with Blessed Bernardo Clausi, with a fellow tertiary and mother, the Venerable Elizabeth Canori Mora. All of these acquaintances, however, were never kept up at the expense of peace and harmony in her marriage and in her family; on the contrary, they were of valuable assistance in maintaining unity and charity.

What led Anne Mary Taigi to sanctity was not her visions, ecstasies, prophecies and miraculous healings; it was rather the care with which she faithfully and perseveringly fulfilled her religious duties and those of her vocation as a wife and mother, to the greater glory of the triune God. If they were to reflect on the life of this exemplary, simple wife and mother, all Christian married people would surely understand without a doubt that sanctity is not the inheritance of a particular group of people or of a special, exalted class of persons. On the contrary, all can and must strive for it, even when they are simple lower-class people and married. It is precisely from the working-class people, who take up the challenges of Christian married life, with its daily work in the household and on the job, with the responsibilities of raising and training children and the everyday give and take of marriage, that the triune God called Blessed Anne Mary Taigi to holiness and to glorify in a special way his trinitarian divine life.

Anne Mary Taigi died in Rome on June 9, 1837, in her sixty-eighth year, a wife, mother, and grandmother. Her husband, who survived her by seventeen years, was able to say of her, "I'm old now, but if I were young and could travel through the whole world, it would be impossible for me to find a wife like her. In her I lost a great treasure." Pope Benedict XV declared this woman blessed on May 30, 1920.

Saint
Elizabeth Ann
(Bayley) Seton
and
William Magee Seton

b. August 28, 1774, in New York
d. January 4, 1821, in Emmitsburg,
  Maryland, near Baltimore

Married 1794
Mother of five children
Beatified March 17, 1963
Canonized September 14, 1975

Elizabeth Ann Seton, née Bayley,[1] was a wife and mother who lived in the United States; after the premature death of her husband, she founded a religious congregation as a widow, while caring for her five children, thus attaining sanctity. She was born on August 28, 1774, in New York, the daughter of the Episcopalian physician Richard Bayley. She received from her parents, who belonged to an American branch of the Anglican Church, a strict Christian upbringing.

At the age of nineteen she married William Magee Seton; during their happy marriage, which lasted a little less than ten years, she bore him five children, whom she raised with great care and love. In the year 1803 she accompanied her invalid husband to Italy. The young couple stayed at first in Livorno (Leghorn) for several months, then in Pisa, where William Magee Seton died in December 1803, a few days after arriving in this city.

In Livorno Elizabeth Ann Seton had become acquainted with

[1] J. Dirvin, C.M., *Mrs. Seton, Foundress of the American Sisters of Charity* (New York, 1962, 1975); idem, *The Soul of Elizabeth Seton: A Spiritual Portrait* (San Francisco: Ignatius Press, 1990).

the Filicchi family. Together with her Italian friends she went to the Catholic worship service on Sundays and even made a pilgrimage to the Marian shrine of the Madonna di Montenero. From that day on Elizabeth, who was not Catholic then, had an especially fervent devotion to our Lord in the Blessed Sacrament of the Altar and a tender devotion to the Blessed Virgin Mary. Upon her return to the United States, the thirty-year-old widow soon severed all her ties with Protestantism and was received into the Catholic Church on March 14, 1805, in New York.

In order to give her children a proper Catholic upbringing, the convert moved to Emmitsburg, near Baltimore. There, at the cost of many sacrifices, she dedicated herself lovingly to raising and educating her own children and a growing number of poor abandoned children. She sought women to assist her in this apostolate of caring for and instructing children. And helpers came. Together with them, she founded in 1809 a religious community in the spirit of the Daughters of Charity of Saint Vincent de Paul. The members of the newly established congregation called themselves the Sisters of Charity of St. Joseph's. They were to be "of the greatest importance for the work of Catholic school sisters and thus for the propagation and preservation of the Catholic faith in the United States".[2]

Elizabeth Ann Seton, who was filled with ardent charity for the children and for her sisters in religion, received excellent guidance and direction herself from Bishops Carroll and Cheverus and the Sulpician Father Dubourg, who stood by her and her foundation, offering their advice and support.

After serving as the general superior of her rapidly growing, flourishing congregation from 1812 to 1820, Elizabeth Ann Seton was called to her eternal reward at the age of forty-seven on January 4, 1821. On March 17, 1963, Pope John XXIII beatified this faith-filled convert, wife and mother of five birth children and countless adopted children. On September 14, 1975, Pope Paul VI canonized Mother Seton. This great North American woman was

[2] E. Krebs, "Elise Anna Seton", in LThK 9:509.

buried in Emmitsburg; beside her grave is that of her nephew, James Roosevelt Bayley (d. October 3, 1877), who likewise converted from the Episcopalian Church to Roman Catholicism in 1842 in Rome and who became the bishop of Newark in 1853 and the eighth archbishop of Baltimore in 1872.

Blessed
Elizabeth
Canori Mora

and

Cristoforo Mora

b. November 21, 1774, in Rome
d. February 5, 1825, in Rome

Married January 10, 1796
Mother of two children
Beatified April 24, 1994

During the "Year of the Family", on April 24, 1994, Good Shepherd Sunday, when Catholics in many churches throughout the world were praying for "holy families and vocations to the priesthood and the religious life" as part of the World Day of Prayer for Vocations, Pope John Paul II beatified a woman born in Rome who was an exemplary wife endowed with heroic virtues, a mother who lovingly cared for her children, and a mystic and penitent whose prayers obtained a religious vocation for one of her two daughters as well as the conversion of her faithless husband and *his* religious vocation, for after his wife's death he became a saintly friar and priest. We are speaking about Blessed Elizabeth Canori, whose married name was Mora.[1]

She was born on November 21, 1774, in the Eternal City, the daughter of the aristocratic landowner Tommaso Canori and Teresa, née Primoli. Even as a child she displayed a particular aptitude for everything religious. So that they might continue their education and receive formation on a religious basis, Elizabeth and her sister Benedetta were sent to the Augustinian nuns in Cascia (Umbria),

---

[1] Raimondo della Purificazione, "Canori-Mora, Elisabetta", in *Bibliotheca Sanctorum* 3:750–51; A. Pagani, *Biografia della Venerabile Elisabetta Canori-Mora* (Rome, 1911); P. Luis Alaminos, "Die selige Elisabetta Canori-Mora", abridged and translated into German in *Schweizerisches Katholisches Sonntagsblatt* 16–20 (1994).

where the widow and penitent Saint Rita had once lived. Here the young Roman girl spent wonderful childhood years (1785–1788) in the seclusion of the convent, and here too she received abundant graces. She liked "to dwell on the things of God", as she herself later explained. About her First Holy Communion she declared, "How contented, peaceful, and full of joy my heart was, O my Jesus, my Bridegroom!"

At the age of twelve Elizabeth began to develop an intimate relationship with Jesus Christ. "At the feet of the Crucified I gave vent to my soul; I opened my heart and begged for light and strength. My soul knew no other director except Jesus Crucified." Everyone marveled at her exemplary conduct and suspected that she had a calling to religious life. She herself later acknowledged, "I dedicated myself entirely to the Lord in prayer and asceticism; I strove to practice the virtues and especially sought interior recollection."

Then she became sick. Her illness was diagnosed as "the initial stage of tuberculosis". Therefore, her parents decided to take Elizabeth home right away. She then lived in the bosom of her family from 1788 to 1795. There, however, the suspected vocation to religious life quickly vanished. At her parents' wishes Elizabeth often took part in gatherings of "genteel society". She soon felt attracted by the things of the world. She later confessed, "No sooner was I back home with my parents, than I forgot about God. I rejected his love and allowed myself to be captivated by the vanities of the world." The young, elegant, and attractive lady was now making plans for marriage, especially since the marriage proposals soon began.

When she was nineteen years old, Elizabeth became acquainted with the young son of a doctor, the law student Cristoforo Mora, and she fell in love with him. After conferring with a priest about the matter, she recognized that she was called, not to religion, but to married life. On January 10, 1796, Elizabeth Canori married the lawyer Cristoforo Mora and in the Sacrament of Matrimony promised to love him and to be faithful until death. Strengthened by the grace of Jesus Christ and sensing that he accompanied, guided, and inspired her, she was determined to redirect her former life onto the path of fidelity and love for her husband.

The first months of their marriage resembled a perpetual honeymoon, with continual tokens of affection and respect and true love for each other. Cristoforo was proud of his wife and took her to important social gatherings so that everyone could marvel at the beauty and excellence of his wife, his "pearl of great price", whom he intended, moreover, to guard jealously. Driven by this jealous love, however, the young lawyer eventually ordered his wife to restrict her communication with her own parents and with her lady friends and male acquaintances—if possible, to give it up entirely. In his jealousy he wanted to have his wife "all to himself". This was difficult for Elizabeth, because she wanted to preserve the happiness of her marriage and maintain a harmonious balance. She armed herself with humility and patience in dealing with her extravagantly jealous husband. After the first years of marriage, though, *his* love suddenly turned into coldness toward his wife. He had fallen for another woman. Infidelity soon developed into a complete lack of interest in his wife and the children they had had.

Elizabeth's life and the home of the Mora family, which until then had been splendidly maintained, were overshadowed in the later years of this marriage by the lamentable adulterous behavior of the unfaithful husband, who distanced himself more and more from his wife and his children and spent his life in pleasures, gambling, and making shady business deals and connections.

For Elizabeth and her two daughters, Marianna and Lucina, there were painful consequences: soon there was not even enough money available to support them. In this tragic family crisis Elizabeth, nonetheless, conducted herself admirably. Her trust in Divine Providence was and remained unshakable, and the same was true for her fidelity to her unfaithful husband. She offered up her life for the salvation and conversion of her husband. Toward him she remained understanding and forgiving. When her husband fell seriously ill, she even sold everything she still owned in order to nurse him back to health and keep him out of debtors' prison. At all times, Elizabeth Canori Mora was true to the promise she had made at her church wedding, and she did not yield to the urgings of her family or of her confessor to separate from Cristoforo Mora. Elizabeth's sisters-in-law would anxiously ask her, "Aren't you afraid to live with an angry man who is overcome with passion and wants to live with another woman at any cost?" The exemplary wife, in unswerving love and fidelity, would answer, "The wife Cristoforo married will always belong to him; his family and his house, too. And the doors of his house are always open for him, so that someday he will again be entirely mine and stay forever with me and the children."

Elizabeth Canori Mora's greatness lay not only in her heroic marital love and fidelity but also in the loving way in which she raised her two daughters, despite all the difficulties. She accompanied the two girls as they grew up, as their religious life unfolded, in their intellectual education and formation, and in discerning their respective vocations. Marianna chose the married state but died very young, leaving a child; Lucina became a religious with the Oblate Sisters of Saint Philip Neri and died a holy death.

Elizabeth had more than her share of sacrifices and crosses to bear in life; she drew the strength she needed from daily attendance at Mass and from a daily Holy Hour during which she worshiped our Lord in the Blessed Sacrament of the Altar. In the last phase of her life, from 1807 until she was called home, Elizabeth's devotions centered above all on the mystery of the Holy Trinity. The Trinitarian priest Padre Fernando de San Luis became her spiritual director in 1807; he enrolled her as a member of the third order Trinitarians at the Roman Church of San Carlino (*San Carlo alle quattro fontane*). From then on she was ever more enraptured by the Holy Trinity. She sensed and experienced in a mystical way how she was being illumined, accompanied, and strengthened by the triune God. Thus in 1804 she could write, "It is not I who live, but God who lives in me and gives me life. He grants to my understanding a special knowledge of the most exalted things concerning the Holy Trinity."

From that time on Elizabeth not only cared for her two daughters, whom she encouraged, as always, to love their father and to forgive him for neglecting his family; spurred on by her life in union with the Blessed Trinity and inspired by the goal of the Trinitarian Order, which has always been dedicated to freeing the imprisoned, she also dedicated herself zealously to the poor and the sick, even to prostitutes and other sinners, because "the triune God", as she would say, "pours out torrents of love for sinners." She also urged the Trinitarian religious at San Carlino in Rome to remain true to their vocation and to carry out their mission generously so as to liberate those who were imprisoned or who had been enslaved because of their faith and their fidelity to the Gospel. Many people from various social classes, even bishops and priests, came to the blessed to ask her for advice. Her lodgings came to resemble a domestic church, especially when she had become ill and received permission from the pope himself to have the Sacrifice of the Mass offered in her house chapel. Then she would unite all her personal and familial sacrifices with the infinitely valuable sacrifice of atonement that was completed on Golgotha, in order to obtain the conversion of sinners, above all, that of her husband, Cristoforo.

When Elizabeth Canori Mora clearly sensed that death was approaching, she called her daughters, Marianna and Lucina, to her side and again recommended that they pray for their father's conversion. He experienced a profound remorse for all his offenses after the death of his holy wife. He went on to become a friar and a priest in the Order of the Conventual Franciscans as Padre Antonio Mora; he lived and died like a saint.

The saintly wife and mother, Blessed Elizabeth Canori Mora, died on February 5, 1825, in Rome. This woman, who was remarkable for the mystical gifts she had received (ecstasies, prophecy, the stigmata, and other charisms), is buried in the church of San Carlino in Rome. Pope John Paul II said of her at her beatification:

For her part Elizabeth Canori Mora, amidst a great many marital difficulties, showed total fidelity to the commitment she had made in the sacrament of marriage, and to the responsibility stemming from it. Constant in prayer and in her heroic dedication to her family, she was able to rear her children as Christians and succeeded in converting her husband. . . . [A] woman who is determined to be consistent with her principles *often feels deeply alone*. Alone in her love, which she cannot betray, and to which she must remain faithful.[2]

[2] John Paul II, "See What Love the Father Has Given Us!", homily at the beatification on April 24, 1994, *L'Osservatore romano*, April 27, 1994, p. 3.

Saint Joachima de Mas y de Vedruna

and

Theodore de Mas

b. April 16, 1783, in Barcelona, Spain
d. August 28, 1854

Married March 24, 1799
Mother of nine children
Canonized April 12, 1959

The holy woman Saint Joachima (Joachina) de Vedruna gave extraordinarily good example in her married life.[1] She was born on April 16, 1783, in Barcelona, the daughter of the nobleman Lawrence de Vedruna and Teresa Vidal.

From early childhood on, she had the desire to give herself completely to God. When she was twelve, she wanted more than anything to enter the Carmelites, but since she had not yet reached the prescribed age, she was turned down. At the age of sixteen she was married, on March 24, 1799, to the twenty-five-year-old nobleman Theodore de Mas. The result of this wedding was an exceptionally happy marriage that lasted for sixteen years. The home of the young couple was filled with peace and harmony. Every day Jesus Christ was quite deliberately invited to be the third party to their marriage covenant, for their daily routine regularly began with attendance at Holy Mass and concluded with the recitation of the family Rosary in the evening.

Nine children arrived, one after the other, in their happy home,

---

[1] Ignacio de Pamplona, *Vida y obra de la insigne educadora S. Joaquina de Vedruna de Mas* (Manresa, 1946); E. Federici, *S. Gioacchina de Vedruna* (Isla del Liri, 1958).

and they were received gratefully, loved dearly, and reared properly. Three children died while still in infancy; four children chose religious life, and two children married and became, like their parents, exemplary spouses.

In the summer months, when the family stayed in the so-called Manso del Escorial on the de Mas estate near the city of Vich, not far from the Pyrenees, people noticed how cheerful and contented they were and how well the older and the younger members of the family got along together. Clearly, they glorified God by keeping his commandments and by their practice of piety and charity. Although the bride and the groom had originally intended to take vows of poverty, chastity, and obedience in religious life, things worked out quite well in their marriage when they followed the wishes of their parents and approached the altar to take marriage vows instead.

Yet, once again, it turned out that the married state can also be a harried state. The happy pair, Theodore and Joachima de Vedruna y de Mas were not spared heartache and suffering. Napoleon and his soldiers invaded the peaceful Iberian Peninsula. By 1808 Napoleon had conquered Portugal. Then he exploited the discord that prevailed between King Carlos IV of Spain and his son Ferdinand, when the two of them called on him to mediate. Napoleon lured them to Bayonne and compelled them both to renounce the Spanish royal throne in favor of his brother Joseph. Many Spaniards revolted and for six long years waged a bloody campaign against the French intruder. Theodore de Mas, too, joined the freedom fighters, as the honor of his noble line demanded. For his wife, Joachima, and their children, though, this meant they had to flee once the French troops had crossed the Pyrenees and were approaching the city of Vich. In this unsettled, tumultuous time Señora Joachima lost her fifth child, to whom she had given birth while in flight.

After the defeat of Napoleon (1813) and the retreat of the French troops, Theodore de Mas was able to return to his family. He rejoiced once more in his large and happy family and resumed his profession as a notary in Barcelona. Their happiness lasted for only three more years, though. Theodore de Mas became seriously ill and died, only forty-two years old, on March 6, 1816. At the time, his wife had come down with erysipelas, a contagious disease, and was in quarantine; before his death, her husband assured her in a moving letter of his true love for her. Joachima, who was only thirty-three years old then, heard the crucified Lord speak to her from the crucifix over her bed: "Joachima, your spouse on earth has died. Come, now I have chosen you to be my bride."

After the death of Theodore de Mas, the young widow was hard pressed by various demands made by the relatives of her late husband. She withdrew at first to the Manso del Escorial near Vich and there—besides tending to the household and her children—led a life of prayer and severe penances. Through a remarkable arrangement of Divine Providence, Joachima became acquainted with the Capuchin Padre Stephen of Olot, who as God's spokesman announced to her that she should found, there in the Manso del Escorial, a congregation of nuns dedicated to the care of the sick and the education of girls. Bishop Corcuera of Vich approved of the plan, but on the condition that this new religious congregation be placed entirely under the protection of Our Lady of Mount Carmel. This was in keeping with Joachima's wishes; as mentioned earlier, she had wanted to become a Carmelite at the age of twelve.

It was very difficult for the foundress, then, to face separation from her children. When the day came, however, the painful farewells were said peacefully. Her son Joseph and her daughter Agnes married; two other daughters felt they were called to religious life. They would have preferred to join the community of the Carmelite Sisters of Charity founded by their mother, but she explained to them, "What sacrifice will you then be offering to your Bridegroom, Jesus Christ, if you stay with your mother?" Mother Joachima was able to entrust her two youngest daughters to the care of her daughter-in-law, Rosita, until they, too, consecrated themselves to God in the religious state.

Mother Joachima de Vedruna, the widowed Señora de Mas, made religious profession with her first companions in 1826. Her religious congregation, the Carmelite Sisters of Charity, grew amidst enormous sacrifices and deprivations. God demanded from the saintly foundress herself the greatest sacrifices of all: imprisonment, deportation to France, removal from office as general superior; finally, a serious illness that led to her death, which took place on August 28, 1854, when the saint was seventy-one years old. On May 19, 1940, she was beatified by Pope Pius XII, and on April 12, 1959, she was canonized. Joachima de Mas y de Vedruna was an exemplary Christian wife for seventeen years and a loving, attentive mother for nine children of her own; then, as a foundress for thirty-eight more years, she spent herself in mothering her spiritual daughters and the children who were entrusted to her congregation of nuns.

Blessed Benedetta (Cambiagio) Frassinello

and

Giovanni Battista Frassinello

b. October 2, 1791, in Langasco, Italy
d. March 21, 1858

Married February 7, 1816
Beatified May 10, 1987

Blessed Benedetta Cambiagio, whose married name was Frassinello, was a wife and widow who became the foundress of a religious congregation and with great love took care of poor girls who were abandoned or at risk. On May 10, 1987, she was raised to the honors of the altar.[1] She was born on October 2, 1791, in Langasco (Italy) into a Christian family that, to all appearances, was well situated. At her parents' recommendation, the pious girl married an upright young man by the name of Giovanni Battista Frassinello. After two years of marriage, during which the young couple were not blessed with any children, they agreed to live in a so-called Josephite marriage. They took a vow of perpetual chastity and resolved from then on to consecrate their lives completely to God and to charitable works. Since they themselves had not had any children, they took in poor abandoned children, especially girls who were at risk. With her husband's consent, Benedetta established a home for abandoned and at-risk girls in Pavia in 1826.

[1] V. Bondiani, *Suor Benedetta Cambiagio* (Genoa, 1925).

Several years later, she founded the Congregation of the Benedictine Sisters of Providence. The apostolate of this community was to provide a Christian education for young people, especially the poor and the abandoned and girls who were at risk, and to establish homes, schools, and workshops for that purpose. She was successful in this work. At the death of Benedetta Cambiagio Frassinello, who, meanwhile, had been widowed, the congregation she had founded numbered thirty-five houses and two hundred nuns; its constitutions were approved by the Holy See in 1937. In all the difficulties she encountered in her charitable work, Blessed Benedetta trusted unswervingly in Divine Providence. She set an example of a life of faith, hope, and love until on March 21, 1858, at the age of sixty-seven, she was called to her eternal reward.

John Francis Vaughan

and

Louisa Elizabeth Rolls

b. 1810
d. December 1880

Parents of fourteen children

Among the married saints and blesseds here, we might also mention an English couple from the nineteenth century who were staunch Catholics, lived a Christian married life, passed on the gift of life to fourteen children, and then gave almost all of their children back to God as priests or religious. Even though it is certain that there will never be a beatification process for this couple, their courage in having such a large family and their constant prayers that their children would have the grace of a vocation to the priesthood or to the religious life make them splendid examples for our time, when so many married couples—affected by a materialistic mentality—are "distinguished" for their aversion to children and are no longer open to the concept that it is a great, exalting, joyful, and consoling thing to have a child with a religious vocation.

John Francis Vaughan[1] was born in 1810 into the noble line of Courtfield, which for generations had been tried by sufferings, persecution, and misunderstanding on account of their fidelity to the Roman Catholic Church. When Catholics were being persecuted during the reign of Queen Elizabeth I, this aristocratic family preferred prison and the loss of property to betraying their Catholic faith. Over the course of decades, in those dangerous but glorious days, Courtfield, the ancestral estate of the Vaughan family, was the refuge and hiding place for priests who were being

[1] J. G. Snead-Cox, *Life of Herbert Vaughan* (London, 1910), 2 vol.; C. C. Martindale, *Bernard Vaughan, S.J.* (London, 1923).

pursued by bounty hunters and who secretly carried out their pastoral work in all sorts of disguises throughout the land, despite the constant threat of martyrdom. Courtfield then was a hallowed place, especially because the Eucharistic Sacrifice was secretly celebrated over and over again in the castle. It is true that this glorious era was almost three centuries in the past, but, meanwhile, nothing had changed in the Vaughan family's loyalty to the faith and to the Church. That is why the family produced so many priestly and religious vocations. For example, an uncle of the young John Francis, on his father's side, William Vaughan, became a priest and eventually the bishop of Plymouth; two of his own brothers became priests, and three of his sisters, nuns. John Francis himself decided on a military career, married, and became the head of an exceptionally large family.

John Francis' wife was Louisa Elizabeth Rolls, the third daughter of the wealthy Anglican landowner John Rolls of the Hendre. The two met in Paris and, despite their different creeds, fell in love. Louisa Elizabeth Rolls must have been very open to the Catholic faith, however, for she converted out of a deep personal conviction. She became Catholic, not only in the externals, but wholeheartedly, and she felt drawn especially to Christ in the Most Blessed Sacrament. The Vaughan family had their own domestic chapel, in which a priest celebrated Holy Mass every day. Besides attending Mass, the young wife spent an hour each day in the chapel in contemplative prayer. Soon she had an interior prompting to pray that God might take back, as priests or religious, all of the children he would send her. She suggested this to her likeminded husband. Colonel Vaughan gladly agreed to his wife's request. God abundantly fulfilled the holy desire of this couple by granting to almost all of their children the grace of a vocation to the priesthood or the religious life.

Louisa Elizabeth Vaughan contrived an exceptionally good religious upbringing for her thirteen children (the fourteenth child of this noble wife died in infancy). On her frequent charitable visits to the poor and the sick tenants of Courtfield Castle, the mother liked to bring one or another of the children along; on such occasions she would prompt the children to offer something to the poor from their own savings or from their collection of toys.

In the case of Herbert Alfred, the oldest son, who was born on April 15, 1832, a priestly vocation began when he was sixteen years old. When he told his mother of his decision, she smiled and replied, "My child, I knew that a long time ago." The boy's father, at any rate, was not so happy about the news, for he had set his hopes on the oldest son as the one who might follow in his footsteps and become a high-ranking officer in the British army. Nevertheless, the father, too, yielded to the will of God, who wanted Herbert to be a priest. At that time, the high-spirited Catholic colonel wrote to a friend, "If Herbert goes [to seminary], then the others can all go, too." Not all of them, but almost all, went. All eight sons, it is true, heard a calling to the clerical state. Herbert Alfred, Roger William Beda, Kenelm, Joseph, Bernard, and John actually were ordained priests, and two of them were consecrated bishops. The two remaining sons, Francis and Reginald, did go to seminary but eventually sensed that they were not called to the priesthood. They married, carried on the Vaughan line, and gave an example of genuine Christian married and family life. Of the five daughters, four became religious, but all of them died young. Only Margaret, the youngest daughter, remained single as a laywoman; she, too, however, spent the last years of her life in the cloister and died, at the age of eighty-five, in 1936.

Their mother, Louisa Elizabeth Vaughan, died at the age of forty and so did not live to see the ordination day of any of her six sons who became priests; surely, though, she implored for them the grace of a vocation many times in prayer. Their father, John Francis Vaughan, died at age seventy in December 1880. In his final illness he had the consolation and joy of attending Masses celebrated daily in his sickroom by two of his six priest sons, namely, Herbert Alfred (then bishop of Salford) and Bernard (then a newly ordained Jesuit priest).

What exactly, now, became of the ten children of the Colonel and Mrs. Vaughan who consecrated their lives to God? Let us begin with the four daughters. Gladys entered the Visitation Order of

Saint Jane Frances de Chantal, Theresa became a Sister of Mercy, Clara became a Poor Clare, and Mary became an Augustinian nun.

The information on the six priest-sons is as follows:

1. Herbert Alfred studied in Brugelette in Belgium from 1846 to 1849, in Downside in 1850, and then in Rome. Having received an eighteen-month papal dispensation, he was ordained a priest at the age of twenty-two on October 28, 1854. In 1855 he became vice-regent in Saint Edmund's College in Ware. In 1857 under H. E. Manning he entered the Oblates of Bayswater. From 1863 to 1865 he made missionary journeys in California and Central and South America, and on March 1, 1866, he founded the St. Joseph's Missionary Society for mission work in South America, with its headquarters in Mill Hill near London. On October 26, 1872, he was made bishop of Salford; on March 29, 1892, archbishop of Westminster; and on January 19, 1893, cardinal. He died on June 19, 1903, in Mill Hill, having performed magnificent services for the Catholic Church in England.

2. Roger William Beda, born on January 9, 1834, became a Benedictine monk in 1854 and was ordained a priest in 1859. He worked as a professor and served as prior at Saint Michael's College in Herefordshire, England. From there he was sent in 1873 to Australia, where he eventually became archbishop of Sidney. He died in Ince Blundell Hall, Lancashire, on August 18, 1883.

3. Kenelm's experience was unique. He was just sixteen years old when he entered the Cistercians. After four years, his health had deteriorated so much that he asked his uncle William Vaughan, bishop of Plymouth, to ordain him so that he could die a priest. The bishop granted the request of his nephew. As a newly ordained priest, Kenelm then made a novena to prepare for his imminent death. On the ninth day, he suddenly was cured during the celebration of Holy Mass. Later, he went to South America and there served the Church admirably for forty-four more years.

4. Joseph became a Benedictine monk; he founded the first Benedictine monastery in Scotland since the Reformation.

5. Bernard, born on September 20, 1847, studied in Stonyhurst College starting in 1859. In 1866 he entered the Jesuits and was

ordained a priest in 1880. He was assigned to the church of the Holy Name in Manchester, then to various other posts. He gradually developed into a highly respected preacher and apologist and traveled in 1910 to Canada; from 1911 to 1913 he toured the United States and, in 1913, the Far East. In 1922 he went to Africa. He died in Roehampton, England, on October 31, 1922.

6. John, the youngest son of John Francis Vaughan and his wife, Louisa Elizabeth, was ordained a priest by his brother, Archbishop Herbert Alfred Vaughan. He served as Rector of Saint Beda College in Manchester and authored twenty-five theological works.

Think of all the blessings that flowed from this extraordinary English married couple, the Vaughans, especially through their six priest-sons!

Blessed
Paula Cerioli
and
Gaetano Buzecchi-Tassis

b. January 28, 1816, in Soncino,
    Bergamo, Italy
d. December 24, 1865

Married April 30, 1835
Mother of three children
Beatified March 19, 1950

Blessed Paula (Paola) Elizabeth Cerioli Buzecchi-Tassis[1] could tell
you many stories about her married life; she was able to cope with
an apparently unbearable situation thanks to her heroic faith. Widowed after nineteen years of marriage, she became the foundress of
a double congregation, thus wisely investing her own funds and
the wealth left to her by her deceased husband.

Constance Cerioli was born on January 28, 1816, in Soncino
(Province of Bergamo); she was the sixteenth child of Francis
Cerioli, a descendant of the old Piedmontese nobility, and his
wife, Frances, née Countess Corniani. At the age of ten, she went
to the Sisters of the Visitation in Alzano and received from them a
proper, faith-based education until she was sixteen. At age nineteen, she was married on April 30, 1835, to the wealthy sixty-year-
old Count Gaetano Buzecchi-Tassis, who was already a sick man
and whose way of thinking was completely unlike that of his pious
Catholic bride.

[1] E. Federici, *Beata Paola Elisabetta Cerioli, vedova Buzecchi-Tassis* (Rome, 1950).

Could a marriage with a husband who was forty-one years older ever work?

Their marriage was blessed with three children, of whom only the firstborn survived childhood—and he died at age sixteen. One child died soon after birth and the other after living for only a year.

As far as marital love and fidelity are concerned, the wife's conduct, at least, was beyond reproach. She was patient with her difficult husband, docile, and generous. The count, however, who likewise loved his young wife faithfully, was jealous of his son; he was always afraid that his wife would love him less than their son, Charles. Both mother and son patiently put up with the count's peculiar moods. He did not allow his son to play or to have any sort of recreation or company. He selfishly monopolized his son, demanding, for example, that the boy listen attentively to him play the piano for hours at a time.

From 1849 on the seventy-five-year-old Count Buzecchi was permanently confined to bed as a result of a stroke. His infirmity aggravated his idiosyncrasies and made him a difficult patient. Nevertheless, his wife, Constance, continued to care for him lovingly; she was his "consoling angel", as he himself used to call her in his reasonable moments. After heroically nursing her sick husband for four years, she learned that her son, Charles, too, was seriously ill with tuberculosis. So Countess Constance had to take care of two invalids, with the father morbidly jealous and afraid that his wife was giving the son more attention than he was getting. Constance Cerioli found the strength to cope with all these difficulties in her marriage through her faith and devotions.

The two people who had been entrusted to the countess' faithful loving care were carried off by death in the same year, 1854. On January 16, 1854, she had to close the eyes of her son, Charles, who died at age sixteen, and on Christmas Day of 1854 she watched her eighty-year-old husband, Count Gaetano Buzecchi, die peacefully in her arms.

Countess Constance had once lamented to her saintly son, Charles, as he was dying, "What will I ever do alone without you?" Though deathly ill, the son spoke to his mother these prophetic words, "The Lord will entrust other children to your care."

The death of her child and that of her husband left Countess Constance Cerioli in possession of a large estate inherited from the aristocratic Buzecchi and Tassis families, as well as her own dowry. This responsibility weighed heavily upon her, for she was uncertain as to what she ought to do with this great wealth. One day, the pastor of Comonte (where the count's palace and the inherited properties were located) said to her, "If I were in your position, I would find poor children, take care of them, and raise them. That would keep you busy and cheer you up."

Later that same day, two orphaned children from the neighboring community of Seriate were brought to the thirty-eight-year-old widow, and she immediately took them in. She thanked God that he had made his will known to her in this way. Because her son was deceased, the orphans would become the heirs of her many properties. The people in that locality and the domestics were, of course, horrified by this decision and declared it foolishness that ragged, neglected children should be sheltered in the palace of a count. The countess, nevertheless, explained: "I wish to God that I really were a fool, but with the foolishness of Christ's love on the Cross! . . . So it is with the ways of the world: If someone in fact behaves foolishly, he is regarded as a reasonable person, but if someone does good, he is considered foolish. In reality, though, people who have the spirit of the world are the fools, for they make themselves slaves to the world. Unfortunately, I, too, was once like that."

In order to care for and rear the ever-increasing number of orphan children, Countess Constance had to look around for suitable helpers; they presented themselves one after the other. Placing her work under the special patronage of Saint Joseph and looking to the Holy Family in Nazareth as a model, she called the orphans "the sons and daughters of Saint Joseph" and set about raising them in simplicity and purity, to love work and to be peaceable and honest in word and deed. From the women who helped her and from the growing children gradually came the members of a religious congregation, the Sisters of the Holy Family. The countess viewed herself as Saint Joseph's co-worker. She had already made a vow of chastity at her husband's wake; now in 1857, along with the name Paula Elizabeth, she took additional vows of poverty and obedience, together with a fourth vow, always to do everything for the greater glory of God. To her companions she said, "From now on you will no longer call me Signora Constance, but rather Sister Paula Elizabeth." In another five years, a men's branch of the congregation developed, even as the blessed foundress fell asleep in the Lord in her fiftieth year in the night between December 23 and 24, 1865.

On March 19, 1950, she was beatified.

The Servants of God
Louis Martin

and

Maria Azelia Guérin

Louis:
b. August 22, 1823, in Bordeaux
d. July 29, 1894, in La Musse

Maria Azelia:
b. December 23, 1831, in Gandelain
d. August 28, 1877, in Alençon

Married July 13, 1858
Parents of nine children

The cause for beatification has been introduced for both the husband and the wife in the case of this saintly married couple, and so it is only right that they should be portrayed here, especially since we are talking about the parents of the much-revered Saint Thérèse of the Child Jesus. Louis Martin and Maria Azelia (Zélie) Martin, née Guérin, have found their final resting place in the shadow of the basilica in Lisieux that was built in honor of their daughter, the Little Flower. Between the two graves stands a statue of the Saint of Lisieux, beneath which her words are captured in bold letters: "Le bon Dieu m'a donné un père et une mère plus dignes du ciel que de la terre [The good God gave me a father and a mother who were more worthy of heaven than of earth]."

1. Louis-Joseph-Aloys-Stanislaus Martin was born on August 22, 1823, in Bordeaux, the third child of Pierre François Martin, a soldier who would advance to the rank of captain and who had been married on April 7, 1818, with the second daughter of Captain Nicolas-Jean Boureau, Marie-Anne-Fanny by name. The vicissitudes of military life led Pierre-François Martin and his

family from Bordeaux to Avignon and then to Strasbourg. On December 12, 1830, Captain Martin, adjutant of the regiment, requested that he be removed from active duty; he planned to spend his retirement with his family in his native town of Athis, in Normandy. On account of the better opportunities for his children's education, however, he moved instead to Alençon, a city then numbering 14,000 inhabitants, and settled there on the rue du Pont-Neuf.

In all of his posts and through all of the vicissitudes of his military career, Captain Martin maintained a steadfast faith, which he then passed on to his children, especially to his favorite son, Louis, by means of a solid Christian upbringing. From his deeply devout father, Louis acquired genuine piety and a good-hearted nature, and he was encouraged, furthermore, to study French literature and to speak the language flawlessly. That is why in later life he was able, not only to talk about religion with his daughters, but also to discuss literary themes. As a youth, Louis also displayed an artistic talent for drawing and painting.

In the city of Rennes, in 1842–1843, Louis learned the watchmaker's trade from Louis Bohard, one of his father's cousins. He then went to Strasbourg, where he had spent his early childhood, and stayed with Aimé Mathey, a friend of his father, for further training in the trade he had learned. Monsieur Louis Martin always had fond memories of his apprenticeship in Strasbourg, where he also learned the German language. After returning to Alençon, he plied his trade there in his own watchmaker's shop.

On July 13, 1858, the pious watchmaker, who was already thirty-five years old, married the twenty-six-year-old lace maker Maria Azelia (Zélie) Guérin. Originally Louis Martin wanted to belong to a religious order. For a long time he thought that he could realize his ideal of consecrating himself totally to God by living in seclusion on Mount Grand-Saint-Bernard in Switzerland. So in autumn 1845 he had set out from Strasbourg on the way to the monastery on Grand-Saint-Bernard. At first the prior benevolently accepted the young man, whose eyes were bright with innocence and purity. When he determined, however, that the

Louis Joseph Martin   *Maria Azelia Martin, née Guérin*

candidate had had no education in the humanities, he advised him to return home and to make it all up by studying privately. Louis bought the required books and also took several courses. An illness, however, forced him to give up his studies and to dedicate himself full-time to the trade he had learned. He stayed for a time in Paris for further training in clock-making and to learn the goldsmith's trade as well. From then on, he had a successful business in Alençon.

2. Maria Azelia Guérin, Louis' young wife, was born on December 23, 1831, in Gandelain, the second child of the gendarme Isidore Guérin and Louise Jeanne Macé. Her older sister later entered the Visitation convent in Le Mans; her younger brother, Isidore, became an apothecary and played an important role in the life of the Martin family in Lisieux.

Her mother, Louise Jeanne Macé, was excessively strict with her daughter Zélie, while she spoiled her son, Isidore. Zélie took comfort in an especially intimate friendship with her older sister, Marie. The two sisters received a very good education from the

Sisters in Alençon at a school run by the Religious of the Congregation of the Sacred Hearts of Jesus and Mary and Adoration (also known as the "Picpus Sisters"). Zélie had a delicate constitution and was almost continuously sick from age seven until she was twelve; she suffered from persistent migraine headaches. Despite her staunch faith, her mother lacked the empathy needed to understand Zélie's idiosyncrasies and her sensitive nature, which was inclined to melancholy. Experiencing so little understanding from her own mother awakened in Zélie a longing to find understanding and security in a cloistered religious community, just as her sister had done in joining the Visitation Convent in Le Mans. Zélie felt drawn to the Daughters of Charity. So she went one day to the hospital in Alençon to introduce herself to the Daughters of Charity there and to express her desire. The interview was not a success, for when she requested admission, the superior replied that it was certainly not the will of God for Zélie to enter the congregation. Was the reason for this answer Zélie's frail health? In any case, she submitted to the superior's better judgment and soon afterward presented a petition to God that is recorded in a letter that has been preserved: "Since I am not worthy to become Thy spouse like my sister, I will enter the married state so as to fulfill Thy holy will, O God. I beg Thee, however, to send me many children, and grant that they may all be consecrated to Thee!"

Now Zélie Guérin had to think about her future. She could not and did not want to continue being a burden to her parents at home. The modest pension that her father received as a retired gendarme was scarcely enough to support the family; besides, the son, Isidore, wanted to study, and that would mean additional expenses for him, the favorite child. So Zélie tried to improve her skills at making the famous Alençon lace, which she had learned from the nuns during her schooldays, so as to earn a living with that sort of work. She entered a school for lace-making and was trained to be an accomplished lace maker, whose work was much in demand. Toward the end of 1853 she even established her own business as a "Manufacturer of Alençon Lace". Until 1856 she produced lace with the help of women who worked at home; in that year she gave up her own business and went to work as an employee of the firm Pigache et Mallat.

Not long after the painful separation from her sister, Marie, when she entered the convent, a marriage prospect presented itself to Zélie Guérin. The wife of the retired Captain Pierre Martin would not be reconciled with the idea that her son Louis, who was already thirty-five years old, would remain a bachelor forever, content with his secluded life as a watchmaker on the rue du Pont-Neuf in Alençon. She admonished him and pestered him to start thinking about getting married. Then Madame Martin heard about the fine qualities of Zélie Guérin and began to dream that the young lace manufacturer would become her son's wife.

As Zélie Guérin was walking over Saint Leonard's Bridge in Alençon one day, her path crossed that of a young man whose noble features, reserved manner, and dignified bearing made a great impression on her. At that very moment she heard an interior voice saying to her, "This is the husband I have destined for you." She became acquainted with Louis Martin. Three months after their first encounter, on July 13, 1858, the two of them exchanged marriage vows before the dean, Monsieur Hurel, in the church of Our Lady in Alençon. Would this marriage go well, when both partners originally intended to consecrate themselves to God in religious life? In contracting marriage with such a virtuous and deeply religious bride, Louis Martin had hopes of entering a so-called Josephite marriage and of living chastely together with his partner as brother and sister. Although Zélie in her generosity was willing to lead such a married life, she was motivated by a strong maternal drive to hand on the gift of life to many children and to raise them up for God.

After ten months of living in a pure, chaste Josephite marriage, the advice of a good confessor prompted the couple to change their way of life; he asked them to consider that they still could see their youthful dream of religious life realized at last in their off-spring. They desired perfection and holiness, and they would go on to prove that this can also be attained by making the right use of marriage, according to God's design, in the mutual self-giving of sexual love. For the Martins, handing on the gift of life to children would be the way to express their love and loyalty for each other, especially since they could raise and educate their children to be willing to seek the greater glory of God on their own. That, in fact, was the magnificent result of their chaste and noble married life.

With the help of God, Louis Martin and his wife, Zélie, gave life to nine children. They are as follows:

1. Marie-Louise (February 22, 1860—January 19, 1940)
2. Marie-Pauline (September 7, 1861—July 28, 1951)
3. Marie-Léonie (June 3, 1863—June 16, 1941)
4. Marie-Hélène (October 3, 1864—February 22, 1870)
5. Marie-Joseph-Louis (September 20, 1866—February 14, 1867)
6. Marie-Joseph-Jean-Baptiste (December 19, 1867—August 24, 1868)
7. Marie-Céline (April 28, 1869—February 25, 1959)
8. Marie-Mélanie-Thérèse (August 16, 1870—October 8, 1870)
9. Marie-Françoise-Thérèse (January 2, 1873—September 30, 1897)

Five of these children consecrated themselves to God as religious, four in the Carmel of Lisieux, namely, Marie-Louise as Sister Marie of the Sacred Heart, Marie-Pauline as Sister Agnes of Jesus, Marie-Céline as Sister Geneviève of the Holy Face, and Marie-Françoise-Thérèse as Sister Thérèse of the Child Jesus. One daughter, Marie-Léonie, became a nun in the Visitation convent in Caen as Sister Françoise-Thérèse. Four children died in infancy or in early childhood, among them two boys who the parents had hoped would glorify God as priests. Instead of the priest-sons they had prayed for so much, God sent these parents their ninth child, who became Saint Thérèse of the Child Jesus, who prayed and sacrificed as a victim-soul for priests and missionaries.

As for the married life of the Martins, we can report the following. The couple enjoyed a reputation in Alençon of being irreproachable. Because of their occupations and their income, they belonged to the upper middle class; in spite of being well off, though, they lived modestly and shunned excess; instead they were socially conscious and generous to the poor and the needy. Their religious sense was based on three pillars: love of God above all things, trust in Divine Providence, and resignation to God's will. In making plans they always had a view to eternity, for "true happiness is not of this world."

Louis Martin liked to get away for a few days to the salutary climate in Mortagne and make a retreat at the Trappist monastery. Attending Mass was part of Louis' and Zélie's daily routine. Madame Zélie Martin frequently visited the Poor Clare convent in Alençon; there she became a member of the Franciscan third order. In her beautiful, well-kept house, daily prayers were recited before a statue of our Lady. During the month of May, this statue was adorned with special care.

The favorite book of this couple was the *Lives of the Saints*. Their entire life revolved around the parish. The typical day began, even after the children started to arrive, at 5:30 in the morning in the church of Saint Pierre de Montfort, later in Notre-Dame. Depending on the circumstances, Monsieur and Madame Martin went once a week or even more often to Holy Communion. On Sundays, the entire family attended High Mass and Vespers. Participating in religious celebrations was a deep-seated need for the Martin couple. Occasionally, Père Martin would also make pilgrimages with his daughters, for instance, to Notre-Dame des Victoires in Paris, to Séez, or to Chartres and Lourdes. The mother would not allow herself to travel with them; she always accompanied her dear ones spiritually on their pilgrimages, though.

Père Martin always approved when his wife would visit the poor and the needy in their cottages, offering them assistance and consolation. It was her special concern to see to it that the dying received the last sacraments. As a member of the Society of Saint Vincent de Paul, Père Martin visited the poor. He set a high standard in his charitable apostolate and helped in whatever way he could. The domestic help in the Martin household were always treated kindly, like members of the family. Mère Martin always took care not to overwork her employees; she herself used to work more than they did, getting up before them and going to bed last.

The unity and harmony in this marriage and this family were remarkable, both between the spouses and between the parents and the children. Jesus Christ was the King of this couple's home and the center of these parents' activities. That is why Saint Thérèse of the Child Jesus was able to write in her *Story of a Soul*, "O, how I love my memories of the blessed days of my childhood! To guard the blossom of my innocence, the Lord always surrounded me with love." In this milieu five religious vocations matured— those of the first, second, third, seventh, and ninth children; furthermore, the last-mentioned attained a degree of sanctity that the Church has solemnly affirmed.

In raising her daughters, Madame Martin tolerated neither self-will nor childish whims; she was strict to a certain extent. Most important, however, she used various occasions, even small, insignificant ones, to form her daughters, to promote good habits, and to lead them on to self-mastery and generosity. She also understood very well how to draw her daughters away from wishful thinking and how to lead them to fulfill conscientiously the duties of their state in life. When the oldest daughter left boarding school at age 15½, her mother initiated her immediately into the ways of running a household. Probably one reason she did this was that she already sensed that her end was near, and therefore the oldest daughter would have to follow her mother in taking responsibility for the younger children.

Bringing up the little ones was also a source of cares and worries for Madame Martin, because one daughter, named Léonie, had a rather difficult and rebellious character and was unpredictable; it seemed that she was born to be contrary. Nevertheless, Madame Martin did not allow herself to become at all discouraged. The youngest daughter, later a saint, might have become a spoiled child had it not been for the vigilance of her parents and all of those fortunate qualities that practically predestined her to be good. Saint Thérèse of the Child Jesus later wrote, "If I, with my disposition, had been raised by parents who were not virtuous, or even if I had been spoiled only by Louise, I would have become very wicked and might even have been lost."

In April 1865 Madame Martin felt the first indications of the breast cancer that was at work in her. For eleven years this malady lay dormant, but frequent headaches, bouts of fever, and strange symptoms of fatigue indicated that this mother, who was in the prime of life—between the years 1866 and 1870 she would bear five more children—was becoming weaker and weaker. She probably begged God not to take her from this earth as long as her children needed her. She maintained her calm composure as she watched the illness progress. Until almost the very end of her life she dragged herself each day to the church of Our Lady in Alençon to attend early Mass. She never ceased caring for her children, especially for the difficult daughter, Léonie, and, finally, for the precious baby of the family, who was to become a great saint. She had many worries and sorrows because of the early deaths of the two boys in 1867 and 1868 and of the next-to-last child in 1870. When Madame Martin's sister, Marie, whose name in religion was Sister Marie-Dosithée, died a holy death at age forty-nine in the Visitation convent of Le Mans on February 24, 1877, this was a heavy blow to Zélie. She had always had a special understanding with her sister, and now she had to deal with the fact that her own life, too, would soon be at an end. Before that occurred, she was able to make one last pilgrimage to Lourdes, which brought her much consolation but not the healing for which she had hoped. After returning from Lourdes, she managed splendidly, despite her great suffering, to continue taking complete responsibility for the household, and until the end of her life she remained the soul of her wonderful home. Finally, the consolations of the faith were her only support during her painful illness. On August 28, 1877, Madame Azelia Martin fell asleep after a short battle with death, shortly before the conclusion of her forty-sixth year. Priests at that time declared openly that there was one more saint now in heaven. Similar things were said by many others who had really known Madame Martin. Of all the testimonies, that of the deceased woman's husband, Monsieur Louis Martin, was especially important; he always described his wife as a saint. Then, too, there are the statements of the daughters who gave testimony under oath as witnesses during the beatification process for their youngest sister, Thérèse, and also attested to their mother's virtues.

Monsieur Louis Martin, now a widower, moved on November 15, 1877, to Lisieux and took up residence in the beautiful villa Les Buissonnets so as to be nearby his dear brother-in-law, the apothecary Isidore Guérin. He no longer worked as a watchmaker; he could afford early retirement and so from then on devoted himself completely to his daughters. He managed the household and determined the family's way of life; he was very strict about order and cleanliness. The oldest daughter, Marie-Louise assumed the role of lady of the house, and, after she entered the convent, Marie-Céline took over her duties.

In Lisieux, as previously in Alençon, the servants were part of the family. Monsieur Martin was always pleasant and kind toward the help. With his daughters he was strict, but always full of extraordinary tenderness and love. After the older daughters had completed their education with the nuns in Le Mans, Père Martin could not bring himself to send his two youngest daughters away to boarding school. Instead, he sent them to school with the Benedictine nuns in Lisieux. Meanwhile, at home they were cared for primarily by their older sisters.

During the years at Lisieux, Monsieur Martin remained a man of prayer and of practical charity who went outside his house only to take walks and, occasionally, to make longer excursions. The spirit of faith and charity informed his entire life in Lisieux also. This included daily Mass, which he usually attended in the cathedral of Saint-Pierre. He received Holy Communion almost every day and also made a daily visit to our Lord in the Blessed Sacrament. Being of Norman descent, Louis Martin was thrifty in managing his finances, yet he displayed the greatest generosity when giving material relief to people in need. The people from his neighborhood in Lisieux, also, were soon impressed by the deep piety and supernatural radiance of this man.

One after the other, the daughters left their father and entered religious life in the Carmel of Lisieux. Pauline went first, on October 2, 1882. Marie-Louise followed on October 15, 1886. A religious vocation became more and more evident in the youngest daughter, Thérèse, as well, although she was still practically a child. The lonely father heroically gave his consent for her to go into the convent, even though it meant losing his "little queen". He agreed to make the pilgrimage to Rome with Thérèse and Céline so as to obtain permission from Pope Leo XIII for Thérèse to join the Carmelites. On April 9, 1888, the fifteen-year-old Thérèse actually entered the Carmel of Lisieux. The "difficult" daughter, Léonie, tried first with the Poor Clares in Alençon, then several times with the Sisters of the Visitation in Caen, before she was finally accepted there on January 28, 1899, as Sister Françoise Thérèse.

Eventually, the only daughter left staying with her father was Céline. On June 15, 1888, she, too, confided in her father that she wanted to follow her sisters and become a Carmelite. Père Martin then said to Céline, "Come, we will go together to visit the Blessed Sacrament, to thank the Lord for the graces he has granted to our family and for the honor he has paid me in choosing all the daughters in my house to be his brides. It is a great, great honor for me that the Good Lord desires to take all of my children. If I had anything better, I would not hesitate to offer it to him." It sometimes happened that he was pitied because of the empty places that now surrounded him. Some considered the sacrifices that were repeatedly demanded of him to be inhumane. He, however, saw the entrance of all his daughters into religious life as a great honor, even though his serious illness began at that time.

Until the sixty-fourth year of his life, Louis Martin was in the best of health; it appeared that he would reach a ripe old age, as his father had done when he died at eighty-eight after a stroke, or at least like his mother, who died at the age of eighty-three. This expectation was dashed, though, by a stroke on May 1, 1887, which was soon followed by two strokes that were less severe. The stroke caused hemorrhaging and brain damage. There was a temporary improvement, but in June 1888 the malady suddenly returned and became worse. From then on, he suffered frequent memory loss; then certain sorts of hallucinations occurred. He was beset with a desire to live as a hermit; he longed to withdraw from the commotion of the world and to flee to some distant refuge. Temporary paralysis would set in, affecting his ability to speak, and he had bouts of depression. Finally, it was necessary to commit him to an institution, the Bon Sauveur [Good Savior] in Caen. Monsieur Martin had to remain there for three years. When the restless compulsion to wander away had finally ceased, the sick man was brought back to Lisieux on May 10, 1892, where he was cared for lovingly by Céline.

On the country estate of La Musse, where Monsieur Martin was staying with his daughter Céline to recuperate, the life of this great, long-suffering man, who had endured a serious illness with complete resignation to the will of God, ended on July 29, 1894; he had received the last sacraments and was well prepared. He was seventy-one years old. Now Céline, too, who had stayed by her father, could take her decisive step and enter the convent. Céline began her postulancy at the Carmel in Lisieux on September 14, 1894, and became Sister Geneviève of the Holy Face and of Saint Teresa.[1]

[1] Further information can be found in P. Stephane-Joseph Piat, O.F.M., *The Story of a Family* (New York: P. J. Kenedy, 1948); Robert Cadéot, *Louis Martin: Père incomparable de Sainte Thérèse de l'enfant Jésus* (Paris, 1985; idem, *Zélie Martin, Mère incomparable de Sainte Thérèse de l'enfant Jésus* (Paris, 1990). From this book we learn that the consultors of the Pontifical Congregation for the Causes of Saints on February 13, 1987, unanimously rendered a positive judgment on the documents forwarded by the diocese of Bayeux concerning the life and death of Louis Martin, and that with only one dissenting vote they likewise rendered a positive judgment on the documents forwarded by the diocese of Séez concerning the life and death of Madame Azelia Martin. Therefore it is to be hoped that the process of beatification can be successfully completed.

Blessed
Bartolo Longo
and
Marianna de Fusco

b. February 10, 1841, in Latiano,
   near Brindisi, southern Italy
d. October 5, 1926

Married April 1, 1885
Beatified October 26, 1980

The famous apostle of the Rosary and founder of New Pompei, Blessed Bartolo Longo, lived in an edifying Josephite marriage. Although his marriage is usually passed over in silence, he deserves to take his place here in the company of married saints and blesseds.

Bartolo Longo was born on February 11, 1841, in Latiano, near Brindisi, in southern Italy, the son of Doctor Longo, the physician, and his wife, Antonia, née Luparelli, and was baptized on February 13, 1841.

As an infant Bartolo had such frail health that—just to be safe—the Sacrament of Confirmation was administered to him at the age of three months. Other than that, Bartolo had a happy and holy childhood in the home of his wealthy, highly regarded parents. He was a lively child, but always well behaved and pious. At the age of six, he was sent to the Piarist Fathers for his schooling. In the Royal Collegium Ferdinandeum in Francavilla Fontana, they gave him a fine education, from the primary grades through secondary school, and also instilled in him a great love of the

413

Blessed Virgin Mary. On June 25, 1858, Bartolo, who had lost his father at the age of ten, received his diploma, qualifying him to enter a university. His mother had married again, after her husband's death, the lawyer Giovanni Campi, who steered young Bartolo toward the legal profession. He began to study law in Lecce and then in 1863 continued at the University of Naples. Besides his studies, Bartolo was involved in the political uprisings of the day inspired by Garibaldi, and also in music; in many respects he was a dashing young student.

The University of Naples at that time was dominated by Freemasonry and by anticlerical professors, some of whom were fallen-away priests, who vigorously attacked the Catholic Church and her doctrines. In particular, Bartolo Longo came under the influence of the apostate Bertrando Spaventa. His faith became weaker and weaker. Moreover, he was impressed by his reading of Renan's *Life of Jesus*. In the year before graduating with a doctorate in law on December 12, 1864, he completely abandoned the Christian faith and became interested in spiritualism, which at that time in Naples had all but taken on the form of an institutionalized religion, with temples, rituals, ceremonies, and cultic attendants, drawing students into contact with demonic powers, almost along the lines of a satanic cult.

Fortunately, Bartolo Longo had not allowed his friendly ties with one believer, Professor Vincenzo Pepe, a deeply spiritual man from his hometown of Latiano, to break off. This man convinced the young law student to confide all of his doubts and difficulties to a highly educated, saintly Dominican priest, Padre Alberto Radente, who was the prior at the church of the Holy Rosary in Portamedina. With the help of a band of prayer warriors, this priest succeeded in bringing the lost sheep back to the Good Shepherd and his Virgin Mother in a thoroughgoing confession and a lasting conversion, so that he began to practice his faith again in earnest and eventually became an extraordinarily zealous lay apostle.

He concluded his professional training for a career as a lawyer and district attorney by passing his bar examinations brilliantly, and he began to practice law. His apostolic activities, however—defending and proclaiming the Catholic faith and charitable social work for the poor and the needy—took up an ever greater part of his daily routine, whereby his relatively large income made it possible for him to offer generous financial help.

Twice during this period Bartolo Longo thought of marriage. At first he was infatuated with the beauty of the baroness Caterina Scazzeri, a relative of his who was very involved in charitable works. He was advised, though, not to marry this close cousin. Then a noblewoman, Annina Guarnieri, the daughter of a banker in Bari, was Bartolo Longo's great "flame". The father of the beautiful, wealthy young lady would have agreed to their betrothal and would have given the young lawyer a large sum of money with which to buy a suitable wedding gift for his bride-to-be. Bartolo Longo himself—as he wrote in a letter to an aunt—had no other desire than "to start a truly Catholic family and, through marriage, to provide the Church with new sons and daughters and God with new worshippers." The groom-to-be finally called off the wedding after conferring with the saintly Redemptorist Padre Emanuel Ribera. When they had discussed the matter thoroughly, this priest advised him to renounce marriage. He spoke these prophetic words to Bartolo Longo: "The Lord wants to do very great things through you; you are called to carry out a very important mission." When the bride learned of Longo's heroic decision to renounce marriage, this chaste virgin said to her father, "O, how inconstant is human love! I will no longer speak of this wedding or about any other marriage. From now on I will love one alone: Jesus, the true Bridegroom." Soon afterward, she died of a short, completely unexpected illness, having gloriously preserved her virginity.

Bartolo Longo now gave up his legal practice in his hometown and went to Naples to do full-time apostolic and charitable work in the slums of that southern Italian metropolis. So as to be well armed for his apostolate in word and in print, he diligently listened to the best preachers in Naples and in 1869 copied down about a hundred sermons. He was especially devoted to the sick people in the "Hospital for Incurables" and performed the lowliest tasks for them, wrote letters to their relatives, and helped in whatever way he could. At the same time, he was edified by two incurable patients who endured their sufferings with impressive resignation to the will of God and peaceful equanimity, thereby attaining sanctity; they were the Servant of God Francesco Maione (d. 1874) and the Servant of God Luigi Avellino (d. 1900). During this time Bartolo Longo also learned much from a religious priest who zealously conducted an apostolate in Naples and the surrounding area, namely, the venerable Servant of God Padre Ludovico da Casoria (d. 1885). "I cannot express in words how much this religious priest influenced me and the course of my whole life by his love of poverty and his love for the poor. He was my instructor in charity", Bartolo Longo would later write.

Another major influence on Bartolo Longo and his apostolic and charitable formation was a saintly woman who had prayed much for his conversion, namely, the venerable Servant of God Caterina Volpicelli (d. 1898), who later founded the Handmaids of the Sacred Heart (*Ancelle del Sacro Cuore*). This wealthy Neapolitan lady gathered together in her ancestral home like-minded women who worked to spread Sacred Heart devotions and the Apostleship of Prayer (founded by Henri Ramière, S.J.) in the city of Naples and who also provided worthy furnishings for poor village churches. Among these women was the young widowed Countess Marianna de Fusco, née Farnararo.

On October 7, 1871, the three hundredth anniversary of the victorious Battle of Lepanto, the lawyer Bartolo Longo was enrolled in the third order of Saint Dominic with the name Fra Rosario (Brother Rosary). Every day he went to the house chapel of Caterina Volpicelli to pray the Rosary in common. Afterward these apostolic lay people would talk about the charitable works in progress. During these discussions Bartolo Longo became acquainted with his future wife and faithful collaborator, Marianna de Fusco. This twenty-four-year-old widowed countess, who had five children [from the deceased count's previous marriage] from eight through sixteen years of age, spent incredible sums on the furnishings and decoration of poor village churches and consequently was in financial difficulty. To be sure, she had large properties in the vicinity of Pompei, but she had no idea how to manage these lands so as to derive a suitable income from them. Caterina Volpicelli had taken the countess and her children into her spacious mansion.

Eventually, Bartolo Longo joined them there and took over the management of the countess' properties. He became the attorney in charge of her estate, her helper and support in the education of her children, and her companion as she traveled to inspect her various properties. On these trips he and the countess became aware of the material poverty and the even greater religious and moral poverty of the small tenant farmers and laborers on the land surrounding Old Pompei. The two of them, the countess and the lawyer, had complementary personalities and were well matched as to age and interests. Neither one, however, thought of getting married. As for the Servant of God Caterina Volpicelli and the Servant of God Padre Ludovico da Casoria, they neither urged the two to marry nor tried to dissuade them from it; of course, they reinforced them in their spiritual lives and in their apostolic works of charity, especially in serving the poor rural inhabitants of Pompei. Both of them recognized that it was necessary to help these people, and not only by social improvements, but also and primarily by leading them out of their religious ignorance and indifference.

Since most of these people could not even read or write, Bartolo Longo planned to counter their ignorance through praying the Rosary. Ever since his conversion, the lay apostle had been convinced that the Rosary could teach these ignorant, uneducated people the fundamental, most important truths about salvation through the events in the lives of Jesus and Mary; that if they would persevere in praying the Rosary and meditating on the mysteries, they would surely become, not only more pious, but also better off. Bartolo Longo tried to gather the inhabitants of the Valley of Pompei in a modest little village church that was nearly in ruins, in order to inspire them to practice their faith. At first he was almost completely unsuccessful. Things improved only in

1873, when Bartolo Longo planned a celebration of the Feast of the Holy Rosary according to the folk traditions. He did the same on an even grander scale for the Feast of the Holy Rosary in 1874. By the Feast of the Holy Rosary in 1875, he had won the complete confidence of the populace, and even the little village church, having been cleaned and decorated, now made a passable impression.

With authorization from the bishop of Nola, Longo organized a popular mission and attempted to found a Rosary sodality on February 13, 1876. At the same time, he managed to receive eleven especially earnest people into the third order of Saint Dominic. To increase the zeal of the Rosary sodality members for praying the Rosary, Bartolo Longo wanted to set up an altar in honor of the Queen of the Holy Rosary in the little village church of Pompei. For this purpose he planned to request permission from the local ordinary, the bishop of Nola. When the latter came, on November 12, 1875, to administer the Sacrament of Confirmation, he considered the attorney's plan and said, "Let's not erect an altar in the village church, which is run-down and much too small; let's combine our resources instead to build a grand new shrine in honor of the Queen of the Holy Rosary." Bartolo Longo liked this plan.

He talked it over with Countess de Fusco, who owned the land on which the church was to be built. She raised serious objections, however, especially on account of the tragic death of her son Errico, who had fallen into a well and drowned wretchedly in the muddy water. She was in mourning and did not know how to respond when she was presented with an unexpected plan for building a church. Bartolo offered to deal with the technicalities. "I will do the worrying for you and for me about this business. Just give me your signature, so that I can make the necessary arrangements, and put me in contact with your relatives. The Madonna will take care of the rest."

The countess replied, "If the Madonna obtains a certain favor for me, then I will do what I can!" The favor she was praying for did not delay in coming. Now the countess' enthusiasm for the construction project knew no bounds. Bartolo Longo later explained how the plans proceeded. "I used the countess' name and her contacts and began by writing various letters asking for donations so as to collect funds for the construction of a church." One of the first actual donors to whom he wrote was Caterina Volpicelli. The project gradually developed into an extensive fundraising campaign, because the planners were no longer content with building a conventional village church. Instead, they planned to construct a grandiose, artistically designed, and magnificently decorated basilica. The driving force, from the laying of the cornerstone on May 8, 1876, to the consecration of the church on May 8, 1891, and beyond, until the completion of the interior decoration of the basilica, was and remained Bartolo Longo. He begged for the money that was required and organized everything out of love for his heavenly Mother.

The former attorney summoned all of his talents to supervise the construction of the Rosary basilica in New Pompei and to promote the recitation of the Rosary in the growing basilica. Not only that, but with astonishing energy he raised the funds that were required and defended, in word and in writing, those truths of the faith and events in salvation history that the Rosary sets forth as subjects for meditation and that, then as now, were often attacked, called into question, disputed, or denied outright. He carried on this apologetic work especially in *Il Rosario de la Nuova Pompei*, a newspaper he founded and edited, and in numerous other publications.

The lay apostle Bartolo Longo, who lived a strictly ascetical life of impressive piety, was not content with fostering the piety of the inhabitants and strengthening their faith. He knew that, if faith is to be genuine, it simply must manifest itself in works of charity on behalf of others. So he established next to the Rosary Basilica an orphanage for boys and girls and a large home for the children of convicted, imprisoned fathers and mothers. His trust in the Queen of the Holy Rosary never failed, even when failures and difficulties, misunderstandings and ingratitude appeared and impeded his apostolic and charitable undertakings. When well-meaning people misinterpreted his selfless efforts in the service of the Queen of the

Holy Rosary, when wicked men mocked him because he lived and worked together with his principal collaborator, the Countess de Fusco, or when in certain circles he was considered to be a swindler and a thief who had embezzled funds or Mass stipends or had misused them to his own advantage, Bartolo Longo persevered courageously, even when sickness and physical frailty came with advancing age.

This courageous, selfless lay apostle had led an exemplary and strictly ascetical life ever since his conversion, when he had made a vow of chastity. Therefore, it was especially painful for him when he was slandered on account of his collaboration with Countess de Fusco. Gradually, these calumnies became unbearable for Bartolo Longo. Finally, he was faced with the dilemma: either he must separate himself from the apostolic works that he had developed together with the countess, or else he would have to ask the countess to distance herself from the entire project, in which she had invested so much effort, most recently, directing the girls' orphanage for ten years. If he were to detach himself from the work, then it would be doomed to failure, for if she were on her own the countess would never be able to deal with the hundred problems, great and small, that had to be solved day in and day out. To remove the countess entirely from the project, on the other hand, would be the worst form of ingratitude toward someone who had sacrificed and worked so much for it.

With whom could Bartolo Longo consult about this dilemma, since his spiritual advisers, Padre Radente and Padre Ludovico da Casoria, were no longer alive? Only Professor Pepe, a layman, was still living. He said to his former protégé, "You still have the Madonna as your best and most faithful adviser!" She advised him, after much prayer, to put everything into the hands of the successor of Peter in Rome. So Bartolo Longo requested an audience with Pope Leo XIII. To His Holiness he explained the entire complex of problems. In reply, however, the Pope asked only two questions: "Are you, Signore, still eligible? And is the countess still a widow and unattached?" On hearing the affirmative answer to both, Leo XIII said, "The entire affair can be put in order very quickly and easily. You two get married, and from then on nobody will have reason to speak ill about your relationship with one another."

After the papal audience, the countess made the brief comment, "We went to Rome as friends and are now returning (to Pompei) as fiancés." The wedding took place in the chapel of the arch-bishop's residence in Naples on April 1, 1885.

Bartolo Longo and Marianna de Fusco, who at that time were both forty-four years old, lived from then on in a Josephite mar-riage in the best sense, as knowledgeable witnesses were able to testify during the beatification process. The spouses always slept in separate quarters. Bartolo Longo had always attached great impor-tance to the vow of perpetual chastity he had taken upon his conversion, and after he was married he continued to observe it strictly. Countess de Fusco, who lost her first husband at age twenty-four, had led an exemplary life of purity during the fol-lowing twenty years as a widow and continued to do so after her second marriage.

The two spouses continued to complement one another very well—as they had done during the twenty years previously—in their fidelity and dedication to the work established in honor of the Queen of the Holy Rosary, although the countess' tempera-ment made her somewhat difficult to get along with. She had always remained conscious of her dignity and authority as a coun-tess, and on occasion she could be short-tempered and abrupt with others. She sought to dampen her husband's ebullient enthusiasm and to restrict his freedom. Be that as it may, she was basically a humble person; above all, she was selfless and generous. For the sake of the work she offered the share of the inheritance that would have been hers upon the sudden death of her son Blasius/Blasio; she sold all of her jewelry for the construction of the basilica, including the diamond brooch that Queen Margaret of Savoy had given her as a present. Bartolo Longo patiently and humbly yielded to the nervous, imperious manner of the countess; he remained silent on those occasions when the countess was unkind and harsh and pronounced injurious words. Once the storm had passed, Bartolo Longo would kindly and lovingly admonish his wife, saying, "Countess, all things pass; let us always think of heaven."

On February 9, 1924, the highly meritorious noblewoman Marianna Longo, the widowed Countess de Fusco, renowned for her charitable work in New Pompei, died, at the age of eighty-three. On October 5, 1926, the eighty-seven-year-old Bartolo Longo followed his faithful collaborator and wife to the grave. They rest side by side, entombed in the crypt of the basilica of the Holy Rosary in New Pompei. Over their common grave stands the altar in honor of Bartolo Longo, who was declared Blessed by Pope John Paul II on October 26, 1980.

On May 30, 1925, when Bartolo Longo received from Augusto Cardinal Sili a special award for the great services he had rendered, the elderly lay apostle said,

> Today . . . I wish to make my last will and testament, since my final hour will soon arrive. I have collected sums of money in the millions and then spent them in order to construct the Rosary basilica and the large charitable institutions in this new city of Mary. I possess nothing now, for I have just given the entire work over to the Apostolic See. All that I have left are the awards that have been given to me. I leave them to my orphans, so as to remind them that one must be valiant as a knight in the practice of virtue, and strong and unshakable in faith. To Your Eminence, on the other hand, since you are the papal delegate and administrator of the basilica and of the works that I founded, I leave my feeble body with the request that it be buried in the sanctuary of the basilica at the foot of the throne of my gracious Queen, whom for over fifty years I have tried to serve faithfully.

At the beatification ceremony Pope John Paul II characterized Blessed Bartolo Longo as follows:

> It is easy to note that his whole existence was an intense and constant service of the Church in the name of, and out of love for, Mary. Bartolo Longo, a Tertiary of the Dominican Order

and founder of the Institution of Sisters "Daughters of the Holy Rosary of Pompei", can really be defined [as] "the man of the Madonna": out of love for Mary, he became a writer, an apostle of the Gospel, propagator of the Rosary and founder of the famous Sanctuary, in the midst of enormous difficulties and adversities; out of love for Mary, he created institutes of charity, went begging for the children of the poor, transformed Pompei into a living citadel of human and Christian goodness; out of love for Mary, he bore tribulations and calumnies in silence, passing through a long Gethsemane, always confident in Providence, always obedient to the Pope and to the Church.[1]

At the conclusion of this striking portrait of Blessed Bartolo we allow ourselves the question: Why is it not mentioned that this admirable man was married for thirty-nine years and for ten years previous to that was already being supported in many ways in his work by his future wife?

---

[1] "A Priest, a Religious, and a Layman Attest That All Are Called to Holiness", *L'Osservatore romano*, November 3, 1908, p. 11.

Blessed
Rafaela Ibarra
and
José de Vilallonga

b. January 16, 1843, in Bilbao, Spain
d. February 23, 1900, in Bilbao

Married 1861
Mother of several children
Beatified September 30, 1984

A daughter was born to a wealthy but devout Basque couple, Gabriel Maria Ibarra y Gutiérrez de Cabiedas and Rosaria de Arambarri y Mancebo, on January 16, 1843, in Bilbao (Spain). The following day she received in Baptism the name Rafaela Maria Stefania and from then on grew to be a shining example among the saints of the Basque people, as Pope John Paul II declared at the beatification on September 30, 1984. Even as a very small child, Rafaela showed extraordinary signs of piety. At the age of eleven, she received her First Holy Communion, which made a truly profound impression upon her, for on that occasion—as she noted in her diary—she wept for joy over the experience of encountering Christ.

If you think that little Rafaela grew up to be a nun, you are wrong. She wanted to demonstrate, in a genuinely Christian marriage, that you can also love God fervently when you deliberately include Christ as the third party to the marriage covenant. At the age of eighteen, Rafaela married a young man from a wealthy Christian family, José Vilallonga, and together with him led a Christian married life in the best sense. She loved her husband in

God and for God's sake, and likewise her children and adopted nieces and nephews. She lovingly took in her aged parents and other relatives as well, not forgetting meanwhile to carry out apostolic work in a wider circle. In the true spirit of the apostolate, she used her great wealth to establish Holy Family Hospice in Bilbao for women in difficult straits and girls at risk. To care for such girls she also founded a religious congregation, the Sisters of the Holy Guardian Angels (*Congregación de los Santos Angeles Custodios*).

Under the prudent spiritual direction of the Jesuit priest Francisco de Sales Muruzabel and with her husband's approval, Señora Rafaela Ibarra de Vilallonga took vows of poverty, chastity, and obedience, to which she added in 1890 the vow of always preferring what is most pleasing to God, which would include—as soon as her family situation permitted—consecrating herself completely to God as a religious. The saintly wife, Rafaela Ibarra Vilallonga, died on February 23, 1900, in her house in Bilbao. She was renowned for her sanctity, which the pope confirmed at her beatification on September 30, 1984.[1]

---

[1] A. Chavarria y Arrondo, *Nació para ser Madre. La vida y la Obra de Rafaela Ibarra de Vilallonga, Fundadora de la Congregación de los Santos Angeles Custodios* (Buenos Aires, 1953).

Blessed Victoria Rasoamanarivo

and

Radriaka Rainilaiarivony

b. 1848, Antananarivo, Madagascar
d. August 21, 1894

Married May 13, 1864
Beatified April 30, 1989

Blessed Victoria Rasoamanarivo,[1] a convert from paganism, took very seriously as a wife the indissolubility of a sacramental marriage; she is the first blessed from the great African island of Madagascar. She was born in 1848 in Antananarivo, on Madagascar, into a very powerful family of the Hovas tribe. Her mother, Rambohinoro, was the daughter of Prime Minister Rainilaiarivony, who ruled for fifteen years. About her father nothing is known; her father's older brother, the military commander Rainimmharavo, adopted Victoria. She received an excellent moral education, but as far as her religious training is concerned, she belonged to an indigenous nature religion until she was thirteen. When the Sisters of Saint Joseph of Cluny settled in Antananarivo, on Madagascar, however, Victoria soon became one of the first girls admitted to the mission school by the nuns. The instructions in the faith and the example of the sisters made a profound impression on the young girl. She asked to be baptized, and the sacrament was conferred upon her on March 1, 1863.

[1] Cf. F. Holböck, *Die neuen Heiligen der katholischen Kirche* (Stein am Rhein, 1994), 3:120–27.

The Christian girl had to fight many difficult battles from then on. Victoria's foster father demanded that she give up the Catholic faith and tried to move her with flattery and threats. Despite these attempts to make her apostatize, she remained true to the Catholic faith. She would have liked to go a step farther and to consecrate herself to God as a religious, but the missionaries advised against it, thinking that such a decision would be extremely imprudent and provocative, given the situation of the Catholic mission on Madagascar at that time. It would be better for Victoria to stay in the world with her relatives at the royal court and discreetly promote the Catholic faith. This she did, with complete dedication.

Soon, though, a wedding was arranged for Victoria, with Radriaka, the son of Prime Minister Rainilaiarivony. She could not prevent this marriage but demanded that the ceremony be conducted in the presence of a Catholic priest.

Victoria's wedding took place on May 13, 1864. Unfortunately, this marriage very soon became a martyrdom for Victoria. Her husband was unprincipled and completely lacking in self-control; he was addicted not merely to alcohol but also to various pagan vices. His life-style gradually became so scandalous that even his own father and the queen repeatedly advised Victoria to divorce the man. She, however, knew that a sacramental marriage, contracted before God, is indissoluble, and she remained true to her dissolute husband. Her main reason was that she had reason to fear the consequences of giving bad example to her newly converted Christian brethren if she, a princess, were to divorce him. So Victoria remained faithful to her husband until his death in 1887, and through her many prayers and her patient sacrifices she prevailed upon him to receive Baptism before he died.

Victoria now endured heroically all the humiliations to which she was subjected. She led a genuinely Christian life as a widow and earned great respect, not only at court, but also among the simple people. The universal admiration in which she was held, on account of her virtuous life and the moral authority that she had acquired, eventually made Victoria a rock-solid support for the Catholic Church on Madagascar, which was repeatedly threatened by persecutions. Her readiness to help her persecuted brothers and sisters in the faith was edifying. She was also an apostle of prayer, often kneeling and praying in a church for hours at a time. And yet, she was not only pious; she was also extremely active in social and charitable works, addressing herself to the needs of poor and abandoned people, the imprisoned and the leprous. She suffered from various illnesses but endured everything with great patience. On August 21, 1894, she died, at the age of forty-six. Pope John Paul II beatified this noble woman during his pastoral visit to Madagascar on April 30, 1989, and on that occasion presented her as a magnificent example of heroic faith. Among other things, the Pope praised her respect for the Sacrament of Matrimony and said,

> We know also what courageous fidelity Victoria has shown *to the Sacrament of Matrimony*. . . . Her commitment had been sealed in the sight of God; she did not wish to question it. With the help of grace, she respected her husband despite everything, and kept her love for him, in the ardent desire that he would turn towards the Lord and be converted; she was granted the consolation of seeing her husband, at the end, accept baptism.[2]

[2] "Passion for Christ in Marriage, in the Church, and in the Service of the Poor and Needy", *L'Osservatore romano*, May 15, 1989, p. 7.

The Servant of God
Ladislaus Batthyány-Strattmann
and
Maria Theresia Coreth

b. October 28, 1870, in Dunakiliti, Wieselburg, Hungary
d. January 21, 1931, in Vienna

Married 1898
Father of twelve children

Even though he is not yet beatified, the Austro-Hungarian prince Dr. Ladislaus Batthyány-Strattmann[1] has every right to be included among the blesseds and saints who can serve as examples for married couples of our time. He was, when he died on January 21, 1931, in Vienna, not only a highly respected physician who put himself at the service of sick people, but also an exemplary Christian husband and father of a large family. Many hope and expect that he will soon be raised to the honors of the altar, to the joy of Catholics in Austria and Hungary.

Ladislaus Batthyány-Strattmann was a descendant of the Hungarian nobility who owned extensive lands and castles in the southern part of the Austrian province of Burgenland. He was born on October 28, 1870, in Dunakiliti in the Hungarian *komitat* [county] of Moson/Wieselburg, the sixth of ten children of Prince N. Batthyány-Strattmann. Because of severe flooding in Dunakiliti from the Danube River, his family had to move in 1876 to Kittsee in what is today Burgenland. The boy's childhood was soon overshadowed by the divorce of his parents. At the age of nine, Ladislaus went to Kalksburg to be educated in the boarding school of the Jesuits. After the six years that he spent there (1879–1885), he attended the secondary school in Kalocsa for three years (1885–

---

[1] R. Kroyer, *Ladislaus Batthyány-Strattmann, ein Leben im Dienste Gottes und der Menschen* (Eisenstadt, 1986).

1888). In Ungvár he continued his studies and earned a diploma there in 1890.

Neither during his school years nor in his university days in Vienna from 1890 to 1900 did Ladislaus show any signs of being a future saint. He was instead—despite the after-effects of his Jesuit education—of a liberal mind-set and rather indifferent toward both the Church and the faith. This was evident in his first years of university studies in Vienna, which he more or less frittered away, especially since he really did not know what he ought to be studying. His father wanted him to study agriculture so as to become an effective manager of the lands belonging to the princedom. He was personally more inclined toward the natural sciences; finally he ended up in medicine and became an extraordinarily competent physician, particularly as a specialist in ophthalmology. He was extremely conscientious and successfully performed around twenty thousand operations, half of them eye operations. The thirty-year-old prince graduated as a doctor of medicine in 1900. He described his student years in Vienna as "unhappy", probably because God, whom he later loved so fervently, meant little to him during that time, and especially because he had also transgressed God's moral laws and sired an illegitimate child.

The great turning point in the life of Dr. L. Batthyány-Strattmann was his engagement in 1898 with Countess Maria Theresia Coreth, whose family was from Southern Tirol. This was the beginning of a proper marriage, lived according to Christian principles, which produced eleven children. It was striking how a happy, harmonious marriage transformed Dr. L. Batthyány-Strattmann into a contented, extremely principled man. He not only practiced his profession as a "doctor of the poor" conscientiously, he also gave an extraordinarily good example of kindness and charity in "spending" himself in his work, all the while remaining a faithful, loving husband and a father who took great care in rearing his children. He had a real partnership with his wife and used to discuss all his concerns with her. She was his assistant, not only in his practice as a physician but also within the family in dealing with the children or the domestic help. They were not at all haughty about their rank; both of them showed respect and Christian courtesy to all people, even to gypsies, beggars, and others who were marginalized by society at that time. Each spouse encouraged the other to make generous donations to charities and often to perform heroic services for the needy. First and foremost, though, the prince loved his children and his patients. It was typical of him to say, "My children and my patients are the only treasures I own."

Another component of the marital and familial life of Prince Ladislaus Batthyány-Strattmann was great piety. One of the prince's sons explained, "Daily Mass and the Rosary were just as much a part of our daily routine as mealtimes." The petition from the Our Father, "Thy kingdom come", was the dominant note in his prayers, whether they concerned personal matters, his family, society, or the world at large. "God was, so to speak, the air he breathed," declared one nurse who used to assist the prince in the operating room. When his son Dr. Josef Batthyány was asked what he thought of his father as a Christian, he replied, "He was a good example, par excellence."

The investigation of the episcopal [diocesan] ordinariate of Eisenstadt for the cause of the prince's beatification emphasized that he zealously cultivated his spiritual life, he very often visited our Lord in the Blessed Sacrament in his private chapel, and that, besides a fervent devotion to the Sacred Heart of Jesus, he also had a childlike love for the Blessed Virgin, the Mother of Christ. In her honor he prayed not only a daily Rosary, but also the "Little Office of the Blessed Virgin, a sort of breviary for laymen.

Dr. Batthyány-Strattmann continued his religious education, mainly through reading periodicals and books. He would carry on in-depth religious conversations with the many priests who were frequent guests at his house. The Franciscans had a great influence on him and also served him and other members of his family as confessors. Because one of his wife's sisters was a Benedictine nun in Bertholdstein in the Steiermark, he felt that he was spiritually related to the Benedictines, who gave him his liturgical formation.

During the fourteen months he spent with a terminal illness in a

Vienna sanatorium, Prince Batthyány radiated a marvelous peace of soul to all who visited him. He had finally learned to pray constantly, and he lived continually in God's presence. Shortly before his death in Vienna, a Jesuit heard his last confession. The priest declared, "I have just heard the confession of a saint." Bishop Mikes von Szombathely/Steinamanger, who was well acquainted with the Batthyány family, said after the death of the prince, "We should pray to him rather than for him."

Hedwig Anthofer
and
Ernst Kronsteiner

Hedwig:
 b. March 2, 1872, in Losenstein, Upper Austria
 d. April 19, 1940

Ernst:
 b. February 9, 1871, in Losenstein, Upper Austria
 d. February 5, 1951

Married May 6, 1901
Parents of eleven children

A simple but exemplary Christian couple from the twentieth century, whose lives were portrayed by one of their priest-sons in a moving book entitled *A Mother and Eleven Children* (which is already in its fifth edition),[1] can be included in this book, *Married Saints and Blesseds*, particularly since many Catholics in the home diocese of this couple thought of recommending for beatification the mother, at least, of this remarkable family.

The husband and father, Ernst Kronsteiner, was born on February 9, 1871, in Losenstein, in the Upper Austrian valley of Ennstal, to a working-class family with liberal and anticlerical views. He learned the clockmaker's trade, which enabled him to feed his large family, despite toils and hardships.

The wife and mother, Hedwig, née Anthofer, was likewise born in Losenstein, on March 2, 1872.

In the home where Hedwig Anthofer grew up, too, a liberal, anticlerical spirit prevailed. During her girlhood years, however, she received such good spiritual direction from a wise and zealous

---

[1] Hermann Kronsteiner, *Eine Mutter und elf Kinder*, 5th ed. (Linz: Verlag Kultur in die Familie, 1989).

Ernst and Hedwig Kronsteiner with their eleven children

chaplain that she entered marriage wearing the crown of virginity. Then, as a staunch believer and a pious wife, she not only brought her husband to practice the Catholic faith but also passed on the gift of life, almost year after year, to a series of eleven children. She raised them well and wisely, so that they became practicing Catholics who lived their faith; eight of the children chose to serve the Church as priests or religious.

Ernst Kronsteiner married Hedwig Anthofer on May 6, 1901, after a traditional engagement that lasted seven years. In the year 1900 he had participated in a pilgrimage to the Holy Land that had a lasting effect on him and helped to liberate him from the anti-clerical spirit he had imbibed at home. Gradually he—like his wife—came to treasure the Catholic faith and its central mystery, the Mass, so much that in the final period of his life he attended Mass not only on Sundays but also on weekdays.

Ernst Kronsteiner's religious sense was deep and genuine, but in his case it was more or less hidden beneath his serious, mild-mannered, taciturn ways. Unlike his wife, he hardly ever gave his children direct religious instructions, but his solemn way of praying, his reverence for everything having to do with religion, his conduct in church, and his profound respect for priests were powerful lessons. For all his tolerance, he would never allow newspapers or magazines that were "risqué" or that might endanger the faith to enter his house. His children recognized that he was the "head" of the family, even though their mother took the guiding role in matters pertaining to education or managing the household. The children also owed their musical training to their father, who had a knack for awakening this sort of talent and gave them instructions in playing a wide variety of instruments and in the rules of harmony.

During the years of marriage that they spent together, the mother took the lead in religious matters, deliberately bringing her husband and children along with her into her world of faith and prayer. She led a life of prayer that was extraordinarily deep. Her prayer life followed a fixed order of an almost monastic sort; she not only said her daily prayers, as was her duty, but, despite her many chores, she recited her Rosary, spent an hour in meditation, and attended Holy Mass each and every day. Moreover, Mother Kronsteiner knew very well how to turn the entire day, with its toils and worries, its work and its cares on behalf of a large family, into a prayer through a "good intention", which she formulated as follows: "You have to do everything for the love of God; anything else is worth nothing!"

This mother raised her children with astonishing wisdom and generous freedom, in keeping, nonetheless, with the twofold principle: "The children don't belong to me, they belong to God", and "Anything rather than a mortal sin!" As a result, eight of the eleven children discerned a vocation to the priesthood or the religious life.

Here are the names and occupations of the eleven children.

(1) Anna (1902–1982) entered the Sisters of Saint Elizabeth in Linz as Sister Cecilia and served there as organist and choir director. (2) Agnes (b. 1904) worked at first as a clockmaker, then she entered the Carmelite monastery in Linz as Sister Theresita and served there as cantor and organist. (3) Hedwig (1905–1988) at first worked at home, then as Sister Lucillia in the missionary

congregation of the Holy Ghost Sisters in Ratibor, Stockerau, and Vienna. (4) Ernst (1906–1981) became a master clockmaker and worked in the parish of Bad Zell (near Zellhof) as director of the church choir. (5) Franz (1907–1981) became a lay brother in the Congregation of the Steyler Missionaries and worked for fifty-three years as a teacher and educator in Argentina and Chile. (6) Berthold (b. 1908) married and worked at first as a clockmaker, then as a policeman in Vienna and Linz. (7) Joseph (1910–1988) became a priest in the diocese of Linz and served for decades as choirmaster at the cathedral and as a highly esteemed composer in Linz. (8) Otto (1911–1982) married and worked as a master clockmaker, serving meanwhile for fifteen years as mayor of Losenstein. (9) Aloisia (1912–1988) became a clockmaker and then entered the Holy Ghost Sisters in Stockerau as Sister Elfriede; she served as organist in Vienna and Bad Hall. (10) Hermann (b. 1914) became a priest of the diocese of Linz and worked as a professor in the *Musikhochschule* [music academy] in Vienna, then as a composer in Linz. (11) Rudolf (b. 1915, since 1943 missing in action in Stalingrad) became a clockmaker and then entered the Benedictine Abbey in Seckau (Steiermark) to become a monk; war prevented him from pursuing this vocation.

In conclusion, let us say a few words about the Christian deaths of Herr and Frau Kronsteiner. The mother, Hedwig Kronsteiner, got up early, at 4:00 A.M., on April 19, 1940, as usual, and had her "conversation with God" in her customary one-hour morning meditation. At 7:00 A.M. she took her missal to attend Mass, as usual, in the parish church in Losenstein and received Holy Communion, unaware that it was her Viaticum. She spent the day as "Grandmother" in the company of her son Otto and his wife, Justina, and watching her little grandson Otto. Around 8:00 P.M. she went with her husband—as she did every evening—into her bedroom to the family photo to bless her children and to pray for each of them. Then the husband and wife, as was their custom, each made the sign of the cross on the other's forehead and prayed the prayer of consecration to the Sacred Heart of Jesus. After this, Frau Kronsteiner went again to the kitchen to make some final preparations. While there she had a fainting spell. After a time, her husband found her unconscious. They brought her to bed, called the doctor and the priest; the latter administered the Anointing of the Sick. At midnight, the courageous woman died in the peace of Christ, after managing to write down a sentence as a sort of testament: "Grant (O God) that I may love Thee always, and do with me what Thou wilt!"

The father, Herr Kronsteiner, survived his wife by eleven years; he died on February 5, 1951. In his final years he became increasingly quiet, resigned, and meek; every morning he approached the Table of the Lord, and to the last he helped his son Otto in his clockmaker's workshop.

In many respects, parallels are evident between the Kronsteiners, who worked as clockmakers, and the French couple Louis and Azelia Martin, the parents of Saint Thérèse of the Child Jesus. Surely we might mention still many other Catholic married couples worldwide who lived an exemplary married life and raised their children very well and also prepared them for priestly and religious vocations.

The Servant of God Charles of Austria

and

Zita

b. August 17, 1887
d. April 1, 1922

Married October 21, 1911
Father of eight children

Charles of Austria (1887–1922) on the occasion of his engagement with Princess Zita of Bourbon-Parma in Pianore, 1911

If we want to include another exemplary, indeed, saintly Christian married couple from the early twentieth century in this book, then we can look to the last emperor of Austria, Charles I, from the House of Habsburg-Lothringen [-Lorraine] and to his wife, Empress Zita, from the royal House of Bourbon-Parma.[1] For all of the vile calumnies—refuted long ago—that have been spread and scattered abroad concerning the emperor and his wife, this couple's good reputation has remained unsullied. From the beginning to the end of their ten years of marriage, which produced eight children, they set an example of marital fidelity. Both noble spouses were true-believing, church-going Catholics who respected and obeyed the hierarchy of the Church, especially the pope, and were devoted, in the best Habsburg tradition, to the Holy Eucharist and to the Blessed Virgin Mary.

1. Charles (Karl) Francis Joseph was born on August 17, 1887, in Persenbeug an der Donau (on the Danube River, in Lower

[1] E. Görlich, *Der letzte Kaiser ein Heiliger?—Kaiser Karl von Österreich*, 3d ed. (Stein am Rhein, 1988).

Austria), the first son of Archduke Otto and Archduchess Maria Josepha, who was the daughter of King Friedrich August III of Saxony, from the House of Wettin. Their marriage was not a particularly happy one. Archduke Otto was largely to blame: a very good-looking man, he cut a fine figure as a monarch, but his character was hardly exemplary. Yet his wife, too, was somewhat at fault: Archduchess Maria Josepha was very highly regarded for her refined manners and her irreproachable conduct; she was much esteemed for her goodness and piety; but she did not know how to get along with her husband. Because of her piety, she may have tried to have too much of a good thing in rearing her children. Otherwise, these aristocratic parents, Otto and Maria Josepha, did all that was deemed necessary to educate their firstborn son and their second son, Archduke Maximilian (1895– 1952), who was born eight years later, to be eventual successors to the throne. In Count Wallis, Charles had an excellent instructor and governor (during the years from 1894 to 1898). Father Norbert Geggerle, O.P., served as a good, inspiring catechist; in his memoirs he later described Emperor Charles as "a very modest child, as pious as he could be, who loved the truth and had a tender conscience. . . . He was never angry, self-willed, self-righteous, or quarrelsome; he didn't hold a grudge." [2]

The young archduke Charles received his secondary schooling from the Benedictines at the *Schottengymnasium* in Vienna; during that time he became more solidly grounded in his knowledge of religion and the humanities. After that, the archduke learned how to command a battalion. On September 1, 1905, after one year of military training, he became a lieutenant in the seventh Dragoon [Cavalry] Regiment. With the exception of four semesters studying law in Prague, he then had to perform military duty in smaller garrisons in Bohemia and Galicia. He always received a good evaluation of his accomplishments from his superiors. In November 1912, Archduke Charles was transferred to the infantry with the rank of major and assigned to the Thirty-Ninth Hungarian

---

[2] E. Feigl, *Kaiser Karl I: Ein Leben für den Frieden seiner Völker* (Vienna, 1990), p. 22.

Infantry Regiment in Vienna. In May 1914 he made lieutenant-colonel, and on July 21, 1914, he was promoted to colonel in the First Hussar Regiment.

With the murder of Archduke Franz Ferdinand d'Este and of his wife, Duchess Sophie von Hohenberg, on June 28, 1914 in Sarajevo, Archduke Charles became the successor to the imperial throne. Emperor Francis Joseph commissioned him to visit the troops at the various fronts, and thus he became acquainted with life in the Army high command, which at first was based in Teschen and later was transferred to Baden. He eventually distinguished himself as a commander of troops in Italy and Romania by his bold and carefully planned campaigns, which were to some extent victorious. During this time at the front, Charles proved to be a worthy combat soldier with genuine *esprit de corps*, who learned firsthand the horrors of war.

On November 21, 1916, Emperor Francis Joseph died, while the First World War was raging, having ruled the double monarchy of Austria-Hungary for sixty-nine years. Archduke Charles, the successor to the throne, now became the emperor of Austria and the apostolic king of Hungary, as well as commander in chief of all

The church wedding of Charles and Zita in Schwarzau, performed by the papal chamberlain Monsignore Bisletti in the presence of Emperor Franz Josef

the armed forces, although he desired peace rather than war. His wife, Empress Zita, astutely observed,

> Emperor Charles could truly say of himself, with full justification, that he did not have the slightest thing to do with this war, no matter how bravely he may have fought at the front as successor to the throne, if for no other reason than that he, as the friend and pupil of Archduke Franz Ferdinand, [the previous] successor to the throne, was opposed to the war, just as [his predecessor] was.

In his proclamation to his subjects, dated November 21, 1916, to which he conscientiously adhered, Emperor Charles declared,

> I will do everything in my power to dispel the horrors and sacrifices of the war as soon as possible and to win back for my peoples the blessings of peace which are so dearly missed. . . . I want to be a just and clement prince for my peoples. I wish to uphold their constitutional freedoms and other rights and to guard carefully the equality of all before the law. It will be my unceasing endeavor to promote the moral and spiritual welfare of my peoples and to protect freedom and order in my countries.

Emperor Charles ruled for only two years. Then, despite enormous efforts to bring about peace, along the lines proposed in the letter on peace by Pope Benedict XV dated August 1, 1917, came the end of the war without any real peace and with the disintegration of the double monarchy, when the Austrian regime compelled the emperor to renounce the exercise of his authority to rule. Next followed the exile of Emperor Charles and his family to Switzerland, which was briefly interrupted by two futile attempts to exercise again his ancestral rights as apostolic king in Hungary.

The sojourn in Switzerland was followed immediately by exile to the Portuguese island of Madeira. There the emperor ended his earthly life, in complete resignation to the will of God, on April 1,

The family of Emperor Charles of Austria at Herthenstein Castle, on Lake Vierwaldstätter, in Switzerland, in the year 1921

1922; he died of influenza and pneumonia while at the mountain estate Quinta do Monte in Funchal, on Madeira.

After his holy death, which was accompanied by many prayers, Emperor Charles left his wife and their seven children in dire need. Zita, who was his equal in everything, especially in her trust in God, was pregnant with their youngest child. The firstborn son, Archduke Otto, who was only ten years old, was present at his father's battle with death at the latter's express wish, because the dying emperor wanted Archduke Otto to see "how a Christian dies".

2. Zita of Bourbon-Parma was born on May 9, 1892, in Villa delle Pianore; she was the seventeenth child of Duke Robert of Parma and the fifth child of the Duke's second wife, Duchess Maria Antonia, a descendant of the Portuguese royal line of Braganza.

Zita grew up in Schwarzau auf dem Steinfeld (Lower Austria) among many brothers and sisters. In the Duke's household there were twenty-four children in all: twelve from the first marriage of Duke Robert of Parma with Princess Maria Pia of Naples and Sicily, and twelve from his second marriage with Duchess Maria Antonia of Braganza. Several of the future empress Zita's brothers became political notables: Sixtus (August 1, 1886—March 14, 1934), Franz Xaver (May 25, 1889—May 4, 1977), Felix (September 28, 1893—April 7, 1970, married to the grand duchess Charlotte of Luxemburg), and Renatus (October 17, 1893—July 30, 1962, married to Margarethe of Denmark). Of Empress Zita's sisters, Adelaide (b. August 5, 1885), Franziska (b. April 22, 1890), and Maria Antonia (b. November 7, 1895) should be mentioned because they became nuns in the Benedictine convent at Solesmes in France. Princess Zita received her education from the school sisters in Zangberg bei Ampfing (Upper Bavaria).

For many years Princess Zita's grandmother, Queen Adelaide of Portugal, had lived as a nun in Sainte Cécile, on the Isle of Wight. More recently, Zita's elder sister, the lovely Adelaide, went there as well. People had said of her that she was certainly "the right one for Archduke Charles". Then, quite suddenly, this temperamental Princess Adelaide went to Sainte Cécile and became a nun.

After her school years in Zangberg, Princess Zita was sent to the Isle of Wight for a one-year stay with the Benedictine nuns of Sainte Cécile. There, under the watchful eye of the prioress, the former Queen Adelaide of Portugal, she was to receive the "finishing touches" in her education. The convent of Sainte Cécile was by no means a boarding school for "daughters of the aristocracy" but, rather, a strictly cloistered Benedictine community for a spiritual elite. In exceptional cases, however, the learned nuns would assume responsibility for imparting a higher education to young girls. This was done

in a manner and using means that could very well be compared to the pedagogy and methodology that we find in Herman Hesse's *Magister Ludi*. This phase in the life of the future empress and queen Zita acquired additional intensity and also spiritual intimacy through the particularly close relationship that she had with her *magistra ludi*, with Queen Adelaide, who, as the mother of many children and also as the queen mother of Portugal in compulsory exile, had herself experienced all the heights and depths of human life.[3]

Soon after Princess Zita left the Isle of Wight and returned to Austria (at first to Franzensbad), Queen Adelaide died. Now that she was dead, she was permitted to return home to Portugal; she was interred in the vault of the Portuguese kings in São Vicente de Fora beside King João VI and Queen Carlota.

In Franzensbad in Bohemia, Princess Zita was accompanied by the archduchess Maria Annunziata, the aunt of Archduke Charles. Together with her companion, the princess met several times with Archduke Charles, who was stationed nearby and used to visit his aunt. Here Zita and Charles became acquainted and started to fall in love. Thus began a marriage of true love, which would continue through joys and sorrows, starting as high-ranking nobility and then, after the death of Emperor Francis Joseph, as imperial consorts, who remained steadfastly faithful to each other in good times and bad.

Zita of Bourbon-Parma proved to be a tender, loving spouse; a truly caring, Christian mother to her eight children and, likewise, an empress who showed maternal concern for the welfare of her peoples during the sorrowful events of the First World War; then a widow who, though abandoned and destitute, courageously bore the burden of raising and educating her eight children during their years of exile in Spain and Belgium and, during the Second World War, in Canada and the United States. With bravery and resignation to the will of God, she carried the heavy cross of calumny and misrepresentation, as well as that of banishment from her beloved Austria, which lasted until 1971.

Seldom have people been so unkindly slandered and misjudged as Empress Zita and Emperor Charles. The empress was branded an "Italian beast in the imperial court of Austria" who betrayed

[3] E. Feigl, *Kaiserin Zita, Legende und Wahrheit* (Vienna, 1977), pp. 84ff.

Empress Zita in widow's garb. On her lap she holds her youngest daughter, Elisabeth. When Elisabeth was born, her father had already been dead for two months.

the interests of Austria-Hungary; the emperor, on the other hand, was slandered as an "alcoholic", as a weakling controlled by his "bigoted" mother and then by his equally "bigoted" wife, and as completely incapable of ruling. He was mocked for turning the "K. & K.", the Austro-Hungarian *Kaisertum und Königreich* [empire and kingdom] into *Kittel und Kutte*, "frock and cowl", insinuating that Charles had delivered himself into the hands of women and clerics. The empress and the emperor were not at all what they were rumored to be; rather, they were above all of the faults and failings they were reputed to have. Both of them were uncommonly pious, but certainly not "bigoted nuns"; they were morally irreproachable, disciplined individual and not at all the slaves of alcohol and other addictions. They were by no means politicians intent on betraying their land and their people but, rather, august rulers who longed for and sought true peace for their peoples and lands. Above all, they were loving spouses who remained completely faithful to each other, provided what was best for their children, and set a fine example of married life and family life.

We can agree entirely with what E. Feigl has written at the beginning of the final chapter of the beautifully illustrated volume *Kaiser Karl I. Ein Leben für den Frieden seiner Völker* [Emperor Charles I: A life dedicated to freedom for his peoples] under the heading, "Emperor Charles—A Blessed, a Saint?"

A comparison will surely occur to the unprejudiced, objective observer when he hears of the perhaps imminent beatification of the "Servant of God Charles from the House of Austria". Repeatedly in the two-thousand-year history of the Church there have been cases in which a child of Adam who originally did not seem cut out for "sainthood" at all was consigned not only to the ash-heap of history but also to death by fire upon a heap of dry wood, and then later, often only centuries later, was raised to the honors of the altar. The quality that seems to distinguish the saints of the past—and certainly those, too, of the present and the future—is their unwavering perseverance. Emperor Charles, who in the two years of his reign and the three subsequent years of exile most assuredly suffered and endured more than all of his illustrious forebears put together, did not for one moment abandon the ancestral faith of his house; in this, certainly, he was supported and strengthened by his incomparable wife. Together they put into practice—and there is no doubt about it among Charles' opponents, either—the ideal of Christian spouses, parents, and rulers, to which even those people who do not belong to Catholic social circles pay their respects.[4]

If the cause for the beatification of Emperor Charles could be introduced and could proceed favorably thus far in Vienna and Rome, then we might wish for and expect the same for Empress Zita, who died at the age of ninety-seven on March 14, 1989, in Zizers (Switzerland). The result would be for ages yet to come a canonized emperor and empress and a very contemporary counterpart to the imperial couple [at the turn of the eleventh century], Saint Henry II and Saint Cunegund.

The children of the imperial couple Charles and Zita are:

1. Otto, b. November 26, 1912, in Wartholz
2. Adelheid, b. January 3, 1914, in Hetzendorf; d. October 2, 1971, in Pöcking am Starnberg

[4] Feigl, *Kaiser Karl I*, p. 245.

3. Robert, b. February 8, 1915, in Vienna-Schönbrunn; d. February 7, 1996, in Basel
4. Felix, b. May 31, 1916, in Vienna-Schönbrunn
5. Karl Ludwig, b. March 10, 1918, in Baden, near Vienna
6. Rudolf, b. September 5, 1919, in Prangins (Switzerland)
7. Charlotte, b. March 1, 1921, in Prangins; d. July 23, 1989, Munich
8. Elisabeth, b. May 31, 1922, in El Prado, near Madrid (Spain); d. January 6, 1993, in Graz

Until the very end, these children were in the thoughts and prayers of the emperor during his final illness. The moving prayer that he pronounced as he was suffering speaks volumes: "Dear Savior, protect our children: Otto, Mädi [Adelheid], Robert, Felix, Karl Ludwig... Who's next?" Empress Zita helped him continue, "Rudolf", and the Emperor went on, "Rudolf, Lotti [Charlotte], and the tiny little one [Elisabeth, who was not yet born]. Keep them in body and soul, and let them die rather than commit a mortal sin. Amen! Thy will be done. Amen!" And the last words that Emperor Charles whispered to his wife were, "I love you endlessly!" Truly, this emperor was a husband who even until the last moment of his tragic earthly life was thinking of his wife with true love and of his children with a father's loving care, but above all of his Lord and Redeemer, to whom he commended himself with the words, "Jesus, Jesus, come!"

Franz Jägerstätter
and
Franziska Schwaninger

*b. May 20, 1907, in Saint
Radegund, Upper Austria*
*d. August 9, 1943, in Brandenburg,
Germany*

Married April 9, 1936
Father to four children

His name[1] was heard throughout the whole wide world for the first time at the Second Vatican Council; this man was so much admired, because in a difficult situation he fearlessly followed the voice of his conscience: Franz Jägerstätter! Archbishop T. D. Roberts spoke to the Council Fathers about him:

> Franz Jägerstätter refused to serve in a war that was later characterized in Nürnberg as a crime against humanity. He was one of those men chosen by the Holy Spirit to manifest truths that are hidden to the powerful and the wise. This young husband and father was called to make clear that a Christian may not serve in a war that he considers unjust, even though it cost him his life. He stood alone in giving this witness. He was convinced that he would be committing a sin if he were to perform military service in this unjust war.

[1] Cf. Georg Bergmann, *Franz Jägerstätter. Ein Leben vom Gewissen entschieden* (Stein am Rhein, 1980; 2d ed., 1988; Erna Putz, *Franz Jägerstätter*, 2d ed. (Linz, 1987); idem, *Gefängnisbriefe und Aufzeichnungen: Franz Jägerstätter verweigert 1943 den Wehrdienst* [Franz Jägerstätter refuses to serve in the military, 1943] (Linz, 1987).

Franz Jägerstätter was a staunch believer in the Catholic faith and a clear-sighted opponent of the godless, anti-religious world view of National Socialism. He became a conscientious objector during Hitler's war of aggression and then a courageous martyr for his Christian convictions and his love of his fatherland, although he thereby caused his wife and their three children much suffering. And yet he was—besides his diligent work as a farmer and a sacristan—a faithful, caring husband and a loving father. He ought to have a place of honor, if only at the conclusion of this book about married saints and blesseds, because he may in the near future be beatified. He himself, as a poor illegitimate child, did not have the good fortune of growing up in the security of a family built upon the foundation of the Sacrament of Matrimony, and he had to suffer as a result. In his own sacramental marriage, therefore, he experienced vividly, if all too briefly, the surpassing value and the fundamental significance of an indissoluble Christian marriage, which is the basis for Christian family life.

Franz Jägerstätter, the illegitimate child of the farm girl Rosalia Huber and the farm boy Franz Bachmeier, was born on May 20, 1907, on the Adam-Sachl farm in the parish of Saint Radegund, near Ostermieting, in the Innsbruck region (Upper Austria). Because his father and mother were too poor even to get married, for the first few years of his life he was brought up by his pious grandmother, who raised him as a Catholic. In 1917, his mother, Rosalia Huber, was able to marry the small farmer Heinrich Jägerstätter. Her husband adopted the ten-year-old Franz, so that from then on he went by the name Jägerstätter.

Franz went to the one-room schoolhouse in his native village but was not a star pupil—not for lack of talent or diligence, but because he was despised and avoided on account of his origins. The basic knowledge of religion that the boy brought with him from home was increased and deepened by the solid instruction in religion imparted by the pastor of the parish, which then numbered five hundred souls, in the classroom and in Sunday school. At a very early age, Franz was obliged to work with his parents on their farm.

In the village, Franz Jägerstätter was considered a happy, outgoing lad who now and then was carried away by youthful frivolity and high spirits, although he never allowed himself to stray into loose relationships with girls.

As a young man at the age of twenty, Franz Jägerstätter wanted to earn something to supplement the meager income of his parents' farm. Therefore, he left home in 1927 and became a laborer, at first on a farm in Teising, a locality between Altötting and Mühldorf in Bavaria. That same year, however, he left that employer and found a better-paying job in the Steirmark iron-ore industry. In that working-class milieu, however, a socialist ideology prevailed; for a short time his religious outlook was shaken, and he gave up the practice of the Catholic faith. Soon, however, he found his way back to the Church and to the faith. In 1930 he had to return to his native village of Saint Radegund, because his foster father and grandfather were no longer strong enough to manage all the work on the farm. The milieu to which he had been accustomed from his childhood followed Christian conventions, and Franz Jägerstätter again began to practice his faith. Moreover, he made an effort to learn about his faith, especially by reading religious periodicals and books.

In so doing, the young farmer gradually realized that, if you really want to take Christianity seriously, it cannot be done by being an average Christian; you must strive for perfection and holiness. This is done most easily in religious life. So the future owner of the tenant farms was faced with the decision: marriage or religious life? In a very significant letter to his godson Franz Huber, from the year 1935, he reflected on the married state and on the importance of religion for marriage and family life; he then went on to write,

> Not every man is called by God to enter the married state. Nor did God institute marriage, as many believe, so that people could live as they please with no restrictions, but rather for the propagation of the human race. Someone who can't control himself in his youth will do no better as a married man, for being married does not mean that everything is permissible.

Franz Jägerstätter consulted with the village pastor, Father Joseph Karobath, about what path he ought to follow in the future, whether in religious life or in marriage. The priest's response was short and to the point: "You are here to look after the tenant farmers' lands. So find yourself a capable wife who is also a good Christian."

The twenty-six-year-old farmer followed this advice. He thought he had already found the right companion for life: he began a relationship with a young woman named Theresia Auer, from Lamprechtshausen-Bürmoos. In doing so he allowed himself to be overcome by passion—quite contrary to his principles—and became the father of a child. His relationship with the mother of the child lasted only a short time; the reason for this is unknown. The woman simply stated, "We separated in peace; he asked me to forgive him." Franz Jägerstätter always considered it a matter of honor to provide for the child's support.

In Franziska Schwaninger, from the parish of Hochburg, whose character reflected her staunch Catholic upbringing, Franz Jägerstätter finally found the woman who was really well-suited to accompany him through life. With his fiancée he spent a half year preparing for the wedding. Both of them acquired a clear understanding of the rights and duties involved in Christian marriage.

Later, in the prison at Berlin-Degel, during the weeks of anxious waiting for a verdict, Jägerstätter wrote down his thoughts—about marriage, among other things. We can read these notes as an echo of his careful considerations while he was preparing to get married. This is especially true of his beautiful meditation on the family,[2] but also of other notes.[3] There it says,

Nowhere is such dignity attributed to the human body as in the religion of Jesus; but that is by no means a cult of the flesh. There is no such thing as a "right to one's body" that would allow misusing it in order to sin. Paul (in 1 Corinthians 7) gives an answer to a question in this regard. When he recommends

[2] Notebook 1, nos. 48–53.
[3] Notebook 4, nos. 101 and 133.

marriage as the God-given means of controlling natural urges, he does not mean to describe its only purpose or its highest one. Both spouses have identical rights and duties toward each other on this account. Neither partner may refuse to render what is due to the other without good reason, but conversely neither may demand what offends against divine law and the sanctity of marital life. God calls some souls to a life of consecrated virginity, but the vocation to marriage is also a grace. The indissolubility of marriage, however, is a commandment of the Lord and is valid for everyone. The Church cannot change it one bit, much less the state.

In marriage the husband is the image of Christ, the Redeemer of his Body, the Church. The wife is the image of the Church, the beloved Bride of Christ, for whom he gave himself up. It is not selfishness that brings them together, but rather the will to sanctify each other. One becomes the second self of the other. And this unity in duality is incorporated into the supernatural fellowship that Christians have with Christ. Marriage, therefore, is infinitely more than a "worldly matter"!

After such considerations about marriage, the bride and the bridegroom, then—purified from all guilt of sin in the Sacrament of Penance and strengthened by the worthy reception of Holy Communion—received the Sacrament of Matrimony on April 9, 1936, in the parish church of Saint Radegund. The bridegroom was at that time twenty-nine years old, the bride twenty-three; both had a firm foundation in the faith and in fidelity to the Church. That is why they went to Rome on their honeymoon and thanked God at the tomb of Saint Peter for the great gift of the faith and of membership in the true Church of Christ.

The marriage of Franz and Franziska Jägerstätter proved to be extremely happy from the start. They were blessed with three healthy children, and—as is movingly demonstrated in the many letters that the husband sent to the wife from his imprisonment in Linz and Berlin—they were filled with a tremendous love for each other. Let us quote a few typical sentences from this series of letters from March 1 to August 9, 1943. They almost always begin with the salutation "Herzallerliebste Gattin [Dearest wife, Love of my heart]!"

In the letter dated March 1, 1943, Franz Jägerstätter writes, "Dearest wife, I thank you with all my heart for your love and faithfulness and for the sacrifices that you have made for me and the whole family." In his letter of April 9, 1943, from the prison in Linz, he writes,

Dearest wife, exactly seven years ago today, in the presence of God and of the priest, we promised that we would love each other and be faithful. I believe that we have faithfully kept this promise to this day, and I believe that God will continue to grant us the grace, even though we are now separated, to remain true to this promise until the end of our life. When I look back and consider all of the happiness and the many graces that have been ours during these seven years, some of them bordering on the miraculous . . . , well, if someone said to me that there is no God, or that God does not love us, and I believed him, then I would have lost all sense of how far I had fallen. Dearest wife, why should the future be so dreadful for us, since he who has preserved and blessed us thus far will not abandon us now, if only we don't forget to thank him and don't grow weary in striving for heaven. Then our happiness will endure into all eternity. Even though I am now sitting behind prison walls, I nevertheless believe that I can continue to build upon your love and fidelity, and even if I depart from this life before you, then [it shall be so] even beyond the grave as well.

For his three daughters, too, Rosalia (b. September 1, 1937), Maria (b. September 4, 1938) and Aloisia (b. May 5, 1940), Franz Jägerstätter found moving words to write in his letters, expressing his love and his sense of paternal responsibility. His family meant more to him than he could say; doing without the company of his wife and children, accordingly, was very difficult for him. "Dear children, we must really thank our Heavenly Father for sending me such a brave wife and giving you such a dear mother. That means you must always show that you love your mother; you can do that only if you are good and obey your mother" (April 9, 1943).

It would be a great joy if we could spend the few days of our life in the circle of a happy family. But if the dear Lord has other plans for us, that is good, too; it is also a joy to be allowed to suffer for Jesus and our faith. We can be glad in the hope that the few days we must live here apart from each other will be repaid a thousandfold in eternity, where there is no sadness, where we will be able to rejoice forever with God and our heavenly Mother. (July 8, 1943)

Even when he lived far away, separated from his wife and children, in imprisonment in Linz and Berlin, Franz Jägerstätter remained spiritually united with his family at all times, especially through prayer. He was confident in the knowledge that he suffered hardships and difficulties, not as a criminal, but because he was true to his faith and to his conscience. Finally, death itself overtook him on August 9, 1943, when he was beheaded in Brandenburg. Archbishop T. D. Roberts, who was quoted at the beginning, is quite right when he says of Franz Jägerstätter, "He offered his life in reparation for the sins of the world and went to his death thanking God for the opportunity to give witness to his faith."

His courageous wife, Franziska, after a difficult struggle, affirmed the separation from her husband and his sacrifice of his life. All alone, she raised their three daughters to be good Christian wives and mothers. Today [1994] this woman, a staunch believer even after such severe trials, lives peacefully as a grandmother of fourteen and still serves—in her husband's stead—as sacristan in the parish church of Saint Radegund. She prays, we can be sure, that her husband's sacrifice will be understood properly and more widely recognized.

Blessed
Gianna Beretta Molla
and
Pietro Molla

b. October 4, 1922, in Magenta,
near Milan, Italy
d. April 28, 1962, in Ponte Nuovo
di Magenta, Italy

Married September 24, 1955
Mother of four children
Beatified April 24, 1994

The physician Gianna (Joan, Joanne) Francisca Beretta and the engineer Pietro Molla were a Christian married couple whose life and work extend into the second half of the twentieth century; they are shining examples, especially the wife and mother, who offered up her life for the sake of her fourth child. The title of an article in a periodical for Italian clergy described Signora Gianna Beretta Molla as follows: "A Mother Sacrifices Her Own Life in Order to Give Life to Her Child."[1] The Pontifical Congregation for the Causes of Saints introduced her cause for beatification on March 15, 1980, and on April 24, 1994, the beatification ceremony took place in Rome.

Gianna Beretta was born on October 4, 1922, in Magenta, 15½ miles north of Milan, the daughter of well-educated, good Catholic parents, Alberto Beretta and Maria de Micheli, who gave life to thirteen children, of whom one daughter became a nun, two sons were ordained priests, and all earned academic degrees.

---

[1] Giuliana Pelucchi, *Gianna Beretta Molla—Una vita per la vita* (Milan, 1994).

In 1925, the family moved to Bergamo, where Gianna received her First Holy Communion at the age of five on April 4, 1928, after having been prepared splendidly by her pious mother and her eldest sister, Amalia. On June 9, 1930, Gianna received the Sacrament of Confirmation at the age of seven. These two sacraments have been mentioned specifically because they were of fundamental importance to her, as the edifying life of the young woman would later prove. Spiritual exercises that she made in March 1938 also left a profound impression on her; she determined to make a twofold resolution, which she kept from then on: "I would rather die than commit a mortal sin", and "I want to do everything for Jesus." The death of her eldest sister, Amalia, at the age of twenty-six, in 1937, may have provided incentives for her to take such a stance. The main influence, though, was the example of her mother, who took her children with her to daily Mass and—as soon as they were old enough—to the Communion rail, if the children themselves wanted to.

The family resettled in 1937 in Quinto al Mare, in the vicinity of Genoa. There Gianna went to secondary school, earning a diploma in 1942. That fateful year, 1942, brought with it two heavy blows that challenged her to attain even greater spiritual maturity. Her mother died at the age of fifty-five, and her father's death followed four months afterward, on September 10, 1942.

The children of the Beretta family returned to Magenta after the death of their parents. Gianna started medical school that same year, 1942; at first she studied for six semesters at the University of Milan; then she continued in Pavia, where, on November 30, 1949, she received a doctorate in medicine.

Immediately after graduation, the young physician began a medical practice in Magenta in order to help sick people. Patients thronged to her office, and she continued her work with great success until her death. She did not restrict her service to the healing of physical illnesses, however. In addition to this, she was involved in programs for social improvement and in Catholic Action, in which she had already participated during her school days and years at the university, even serving as the president of one youth association. From her mother she had inherited the ability to inspire young people for the Catholic faith. She often gave lectures and organized retreat days and spiritual exercises, social evenings, excursions, and hikes for the Catholic youth groups.

Soon, however, she was no longer content with her medical practice. She wanted to become a medical missionary in Brazil. One of her brothers was already serving there as a missionary in the jungle mission stations. He, too, had studied medicine, but then he became a priest as well, entered the Capuchin Fathers as Padre Alberto, and went to Brazil to evangelize the indigenous population. Another brother, who had become a civil engineer, was also in Brazil, helping Padre Alberto to build a hospital in the rain forest. There—as young Dr. Gianna Beretta thought and planned—a wide field of activity was awaiting her efforts as a physician and a missionary.

An encounter took place meanwhile with a man who thought just as she did: the engineer Pietro Molla. While she was a medical student, Gianna had met this man a few times; he had advanced to a position of importance in a large industrial firm and later became their general manager. As a physician, Gianna now occasionally had professional dealings with Signor Molla, since he did volunteer work with various social programs in Mesero-Magenta and was also very much involved in Catholic Action.

At first, the engineer made no particular impression on the young physician; he, on the other hand, was extremely impressed by her. After meeting him several times, however, Gianna began to discern on the horizon the possibility of marriage. She kept wondering what the will of God was in her case. As a medical missionary in Brazil, she could help many people physically and spiritually and, together with her priest-brother, lead them to God; as a Christian wife and mother, however, she would be able to hand on the gift of life to children and bring them up to love and praise God. What was she to do? She prayed a lot during this time and asked her friends and siblings to pray for her. They made novenas for this intention. Her confessor was wise enough not to give her any direct advice; he did say, though, "If all good Catholic girls went into the convent, then where would we get our Christian mothers?"

Then came the month of December during the Marian Year 1954, which commemorated the one hundredth anniversary of the dogmatic definition, by Pope Pius IX, of the Immaculate Conception of the Blessed Virgin Mary. The now thirty-two-year-old physician accompanied a pilgrimage of the sick to Lourdes. On that occasion, on the eighth of December, she received an inner light: Her path according to the will of God was via Christian marriage. In February 1955 the engineer Pietro Molla asked Dr. Gianna Beretta to be his wife. On Easter Sunday, April 11, 1955, they were engaged. The bridegroom suggested to the bride that after the wedding she should give up her medical practice and devote herself to her family. Gianna, however, would hear nothing of it. Until her death, she remained true to her vocation as a physician and continued to practice medicine in Mesero, near Magenta.

The months leading up to the wedding on September 24, 1955, in Magenta passed very quickly. Everything they needed was purchased for the apartment where the newlyweds would live; the most beautiful and costly material was obtained for the bridal gown, with the remark, "If a son of mine becomes a priest, I would like to make vestments for him out of my bridal gown." The bride, who was already thirty-three years old, and the groom, who was forty-three, prepared themselves to receive the Sacrament of Matrimony by a triduum of prayer and by making a good confession and going to Holy Communion. "If we are going to have children, we had better hurry", the newlyweds said, and they had the right idea. They resolved to avoid any sort of abuse in their marital relations and to start a good Catholic family, to build a genuine "domestic church". After their honeymoon, which took them via Rome to Sicily, they moved into their new home and made the family consecration to the Sacred Heart of Jesus, promising to recite the Rosary together daily. And so they did, even when they had to travel abroad together—something the husband was often required to do for business reasons—to Germany, Great Britain, Denmark, Sweden, or Switzerland.

The Beretta family in 1933. First row (left to right): Giovanna ("Gianna"), Maria (the mother), Virginia, Amalia, Albert (the father), and Giuseppe; second row: Francesco, Ferdinando, Zita, and Enrico.

They were not married long when the first child arrived, a boy, Pierluigi, who was born in 1956; then in 1957 came the second child, a girl, Mariolina, and in 1959 the third child, another girl, Laura. All three were born in their own residence in Ponte Nuovo di Magenta.

Then, regrettably, two miscarriages followed. In 1961 the doctor became pregnant again. During a physical examination a dangerous cyst was discovered on her uterus. Surgery was absolutely necessary, and so it was scheduled for September 6, 1961, at the hospital in Monza. Before undergoing this very risky procedure, the patient gave strict orders to the doctors: "Save my child!" Contrary to the doctors' expectations, Signora Dottore Gianna Molla gave birth on April 21, 1962, to a perfectly healthy little girl, who at her Baptism received the name Gianna Emanuela. This child, however, owed her life to the unselfish sacrifice of her mother, who died one week later, on April 28, 1962, in her house in Ponte Nuovo di Magenta. All of her deliveries were very difficult and took place after extremely troublesome pregnancies. The mother, who was also a physician, always stood by her child and willingly and lovingly endured the discomfort and the labor pains. When the fourth child was on the way, she was completely aware of her condition and of the fact that she was in danger of losing her life. And when the surgeon asked about her impending operation, "What should we do, Signora Dottore? Do we save you, or do we save the child?", she replied without much hesitation, "First you must save the child and then, if possible, the mother. There are no two ways about it, so it is!"

No one should imagine, though, that the decision to save her child at the expense of her own life was easy for Gianna. She loved her three children dearly; she loved her husband with all her heart. Above all, though, she loved life. And yet she was willing to renounce her own life so as to save the life of her child.

Signora Gianna Molla prayed much, not only for the child she bore in her womb, but also for herself: that God might keep her alive, so that she could continue to dedicate herself to the Christian upbringing of her children and to her beloved husband. Nevertheless, she resigned herself completely to whatever God might will. And in case she did not survive the delivery, she made provisions. She asked her sister Zita, who was a pharmacist, to take charge of the household and of the children after her death. She asked her sister Virginia, who was a nun and worked as a missionary in India, to request an assignment back in Italy, so that she, too, could help to raise the children.

The death of this courageous wife and mother was very difficult, not only for her, but especially for her husband. Yet both of them managed, on the basis of their profound faith, to say a magnificent Yes to the unfathomable will of God. They drew their strength—the one to die, the other to live—from the grace of the Church's sacraments and from much prayer. Gianna received from the hand of her second priest-brother, Giuseppe, the sacraments of the Anointing of the Sick, Reconciliation, and Holy Eucharist to see her safely home. Then she asked her husband, Pietro, to let her die, not in the hospital, but rather back home, in the room where seven years before she had moved in as a bride and begun a happy marriage and a joyful family life. Though she was near death, the patient was brought at night by ambulance from the hospital to her home, and she died there on the morning of April 28, 1962. On

April 30, 1962, she was buried during a funeral attended by an enormous number of people from Mesero di Magenta.

What became of the children of these courageous Christian parents? Pierluigi became an economist with a doctor's degree; Mariolina died in childhood; Laura likewise took a doctorate in economics, and Gianna Emanuela, whom her priest-uncle Don Giuseppe Beretta described as "the living relic of her mother, Gianna", became a physician like her mother. She had every right to be proud on April 24, 1994, when she was permitted to participate in the beatification ceremony for her mother in the basilica of Saint Peter in Rome.

The Pope said the following about this exemplary Christian wife:

Gianna Beretta Molla, crowning an exemplary life as a student and a committed young woman in the ecclesial community, and as a happy wife and mother, knew how to offer her life as a sacrifice so that the baby she bore in her womb might live, and she is with us here today! As a surgeon, she was well aware of what to expect, but did not falter before [that is, when faced with] sacrifice, confirming in this way the heroic nature of her virtues. . . . In the name of progress and modernity the values of fidelity, chastity, sacrifice, in which a host of Christian wives and mothers have distinguished and continue to distinguish themselves, are presented as obsolete.[2]

[2] "See What Love the Father Has Given Us!", *L'Osservatore romano,* April 27, 1994, p. 3.

Niklaus Wolf von Rippertschwand

and

Barbara Müller

b. May 1, 1756, in Neuenkirch, Lucerne Canton

d. September 18, 1832, in Saint Urban's Abbey, Lucerne Canton

Father of nine children

Niklaus Wolf von Rippertschwand lived in the tumultuous times following the French Revolution. He became a farmer and the town councillor in Lucerne. Niklaus Wolf von Rippertschwand married Barbara Müller, who gave him nine children. Three daughters went into the convent, which especially pleased their father, since he had once declared, "Monasteries are the fortress of the faith." Every evening, he conducted a domestic liturgy with his family. Besides this, he organized prayer groups. One day he received the charism of healing the sick: "I prayed for help in the Name of Jesus, and it was granted to me. However often I would knock, it was opened to me." Niklaus Wolf von Rippertschwand, like his namesake, Nicholas von Flüe, became a popular saint among simple folk. His cause for beatification has been under way since 1955 and is near its conclusion. Pope John Paul II has expressed his wish that Niklaus Wolf von Rippertschwand might be beatified soon. Therefore we introduce this father of a family briefly.

Saint Stephen of Hungary,

and

Blessed Gisela

Stephen:
b. ca. 970–975
d. August 15, 1038

Canonized 1083

Gisela:
b. ca. 985
d. May 7, 1060

On the feast of Christmas, in the year 1000, Stephen was anointed and crowned apostolic king of Hungary. His royal crown is valued as the supreme symbol of the Hungarian state.

At the beginning of Christian history in Hungary stands the saintly couple Stephen and Gisela, with their saintly son, Emeric. These three personages led exemplary lives and merit particular attention, because in many respects they resemble the Holy Family of Nazareth.

Géza of the Arpad dynasty, one of the leading Hungarian princes in the second half of the tenth century, married a Christian wife, Sarolt, from the Siebenbürgen region, and under her influence became more open to Western Christendom. He had himself and his son, Vaik (born between 970 and 975), baptized around the year 985 by a priest from the diocese of Passau. On that occasion his son received, instead of the pagan name Vaik, the name of the

463

diocesan patron of Passau, the holy deacon and proto-martyr Stephen.

While Géza's conversion to the Christian faith was not that deep, it was quite a different story with that of his son, Stephen.

Though he was small in stature, he had great energy, courage, and openness to the faith, and he strove to live according to Christian principles. In this he was directed and formed by the holy bishop Adalbert, who had been summoned from Prague. The latter also arranged that his pupil would have a suitably noble and like-minded spouse, and in 995 the young prince married Gisela, the sister of Henry II, who later became emperor and a saint. Both spouses made sincere efforts to lead an exemplary Christian married life.

In 997 Stephen succeeded his father, Géza, as ruler of the Hungarian people. Formerly nomadic, they had only recently settled down, and their conversion from pagan ways was just beginning. Stephen, however, resolutely promoted the cause of Christianity. He provided the necessary organization for the Church in Hungary by founding two archdioceses (Gran and Kalocsa) and eight dioceses (Csanad, Eger, Bihar /Grosswardein, Pics, Raab, Alba Julia, Veszprem, and Waizen). Similarly, Stephen founded several monasteries, for example, Panonhalma, as communities dedicated to the glory of God, as cultural centers, and as schools for the formation and training of priests and teachers. In order to consolidate his rule as a Christian prince against the presence of pagan rivals, Stephen turned to Pope Sylvester II with a request for confirmation of his political and ecclesiastical works.

His advisor in this was the monk Astrik, who had come from Prague in 993. He obtained for Stephen from Rome the royal crown, the processional cross, and the apostolic privilege of founding additional dioceses and appointing their spiritual leaders. Then, on the feast of Christmas in the year 1000, King Stephen was anointed and crowned apostolic king in Gran. From then on he strove constantly in his personal life to set an example for his people as a Christian ruler. This he did also in his marriage with Gisela, who in every respect was always a faithful helpmate to

Hungarian stamps commemorating the thirty-fourth
World Eucharistic Congress in Budapest.
Row 1: King Saint Stephen, Saint Emeric, Saint Ladislaus.
Row 2: Chalice and Host, symbol of the World Eucharistic Congress.
Row 3: Blessed Elizabeth of Hungary, Saint Maurus, O.S.B. (bishop of Fünfkirchen),
Saint Margaret of Hungary, O.P.

Hungarian stamps commemorating the life and death of Saint Emeric (István).
In the middle: Mary, the patroness of Hungary.

him and bore him a worthy successor to the throne: Emeric
(in Hungarian, Imre). Their son was born in the coronation year
1000 or—as many historians think—in the year 1007, in Stuhl-
weissenburg. The father found a suitable tutor and educator for
him in the saintly Gerhard von Csánad. He gave the young Emeric
a strict, ascetical upbringing, so that the biographical chronicle
(*vita*) dated 1109–1116 reported that from his youth he distinguished himself by his eminent virtues and graces. Then, as the
husband of a Greek princess, Emeric practiced continence within
marriage.

Emeric attained such a remarkable degree of maturity that his
father, Stephen, elected him to be co-regent during his own lifetime. In 1031, however, before his coronation as co-regent, Emeric
was attacked by a wild boar while hunting and was killed. King
Stephen died on August 15, 1038. He was canonized *anno Domini*
1083 together with his son, Emeric.

Gisela of Hungary was born around the year 985 at Regensburg.

Gisela of Hungary

Her father was Count Henry II of Bavaria; her brother was later Emperor Henry II, the husband of Saint Cunegund. Henry II was the German emperor second to none in promoting the Christian life through the construction of many monasteries and churches.

When Gisela was around eleven years old, emissaries from Hungary came to Regensburg to request her hand in marriage for Vaik, who in Baptism had received the name Stephen. The marriage took place in Burg Scheyern, the ancestral castle of the Wittelsbachers, around the year 995. The young married couple then traveled to Hungary, where Stephen was anointed and crowned the first Christian king of Hungary, and Gisela, the queen. The new royal couple now energetically set about Christianizing their land. Advised by his wife, Gisela, Stephen constructed many churches and monasteries and erected the first diocese in Vesprem on Lake Balaton.

When King Stephen died, on August 15, 1038, the pagan princes in Hungary rebelled against the widowed queen; accused of being a "foreigner", she was mistreated, imprisoned, and disinherited. Eventually, King Henry III succeeded in freeing Gisela, in 1045, and bringing her back to Passau, where she entered the Benedictine convent of Niedernburg and where she was elected by the nuns in 1054 to rule as the third abbess. On May 7, 1060, she was called by God to her eternal reward. She was laid to rest in a magnificent tomb in the Parz Chapel. Although she was never formally beatified, she was revered as a blessed. Her canonization is expected soon. Her emblems are a royal throne and the Hungarian coronation mantle. She is depicted as carrying a cross or a rosary and a model of a church.

Saint
Philip Howard
and
Anne

b. June 28, 1557, in Arundel House, London
d. October 19, 1595, in the Tower of London

Beatified 1929
Canonized 1970

The theological concept of grace has been much discussed in the Church. In spite of all the disputes, it is possible to declare that grace means, essentially, the loving encounter of man with his Creator. A man can be described as "favored" or "graced" when he lives his life face to face with God and conducts himself according to his Commandments and his Word. Grace can accomplish much in us and through us. It can move the remorseful sinner to conversion; it can heal, revive the hardened heart, and reunite what is separated.

The grace of the Lord was at work in the life of the English husband, father, and martyr Philip Howard. His life is not yet well known in the Church, but it deserves a special consideration, prominence, and imitation, because the grace of the Lord "struck his heart" [1] and gave him the strength "not only to believe in Christ but also to suffer for his sake".

Philip Howard was born on June 28, 1557, in Arundel House, the son of Thomas, Duke of Norfolk. At this time the Catholic Queen Mary was still reigning, under whose rule England again became Catholic, after Henry VIII had broken from Rome and

---

[1] Council of Trent, Decree on Justification, chap. 5.

declared himself the head of the new state church (Church of England). Philip, who was baptized by the Catholic archbishop of York, was educated at Cambridge University. Meanwhile, much took place in England and in his parents' house. Queen Elizabeth I took over the government in 1558, and with that the English state church was reestablished and Catholicism was forbidden. Howard's father joined this church again. Thomas of Norfolk was married a third time, this time to the widow Elizabeth Dacre of Gillesland.

Elizabeth brought three daughters with her into this marriage. These daughters were married to Thomas' three sons. Thus Philip Howard, who belonged now to the Anglican Church like his father, was married at the age of fourteen to Anne Dacre of Gillesland. She was a pretty, clever woman, quick-witted and re-markably generous to all people. It is hardly surprising that this marriage was built on sandy ground, for how is a youngster sup-posed to be able to understand the full significance of the Sacra-ment of Matrimony?

Philip cared only for worldly things, about his own advance-ment. So he neglected God and his wife. It was more important for him to pursue his career than to bother about marital concerns in addition to his professional ones. Anne, on the other hand, honestly loved her husband and remained faithful to him. And this might seem miraculous, for not only was she neglected by him, but she also suffered severely from his moods. Her love must have been truly deep and great for her to endure such a life patiently without a word of complaint. To make matters worse, she was despised by the English queen. Cardinal Basil Hume described her on one occasion as having achieved "the highest degree of sanc-tity", even if this has not been officially recognized.

Philip pursued his career at his wife's expense. In 1580 he be-came Earl of Arundel. In his blindness, he did not yet recognize that God puts down the mighty and exalts the lowly (cf. Lk 1:52). So with his title he enjoyed great honors. Frequently, he was a guest at the English court, and he became the favorite of the power-hungry, egotistical Queen Elizabeth I. Surely there would have been no end to Philip's career had it not been for the year

1581. In that year the word of the prophet Jesus Sirach was fulfilled in the life of the earl of Arundel: "But to the penitent he hath given the way of justice, and he hath strengthened them that were fainting in patience, and hath appointed to them the lot of truth" (Sir 17:20 Douay-Rheims; cf. Sir 17:24 RSVC).

At the queen's court Philip witnessed a theological dispute between Anglican theologians and the Jesuit priest Saint Edmund Campion. Although the words of the Catholic priest did not bring about his conversion immediately, he was confronted with a kind of truth that set him free interiorly (cf. John 8:32). This theological dispute, which resulted in Campion's martyrdom, took hold of Philip. It became ever clearer to him that the Church of England was merely a contrivance of the queen and not the work of God, who had built his Church on Peter and his successors, certainly not on the English crown. For three years he struggled with these thoughts. In his mind his personal career receded more and more into the background. In thinking over these things, he began to follow Jesus. The more he recognized Christ in the Catholic Church, the more he recognized also how much he had neglected his wife for all those years. His marital life from that moment on can be described as heroic. Their life together was marked by love and understanding. This love became so great that all the difficulties to come were also conquered by love. His wife, Anne, who was devoted to the Catholic faith, turned her back on the Anglican Church and converted openly. This step was the catalyst for Philip's own conversion to Catholicism, which he completed in 1584. Philip became, in fact, an ardent Catholic whose heart was set on nothing else but serving Christ in his Church. Knowing that Christ's Passion was an injustice, but necessary for salvation, he knew that his own passion was now beginning. The further course of Philip's life displays incredible parallels with the sufferings of the Redeemer.

The English royal court took note of Howard's transformation. Philip very soon sensed that the Queen was turning away from him as her favorite and that many dangers were lurking. Yet with Christ he was able to say, "The hour has come" (Mk 14:41). In a passionate letter to the queen, the young earl depicted his motives and explained to her what truth meant and continued to mean for him. With this letter he sealed his fate, which for him meant more happiness than suffering. After writing this letter he fled. And, once again, the words of Jesus were fulfilled, "See, my betrayer is at hand" (Mk 14:42), when someone in the service of the queen betrayed Howard, and he was apprehended at sea and brought to the Tower of London. From then on he would not leave prison again. He was tried and sentenced, first to pay a fine of 10,000 pounds, and then—to the Queen's delight—to imprisonment. It was only thanks to his title as earl and to his noble lineage that he was not condemned to death. In a new trial, which was never intended to result in acquittal, he was accused of praying for the enemies of the royal house. Philip's cell in the Tower became his church. Every day, he spent several hours in prayer and meditation. Later on, witnesses reported that he repeatedly prayed with the words of Jesus, "Father, into thy hands I commit my spirit" (Lk 23:46). Although the queen never signed his death sentence, he was ready at any time to accept martyrdom. Every footstep, every tolling of the bell could mean his death. And every time he was ready to take that step of grace. For more than ten years Christ asked him, "Philip, do you love me?" And Philip answered, for more than ten years, "Lord, you know everything; you know that I love you" (cf. Jn 21:15–23). His request to be allowed to see his wife was refused, and he never looked upon his only son, who was born after his arrest. Only if he would convert again to Protestantism would he be able, not only to see his wife and his child, but also to regain his freedom. Yet Howard refused. In prison he suffered much from the thought that he had neglected his wife for so long and now could not care for her any more. Still, just as Christ assured the repentant thief of paradise, so too he called out in the Tower of London, "Today you will be with me in Paradise" (Lk 23:43).

The last will and testament that Philip left for all of us can still be seen by visitors to the Tower. They are Latin words that he scratched into the wall in the Tower. The text is: "Quanto plus afflictiones pro Christo in hoc saeculo, tanto plus gloriae cum Christo in futuro [The more afflictions we bear for Christ in this world, the more glory we attain with Christ in the world to come]." His sufferings came to an end on October 19, 1595, when at the age of thirty-eight he was set free by God in the Tower of London. Pope Paul VI canonized him in 1970 as one of the Forty Martyrs of Wales and England. He is the patron of the diocese of Arundel.

Don Bosco once said, "Grace is a free gift of God." And Saint Philip Howard, earl of Arundel, accepted it gratefully. From the moment of his conversion he felt that he was really a *cooperator veritatis* (3 Jn 8), a fellow worker in the truth. As blind as he was for many years, he fought all the more for this truth, to which he felt obliged. Finally, it was truth that caused him to see his wife, his Church, and his world with new eyes.

It was a freedom that sets free, that made him free. And who is not glad to be a fellow worker with such a liberating truth? Through Saint Philip Howard, Christ also asks the families of today, "And you, do you love me?" How will they answer?[2]

[2] The Diocese of Arundel and Brighton, "St Pilip Howard" (1995), <http://www.dabnet.org/p_howard.htm>; J. H. Pollen, "Ven. Philip Howard", Catholic Encyclopedia, vol. 7 (1910), online ed. (1999), <http://www.knight.org/advent/cathen/07503a.htm>.

Blessed
Frédéric Ozanam

and

Amélie Soulacroix

b. April 23, 1813, in Milan
d. September 8, 1853, in Marseilles

Married June 23, 1841, in Lyons
Beatified August 22, 1997

"I am weary of words—let us act." Those are words of Antoine Frédéric Ozanam, whose entire life was a wonderful witness to the practice of the Christian faith. A closer look at this short but highly concentrated life makes it clear that its goal was the fulfillment of the primary Christian precept: "God is love" (1 Jn 4:16). The commandment of love animated Frédéric to undertake deeds that we can only marvel at today.

Ozanam was born on April 23, 1813, in Milan, the son of French parents. He spent his childhood and youth in Lyons, where he also completed his schooling. If we wish to understand Frédéric's concept of the Church, we must become better acquainted with his family.

His father, Jean-Antoine Ozanam, was a physician. He performed his professional duties passionately, as a service to humanity. One-third of his patients were poor, isolated people, whom he treated free of charge. Frédéric's mother, Marie, whom he described as his "church", was very much involved in charitable works and, as the doctor's wife, cared for many sick people in the neighborhood. "She was the one whose first instructions gave me the gift of faith; she was a living image of Holy Mother Church",

473

he would later write. And how he must have had his mother before his eyes when he later described Christian charity as follows: "Charity is a tender mother, who turns her eyes to the child whom she clasps to her heart. She no longer thinks of herself, and forgets all thought of her own beauty, so as to live only for love." Besides a practical love of neighbor, little Frédéric also learned patient endurance of the vicissitudes of fortune. Of the fourteen children in the Ozanam family, eleven died shortly after birth or else in early childhood. In spite of all these adversities, the parents' faith grew stronger. This unshakable faith shaped Frédéric's future.

During Ozanam's lifetime, in the mid-nineteenth century, his country, France, faced many challenges. France as yet had no organized system of social assistance for needy people. The country was torn by political disputes, and hardly anyone seemed interested in basic democratic structures. The advance of industrialization benefited only the factories and their power-hungry owners, but not the working men. Despite the prevailing Enlightenment ideas, education was a foreign word in many regions. The French Revolution had left scars and had deprived the Church of her sense of Christian identity. Then, as if the French Revolution had not been enough, the country was afflicted with further bloody revolutions, which claimed more victims while bringing no improvement. In this way the country's plight was debated in its institutions of higher learning. The young law and literature student Frédéric, who had begun his studies in Paris, pondered which way would be the right one for society and the Church. All these thoughts contributed to his later decision as to the path that he himself would follow.

But first, as a student, Frédéric was prey to great doubts. The words of the Psalmist, "Out of the depths I cry to thee" (Ps 130:1), seem to have been on his lips. Law school did not suit him; he completed it only to please his father. He preferred and enjoyed the study of literature. At the same time, he exhausted himself worrying about his future; he was oppressed by doubts about the faith. He expressed these thoughts in 1834 in a letter to a friend: "At this moment I am experiencing one of the greatest anxieties of my life, uncertainty about my vocation. . . . There is scarcely a field of study or an occupation that would not have its attractions for me. . . . I cannot busy myself with a subject without thinking of a thousand others at the same time." Despite these doubts, Ozanam kept his troubles to himself.

In the midst of all this emptiness, it seems that God revealed himself to him. In the midst of all these doubts, Frédéric was convinced of this idea. The year 1833, when Frédéric was twenty years old, became the year in which the so-called Saint Vincent de Paul Conferences were founded. With all the social disorders of his day, the young man recognized that more was being said than done about them. The challenge of Sacred Scripture from the First Letter to the Corinthians, "Make love your aim!" (1 Cor 14:1), may best express the student's inner disposition when he said to several students in the midst of hopeless discussions, "It really is high time to combine deeds with words. The vital power of our faith must prove itself in works of charity! Let us not *talk* so much about charity! Instead we ought to *practice* it and really help the poor!" Indeed, it seems as though he meant to say, in short, "Let us make love our aim." He was so enthusiastic about Saint Vincent de Paul (1581–1660), the great social apostle of France, that he chose him to be the patron of this new "union". Frédéric Ozanam's enthusiasm inspired the other six students so much that the "Conferences of Saint Vincent de Paul" were founded. One of the students left a written account of the occasion: "I can still see it, that gleam in Ozanam's eyes! The sound of his voice still echoes in my ear—it trembled with spiritual excitement in that evening hour, and I hear how he explained to us his plan for a Vincentian society, a Catholic charitable union. He found such ardent, moving words for what he wanted to do! We had to pledge ourselves right away to such an undertaking." On the same evening, what had been discussed was put into action, when they, the first members, dropped off the remaining firewood at the house of an elderly lady.

Despite all his doubts concerning his life and his future, he was convinced about the Saint Vincent de Paul Society. Nevertheless, it was not easy going for this new initiative, which expanded into ever-wider circles. The members were not spared attacks by the Church and by politicians. Although these men did nothing but love one another and their neighbors (cf. Jn 15:12), these honorable charitable workers—who, furthermore, were supported by the Servant of God Rosalie Rendu, a Daughter of Charity—were reproached as being "unauthorized Catholics", and the Society itself was suspected of being an "organ of dangerous political currents and liberal tendencies". Yet these attacks did not cause Frédéric to doubt. "God is love." That was sufficient foundation for him. And he pursued this God as his aim until his death.

With the passage of time Ozanam's doubts subsided, and his thoughts turned in Christian hope to the future. He took a degree in jurisprudence, became an advocate at the Court of Appeals in Paris, then in 1839 completed a doctorate in philosophy in Paris and became a professor of commercial law in Lyons. In the meantime, his father and mother died.

Frédéric was sure that he wanted to marry. Yet he also knew that his future wife would have to be a suitable match for him. In 1835 he wrote to a friend,

My poor head has already suffered much. . . . Still, for some time now I have been experiencing the first signs of a new life of sentiment, and I am alarmed: I sense within me a great void, which neither friendship nor study can fill. I do not know who will fill it: God, or a creature? If it is to be a creature, then I pray that it will be later, when I am worthy of her. I pray that, besides what she brings with her by way of external charm and material goods, there will be no room for any regret, but above all I pray that she will be a pure soul, quite different from me; that she will draw me upward and not downward; that she will be magnanimous, since I am so often mean and petty; that she will be zealous for the faith, since I am so often lukewarm about God's concerns.

What deep, humble words! This great founder of charitable works in the nineteenth century emphasizes how little he is. And in everything he writes, he longs for a "thou", in relation to whom he can become an "I" (Martin Buber). God heard Frédéric's prayers, and so Frédéric made the acquaintance of Amélie Soulacroix, the daughter of the rector of the university in Lyons. Each one sensed immediately that he had found in the other the person for whom he had been looking. Before the wedding, he wrote her a letter:

> I cannot offer you the conveniences of an amiable life of leisure or the prestige of a large income or tranquility or anything especially remarkable, none of the things that seduce most people. Nevertheless, I hope that my gift, as modest as it may be, will be accepted kindly, for it is the thing that God's eternal majesty wants of us, that it prefers to everything else, the only thing that it desires, the only thing that deserves to be presented to you: I give you the will of a man, an upright and honest will, the will to be good so as to make you happy.

So strong and firm was their confidence in their love, that on June 23, 1841, in the church of Saint Nizier in Lyons, they said Yes to one another in the presence of God and the Church. In remembrance of this beautiful day, Frédéric made a custom of giving his wife a bouquet of flowers on the twenty-third of each month. They lived their married life completely, in love and respect and harmony. It is not presumptuous to compare their married life with the life of the early Church, for Frédéric and Amélie were Church in deed and in love, "were together and had all things in common . . . , praising God and having favor with all the people" (Acts 2:44, 47). Therefore it went without saying that the Ozanams took in Amélie's handicapped brother. Indeed, "the Lord added to their number . . . those who were being saved" (Acts 2:47). After two miscarriages, difficult times for the family, a daughter was born to them in 1845, little Marie.

Frédéric, who was richly endowed by God with "all wisdom and insight" (Eph 1:8), pursued a career as a scholar. In 1844 he became a full professor at the Sorbonne, the renowned university in Paris, in the department of foreign literature. Besides his family and his academic work, Professor Ozanam also served the universal Church; in 1840 he took over the work of editing the *Annals of the Propagation of the Faith*.

In 1848, another revolution broke out in France that, while ending the reign of the "Bourgeois King", still did not establish any practicable form of government. Frédéric Ozanam saw and emphasized the urgent need for the Church to insist more and more upon democracy and to take a firmer stance with respect to the people's welfare. He understood these goals, not as the French Revolution had done, but rather in light of the gospel, for "liberty, equality, and fraternity" appeared to him to be practical evangelical counsels, directly called for by Jesus. Yet Ozanam's optimism was severely shaken. Democracy was not seen as the ultimate solution, neither in the Church nor in society. He had meditated profoundly on the thesis "Christianity is democracy", but his formula was not taken seriously and was often ridiculed. Just two years before his death, he had to witness the complete destruction of the tender plant of democracy through the coup d'état of Napoleon III. Politically, he was considered defeated, but from a Christian perspective he was viewed as a prophet and an innovator of an "intellectual and spiritual democracy", even though the French Church could not and would not follow him. Ultimately, like the great social bishop in Germany, Wilhelm Emmanuel von Ketteler, he was condemned to be a voice crying out in the wilderness. Perhaps he found some comfort in the thought that a prophet is never (or rarely) honored in his own country (cf. Mt 13:57).

As a professor, he was always very well liked by his students. The power of his lectures became proverbial. Statements such as "Oh, that Ozanam—how we all loved him!" or, "Love of neighbor surrounded Ozanam like an aura", testified to his popularity and his charisma. His lectern was also his pulpit, as is evident from the testimony of one of his students, who said to Ozanam, "What many sermons could not accomplish, you have brought about with one lecture in a single day: You have made me a Christian."

Despite his immense workload (he also managed to travel extensively in Europe), he himself always remained the simple "Vincentian brother" who visited needy people, for instance, working-class families, as part of his volunteer work. On his journeys he lectured, founded new Saint Vincent de Paul Conferences, and admonished everyone never to lose sight of practical love of neighbor.

Yet failing health put an abrupt end to his plans. In 1852, with a heavy heart, he resigned from his professorate at the Sorbonne for health reasons. In the year in which Brother Death was to call him, he joined the Franciscan Order as a tertiary.

Frédéric Ozanam was deathly ill. His wife, who was caring for him, wrote to friends, "God apparently wants to purify him even more before he takes him. The more his body is weakened by his suffering, the more beautiful his soul grows and develops. Never was his heart warmer; never was his spirit livelier. Not a word of complaint!" To a priest who was encouraging him, he said, "How could I doubt God, when I love him so much?" He drew strength from reading the Bible each day. The words of encouragement he found he would write on slips of paper. One of them reads, "I will go, Lord, when you call me." And he called him on September 8, 1853, in Marseilles, at the age of forty.

Frédéric Ozanam has died. Yet he lives on in the approximately 800,000 members of the 47,000 Saint Vincent de Paul Conferences worldwide—in 132 countries, to be precise—which put Ozanam's idea of charitable service into practice. True, he has died, but as a heavenly intercessor he lives on; this is the message of his beatification in 1997 in Paris. We should be grateful that he translated anew the gospel of the Good Samaritan (cf. Lk 10:25–37) for our time. His life teaches us that serving one's neighbor is the continuation of the eucharistic celebration. He teaches us that all service to one's fellowman is another expression of divine worship. "Make love your aim!", Frédéric Ozanam cries out to us Christians, to the Church, and to every form of society or government. "Make love your aim!", he cries out to families as well. This motto is more than a challenge; it is an opportunity. Every situation, every conflict in the family or in society must and can be endured, when it is endured with love. "Make love your aim!", he cries out to united Europe, which he dreamed so much about and for which he longed. May his call not remain unheard.[1]

---

[1] Victor Conzemius, *Frédéric Ozanam: Solidarität statt Klassenkampf* (Fribourg: Imba, 1983); Bernhard Hanssler, *Friedrich Ozanam* (Cologne: Gemeinschaft der Vinzenz-konferenzen Deutschland e.V., n.d.); Gisbert Kranz, *Frédéric Ozanam* (Regensburg: Friedrich Pustet, n.d.).

Blessed
Giuseppe Antonio Tovini

and

Emilia Corbolani

*b. March 14, 1841, in Cividate
    Camuno*
d. January 16, 1897, in Brescia

Married January 6, 1875
Father of ten children
Beatified September 20, 1998

A man who lived for only fifty-six years nevertheless labored with unbelievable energy and made immense sacrifices in the interests of his fellowmen. Giuseppe Antonio Tovini, who worked in Brescia and in the Piedmont region, was a real boon for the people, because he, living as a fine, upstanding Christian, gratefully accepted his charisms from God and used them to do vital apostolic work for the people of his time.[1] Aware of these gifts of the Holy Spirit granted to him by God, Giuseppe Tovini recognized his duty to use them, not for himself, but rather "for the welfare of the people and for the upbuilding of the Church".[2] Though he was taken from the people of Piedmont by an early death in 1897, after standing up so courageously for their social needs and combating poor conditions, he was given back to them by God a hundred years later as a heavenly intercessor when Pope John Paul II enrolled this lawyer, school principal, politician, husband, and father in the list of the blesseds in 1998 in Brescia.

Giuseppe was born on March 14, 1841, in Cividate Camuno, the firstborn son of his parents, Mosé Tovini and Rosa Malaguzzi.

[1] Cf. *Catechism of the Catholic Church*, no. 800.
[2] Vatican Council II, Decree on the Apostolate of Lay People, *Apostolicam actuositatem*, November 18, 1965, no. 3.

In the Tovini household, Giuseppe experienced love of the Christian faith and devotion to the Catholic cause. Giuseppe went to school in his hometown, in Breno, Lovere, and in Verona. One of his schoolmates in Lovere later became a Capuchin father, Blessed Innocent of Berzo (1844–1890). While he was still a student, he and his family suffered a tragic loss in 1859 when his father died.

This death brought on financial difficulties, and so Giuseppe soon sensed an obligation to support his mother in raising his younger brothers and sisters. One year later, Giuseppe passed his secondary school examination, after which he went on to study law at Padua and Parma. He completed his studies brilliantly in 1865 and in that same year experienced again how close happiness and sorrow are to each other: his mother died.

The lawyer settled at first in Lovere. There he soon became the assistant principal and a teacher at the technical school in that locality. During this period, Tovini quickly realized how important education is. As a pedagogue, he felt obliged to strive personally to give each student the opportunity to pursue the goal set for him by his Creator.[3] Just as he applied his aptitudes and talents for the good of his students, so, too, as an educator he did not want to hinder them in any way.[4] Rather, he tried to encourage each one to make full use of his talents.

In 1867, he went to Brescia, the city that was to become the vineyard in which he would work for the Lord. There he soon became acquainted with the Corbolani family. Giordano Corbolani was an attorney in Brescia and had a daughter named Emilia. Giuseppe and Emilia met and fell in love, and in this woman Giuseppe "found a wife, found happiness, and obtained favor from the Lord" (cf. Prov 18:22).

In the meantime, specifically, from 1871 to 1874, Giuseppe became mayor of Cividate Camuno. As chief servant of his hometown community, his strength of character, his quick mind, and his deeply rooted faith stood him in good stead. He did not want to be the sort of politician that says one thing and does another. He

[3] Paul VI, encyclical letter *Populorum progressio*, March 21, 1967, no. 15.
[4] Ibid.

wanted to set an example of a faith that expresses itself in good works and is thus alive (cf. Jas 2:14–17). Concretely, for him, that meant improving the living conditions of the people entrusted to his care. Thus he carried out several plans, for instance, the construction of railroad lines to connect the rural areas with each other and with the city. In order to give a more definite form to the financial affairs of the people, too, he founded the Banca di Valle Camonica [Camonica Valley Bank] in Breno.

On January 6, 1875, Giuseppe Tovini and Emilia Corbolani exchanged vows in the presence of God in the church of Santa Agata in Brescia, pledging each other lifelong love, honor, and fidelity and promising to accept the children God might send them and to raise them to be followers of Christ and members of his Church.[5] They had spent eight years getting to know each other and testing their vocation. And they became a happy family, which God blessed with ten children. With this disposition, they fulfilled God's creative will that they should pass on human life.[6] Emilia and Giuseppe were good parents who set an example for their children of deep and mutual love. Strict discipline and love characterized their family life. In teaching their children about the faith, they gave them "a firm confidence in Divine Providence".[7]

This education was no external routine, no pretense but, rather, a genuine, living witness; the proof is that three of their children entered religious life. Yet it must also be mentioned that Emilia was a strong woman, for her husband's activities demanded that she be present for her family and, despite Giuseppe's frequent absences, faithfully devoted to him. Her love was patient and kind. She bore all things, endured all things. Her love never ceased (cf. 1 Cor 13:4, 7). It can really be said that the love of this couple for each other and the long-suffering love of Emilia were an image of the divine, eternal, long-suffering, and all-surpassing love of the Lord. This love was also Giuseppe's mainstay in his various and incredibly numerous activities.

---

[5] From *Die Feier der Trauung* (Benziger, Pustet, St. Peter, Veritas, 1975).

[6] John XXIII, encyclical letter *Mater et Magistra*, May 15, 1961, no. 193.

[7] Ibid., no. 195.

As a city councilman in Brescia and provincial councilor in the rural areas, Giuseppe became the founder or initiator of numerous works in a wide range of fields. "The recent past, down to this day, can testify as to how many blessings they brought about."[8] He recognized that, in his time, illiteracy, lack of education, poverty, and the exploitation of the working man must come to an end. Pope Paul VI, who came from Brescia and was acquainted with Tovini's works, later formulated the aspirations of all men in his social encyclical *Populorum progressio* as follows: "Freedom from misery, the assurance of a livelihood, health, steady employment, protection from situations that injure human dignity, the continual development of skills, better education, in a word: to work more, to learn more, to own more, so as to have greater worth."[9] Tovini worked persistently so that these reasonable aspirations would not be castles in the air but, rather, would become concrete, practical reality. Thus he founded schools, for example, a girls' school in his hometown community. He promoted the publication of newspapers such as *Cittadino di Brescia* (a daily newspaper), *La Voce di Popolo* (a Catholic weekly), and *Scuola Italiana Moderna* (a pedagogical journal). As a politician, Tovini was to some extent a prophet of what was formulated by the Second Vatican Council in the twentieth century as follows: "Above all, good publications are to be promoted."[10] Man should be able to form his own opinion; he should be the subject, not the object of his everyday life.[11] For the poor and the needy, who in his eyes were Christ himself (cf. Mt 25:45), and to whom he considered himself so closely connected as a tertiary of the Franciscan order, he founded countless establishments. In the cities of Padua and Rome, he founded international student residences so that everyone would have the opportunity to study without great financial expenditures. He himself had not had that advantage, and he wanted things to be different for the generations to come.

[8] Leo XIII, encyclical letter *Rerum novarum*, May 15, 1891, no. 39.

[9] Paul VI, *Populorum progressio*, no. 6.

[10] Vatican Council II, Decree on the Means of Social Communication, *Inter mirifica*, December 4, 1963, no. 14.

[11] John Paul II, encyclical letter *Laborem exercens*, September 14, 1981, no. 6.

Tovini was a realist. And so he soon recognized that financial support would have to be secured for all the works mentioned here and for those not mentioned. Furthermore, he wanted to protect people from exploitation in their financial dealings and to lay a financial foundation for the Catholic Church and all her manifold projects. Therefore, he founded Church-affiliated credit unions, which would be centered on people and not on money. These institutions still exist today; they are the *Banca San Paolo* in Brescia (founded 1888) and the *Banco Ambrosiano* in Milan (founded 1896).

A further concern of Tovini's were the so-called *Opera dei Congressi e dei Comitati Cattolici*, which we will refer to here briefly as the Catholic congresses. These congresses set out to observe and analyze developments in the Church, in society, and in everyday life and to intervene in areas where help was needed. Tovini saw them as an opportunity for the Church to be present in society and actively involved in remedying abuses. As Pope Leo XIII so aptly put it in the first social encyclical, *Rerum Novarum*, "Without the help of religion and the Church, no way can be found out of the chaos." [12] Giuseppe Tovini was appointed a member of the permanent council of these congresses in 1885; president of the third section for "Education and Instruction" in 1888; in that same year a member of the committee for Lombardy; in 1891 a member of the board of directors and again of the permanent council; in 1893 vice president; and in 1895 president of the committee.

Considering all of these activities, one could easily get the impression that Tovini the politician was an activist and a populist. That would be misjudging the man, however, since he was a Christian through and through. For his spiritual life was by far even more extensive than his social and political accomplishments.

Giuseppe Tovini read from Sacred Scripture daily and took his inspiration from the Word, the beginning of all being and action (cf. Jn 1:1–5). He was aware that "without [the Word] was not anything made that was made" (Jn 1:3); thus without God's Word nothing could come about, no matter how well planned it was.

---

[12] Leo XIII, *Rerum novarum*, no. 13.

Furthermore, Tovini attended Mass every day and received Holy Communion daily, which was rare at that time. He thereby immersed himself entirely in Christ, and, through the working of the Spirit and his devotion to the Sacrament of the Eucharist, he gradually "attained spiritual perfection".[13] He not only participated in perpetual adoration of the Blessed Sacrament; he also initiated it in the church of San Luca in Brescia, where he was later buried.

All too soon, exhausted by all his activities, Giuseppe Antonio Tovini died, on January 16, 1897.

Nineteenth-century Brescia could feel fortunate to have had this man in the ranks of its leading citizens. The city can consider itself blessed forever to have him in the ranks of its heavenly intercessors. His beatification is a sure sign that his lay apostolate was a successful one. His was the gift of seeing needs, misery, abuses, and injustices and addressing them. He was aware that the Church of his time could not draw back, as has, unfortunately, so often been the case. His Church had the obligation of making a public appearance, with all her living members, as a spokesman of an eternally valid message, so that the gospel could be heard by everyone. When we speak today of Catholic social teaching, then we are certainly indebted to him as well, since he took such initiatives at a time when as yet there were no social encyclicals, guidelines, or model programs. It was the Holy Spirit alone to whom he entrusted himself. It was the example of the *poverello d'Assisi*, of Francis the poor man, whom he imitated as a *poverello di Brescia* by joining the third order Franciscans. It was the gifts that God had entrusted to him, which he used for the good of all and increased by his faith (cf. Lk 19:11–27). It was his wife, Emilia, and his children, whose love provided him with an "emotional driving force" for all his activity. As a "true apostle of Brescia", who with the eyes of Jesus' disciples recognized the Risen One in his fellowman (Lk 10:23), he was not content with activity alone, but "strove above and beyond that to proclaim Christ to his neighbors by his words as well."[14]

[13] Council of Florence, *Decree for the Armenians*, 1439.
[14] Cf. Vatican Council II, *Apostolicam actuositatem*, no. 13.

The kingdom of heaven is at hand, not at any one place, but within us in every place on the earth. Once we have learned that from Giuseppe Antonio Tovini, then the kingdom comes in our hearts.[15]

---

[15] *Feier der Trauung; Catechism of the Catholic Church*; Karl Rahner and Herbert Vorgrimler, *Kleines Konzilskompendium*, 21st ed. (Herder, 1989); John XXIII, *Mater et Magistra*, from <www.198.62.75.1/www1/overkott/mater.htm>; Paul VI, *Populorum Progressio*, from <www.198.62.75.1/www1/overkott/populo.htm>; John Paul II, *Laborem exercens*, from <www.198.62.75.1/www1/overkott/laborem.htm>; <www.numerica.it/tovini/beato.htm>; Leo XIII, *Rerum novarum*, from <www.198.62.75.1/www1/overkott/rerum.htm>.

Blessed
Anna Rosa Gattorno
and
Gerolamo Custo

b. October 14, 1831, in Genoa
d. May 6, 1900, in Rome

Married November 5, 1852
Beatified April 9, 2000

Anna Rosa Gattorno was born in Genoa on October 14, 1831, into a deeply religious family. On that same day she was baptized in the parish church of San Donato and received the name of Rosa Maria Benedicta. Her parents provided her with her first examples of well-founded, exemplary Christian life. In this religious atmosphere was nurtured a life that would become a model for all Catholics. She received her schooling at home, as was the custom at that time in wealthy families. She had an aptitude for learning and good manners, but also for the Word of God, which she tried to follow in everything. During the years of her childhood and youth, she was confronted with the faithless, anticlerical trends of her time, which affected even some members of the Gattorno family.

At the age of twenty-one, Anna Rosa married her cousin Gerolamo Custo and moved with him to Marseilles. Unforeseeable financial difficulties troubled the fortunes of the young family and forced them to return to Genoa. Besides poverty, fate dealt Anna Rosa's family other blows. Her first child, Carlotta, came down with a serious illness that left her deaf and mute for the rest of her life. Gerolamo's attempt to find fortune and success abroad ended with his return to Genoa. He died when Anna Rosa and he had been married for only six years. A few months later their youngest son died, too. The young widow did not despair, in spite of all these shadows that darkened her life. She herself described this time as one of "conversion". From now on, her life would belong to her Creator alone.

Anna Rosa Gattorno understood the meaning of her spiritual sufferings: God wanted to test his servant. She became a Franciscan tertiary. Through daily Communion, which was very unusual at that time, she became more and more devoted to her Lord and desired to follow him in all things. The Lord gave her a sign that she was on the right path: she received invisible stigmata. The marks of Christ's wounds became, so to speak, the spiritual crowning of her earthly journey. In Piacenza she founded a congregation, the Daughters of Saint Anne. She established schools for the poor and for nurses, houses for the newborn babies of workers in the tobacco fields, women's shelters for former prostitutes, and so on. At her death, the religious institute already numbered 368 houses, in which 3,500 sisters worked and prayed.[1]

[1] Cf. Johannes Maria Höcht, *Träger der Wundmale*, 5th ed. (Stein am Rhein: Christiana-Verlag, 2001): "If one considers the path of Saint Rosa's rich life, one could characterize her whole life as a stigmata. Earthly joys and family happiness were overshadowed by hard and unmitigated blows. While many would have despaired of God, not so Rosa Gattorno. She felt every valley, despite all sadness and pain, to be the will and pointed finger of God. She did not despair of God's plan, rather she was molded by it. The stigmata, even though she experienced this invisibly, was the divine confirmation of Rosa's life, molded as it was by pain. The wounds of Jesus thereby became hers. The Passion was something she could perceive and touch. For her following Jesus meant suffering in order to love. In this, she became an example for many" (pp. 530ff.).

Blessed
Ceferino Giménez Malla

and

Teresa Giménez Castro

b. ca. August 26, 1861, in Fraga, Huesca, Spain
d. August 8, 1936, in Barbastro, Spain

Beatified 1997

What a joy it was for the Gypsy people in 1997, when Pope John Paul II beatified in Rome a man who was one of them. The Holy Father was also presenting to all the other faithful, as an example, a man who was a husband and a businessman, an upright Christian, and even a martyr for his Church. We mean Ceferino Giménez Malla, who became truly just in the eyes of the Lord. But who is this "first blessed Gypsy" who has so much to say to us?

The exact date of Ceferino's birth is not certain. He was born in the year 1861 in Fraga (Spain) to parents named Juan and Teresa. The first certain date that is known, from the Christian perspective, his actual birthday, is August 26, 1861. On that day he was reborn as a Christian in the Holy Sacrament of Baptism. It was on the memorial of Pope Saint Zephyrinus, who led the Church from 199 to 217 as her chief shepherd. Pope Zephyrinus was of poor, humble origins and protected the Church against her foes. The traits found in this rough sketch of his patron saint's life are not uninteresting as we consider Blessed Ceferino.

Ceferino was not the only child in his family. Little Ceferino grew up with three siblings: a brother and two sisters. At an early age the boy sensed that he really was a Gypsy. His family had no permanent home. They traveled through the Spanish provinces of Catalonia and Aragon and also through southern France. Just as the patriarch Abraham was always journeying in search of the presence of God, and as the Holy Family was constantly in flight, so too did he experience homelessness. He used to say of himself ironically, "I am half Catalonian, half Aragonese."

When he was eighteen years old, he married the twenty-year-old Teresa Castro, who was likewise a Gypsy, originally from Lérida. It was customary among the Gypsies to marry at an early age. Although his beloved hesitated at first when he asked for her hand in marriage, she did consent. The marriage, which was not regularized in the Church until 1912, in Lérida, immediately encountered burdensome difficulties. Ceferino's father left the family. Shortly afterward, his mother gave birth to little Felipe. As the oldest son of the family, Ceferino supported his mother in raising the children and industriously helped with the daily routine. Teresa and Ceferino themselves, unfortunately, never had children of their own. Still, they became good Christian parents in 1909 by adopting Josefina, a niece of Teresa. "Pepita", as she was called, received from her adoptive parents everything children need: love, affection, and a well-grounded education. Among the Gypsies it is recounted even today how Ceferino used to ride on a horse, standing, with Pepita behind him, holding on tight.

After forty years of wandering and upheaval, the Giménez Malla family settled down in the city of Barbastro, the see of a Spanish bishop. In the "San Hipólito" quarter of the city, where they lived, the family was well liked and recognized as being dear, good, and helpful neighbors. They were also in close contact with those who shared their Gypsy background, the people of Kalós. Ceferino became a horse trader and as such was an upright and honorable businessman. The sorts of deception that are often practiced in this profession were far from his thoughts. Doing business with "El Pelé", as Ceferino was called, meant reliability and guaranteed quality. This reputation quickly made the rounds, but it also gave rise to envy.

His family life was characterized by the religiosity and deep devotion of both spouses. Among Ceferino's friends were both rich and poor. To children and young people he used to tell stories from Sacred Scripture, and he would teach them the most important prayers. He helped the poor in whatever way he could. He prayed the Rosary with the elderly and accompanied the priests who brought Viaticum to the dying. In the truest sense of the word he was "all things to all men".

We know that Ceferino went to church every Sunday and received the Holy Eucharist. As a regular communicant, he surely recognized that in that sacrament he could "receive Christ, fill his soul with grace, and have a pledge of future glory." [1] He appreciated more and more deeply the wealth with which the eucharistic Lord filled him. This love continued to increase, so that Ceferino often attended Mass on weekdays as well. Yes, he received and enjoyed Christ more and more; his soul was filled more and more with grace; and he did attain the pledge of eternal glory, though it was in tragic, albeit salutary circumstances.

We should not continue his story, however, without mentioning one thing: his love for the Rosary. In praying the Rosary daily, he felt united with the Mother of Jesus, whose "Fiat voluntas tua", in devoted surrender to the will of her Son, became Ceferino's *fiat*. He spoke this *fiat* in everything; and he also spoke it to the end. The Rosary reminded him of God's loving offer, which is guaranteed by the Sorrowful Mother. This is the only explanation for Ceferino's equanimity in his family and in his line of work. This is the only way to explain why he was summoned to be a reliable mediator between the Catalonian farmers and the Roma [Gypsies] and was successful. He took to heart and lived the advice given to all of us in Sacred Scripture: "My son, keep sound wisdom and discretion. . . . Then you will walk on your way securely and your foot will not stumble" (Prov 3:21, 23). With Christ in his heart and the Rosary in his hand, "El Pelé" became a saint. The people around him sensed this.

His attorney, too—a friend of his who was a law professor— sensed this and defended Ceferino in 1922, when he was unjustly

[1] Vatican Council II, Dogmatic Constitution on the Church, *Lumen Gentium*, November 21, 1964, no. 47.

imprisoned for theft. The lawyer said, "El Pelé is not a thief; he is Saint Ceferino, the patron of Gypsies." At any rate, he overcame this time of interior desolation and helplessness in the same way as did the crucified Christ. His acquittal was the fulfillment of the theological truth expressed in the Letter to the Romans: "This was to show God's righteousness . . . ; it was to prove at the present time that he himself is righteous and that he justifies him who has faith in Jesus" (Rom 3:25–26).

Yet it seemed that he was permitted to continue following the Sorrowful Mother of the Rosary, as he suffered many tragic situations. During that same year of his imprisonment, his beloved wife, Teresa, died, on December 4.

"El Pelé" became more and more lonely. Nevertheless, he bore this cross in an exemplary way, ever more fully united to Christ, whom he imitated more and more closely as a layman. In 1926 he joined the third order of Saint Francis that the Capuchins in Barbastro had just founded. He was also a member of the Saint Vincent de Paul Society, which had been founded in France by Blessed Frédéric Ozanam. The widower could be seen at any church event, especially at nocturnal adoration. Yet the crowning of his life had not yet come. In spite of all that he had gone through, it seems that something was still lacking in Ceferino's life, the final accomplishment in his imitation of Christ and his devotion to the sorrowful but glorious Mother of the Redeemer.

In July 1936, when El Pelé was seventy-five years old, the unholy Civil War broke out in Spain. As in the early period of the Church, Christians were persecuted and oppressed, and their faith was put to the test. Yes, Christ also had the church of Spain in mind, and the local church of Barbastro, too, when he warned his listeners, "Blessed are you when men revile you and persecute you and utter all kinds of evil against you falsely on my account" (Mt 5:11).

Indeed, blessed too was Ceferino, "El Pelé", when he defended a priest, in whom he recognized Christ, and became a victim himself. Blessed was Ceferino when he was thrown into prison and tortured. Blessed was he when freedom was offered to him, provided he stop praying the Rosary, and he refused. Blessed was

"El Pelé" when, in front of the Communist soldiers, he cried out, "Viva Christo rey!" (Long live Christ, the King!) and was executed early in the morning of August 8, 1936.

What a terrible, what a fortunate end for this Gypsy, this family man, this businessman! From a human perspective, we would call it an injustice, that this difficult life of Ceferino had to end so dramatically as well. And yet it was the resolution foreordained by God, as it were, the divine completion of a profound life led in imitation of Christ. Just as Jesus was born poor, was close to the needy, preached love, and redeemed the world out of love, so, too, the imitation of Christ became for this Gypsy a practice, a gift, and a duty: born poor, loving his wife, and charitable toward all men, dying in obedience to God. His motivation, though, came from the Mother of God. Saint Irenaeus of Lyons writes so wonderfully about her: "The knot of Eve's disobedience was untied by Mary's obedience." [2] To be sure, the illiterate Ceferino Giménez Malla, who had never been to school, could not have expressed it like that. But that is not important, either. The blessed untied the knot of the disobedience of his time, of those who envied and persecuted him, through his obedience unto death. Rightly was he officially beatified, and on that day it seemed as if Christ proclaimed to Ceferino the words that he had once spoken to Peter: Blessed are you, Ceferino Giménez Malla, for you have believed (cf. Mt 16:17). Through the intercession of this blessed, may many knots in our time, especially those that affect our families, be untied. Through his example, may families more and more "mature in their love and fidelity, keep the Commandments and live a blameless life." [3]

Incidentally, when Ceferino was shot, he was holding his rosary in his hand.[4]

[2] *Adv. haer* 3, 22.

[3] From *Die Feier der Trauung* (Benziger, Herder, Pustet, St. Peter, Veritas, 1975).

[4] Wolfgang Beinert. ed., *Mariologie*, Texte zur Theologie-Dogmatik (Graz, Vienna, Cologne: Styria, 1991); *Die Feier der Trauung*; Karl Rahner and Herbert Vorgrimler, *Kleines Konzilskompendium*, 21st ed. (Herder, 1989); <www.augustea.it/pele>; <www.kath-zigeunerseelsorge.de>.

1. Ceferino: his work and his faith. 2. Begging—as many children do. 3. In Catalonia and Aragon. 4. Horse trader. 5. Life on the street. 6. Raising a niece. 7. Marriage in the Church. 8. As a Franciscan tertiary. 9. Visiting the sick and the elderly. 10. Friend of youth. 11. Imprisoned as a witness to the faith. 12. Death as a martyr.

Blessed
Vicente Vilad David
and
Isabel Rodes Reig

b. June 28, 1889, in Manises, Spain
d. February 14, 1937, in Manises

Married November 30, 1922
Beatified October 1, 1995, in Rome

This exemplary lay apostle and martyr was born on June 28, 1889, in Manises (Valencia, Spain), the youngest of the eight children of the ceramics manufacturer Justus Vilar and his pious wife, Carmen, and he received a model upbringing in the Christian faith. This foundation was deepened during the time he attended secondary school with the Piarist Fathers. Vicente then studied at the technical institute and became an industrial engineer.

On November 30, 1922, he was married to Isabel Rodes Reig and led an exemplary Christian married life. He not only practiced his Catholic faith as a believer and a husband, he also helped the priests of the parish in their pastoral work in whatever way he could—without neglecting his worldly occupation, for he successfully managed the ceramics factory that he took over from his father. In this he proved to be a model employer and entrepreneur, concerned about social justice for his employees and workers.

In August 1936, the persecution of the Church and of Christians that had broken out with the Spanish Civil War reached its climax in Manises. Vicente Vilar David was dismissed as professor at the ceramics trade school—not because of professional incompetence, but merely on account of his Catholic views. In these

496

weeks he fearlessly sought to help the priests and to encourage his fellow Christians to be optimistic and to trust in God. He himself was increasingly harassed, on account of his stance as a Catholic, by the Red regime that had come to power. On February 14, 1937, he was summoned before a tribunal and ordered to give up his activities on behalf of the Church and the Catholic faith. He vehemently refused, however, and declared that being a Catholic and a member of Christ's Church was his most honorable vocation and that he would remain true to it until death. For this and for this alone he was sentenced to death on the spot. Before he was shot, on February 14, 1937, in his hometown, he expressly forgave his enemies, above all, his murderers. When he was allowed to see his wife once more, he encouraged her lovingly with consoling words. That was how this valiant hero for the faith took leave of this world.

When the employees and workers of the ceramics firm went on strike for three days in protest, the socialist officials tried to prohibit and prevent the action. The workers, though, declared, "You have robbed us, not only of our boss, but of a faithful, caring father. Because of his concern for social justice, his prudence, and his kindness, we not only respected him; we loved him." In the beatification process, which was started on September 4, 1963, in Valencia, his violent death was recognized as a genuine martyrdom for the sake of the faith. On October 1, 1995, Vicente Vilar David was beatified.

Blessed
Peter To Rot
and
Paula Ia Varpit

b. 1912 in Rakunai, Papua New Guinea

d. July 17, 1945, in the Vunaiara concentration camp

Father of three children
Beatified January 17, 1995, in Port Moresby, on Papua New Guinea

During World War II, a catechist, husband, and father of a family was incarcerated by the Japanese for his activities on behalf of the Catholic faith and its moral principles, especially with regard to marriage, and was then executed without trial. Peter To Rot was born in 1912 in Rakunai, a village in New Britain, today the eastern province of Papua New Guinea; the son of Angelo To Puia and Marie Ia Tumul, he was the third of six children.

His parents were among the very first converts on this island who left paganism for the Catholic faith. His father, Angelo To Puia, in particular, the "big chief" of the village, was a thoroughly honest and upright man who took his conversion very seriously and therefore had all of his children baptized and brought up properly. Peter first attended the mission school in the village of Rakunai. Then he participated in the catechist training course at Saint Paul's College in nearby Taliligap and completed the requirements for a catechist's diploma. From then on he zealously helped the missionary in Rakunai with his pastoral duties.

At the age of twenty-two, Peter To Rot married the sixteen-year-old Paula Ia Varpit, who bore him two children; a third was born only after the father had suffered a martyr's death. The pastoral work of the lay catechist Peter To Rot was especially in demand

498

in 1942, when the Japanese invaded New Guinea and detained all the missionaries. The entire responsibility for the Catholic community weighed now upon the shoulders of this courageous lay catechist, who carried on his work very prudently. He organized prayer services and instructed adults and children in the catechism; he visited the sick and the dying and brought them the Viaticum; he witnessed marriages.

When the Japanese prohibited all religious activity, at the beginning of 1945, Peter To Rot continued, nonetheless, to fulfill his duties, though with greater caution. When he opposed the legalization of polygamy, which the Japanese were demanding, he was locked up for a few days the first time. Soon after his release, he was sentenced again, to three months imprisonment. During his compulsory stay in the concentration camp at Vunaiara, he was fully aware that this meant he might very well witness to the Catholic faith with a martyr's death.

After six weeks of internment, he was supposed to be set free again; then one night during the month of July 1945 he was murdered by two Japanese military guards who hated the Catholic faith.

When the death of Peter To Rot became known in the village of Rakunai, the entire population mourned him. Everyone was convinced that Peter had been put to death for his faith and was an authentic martyr. Pope John Paul II confirmed this by declaring him blessed. What took place on the island of Papua New Guinea during the beatification ceremony is interesting to relate. For seven long months it had not rained in the southeast of Papua New Guinea. When the Pope arrived on January 17, 1995, the floodgates of heaven were opened, pouring down the long-awaited rain. The people immediately nicknamed John Paul II "Piri-Piri-Man" (rainmaker). Despite the torrential rainfall, a colorful liturgy was celebrated, in which the Pope raised the first blessed of the land, Peter To Rot, to the honors of the altar.

Among the approximately fifteen thousand faithful at the John Guise Stadium in Port Moresby, the one surviving daughter of the new blessed was also present. She had the privilege of hearing from the Pope's own lips the following eulogy of her brave father.

Blessed Peter understood the value of suffering. Inspired by his faith in Christ, he was a devoted husband, a loving father and a dedicated catechist known for his kindness, gentleness and compassion. Daily Mass and Holy Communion, and frequent visits to our Lord in the Blessed Sacrament, sustained him, gave him wisdom to counsel the disheartened, and courage to persevere until death. In order to be an effective evangelizer, Peter To Rot studied hard and sought advice from wise and holy "big men". Most of all he prayed—for himself, for his family, for his people, for the Church. His witness to the Gospel inspired others, in very difficult situations, because he lived his Christian life so purely and joyfully. Without being aware of it, he was preparing throughout his life for his greatest offering: by dying daily to himself, he walked with his Lord on the road which leads to Calvary (cf. Mt 10:38–39).

During times of persecution the faith of individuals and communities is "*tested by fire*" (1 Peter 1:7). But Christ tells us that there is no reason to be afraid. Those persecuted for their faith will be more eloquent than ever: "*it is not you who will be speaking; the Spirit of your Father will be speaking in you*" (Mt 10:20). So it was for Blessed Peter To Rot. When the village of Rakunai was occupied during the Second World War and after the heroic missionary priests were imprisoned, he assumed responsibility for the spiritual life of the villagers. Not only did he continue to instruct the faithful and visit the sick, he also baptized, assisted at marriages and led people in prayer.

When the authorities legalized and encouraged polygamy, Blessed Peter knew it to be against Christian principles and firmly denounced this practice. . . . During his final imprisonment Peter To Rot was serene, even joyful. He told people that he was ready to die for the faith and for his people.

On the day of his death, Blessed Peter asked his wife to bring him his catechist's crucifix. It accompanied him to the end. Condemned without trial, he suffered his martyrdom calmly. Following in the footsteps of his Master, the "Lamb of God who takes away the sin of the world" (Jn 1:29), he too was "*led like a lamb to the slaughter*" (cf. Is 53:7). And yet this "grain of wheat" which fell silently into the earth (cf. Jn 12:24) has produced a harvest of blessings for the Church in Papua New Guinea! [1]

[1] John Paul II, "Peter Knew Value of Suffering", homily at the beatification of Peter To Rot, January 17, 1995, in *L'Osservatore romano*, January 25, 1995, p. 8.

INDEX